PEREGRINE BOOKS

Y68

MILTON'S EPIC POETRY

EDITOR: C. A. PATRIDES

D1580233

MILTON'S EPIC POETRY

Essays on *Paradise Lost* and *Paradise Regained*

EDITED WITH AN
ANNOTATED READING LIST BY
C. A. PATRIDES

PENGUIN BOOKS

Penguin Books Ltd, Harmondsworth, Middlesex, England
Penguin Books Australia Ltd, Ringwood, Victoria, Australia

—

First published 1967
Copyright © C. A. Patrides, 1967

—

Made and printed in Great Britain by
Cox & Wyman Ltd,
London, Fakenham and Reading
Set in Monotype Garamond

FOR YANNI AND LULA

μιὰ ἀπολαμπίδα ἀπὸ χαρὰ θεΐκὴ

CONTENTS

PREFACE

MILTON's own words, misappropriated from their context it is true, very suitably describe the vagaries of his status among major English poets. Early on in our century he was removed to regions thrice as far as is the centre from the utmost pole. In the late nineteen-thirties, however, he was again descried through many an optic glass. By 1944 we could even say that 'the simultaneous expansion of Donne's and the shrinkage of Milton's reputations, more and more seem to have been a critical aberration'. Nearly twenty years later the scales appear to have inclined the other way. One authority on *Paradise Lost* claims even that 'it is Milton, not Donne, who is the poet of our time, who speaks in our idiom'.

If I do not assent to this proposition it is because I dare not boast confident knowledge about the exact preferences of 'our times'. But I have at least observed in my students a readiness to accept that 'our idiom' is spoken by Milton as much as it is by Donne. They voice, too, their surprise that our most eminent critics should so obstinately tilt the scales now in favour of Donne, now of Milton. But can we afford to ignore the voices raised in the cause of either, or in opposition to either?

My decision to include in the present volume a whole range of views from laudatory to adverse is the result of my conviction that every worthwhile criticism of Milton awakens us to the infinite complexity of his poetry. This range of views demonstrates also the impressive wealth of modern critical strategies, the divers paths we may tread as students of great literature. The essays reprinted here may in collision let out discordant notes that jar upon our ears. Yet I hope – and believe – that each has its contribution to make toward that harmony which is the aesthetic experience of reading *Paradise Lost* and *Paradise Regained*.

Milton's Epic Poetry

George Eliot once wrote that 'the grace of prefaces seems to lie in reticence of all but useful indications or explanations'. I cannot end without acknowledging the generous co-operation of everybody whose assistance I sought. F. R. Leavis was the first to be approached. His enthusiastic response set a pattern of generosity to which all subscribed. I am grateful to A. R. Cirillo, B. K. Lewalski and Kingsley Widmer for the alacrity with which they undertook revisions of their essays; and to Douglas Bush, William Empson, L. L. Martz, B. Rajan, Christopher Ricks and Arnold Stein for the readiness with which they attended to various aspects of their contributions. I am pleased also to acknowledge the advice and encouragement I received from M. H. Abrams, A. E. Barker, M. Y. Hughes, W. B. Hunter, L. L. Martz, J. T. Shawcross, and Kester Svendsen. Finally, I wish to express my thanks to James Cochrane, who welcomed the present volume on behalf of Penguin Books and warmly supported its publication; and to Marian J. McKellar, also of Penguin Books, who patiently attended to countless details of my manuscript.

Langwith College   C.A.P.
University of York
3 October 1966

ACKNOWLEDGEMENTS

ACKNOWLEDGEMENT is gratefully made to the following publishers and individuals who have given permission to reprint the material used in this volume:

ASIA PUBLISHING HOUSE and Professor B. Rajan for permission to reprint, with some changes, the better part of his 'Introduction' to *Paradise Lost, Books I and II* (London, 1964).

CAMBRIDGE UNIVERSITY PRESS for permission to reprint the better part of Chapter III from A. J. A. Waldock's '*Paradise Lost' and its Critics* (Cambridge, 1947).

CHATTO AND WINDUS LTD. and the authors of the following works for permission to reprint the sections indicated: pages 42–58 from F. R. Leavis's *Revaluation* (London, 1936); Chapter V from Joseph H. Summers's *The Muse's Method* (London, 1962); and, with some changes, pages 135–57 from J. B. Broadbent's *Some Graver Subject* (London, 1960), and pages 147–74 from William Empson's *Milton's God* (London, 1961; rev. ed., 1965).

THE CLARENDON PRESS and Mr Christopher Ricks for permission to reprint, with some slight changes, pages 78–102 from his *Milton's Grand Style* (Oxford, 1963).

CORNELL UNIVERSITY PRESS and Professor Douglas Bush for permission to reprint, with some changes, Chapter IV from his '*Paradise Lost' in Our Time* (Ithaca, N.Y., 1945). Copyright 1945 by Cornell University Press.

THE JOHNS HOPKINS PRESS for permission to reprint, with reduced documentation, Arthur O. Lovejoy's 'Milton and the Paradox of the Fortunate Fall' from his *Essays in the History of Ideas* (Baltimore, 1948); and the same Press, the editors of the *Journal of English Literary History* and the authors of the following works for permission to reprint, in revised form, Kingsley Widmer's 'The Iconography of Renunciation: The Miltonic Simile' from the *Journal of English Literary History*, XXV (1958), 258–69, and Louis L. Martz's '*Paradise Regained*: The Meditative Combat' from the

Journal of English Literary History, XXVII (1960), 223–47 [cf. below under Yale University Press]; and a condensed version of Albert R. Cirillo's 'Noon-Midnight and the Temporal Structure of *Paradise Lost*' from the *Journal of English Literary History*, XXIX (1962), 372–95.

PROFESSOR F. T. PRINCE for permission to reprint his essay 'On the Last Two Books of *Paradise Lost*' from *Essays and Studies 1958* by Members of the English Association (London, 1958).

THE UNIVERSITY OF CHICAGO PRESS and Professor Northrop Frye for permission to reprint his essay 'The Typology of *Paradise Regained*' from *Modern Philology*, LIII (1956), 227–38.

THE UNIVERSITY OF MINNESOTA PRESS and Professor Arnold Stein for permission to reprint, with some changes, the better part of pages 119–62 from his *Answerable Style* (Minneapolis, 1953). Copyright 1953 by the University of Minnesota.

THE UNIVERSITY OF NORTH CAROLINA PRESS and Professor Barbara K. Lewalski for permission to reprint a condensed version of her essay 'Theme and Structure in *Paradise Regained*' from *Studies in Philology*, LVII (1960), 186–220.

YALE UNIVERSITY PRESS for permission to reprint, with some slight changes, Chapter IV from Louis L. Martz's *The Paradise Within* (New Haven, 1964).

On *Paradise Lost*

F. R. Leavis

MILTON'S VERSE*

MILTON's dislodgement, in the past decade, after his two centuries of predominance, was effected with remarkably little fuss. The irresistible argument was, of course, Mr Eliot's creative achievement; it gave his few critical asides – potent, it is true, by context – their finality, and made it unnecessary to elaborate a case. Mr Middleton Murry also, it should be remembered, came out against Milton at much the same time. His *Problem of Style* contains an acute page or two comparing Milton with Shakespeare, and there was a review of Bridges's *Milton's Prosody* in *The Athenaeum* that one would like to see reprinted along with a good deal more of Mr Murry's weekly journalism of that time. But the case remained unelaborated, and now that Mr Eliot has become academically respectable those who refer to it show commonly that they cannot understand it. And when a writer of Mr Allen Tate's repute as critic, poet, and intellectual leader, telling us that Milton should be 'made' to 'influence poetry once more', shows that he too doesn't understand then one may overcome, perhaps, one's shyness of saying the obvious.[1]

Mr Tate thinks that if we don't like Milton it is because of a prejudice against myth and fable and a preference for the fragmentary: 'When we read poetry we bring to it the pseudo-scientific habit of mind; we are used to joining things up in vague disconnected processes in terms that are abstract and thin, and so our sensuous enjoyment is confined to the immediate field of sensation. We are bewildered, helpless, confronted with one of those immensely remote, highly sensuous, and perfectly make-believe worlds that rise above our scattered notions of process.'[2]

*From *Revaluation: Tradition and Development in English Poetry* (1936), pp. 42–58; first published in *Scrutiny*, II (1933), 123–36.

Not everyone will find this impressive. If we are affected by the pseudo-scientific habit of mind to that degree, some would suggest, we probably cannot read poetry at all. But if we can and do read poetry, then our objection to Milton, it must be insisted, is that we dislike his verse and believe that in such verse no 'highly sensuous and perfectly make-believe world' could be evoked. Even in the first two books of *Paradise Lost*, where the myth has vigorous life and one can admire the magnificent invention that Milton's verse is, we feel, after a few hundred lines, our sense of dissatisfaction growing into something stronger. In the end we find ourselves protesting – protesting against the routine gesture, the heavy fall, of the verse, flinching from the foreseen thud that comes so inevitably, and, at last, irresistibly: for reading *Paradise Lost* is a matter of resisting, of standing up against, the verse-movement, of subduing it into something tolerably like sensitiveness, and in the end our resistance is worn down; we surrender at last to the inescapable monotony of the ritual. Monotony: the variety attributed to Milton's Grand Style in the orthodox account can be discoursed on and illustrated at great length, but the stress could be left on 'variety', after an honest interrogation of experience, only by the classically trained.

Here, if this were a lecture, would come illustrative reading-out – say of the famous opening to Book III. As it is, the point seems best enforcible (though it should be obvious at once to anyone capable of being convinced at all) by turning to one of the exceptionally good passages – for everyone will agree at any rate that there are places where the verse glows with an unusual life. One of these, it will again be agreed, is the Mulciber passage at the end of Book I:

> The hasty multitude
> Admiring enter'd, and the work some praise
> And some the Architect: his hand was known
> In Heav'n by many a Towred structure high,
> Where Scepter'd Angels held their residence,
> And sat as Princes, whom the supreme King

Exalted to such power, and gave to rule,
Each in his Hierarchie, the Orders bright.
Nor was his name unheard or unador'd
In ancient Greece; and in Ausonian land
Men called him Mulciber; and how he fell
From Heav'n, they fabl'd, thrown by angry Jove
Sheer o're the Chrystal Battlements: from Morn
To Noon he fell, from Noon to dewy Eve,
A Summers day; and with the setting Sun
Dropt from the Zenith like a falling Star,
On Lemnos th' Aegaean Ile: thus they relate,
Erring . . . .

The opening exhibits the usual heavy rhythmic pattern, the hieratic stylization, the swaying ritual movement back and forth, the steep cadences. Italics will serve to suggest how, when the reader's resistance has weakened, he is brought inevitably down with the foreseen thud in the foreseen place:

>   The hasty multitude
> Ad*mir*ing enter'd, and the work some praise
> And *some* the Architect: his hand was known
> In Héav'n by many a Tówred structure high,
> Where Scépter'd Angels held their résidence,
> And *sat* as Princes . . . .

But from 'Nor was his name unheard' onwards the effect changes. One no longer feels oneself carried along, resigned or protesting, by an automatic ritual, responding automatically with bodily gestures – swayed head and lifted shoulders – to the commanding emphasis: the verse seems suddenly to have come to life. Yet the pattern remains the same; there are the same heavy stresses, the same rhythmic gestures, and the same cadences, and if one thought a graph of the verse-movement worth drawing it would not show the difference. The change of feeling cannot at first be related to any point of form; it comes in with 'ancient Greece' and 'Ausonian land', and seems to be immediately due to the evocation of that serene, clear, ideally remote classical world so potent upon Milton's sensibility.[3] But what is most important to note is that the heavy stresses, the characteristic cadences, turns, and returns of the verse, have here a peculiar expressive felicity. What would elsewhere have been the routine thump of 'Sheer' and 'Dropt' is here, in either case, obviously functional, and the other rhythmic features of the verse are correspondingly appropriate. The stress given by the end-position to the first 'fell', with the accompanying pause, in what looks like a common, limply pompous Miltonicism –

> and how he fell
> From Heav'n, they fabl'd, thrown . . .

– is here uncommonly right; the heavy 'thrown' is right, and so are the following rise and fall, the slopes and curves, of the verse.

There is no need to particularize further. This much room has been given to the fairly obvious merely by way of insisting that the usual pattern of Milton's verse has here an unusual expressive function – becomes, indeed, something else. If anyone should question the unusualness, the doubt would be soon settled by a little exploration. And to admit the unusualness is to admit that commonly the pattern, the stylized gesture, and movement, has no particular expressive work to do, but functions by rote, of its own momentum, in the manner of a ritual.

Milton has difficult places to cross, runs the orthodox eulogy, but his style always carries him through. The sense that Milton's style is of that kind, the dissatisfied sense of a certain hollowness, would by most readers who share it be first of all referred to a characteristic not yet specified – that which evoked from Mr Eliot the damaging word 'magniloquence'. To say that Milton's verse is magniloquent is to say that it is not doing as much as its impressive pomp and volume seem to be asserting; that mere orotundity is a disproportionate part of the whole effect; and that it demands more deference than it merits. It is to call attention to a lack of something in the stuff of the verse, to a certain sensuous poverty.

This poverty is best established by contrast, and tactical considerations suggest taking the example from Milton himself:

Wherefore did Nature powre her bounties forth,
With such a full and unwithdrawing hand,
Covering the earth with odours, fruits, and flocks,
Thronging the Seas with spawn innumerable,
But all to please, and sate the curious taste?
And set to work millions of spinning Worms,
That in their green shops weave the smooth-hair'd silk
To deck her Sons, and that no corner might
Be vacant of her plenty, in her own loyns
She hutch't th' all-worshipt ore, and precious gems
To store her children with; if all the world
Should in a pet of temperance feed on Pulse,
Drink the clear stream, and nothing wear but Frieze
Th' all-giver would be unthank't, would be unprais'd,
Not half his riches known, and yet despis'd,
And we should serve him as a grudging master,
As a Penurious niggard of his wealth,
And live like Natures bastards, not her sons,
Who would be quite surcharged with her own weight,
And strangl'd with her waste fertility;
Th' earth cumber'd, and the wing'd air dark't with plumes,
The herds would over-multitude their Lords,
The Sea o'refraught would swell, and th' unsought diamonds
Would so emblaze the forhead of the Deep,
And so bestudd with Stars, that they below
Would grow inur'd to light, and com at last
To gaze upon the Sun with shameless brows.

This is very unlike anything in *Paradise Lost* (indeed, it is not very like most of *Comus*). If one could forget where one had read it, and were faced with assigning it to its author, one would not soon fix with conviction on any dramatist. And yet it is too like dramatic verse to suggest Milton. It shows, in fact, the momentary predominance in Milton of Shakespeare. It may look less mature, less developed, than the verse of *Paradise Lost*; it is, as a matter of fact, richer, subtler, and more sensitive than anything in *Paradise Lost, Paradise Regained,* or *Samson Agonistes.*

Its comparative sensuous richness, which is pervasive, lends itself fairly readily to analysis at various points; for instance:

> And set to work millions of spinning Worms,
> That in their green shops weave the smooth-hair'd silk . . . .

The Shakespearian life of this is to be explained largely by the swift diversity of associations that are run together. The impression of the swarming worms is telescoped with that of the ordered industry of the workshop, and a further vividness results from the contrasting 'green', with its suggestion of leafy tranquillity. 'Smooth-hair'd' plays off against the energy of the verse the tactual luxury of stroking human hair or the living coat of an animal. The texture of actual sounds, the run of vowels and consonants, with the variety of action and effort, rich in subtle analogical suggestion, demanded in pronouncing them, plays an essential part, though this is not to be analysed in abstraction from the meaning. The total effect is as if words as words withdrew themselves from the focus of our attention and we were directly aware of a tissue of feelings and perceptions.

No such effect is possible in the verse of *Paradise Lost*, where the use of the medium, the poet's relation to his words, is completely different. This, for instance, is from the description, in Book IV, of the Garden of Eden, which, most admirers of Milton will agree, exemplifies sensuous richness if that is to be found in *Paradise Lost*:

> And now divided into four main Streams,
> Runs divers, wandering many a famous Realme
> And Country whereof here needs no account,
> But rather to tell how, if Art could tell,
> How from that Sapphire Fount the crisped Brooks,
> Rowling on Orient Pearl and sands of Gold,
> With mazie error under pendant shades
> Ran Nectar, visiting each plant, and fed

Flours worthy of Paradise which not nice Art
In Beds and curious Knots, but Nature boon
Powrd forth profuse on Hill and Dale and Plaine,
Both where the morning Sun first warmly smote
The open field, and where the unpierc't shade
Imbround the noontide Bowrs: Thus was this place,
A happy rural seat of various view:
Groves whose rich Trees wept odorous Gumms and Balme,
Others whose fruit burnisht with Golden Rinde
Hung amiable, Hesperian Fables true,
If true, here onely, and of delicious taste . . . .

It should be plain at once that the difference was not exaggerated. As the laboured, pedantic artifice of the diction suggests, Milton seems here to be focusing rather upon words than upon perceptions, sensations, or things. 'Sapphire', 'Orient Pearl', 'sands of Gold', 'odorous Gumms and Balme', and so on, convey no doubt a vague sense of opulence, but this is not what we mean by 'sensuous richness'. The loose judgement that it is a verbal opulence has a plain enough meaning if we look for contrast at the 'bestudd with Stars' of Comus's speech; there we feel (the alliteration is of a different kind from that of the Grand Style) the solid lumps of light studding the 'forehead of the Deep'. In the description of Eden, a little before the passage quoted, we have:

> And all amid them stood the Tree of Life,
> High eminent, blooming Ambrosial Fruit
> Of vegetable Gold . . . .

It would be of no use to try and argue with anyone who contended that 'vegetable Gold' exemplified the same kind of fusion as 'green shops'.

It needs no unusual sensitiveness of language to perceive that, in this Grand Style, the medium calls pervasively for a kind of attention, compels an attitude towards itself, that is incompatible with sharp, concrete realization; just as it would seem to be, in the mind of the poet, incompatible with an interest in sensuous particularity. He exhibits a feeling *for* words rather than a capacity for feeling *through* words; we are often, in reading him, moved to comment that he is 'external' or that he 'works from the outside'. The Grand Style, at its best, compels us to recognize it as an impressive stylization, but it functions very readily, and even impressively, at low tension, and its tendency is betrayed, even in a show piece like the description of Eden, by such offences as:

> Thus was this place,
> A happy rural seat of various view:
> Groves whose rich Trees wept odorous Gumms and Balme,
> Others whose fruits burnisht with Golden Rinde
> Hung amiable, Hesperian Fables true,
> If true, here onely, and of delicious taste . . . .

– If the Eighteenth Century thought that poetry was something that could be applied from the outside, it found the precedent as well as the apparatus in Milton.

The extreme and consistent remoteness of Milton's medium from any English that was ever spoken is an immediately relevant consideration. It became, of course, habitual to him; but habituation could not sensitize a medium so cut off from speech – speech that belongs to the emotional and sensory texture of actual living and is in resonance with the nervous system; it could only confirm an impoverishment of sensibility. In any case, the Grand Style barred Milton from essential expressive resources of English that he had once commanded. Comus, in the passage quoted, imagining the consequences of the Lady's doctrine, says that Nature

> would be quite surcharged with her own weight,
> And strangl'd with her waste fertility;
> Th' earth cumber'd, and the wing'd air dark't with plumes,
> The herds would over-multitude their Lords,
> The Sea o'refraught would swell . . . .

To cut the passage short here is to lame it, for the effect of Nature's being strangled with her waste fertility is partly conveyed by the ejaculatory piling-up of clauses, as the reader, by turning back, can verify. But one way in which the verse acts the meaning – not merely says but does – is fairly represented in the line

Th' earth cumber'd, and the wing'd air dark't with plumes,

where the crowding of stressed words, the consonantal clusters, and the clogged movement have a function that needs no analysis. This kind of action in the verse, together with the attendant effects of movement and intonation in the whole passage, would be quite impossible in the Grand Style: the tyrannical stylization forbids. But then, the mind that invented Milton's Grand Style had renounced the English language, and with that, inevitably, Milton being an Englishman, a great deal else.

'Milton wrote Latin as readily as he did English.' And: 'Critics sometimes forget that before the *Nativity Ode* Milton wrote more Latin than English, and one may suggest that the best of the Latin is at least as good as the best of the English.' At any rate, one can believe that, after a decade of Latin polemic, Latin idiom came very naturally to him, and was associated with some of his strongest, if not necessarily most interesting, habits of feeling. But however admirable his Latin may be judged to be, to latinize in English is quite another matter, and it is a testimony to the effect of the 'fortifying curriculum' that the price of Milton's latinizing should have been so little recognized.

'This charm of the exceptional and the irregular in diction', writes Mr Logan Pearsall Smith in his extremely valuable essay on English idioms (*Words and Idioms*, p. 267), 'accounts for the fact that we can enjoy the use of idiom even in a dead language which we do not know very well; it also explains the subtlety of effect which Milton achieved by transfusing Greek or Latin constructions into his English verse.' But Milton's transfusing is regular and unremitting, and involves, not pleasant occasional surprises, but a consistent rejection of English idiom, as the passage quoted from Book IV sufficiently shows. So complete, and so mechanically habitual, is Milton's departure from the English order, structure, and accentuation that he often produces passages that have to be read through several times before one can see how they go, though the Miltonic mind has nothing to offer that could justify obscurity – no obscurity was intended: it is merely that Milton has forgotten the English language. There is, however, a much more important point to be made: it is that, cultivating so complete and systematic a callousness to the intrinsic nature of English, Milton forfeits all possibility of subtle or delicate life in his verse.

It should be plain, for instance, that subtlety of movement in English verse depends upon the play of the natural sense movement and intonation against the verse structure, and that 'natural', here, involves a reference, more or less direct, to idiomatic speech. The development in Shakespeare can be studied as a more and more complex and subtle play of speech movement and intonation against the verse. There is growing complexity of imagery and thought too, of course, but it is not to this mainly that one could refer in analysing the difference between a characteristic passage of *Othello* and Romeo's dying lament: the difference is very largely a matter of subtle tensions within, pressures upon, the still smooth curves of the still 'regular' verse of *Othello*. No such play is possible in a medium in which the life of idiom, the pressure of speech, is as completely absent as in Milton's Grand Style. That is why even in the most lively books of *Paradise Lost* the verse, brilliant as it is, has to the ear that appreciates Shakespeare a wearying deadness about it. That skill we are told of, the skill with which Milton varies the beat without losing touch with the underlying norm, slides the caesura backwards and forwards, and so on, is certainly there. But the kind of appreciation this skill demands is that which one gives – if one is a classic – to a piece of Latin (we find writers on Milton 'appreciating' his Latin verse in the same tone and spirit as they do his English).

'An appreciation of Milton is the last reward of consummated scholarship.' Qualified as Mark Pattison prescribes, one may, with Raleigh, find that Milton's style is 'all substance and weight', that he is almost too packed to be read aloud, and go on to acclaim the 'top of his skill' in the choruses of *Samson Agonistes*. But the ear trained on Shakespeare will believe that it would lose little at the first hearing of a moderately well-declaimed passage, and that *Samson Agonistes* read aloud would be hardly tolerable, because of its desolating exposure of utter loss – loss in the poet of all feeling for his native English.[4] The rhythmic deadness, the mechanical externality with which the movement is varied, is the more pitifully evident because of the personal urgency of the theme and the austerity: there is no magniloquence here. To arrive here, of course, took genius, and the consummation can be analytically admired. But then, there have been critics who found rhythmic subtlety in *Phoebus with Admetus* and *Love in the Valley*.

Up to this point the stress has fallen upon Milton's latinizing. To leave it there would be to suggest an inadequate view of his significance. His influence is seen in Tennyson as well as in Thomson, and to say that he groups with Tennyson and Spenser in contrast to Shakespeare and Donne is to say something more important about him than that he latinized. The force of associating him with Spenser is not that he was himself 'sage and serious'; and in contrasting him with Donne one is not, as seems also commonly to be thought, lamenting that he chose not to become a Metaphysical. The qualities of Donne that invite the opposition are what is shown in this:

> On a huge hill,
> Cragged and steep, Truth stands, and hee that will
> Reach her, about must, and about must goe;
> And what the hills suddenness resists, winne so;
> Yet strive so, that before age, deaths twilight,
> Thy Soule rest, for none can worke in that night.

This is the Shakespearian use of English; one might say that it is the English use – the use, in the essential spirit of the language, of its characteristic resources. The words seem to do what they say; a very obvious example of what, in more or less subtle forms, is pervasive being given in the image of reaching that the reader has to enact when he passes from the second to the third line. But a comparison will save analysis:

> For so to interpose a little ease,
> Let our frail thoughts dally with false surmise.
> Ay me! Whilst thee the shores, and sounding Seas
> Wash far away, where ere thy bones are hurld,
> Whether beyond the stormy Hebrides,
> Where thou perhaps under the whelming tide
> Visit'st the bottom of the monstrous world;
> Or whether thou to our moist vows denied,
> Sleep'st by the fable of Bellerus old,
> Where the great vision of the guarded Mount
> Looks toward Namancos and Bayona's hold . . . .

The contrast is sharp; the use of the medium, the attitude towards it in both writer and reader, is as different as possible. Though the words are doing so much less work than in Donne, they seem to value themselves more highly – they seem, comparatively, to be occupied with valuing themselves rather than with doing anything. This last clause would have to be saved for Tennyson if it were a question of distinguishing fairly between Milton and him, but, faced with the passage from Donne, Milton and Tennyson go together. Tennyson descends from Spenser by way of Milton and Keats, and it was not for nothing that Milton, to the puzzlement of some critics, named Spenser as his 'original': the mention of Tennyson gives the statement (however intended) an obvious significance.

The consummate art of *Lycidas*, personal as it is, exhibits a use of language in the spirit of Spenser – incantatory, remote from speech. Certain feelings are expressed, but there is no pressure behind the words; what predominates in the handling of them is not the tension of something precise to be defined and fixed, but a concern for mellifluousness – for liquid sequences and a pleasing opening and closing of the vowels. This is the bent revealed in the early work; the Shakespearian passage in *Comus* is exceptional. Milton, that is, someone will observe of the comparison, is trying to do something quite other than Donne; his bent is quite different. Exactly: the point is to be clear which way it tends.

The most admired things in *Comus* – it is significant – are the songs.

> Sweet Echo, sweetest Nymph that liv'st unseen
> Within thy airy shell
> By slow Meander's margent green,
> And in the violet imbroider'd vale
> Where the love-lorn Nightingale
> Nightly to thee her sad Song mourneth well . . .

Quite plainly, the intention here is not merely to flatter the singing voice and suit the air, but to produce in words effects analogous to those of music, and the exquisite achievement has been sufficiently praised. The undertaking was congenial to Milton. Already he had shown his capacity for a weightier kind of music, a more impressive and less delicate instrument:

> Blest pair of Sirens, pledges of Heav'ns joy,
> Sphear-born harmonious Sisters, Voice, and Vers,
> Wed your divine sounds, and mixt power employ
> Dead things with inbreath'd sense able to pierce,
> And . . . .

We remember the Tennysonian felicity: 'God-gifted organ voice'. *At a Solemn Musick*, though coming from not long after 1630, anticipates unmistakably the 'melodious noise' of *Paradise Lost*, and suggests a further account of that sustained impressiveness, that booming swell which becomes so intolerable.

This, then, and not any incapacity to be interested in myth, is why we find Milton unexhilarating. The myth of *Paradise Lost*, indeed, suffers from deficiencies related to those of the verse. 'Milton's celestial and infernal regions are large but insufficiently furnished apartments filled by heavy conversation', remarks Mr Eliot,[5] and suggests that the divorce from Rome, following the earlier breach with the Teutonic past, may have something to do with this mythological thinness. But it is enough to point to the limitations in range and depth of Milton's interests, their patent inadequacy to inform a 'sense of myth, of fable, of ordered wholes in experience'. His strength is of the kind that we indicate when, distinguishing between intelligence and character, we lay the stress on the latter; it is a strength, that is, involving sad disabilities. He has 'character', moral grandeur, moral force; but he is, for the purposes of his undertaking, disastrously single-minded and simple-minded. He reveals everywhere a dominating sense of righteousness and a complete incapacity to question or explore its significance and conditions. This defect of intelligence is a defect of imagination. He offers as ultimate for our worship mere brute assertive will, though he condemns it unwittingly by his argument and by glimpses of his own finer human standard. His volume of moral passion owes its strength too much to innocence – a guileless unawareness of the subtleties of egotism – to be an apt agent for projecting an 'ordered whole of experience'. It involves, too, a great poverty of interest. After the first two books, magnificent in their simple force (party politics in the Grand Style Milton can compass), *Paradise Lost*, though there are intervals of relief, becomes dull and empty: 'all', as Raleigh says, 'is power, vagueness, and grandeur'. Milton's inadequacy to myth, in fact, is so inescapable, and so much is conceded in sanctioned comment, that the routine eulogy of his 'architectonic' power is plainly a matter of mere inert convention.

But even if the realized effect were much less remote than it actually is from the abstract design, even if the life and interest were much better distributed, the orthodox praise of Milton's architectonics would still be questionable in its implications. It would still be most commonly found to harbour the incomprehensions betrayed by the critic cited in the opening of this chapter.

F. R. Leavis

In his time (as in ours) there was a good deal to be said for the Spenserian school against the technical breakdown to which the Jacobean dramatists had ridden English verse. Webster is a great moment in English style, but the drama was falling off, and blank verse had to survive in a non-dramatic form, which required a more rigid treatment than the stage could offer it. In substance, it needed stiffer and less sensitive perceptions, a more artificial grasp of sensation, to offset the supersensitive awareness of the school of Shakespeare, a versification less imitative of the flow of sensation and more architectural. What poetry needed, Milton was able to give. It was Arnold who, in the 1853 preface to his own poems, remarked that the sensational imagery of the Shakespearian tradition had not been without its baleful effect on poetry down to Keats: one may imitate a passage in Shakespeare without penetrating to the mind that wrote it, but to imitate Milton one must be Milton; one must have all of Milton's resources in myth behind the impulse: it is the myth, ingrained in his very being, that makes the style.

If that is so, the style, as we have seen, condemns the myth. Behind the whole muddled passage, of course, and not far behind, is the old distinction (see, for instance, Raleigh) between the 'Classical style' and the 'Romantic' – the 'Romantic' including Shelley (and, one presumes, Swinburne) along with Shakespeare. It is enough here to say that the inability to read Shakespeare (or the remoteness from the reading of him) revealed in such a passage and such a distinction throws the most damaging suspicion upon the term 'architectural'. The critic clearly implies that because Shakespeare exhibits 'more sensitive perceptions', and offers a 'versification more imitative of the flow of sensation', he is therefore indifferent to total effect and dissipates the attention by focusing, and asking us to focus, on the immediate at the expense of the whole. As a matter of fact, any one of the great tragedies is an incomparably better whole than *Paradise Lost*; so finely and subtly organized that architectural analogies seem inappropriate (a good deal of *Paradise Lost* strikes one as being almost as mechanical as bricklaying). The analysis of a Shakespeare passage showing that 'supersensitive awareness' leads one into the essential structure of the whole organism: Shakespeare's marvellous faculty of intense local realization is a faculty of realizing the whole locally.

A Shakespeare play, says Professor Wilson Knight, may be considered as 'an extended metaphor', and the phrase suggests with great felicity this almost inconceivably close and delicate organic wholeness. The belief that 'architectural' qualities like Milton's represent a higher kind of unity goes with the kind of intellectual bent that produces Humanism – that takes satisfaction in inertly orthodox generalities, and is impressed by invocations of Order from minds that have no glimmer of intelligence about contemporary literature and could not safely risk even elementary particular appreciation.

NOTE I
Proserpin Gath'ring Flow'rs

Another of the finest of those passages (it is rightly one of the most current pieces of Milton) in which life suddenly flows is that with which the description of the Garden of Eden closes (Bk IV, l. 268). To bring out the contrast with the stylized literary opulence of what goes before (see p. 22 above) quotation had better start a dozen lines earlier – I use the Grierson text:

> Another side, umbrageous Grots and Caves
> Of cool recess, o'er which the mantling Vine
> Lays forth her purple Grape, and gently creeps
> Luxuriant; meanwhile murmuring waters fall
> Down the slope, hills, disperst, or in a Lake,
> That to the fringed Bank with Myrtle crown'd,
> Her chrystal mirror holds, unite thir streams.
> The Birds thir quire apply; airs, vernal airs,
> Breathing the smell of field and grove, attune
> The trembling leaves, while Universal Pan
> Knit with the Graces and the Hours in dance

Led on th' Eternal Spring. Not that fair field
Of Enna, where Proserpin gath'ring flow'rs
Herself a fairer Flow'r, by gloomy Dis
Was gather'd, which cost Ceres all that pain
To seek her through the world; not that sweet Grove
Of Daphne by Orontes, and th' inspir'd
Castalian Spring might with this Paradise
Of Eden strive; nor that Nyseian Isle
Girt with the River Triton, where old Cham,
Whom Gentiles Ammon call and Lybian Jove,
Hid Amalthea and her Florid Son
Young Bacchus from his Stepdame Rhea's eye;
Nor where Abassin Kings thir issue Guard,
Mount Amara, though by this some suppos'd
True Paradise under the Ethiop Line
By Nilus head, enclos'd with shining Rock,
A whole day's journey high, but wide remote
From this Assyrian Garden . . . .

The effect, when we come to the Proserpin passage, is like a change from artificial flowers and elaborated decoration to something alive with sap that flows from below.

> Not that fair field
> Of Enna, where Proserpin gath'ring flow'rs
> Herself a fairer Flow'r, by gloomy Dis
> Was gather'd . . .

– that might, in its simple, inevitable rightness and its fresh bloom, have come from Shakespeare, the Shakespeare of the pastoral scene in *The Winter's Tale*. It is in the repeated verb that the realizing imagination is irresistibly manifested; it is the final 'gathered' that gives concrete life to a conventional phrase and makes Proserpin herself a flower. And to make her a flower is to establish the difference between the two gatherings: the design – the gathered gatherer – is subtle in its simplicity. The movement of the verse seems to be the life of the design, performing, in fact, in its suggestive appropriateness, something of the function of imagery. The phrasing – e.g.,

which cost Ceres all that pain
To seek her through the world

– has a direct and sensitive naturalness.

It is notable that the inspiration here is of the same kind as in the Mulciber passage – 'the freshness of the early world', the 'wonder and bloom' of the legendary classical morning. In the lines that follow, about Abassin Kings and Mount Amara – lines so curiously echoed in *Kubla Khan* – the delighted romantic wonder is plain.

In contrast with this snuggled-in (for such it is with reference to the theme of *Paradise Lost*) piece of imaginative indulgence, the famous description of Adam and Eve –

Two of far nobler shape, erect and tall,
God-like erect

– that comes immediately after is, in its conscious and characteristic moral solemnity and poetic decorum, more distasteful than it might otherwise have been.

NOTES

1. It is fair to add that Mr Tate objects to the representation of him given here, and that he does not, I gather, now hold the position with regard to Milton set forth in the essay referred to.
2. *The New Republic*, 21 October 1931.
3. See NOTE 1 ['Proserpin Gath'ring Flowers', above, p. 30].
4. See NOTE 2 ['The Verse of *Samson Agonistes*' – not reprinted in this volume. – Ed.].
5. See the essay on Blake, now to be found in *Selected Essays*.

Douglas Bush

PARADISE LOST: THE POETICAL TEXTURE*

In the nineteenth century critics were commonly given to re-
gretting Milton's beliefs and ideas (which they commonly did
not understand) and to exalting his art. When in the 1920s the
metaphysical vogue became dominant, even Milton's art came
under the ban. It now appeared that there was only one vital
kind of poetry, that which simultaneously embraces diverse
planes of experience and is characterized by realistic immediacy,
particularity, and complexity, by a fusion of thought and feeling, by the interplay of irony and wit, and by diction, syntax,
and rhythms which belong to the genius of common speech.
To summarize the verdict of Mr Leavis, the so-called grand
style of *Paradise Lost* is in the main a heavy and monotonous
stylization, a dead external grandiosity which reflects its author's
narrow and rigid simple-mindedness.

During the past decade or two the metaphysical vogue has
subsided to rational proportions, and the main movement in the
criticism of seventeenth-century poetry has been a renewed
appreciation of Milton's art, an appreciation much more penetrating and subtle than the older kind and carried on with sympathetic awareness of the beliefs and ideas that art was
employed to utter. Much of this criticism has had no special
bias (apart from some critics' concern with baroque), and has
treated *Paradise Lost* as a supreme English poem, conditioned
but not confined by its period. This has been all to the good. It
may be old-fashioned, though perhaps not amiss, to recall
Milton's former status as the supreme 'classical' artist in
English poetry, in both the narrow and the broad sense of the
term. The following pages offer only a few reminders of that

* From *'Paradise Lost' in our Time* (1945), ch. IV. Revised in part for the
present volume by the author.

quality, of the tradition in which Milton has his poetic being. If those pages (written in 1944) are unduly polemical, it may be remembered that some critics of high authority had been conducting a prolonged and sometimes violent anti-Miltonic campaign. (Just for the record – not that it matters to anyone but me – I may say that my objections to Eliot the anti-Miltonist have gone along with immense admiration for Eliot the poet.)

*

As a poet whom we enjoy or do not enjoy reading, Milton must of course stand on his own feet. At the same time, as the greatest English representative of a great tradition, a central kind of poetic sensibility and technique, Milton does not stand or fall alone. He had, as our critics reluctantly admit, his own powerful individuality, yet the essential qualities of his poetic art are the same in kind as those of the ancients among whose heirs he hoped to rank. I do not mean to say that Milton deserves high marks because he imitated and echoed the classics. What I do mean, though it may seem too obvious to state, is that, since Milton's art is of the ancient kind, the charges brought against him must be brought likewise against nearly all the Greek and Roman poets. And it is doubtful if even our iconoclasts would venture to dismiss nearly all ancient poetry as bad, although that great body of writing, lyrical as well as epic, was very thoroughly stylized and artificial. But if we agree that most ancient poets were entitled to wear their singing robes, so assuredly was their English affinity and peer.

We may again recall Mr Leavis's general view, a view evidently shared by Mr Eliot and others, that Milton was a man of moral force and grandeur, with a dominating sense of righteousness, a single-minded and simple-minded egoism, which made him incapable of exploring the significance and conditions of righteousness and led him to impose a merely artificial order upon experience. One might, if one's mind worked in that way, use the same words about Pindar or Aeschylus. The critics' moral judgement of Milton seems to be in part a reflection of their aesthetic judgement, and their aesthetic judgement indicates either unwillingness or incapacity to understand the methods of classical art. A poet like Donne develops his theme through a network of heterogeneous particulars and thereby displays what is called a unified sensibility, though the adjective might better be 'multiple'. Milton on the other hand was always governed by the traditional principle which Ben Jonson stated simply, that 'the learned use ever election, and a mean; they look back to what they intended at first, and make all an even, and proportion'd body.' We have a signal example of that in the beautiful lines Milton cut out of the beginning of *Comus*, apparently because they blurred his main idea; if the author of the *Anniversaries* had written such lines, or their equivalent, he would have retained and amplified them. In Milton and other truly classical artists the artistic creed, like the philosophic creed, rests on a hierarchical scale of values, not on the assumption that all the facts of experience or erudition are born free and equal. The ancient poets would have been astonished if told that their method betrayed a single-minded simplicity and ignorance of the complexities of human nature and life. They would have replied that it was the artist's job to order nature, not merely to reproduce it or leave it half-finished. I am not saying that the one method is at all times and for all purposes better than the other, I am only saying that it is foolish to confuse the self-imposed limitations of classical art with a limitation of intelligence and sensibility, and doubly foolish to write as if Milton's method were a deplorable invention of his own. When we boil down the hostile criticism of Milton's technique, much of it only amounts to the usual romantic feeling that classical art is cold and dead. There are always critics who, seeing the surface of the ocean smooth, take it for a pond, and, seeing a pond agitated by the wind, take it for the ocean. To appreciate the complexity and depth of emotional suggestion in Milton we must learn his language – as, on a somewhat lower level, we willingly learn to interpret the hints and nuances of Henry James.

One pervasive element in classical art which devotees of metaphysical particularity cannot abide is its generalizing habit, its refusal to number the streaks of the tulip. In Milton, as in the ancients, that habit springs from the instinct for rendering the normal and universal, not the peculiar. The result may appear 'simple', but it is not thin. One perfect example of classical writing is the invocation to Light:

> Thus with the Year
> Seasons return, but not to me returns
> Day, or the sweet approach of Ev'n or Morn,
> Or sight of vernal bloom, or Summer's Rose,
> Or flocks, or herds, or human face divine;
> But cloud instead, and ever-during dark
> Surrounds me, from the cheerful ways of men
> Cut off, and for the Book of knowledge fair
> Presented with a Universal blanc
> Of Nature's works to mee expung'd and ras'd,
> And wisdom at one entrance quite shut out.
> So much the rather thou Celestial light
> Shine inward, and the mind through all her powers
> Irradiate, there plant eyes, all mist from thence
> Purge and disperse, that I may see and tell
> Of things invisible to mortal sight.

In the first lines the generalized items – the round of seasons, 'Day', so suggestively poised, 'Ev'n or Morn', and the rest, including the profoundly moving surprise of the inverted 'divine' – all these are packed with emotion because they are merely registered with impersonal restraint as the commonplace phenomena of every day. We feel the reserve of power behind such quietness. We are compelled to realize for ourselves what deprivation means, and we can do so because Milton universalizes his own feelings, the normal feelings of the cheerful human race to which he belongs. He feels, to be sure, as John Milton, but he writes as 'the blind poet'.[1] Both in temper and manner

Milton's humble prayer – the prayer of a man whose imagination, according to Lord David Cecil, is 'unlit by heavenly gleams' – is a world away from the passionate egoism of Donne's religious poems.

These lines, and countless others in *Paradise Lost*, are written with more or less natural and almost prosaic simplicity. But a generalized style of more ritualistic remoteness is appropriate and necessary in a long poem about God and Satan, Everyman and Everywoman, on the stage of the world. Milton's stage is completely different from Dante's and demands in general the opposite of realistic minuteness. What Milton needs to give is the idea of hell, not a road map, the idea of an earthly paradise, not a recognizable description of a spot in Mesopotamia. His generalizing habit very rarely becomes routine classicism or inflation, and the critics' expressions of dislike, when attached to actual examples and not left in a hazy grandeur of generality, usually reveal a failure to understand the poet's intention and achievement. We might look at two passages from the picture of Eden which are condemned by Mr Leavis. One is this:

> And all amid them stood the Tree of Life,
> High eminent, blooming Ambrosial Fruit
> Of vegetable Gold.

While the critic seems to think the Tree of Life should have been presented in terms acceptable to the horticulturist, Milton wishes, with an oblique glance at the apples of the Hesperides, to suggest a mysterious growth hardly to be approached in words. In the paradoxical phrase 'vegetable Gold', which Mr Leavis especially scorns, each word is altered and quickened by the other; the richness of 'Gold' glorifies the simple product of nature, and the rich natural life implied in 'vegetable' gives pliant form and vitality to metallic hardness and removes the idea of unhealthy artifice and evil which in *Paradise Lost* is associated with gold.

Mr Leavis's other horrible example is a longer neighbouring passage:

> How from that Sapphire Fount the crisped Brooks,
> Rolling on Orient Pearl and sands of Gold,
> With mazy error under pendant shades
> Ran Nectar, visiting each plant, and fed
> Flow'rs worthy of Paradise which not nice Art
> In Beds and curious Knots, but Nature boon
> Pour'd forth profuse on Hill and Dale and Plain,
> Both where the morning Sun first warmly smote
> The open field, and where the unpierc't shade
> Imbrown'd the noontide Bow'rs: Thus was this place,
> A happy rural seat of various view:
> Groves whose rich Trees wept odorous Gums and Balm,
> Others whose fruit burnisht with Golden Rind
> Hung amiable, Hesperian Fables true,
> If true, here only, and of delicious taste.

The laboured, pedantic artifice of the diction, says Mr Leavis, suggests that Milton is focusing rather upon words than upon perceptions, sensations, or things; the conventional items 'convey no doubt a vague sense of opulence, but this is not what we mean by "sensuous richness".'[2] In other words, Milton was trying, or should have tried, to create the sensation of being in a garden, like Marvell's perhaps, and only produced a tissue of unreal generalities. (If, by the way,

> A happy rural seat of various view

is bad eighteenth-century diction, so too perhaps is Marvell's

> Waves in its plumes the various light.)

While wrong-headed on the main point, Mr Leavis has a glimmer of the truth in his vague sense of opulence. Milton knew quite as well as his critic that he was assembling the stock properties of traditional earthly paradises. Far from trying to render the sensation of being in a garden, he was suggesting, through conventional symbols, a golden age more perfect than even the classical poets had imagined. He is gathering us, in the language of Yeats, into the artifice of eternity. A localized sharpness of sensation would have both cramped and dissipated that half-abstract impression of an ideal world, an ideal state both cosmic and human, external and mental. Mr Leavis deplores the contrast between such writing and the uniquely complex and dynamic particularity of Comus's speech on the bounties of nature. But in that speech, in writing for once in a way which would win Mr Leavis's applause, Milton was conveying the idea of vast sprawling disorder in keeping with the spiritual disorder of his naturalistic speaker.

Milton's emphasis on the fresh fertility and unspoiled simplicity of Eden is a notable instance of a general device, though 'device' is hardly adequate for what is a religious and philosophic as well as an artistic principle. That is the kind of contrast which his master Spenser had first used on a large scale. In *Paradise Lost* as in *The Faerie Queene*, and to an even greater degree, there is a continuous antithesis, direct or indirect, between simplicity, purity, goodness, health, light, life, and love on the one hand, and luxury, corruption, evil, disease, darkness, death, and hate on the other. It is, however different the manner, much the same as the continuous contrast in *The Waste Land* between water and aridity as symbols of spiritual life and death. And Milton's all-embracing network of contrasts, the imaginative and pictorial illustration of right and wrong, is one of the richest elements in that power of architectural design which Mr Leavis likens to bricklaying. When the simpleminded old poet appears to be merely letting himself go in ornamental opulence, he may be doing something more than that. Let us look first at a passage in *The Waste Land*:

> The Chair she sat in, like a burnished throne,
> Glowed on the marble, where the glass
> Held up by standards wrought with fruited vines
> From which a golden Cupidon peeped out
> (Another hid his eyes behind his wing)
> Doubled the flames of sevenbranched candelabra
> Reflecting light upon the table as
> The glitter of her jewels rose to meet it,

> From satin cases poured in rich profusion;
> In vials of ivory and coloured glass
> Unstoppered, lurked her strange synthetic perfumes,
> Unguent, powdered, or liquid – troubled, confused
> And drowned the sense in odours; stirred by the air
> That freshened from the window, these ascended
> In fattening the prolonged candle-flames,
> Flung their smoke into the laquearia,
> Stirring the pattern on the coffered ceiling.[3]

Here, through a picture of physical objects (a picture perhaps somewhat overloaded for its purpose), Mr Eliot is describing their owner's spiritual desiccation and blindness and irreligious pride. That is precisely what Milton does in describing the palace of Pandemonium built by the fallen angels in hell:

> Anon out of the earth a Fabric huge
> Rose like an Exhalation, with the sound
> Of Dulcet Symphonies and voices sweet,
> Built like a Temple, where Pilasters round
> Were set, and Doric pillars overlaid
> With Golden Architrave; nor did there want
> Cornice or Frieze, with bossy Sculptures grav'n,
> The Roof was fretted Gold. Not Babylon,
> Nor great Alcairo such magnificence
> Equall'd in all thir glories, to inshrine
> Belus or Serapis thir Gods, or seat
> Thir Kings, when Egypt with Assyria strove
> In wealth and luxury.

Since we hear a good deal about the poverty of Milton's rhetorical texture, we may look at a few details in this description. The supernatural power and speed of the diabolic builders are conveyed in the rhythm of 'out of the earth' and 'Rose like an Exhalation', and in the substance of the simile. 'Exhalation' was a generic name for hot, dry 'smokes' ascending from the earth, thinner and lighter than watery 'vapors'; besides, exhalations, in themselves suggestive of diseased nature, might be kindled into comets and other portentous apparitions. The mention of 'Symphonies' recalls the miraculous building of Ilion and Thebes, although, in contrast with the noble music of Apollo and Amphion, the words 'Dulcet' and 'sweet' suggest unhealthily sensuous Lydian airs; Milton may have remembered too, as he had in an early sonnet, the so-called beginning of Greek liberty, the Spartans' destruction of the walls of Athens to the music of women flute players. 'Built like a Temple' reminds us how far this gorgeous palace is from the simplest of true temples,

> an Island salt and bare,
> The haunt of Seals and Orcs, and Sea-mews' clang,

how far from Him who prefers

> Before all Temples th' upright heart and pure.

'Doric pillars', which imply heroic strength, are 'overlaid with Golden Architrave' and an excess of luxuriant ornament, as the builders' angelic strength has been corrupted. Finally, here as elsewhere, Milton links Satan and his host with the barbarous and mighty empires of the heathen orient, empires which are the very synonym of human pride long since overthrown, as such things must always be. Thus we visualize and feel the evil degradation of angelic powers, but at the same time the whole description and the main metrical movement reflect the angels' renewed energy and confidence. And though the general impression is quite clear, a full impression depends upon details and overtones which do not bear out the charge of Milton's insensitivity to the smaller effects of words and rhythms. His wealth of traditional and emotional association, while very different from that of Donne or Mr Eliot, has its own complexity, a complexity, however, not tangential, as in both those poets it often is, but so coherently integrated that it seems simple.

One could not very well, in the briefest sketch of Milton, overlook his classical adaptations, although these are much less important than his classicism in the more general and deeper sense of the word. I shall not speak here of large elements in his fable, like the roll call and council of leaders, the use of celestial agencies, and so on. These things are interesting, since Milton does not imitate without re-creating, but we are concerned with the minuter threads of texture.

Of Milton's heterogeneous allusions those which spring first to mind are the mythological. Three of the four passages in Milton which Mr Leavis is able to praise are of that kind. In Milton as in other Renaissance poets the ancient myths are generally symbols of an ideal world of ideal beauty, and the description of Eden is naturally studded with them. Mr Eliot, in his earlier verse, was in the habit of juxtaposing a sordid present and an ideal past, and Milton, though never a romantic in the sense that Mr Eliot was, could feel a partly similar nostalgia, sometimes in a simply idealistic mood, sometimes not. His description of the loveliest of earthly paradises was given after Satan had entered it, so that there was a tragically ironic contrast between ideal beauty and imminent evil. And in his pictures of Adam and Eve there is a frequent revelation, especially moving from an upholder of conscious virtue, of the desire to believe in an ideal state of unconscious innocence. Both nostalgic idealism and tragic irony are fused in the most beautiful and famous of all Milton's similes:

> Not that fair field
> Of Enna, where Proserpin gath'ring flow'rs
> Herself a fairer Flow'r by gloomy Dis
> Was gather'd, which cost Ceres all that pain
> To seek her through the world.

One cannot fully analyse the power of these lines – the poignant pattern of idea and rhythm, the pathos of familiarity in 'all that pain', the implied likeness between the beauty and the fate of Proserpine and Eve, and the pervasive and suggestive economy and understatement.

While there is no central antinomy in *Paradise Lost*, there may be incidental antinomies, for often, in writing a sacred poem, Milton feels obliged to label as pagan fiction what his imagination cannot resist. Perhaps the best example is the passage on Mulciber, in which he is recalling, in a serious and romantic mood and with an un-Homeric sense of space, a bit of Homeric comedy:

> how he fell
> From Heav'n, they fabl'd, thrown by angry Jove
> Sheer o'er the Crystal Battlements: from Morn
> To Noon he fell, from Noon to dewy Eve,
> A Summer's day; and with the setting Sun
> Dropt from the Zenith like a falling Star,
> On Lemnos, th' Ægæan Isle: thus they relate,
> Erring . . . .[4]

The allusion is opened and closed with hostile phrases, and Mulciber is one of the fallen angels, yet the imaginative and visual richness and the rhythmical movement of the lines show the poet succumbing to the spell.

Milton's direct treatment of ancient myth is the culmination of Renaissance art and it has lost nothing of its magical beauty. But I should like to mention a few examples of a device which is much more in favour with modern poets, the half-concealed or altered allusion. At the beginning of Satan's first speech he greets his lieutenant, Beelzebub, with

> If thou beest he; But O how fall'n! how chang'd
> From him, who in the happy Realms of Light . . . .

We are certainly intended to remember Isaiah's 'How art thou fallen from heaven, O Lucifer, son of the morning!' and almost certainly the appearance to Aeneas, at the fall of Troy, of the blood-stained ghost of Hector, *'lux Dardaniae'*, *'quantum mutatus'* from that Hector who had been the tower of Trojan strength. The double allusion conveys a simultaneous effect of superhuman remoteness and grandeur and of something like concrete human reality, and also, as in Virgil, the suggestion of the end of an epoch in the world's history.

In a biblical poem classical allusions are likely to add either a romantic or a humanizing note or often, as in the simile of

Proserpine, both together. The account of the creation of the universe and of men concludes with

> thrice happy if they know
> Thir happiness, and persevere upright.

Milton is clearly echoing the famous passage at the end of Virgil's second *Georgic*, in praise of the happy life of the early Italian farmers:

> O fortunatos nimium, sua si bona norint,
> agricolas!

The echo not only calls up a human and historical image of bucolic felicity but adds an overtone to the angelic warning against corrupt ambition. Another part of the same Virgilian passage appears in the invocation to Light. Even blindness, Milton declares, has not cut him off from his beloved classical authors, although they, as always, are ranked below the Bible:

> Yet not the more
> Cease I to wander where the Muses haunt
> Clear Spring, or shady Grove, or Sunny Hill,
> Smit with the love of sacred song; but chief
> Thee Sion and the flow'ry Brooks beneath
> That wash thy hallow'd feet, and warbling flow,
> Nightly I visit.

The first lines are a free paraphrase of Virgil's invocation to the learned Muses:

> Me vero primum dulces ante omnia Musae,
> quarum sacra fero ingenti percussus amore,
> accipiant . . .

'And the effect', says Mr Tillyard,

is prodigious. Occurring, as both passages do, in contexts of a poetic intensity almost unbearable, they are like the two extremities of a flash of lightning, spots united by a blinding stream of electric fluid. In the common love of their art the two great poets as it were mingle their minds, each gaining sustenance from the other. In plainer prose, we feel Milton's context to be enriched through the reference and we trust Virgil's lines the more because they have animated the later poet.[5]

We might observe how Milton turns one Homeric passage to different uses. In the fourteenth book of the *Iliad* Hera has made herself seductive for a purpose, and succeeds.

So spake he, and the son of Kronos clasped his consort in his arms. And beneath them the divine earth sent forth fresh new grass, and dewy lotus, and crocus, and hyacinth, thick and soft, that raised them aloft from the ground.

The nuptial bower of Adam and Eve is the perfection of natural beauty:

> underfoot the Violet,
> Crocus, and Hyacinth with rich inlay
> Broider'd the ground.

Incidentally, the artificial words 'inlay' and 'Broider'd' are employed precisely for their artificial value; the terms of sophisticated art emphasize the natural simplicity of Eden. Later Milton uses the same episode of Zeus and Hera (and a similar episode in Homer's third book, when Paris, remaining away from battle, urges Helen to dalliance). After Eve and Adam have eaten the fruit, they are both stirred by fleshly desire and Adam ends a speech of hard-boiled levity with sensual invitation:

> For never did thy Beauty since the day
> I saw thee first and wedded thee, adorn'd
> With all perfections, so inflame my sense
> With ardor to enjoy thee, fairer now
> Than ever, bounty of this virtuous Tree.

'For never once as thus,' Zeus declares, 'did the love of goddess or woman so mightily overflow and conquer the heart within my breast,' and, after a complacent list of his conquests, he says that never before had he desired Hera herself so much. Quite apart from Homer, Adam's words, in particular the possessive animalism of 'enjoy', reveal the extent of his corruption. But we may feel the irony of Adam's contrasting, in the sensual language of Zeus and Paris, his first pure and happy union with the rapture of his present carnality; even if we do not recall Homer, and if Milton did not expect us to, his own recollection was a potent factor in the result. And this is not all. Adam leads the willing Eve to a couch of flowers,

> Pansies, and Violets, and Asphodel,
> And Hyacinth, Earth's freshest softest lap.

Again we remember their first wedding, the natural beauty of their Homeric bower, and both former purity and present impurity are concentrated and contrasted in the one phrase, another ironic echo of Homer, 'Earth's freshest softest lap'. The whole episode, with its interplay of ideal and actual, is not less complex than, say, the coming home at the violet hour of Mr Eliot's typist and her encounter with the small carbuncular house-agent's clerk. Indeed it might be thought more complex, since the modern episode is wholly ugly, whereas in Milton it occurs in an earthly paradise and the sensual Adam thinks he is a loving husband.

We noticed before the use of the dramatic irony of ideas in the speeches of Satan and his followers, that is, the revelation of evil attitudes which the reader is expected to assess at their true value, and that strain might be illustrated at length. Sometimes also irony is embodied, as in Mr Eliot, in more or less veiled allusion. Adam, when rebuked by Raphael for his excessive passion for Eve, tries to put things right and affirms that, still free, he approves the best and follows what he approves. The altered version of a familiar Ovidian tag has the effect, for the reader, of ironically puncturing Adam's self-confidence and preparing for what is to come. A more arresting instance occurs when Eve, after Adam has avowed his readiness to share her fate, exclaims,

> O glorious trial of exceeding Love!

– a phrase which at once evokes the infinite contrast between Adam's misguided love and the love of Christ for man.

It may be said that such examples of Milton's allusiveness and complexity – a few which must represent the general texture of *Paradise Lost* – only confirm the notion that he is not for every reader and everyday reading. On the other hand, for the complex sensibilities of the anti-Miltonists, he is much too simple. As a matter of logic or probability, neither position can be quite right. For many people, certainly, there does hang about Milton a forbidding austerity not only of Puritanism but of learning. It is a fact that for centuries before him, and for perhaps two centuries after him, a poet could assume in his readers, as Milton assumed, a fair amount of classical – and biblical – knowledge. If that is no longer true, we can hardly claim a large and peculiar fault in Milton or a large and peculiar merit in ourselves. But the decline of classical education, and the metaphysical revival, have brought about an odd result in a number of critical minds. Scholasticism replaced the classics as the really respectable source of images and ideas for the older poets – with this very important difference, that whereas 'the classics' generally meant classical literature and thought, scholasticism has hardly ever meant scholastic philosophy but only a dialectical texture and isolated scraps of curious learning. The anti-Miltonists, however, have little interest in the ideas of Milton, they merely express abhorrence and pass on to his craftsmanship. And on that level, when Milton employs an image or idea or idiom not immediately intelligible, it is characteristic Miltonic pedantry; when Dante or Donne or Mr Eliot does so, it is characteristic metaphysical subtlety.

It is true of course that the more one knows of all thought and learning and literature, the richer one's understanding and enjoyment of Milton are. But the same thing may and must be said about any serious writer, the learned Donne and the unlearned Shakespeare among others. The more important fact is that Milton used to be, and still is, an essentially popular poet. For many generations a great many ordinary people read *Paradise Lost* – very often, no doubt, with a more or less unaesthetic scale of values – as ordinary people never did or could read

Donne's *Anniversaries*. If those fastidious intellectuals whose noses are in great indignation at anything popular are moved to ejaculate, 'So much the worse for Milton!' they must also outlaw most of the really great writings of the world, from Homer and the Bible onward. After we have listened to all that is said about Milton's remote learning and his un-English obscurity of style, we may still safely guess that about ninety per cent of his verse can be understood with sufficient ease and fullness by a modern reader of normal education and intelligence without special literary training. That reader might miss much in the way of aesthetic and philosophic refinements, though perhaps not more than sophisticated anti-Miltonists miss, and he might see a good deal more than they of what Milton strove to utter.

Then there is the complaint that *Paradise Lost* is full of dull, heavy, 'unpoetic' stretches. That some parts of the poem may deserve those labels we need not deny, but they are not nearly so numerous or so long or so dull as hostile generalizations would lead one to believe. Every sympathetic reader has had the experience of finding, through his own eyes or another's, vitality and beauty in passages he had too hastily skimmed because they looked or were said to be unrewarding. Not all parts of Homer and Virgil, or even of Dante and Shakespeare and Donne, are alive for us, though anti-Miltonic references to the last three imply that these poets always thought and felt and wrote on their highest level. Dante's poetical technique does not alleviate the sour tedium of his many dull stretches, and his preoccupation with the tortures of his personal and political enemies is not more inviting to the modern reader than Milton's account of Hebrew and later history (which, if perhaps somewhat too full, is as a whole requisite for Adam's moral and spiritual education and is a very grim picture of the course of human existence).

If there are in *Paradise Lost* layers of material, large or small, which to us seem recalcitrant or irrelevant to the spiritual theme, we should not forget that a Renaissance epic was expected to comprehend a wide range of general learning, to embody, in a sense, the sum of knowledge. Both poets and critics believed, not without reason, that a heroic poem required a broad and solid and 'prosaic' substratum. That historical reason has, to be sure, no aesthetic validity for a modern reader, but we may ask how the modern equivalent of a heroic poet meets the same problem. Milton, like all great poets before him and most poets after him, put into his text everything necessary for the understanding of the whole and the parts. Mr Eliot, who is a very good poet, possibly a great one, achieved condensed brevity and continuously 'poetic' vitality by cutting out all the expository and 'prosaic' elements which the traditional epic needed. But readers of *The Waste Land* could not get very far before – and some did not get very far after – they had read his notes and gained or regained a pretty minute knowledge of Dante, Jessie Weston's *From Ritual to Romance,* Frazer's *Golden Bough,* and a multitude of casual items, like the Tarot pack of cards, from the ragbag which every individual mind contains. One may be greatly stirred by that poem without thinking that the poet's method, the often arbitrary selection of more or less private symbols, linked by an almost invisible thread of emotional and literary associations, is altogether superior to Milton's use of the central, mainly familiar, and self-sufficient traditions of mankind. Although Milton is not only richly allusive but builds on such ideas as 'right reason' which are no longer familiar, while Mr Eliot belongs to our own world, it is the contemporary poet who requires footnotes and commentary. Milton's incidental effects may be heightened by our recognition of sources, but they do not depend, as Mr Eliot's central effects do, upon such recognition. And on the practical if not the critical plane, is the reading of Milton's occasional 'prosaic' passages of verse more, or less, remote from poetic experience than the getting up of Mr Eliot's prose authorities? It may be added, too, that in Mr Eliot's latest work, *Four Quartets,* there is a high proportion of plain prosaic statement of a kind which the author of *The Waste*

Land and many critical essays might have condemned as unpoetical.

We have not much time left to consider the charge of heavy artifice and monotony in rhythm. Those readers who have an ear for the grand style, who can hardly imagine the gap there would be in English poetry and in their own experience if *Paradise Lost* were not there, do not need any defensive comment, long or short. But, without going into technicalities, we may register a few general facts and impressions. In rhythm as in other things Milton executed *Paradise Lost* in the grand manner because nothing less than superhuman and ritualistic grandeur would be in keeping with his characters, his vast stage, and his assertion of divine order. No Renaissance poet had so critical and creative an understanding of the great principle of 'decorum' as Milton. Yet within the limits of epic decorum he achieved a wide variety of tone and movement. Granted a general and necessary stylization of rhythm as of language, 'the enormous onward pressure of the great stream on which you are embarked',[6] there are more or less audible differences of rhythm in Milton's descriptive, narrative, and dramatic passages. And, within those divisions, there are differences in the descriptions of hell, celestial space, and Eden, between public oratory and private dialogue and, to subdivide still further, among the several orators and between the earlier and the later dialogue of Adam and Eve. Some of the passages cited already furnish partial illustration, and out of the wealth of material we can add only two or three more. Here is the picture of Christ, the Logos, clothed with His Father's omnipotence, leaving heaven to begin the great task of creation:

> Heav'n op'n'd wide
> Her ever-during Gates, Harmonious sound
> On golden Hinges moving, to let forth
> The King of Glory in his powerful Word
> And Spirit coming to create new Worlds.
> On heav'nly ground they stood, and from the shore

> They view'd the vast immeasurable Abyss
> Outrageous as a Sea, dark, wasteful, wild,
> Up from the bottom turn'd by furious winds
> And surging waves, as Mountains to assault
> Heav'n's highth, and with the Centre mix the Pole.
> Silence, ye troubl'd waves, and thou Deep, peace.

Every rhythmic phrase reinforces the verbal picture – first the majestic order of heaven, then the vast disorder of chaos, and then, with the tremendous effect of a more drastic change of pace, the divine creation of order.

Or let us take this, from the catalogue of the fallen angels, whom old tradition transformed into the gods of the pagan religions:

> Thammuz came next behind,
> Whose annual wound in Lebanon allur'd
> The Syrian damsels to lament his fate
> In amorous ditties all a Summer's day.
> While smooth Adonis from his native Rock
> Ran purple to the Sea, suppos'd with blood
> Of Thammuz yearly wounded: the Love-tale
> Infected Sion's daughters with like heat,
> Whose wanton passions in the sacred Porch
> Ezekiel saw, when by the Vision led
> His eye survey'd the dark Idolatries
> Of alienated Judah.

Here, not through any obvious onomatopoeia but through the altered weight and tempo of rhythm, we feel the contrast between the sensuous levity of popular paganism and the passion for righteousness which inspired the Hebrew prophets.

For a specimen of dialogue we might read this early speech in which Eve is declaring her love for Adam and in which she winds and unwinds a beautiful lyrical pattern:

> With thee conversing I forget all time,
> All seasons and thir change, all please alike.
> Sweet is the breath of morn, her rising sweet,

> With charm of earliest Birds; pleasant the Sun
> When first on this delightful Land he spreads
> His orient Beams, on herb, tree, fruit, and flow'r,
> Glist'ring with dew; fragrant the fertile earth
> After soft showers; and sweet the coming on
> Of grateful Ev'ning mild, then silent Night
> With this her solemn Bird and this fair Moon,
> And these the Gems of Heav'n, her starry train:
> But neither breath of Morn when she ascends
> With charm of earliest Birds, nor rising Sun
> On this delightful land, nor herb, fruit, flow'r,
> Glist'ring with dew, nor fragrance after showers,
> Nor grateful Ev'ning mild, nor silent Night
> With this her solemn Bird, nor walk by Moon,
> Or glittering Star-light without thee is sweet.

It would not be easy to find the equal of that in English pastoral verse, but it is clearly not human dialogue. It is a carefully composed poem on the beauty of human love and its harmony with nature, and that is in keeping with the ideal and regal order of primitive innocence. But after Adam and Eve have sinned, their mode of utterance changes to the natural, colloquial, and dramatic. We might recall again that soliloquy in which we heard Eve thinking aloud:

> But to Adam in what sort
> Shall I appear? shall I to him make known
> As yet my change, and give him to partake
> Full happiness with mee, or rather not,
> But keep the odds of Knowledge in my power
> Without Copartner? so to add what wants
> In Female Sex, the more to draw his Love,
> And render me more equal, and perhaps,
> A thing not undesirable, sometime
> Superior.

Or, to hear Eve in a more attractive mood of wifely contrition, she can speak in these faltering human accents:

> Forsake me not thus, Adam, witness Heav'n
> What love sincere, and reverence in my heart
> I bear thee, and unweeting have offended,
> Unhappily deceiv'd.

Finally, for Milton's subtlest and most inspired control of word and rhythm, there is no greater example than the last lines of the poem, when Adam and Eve depart from the garden with the angel's sword flaming above the gate behind them:

> Some natural tears they dropp'd, but wip'd them soon;
> The World was all before them, where to choose
> Thir place of rest, and Providence thir guide:
> They hand in hand with wand'ring steps and slow,
> Through Eden took thir solitary way.

Every phrase and rhythm, with a marvellous depth of suggestion, rings the changes on the mingled feelings of sadness and hope, frailty and trust, loneliness and divine help. In this quiet and impersonal vision of human life beginning its course on earth are concentrated all the poet's tender pity for mankind and his unshakeable faith in God and goodness. What Milton is saying indirectly in those simple descriptive lines is not very far from what Mr Eliot says directly:

> Blessèd sister, holy mother, spirit of the fountain,
>   spirit of the garden,
> Suffer us not to mock ourselves with falsehood
> Teach us to care and not to care
> Teach us to sit still
> Even among these rocks,
> Our peace in His will
> And even among these rocks
> Sister, mother
> And spirit of the river, spirit of the sea,
> Suffer me not to be separated

And let my cry come unto Thee.[7]

NOTES

1. C. S. Lewis, *A Preface to 'Paradise Lost'* (London, 1942), p. 58.
2. *Revaluation* (London, 1936), p. 50 [above, p. 21].
3. *The Waste Land*, ii; in *Collected Poems* (London and New York, 1936).
4. In quoting this brief passage as a basis for comment, the acute author of *Seven Types of Ambiguity* (p. 15) rewrites it by altering two individual words and telescoping the last two lines into one:

> *flung* by angry Jove
> Sheer o'er the crystal battlements; from *dawn*
> To noon he fell, from noon to dewy eve,
> A summer's day; and with the setting sun
> Dropped into Lemnos the Ægean isle.

It is difficult to understand a sensitive critic's omitting 'from the Zenith like a falling Star' or having Milton end with 'Dropped into Lemnos', as if Mulciber had come to call.

5. *Poetry Direct and Oblique* (London, 1934), p. 190. On the Homeric item (below), see ibid., pp. 186–7.
6. C. S. Lewis, op. cit., p. 45.
7. *Ash-Wednesday*, vi; in *Collected Poems* (London and New York, 1936).

Arthur O. Lovejoy

MILTON AND THE PARADOX OF
THE FORTUNATE FALL*

To many readers of *Paradise Lost* in all periods the most surprising lines in the poem must have been those in the Twelfth
Book in which Adam expresses a serious doubt whether his
primal sin – the intrinsic enormity and ruinous consequences of
which had elsewhere been so copiously dilated upon – was not,
after all, rather a ground for self-congratulation. The Archangel
Michael, it will be remembered, has been giving Adam a prophetic relation of the history of mankind after the Fall. This,
though for the greater part a most unhappy story, concludes
with a prediction of the Second Coming and the Final Judgement, when Christ shall reward

> His faithful and receive them into bliss,   (462)
> Whether in Heav'n or Earth, for then the Earth
> Shall all be Paradise, far happier place
> Than this of Eden, and far happier days.
>   So spake the Archangel Michael; and then paused,
> As at the world's great period, and our Sire
> Replete with joy and wonder thus replied:
> 'O Goodness infinite, Goodness immense,
> That all this good of evil shall produce,
> And evil turn to good – more wonderful
> Than that which by creation first brought forth
> Light out of darkness! Full of doubt I stand,   (473)
> Whether I should repent me now of sin
> By me done or occasioned, or rejoice
> Much more that much more good thereof shall spring –
> To God more glory, more good will to men
> From God – and over wrath grace shall abound.'   (478)

* From *Essays in the History of Ideas* (1948), pp. 277–95; first published in
the *Journal of English Literary History*, IV (1937), 161–79.

The last six lines are Milton's expression of what may be called the Paradox of the Fortunate Fall. It is a paradox which has at least the look of a formal antinomy. From the doctrinal premises accepted by Milton and implicit in the poem, the two conclusions between which Adam is represented as hesitating were equally inevitable; yet they were mutually repugnant. The Fall could never be sufficiently condemned and lamented; and likewise, when all its consequences were considered, it could never be sufficiently rejoiced over. Adam's eating of the forbidden fruit, many theologians had observed, contained in itself all other sins;[1] as the violation by a rational creature of a command imposed by infinite wisdom, and as the frustration of the divine purpose in the creation of the earth, its sinfulness was infinite; and by it the entire race became corrupted and estranged from God. Yet if it had never occurred, the Incarnation and Redemption could never have occurred. These sublime mysteries would have had no occasion and no meaning; and therefore the plenitude of the divine goodness and power could neither have been exercised nor have become known to men. No devout believer could hold that it would have been better if the moving drama of man's salvation had never taken place; and consequently, no such believer could consistently hold that the first act of that drama, the event from which all the rest of it sprang, was really to be regretted. Moreover, the final state of the redeemed, the consummation of human history, would far surpass in felicity and in moral excellence the pristine happiness and innocence of the first pair in Eden – that state in which, but for the Fall, man would presumably have remained.[2] Thus Adam's sin – and also, indeed, the sins of his posterity which it 'occasioned' – were the *conditio sine qua non* both of a greater manifestation of the glory of God and of immeasurably greater benefits for man than could conceivably have been otherwise obtained.

Necessary – upon the premises of orthodox Christian theology – though this conclusion was, its inevitability has certainly not been always, nor, it may be suspected, usually, apparent to those who accepted those premises; it was a disturbing thought upon which many even of those who were aware of it (as all the subtler theologians must have been) were naturally reluctant to dwell; and the number of theological writers and religious poets who have given it entirely explicit and pointed expression has apparently not been great. Nevertheless it had its own emotional appeal to many religious minds – partly, no doubt, because its very paradoxicality, its transcendence of the simple logic of common thought, gave it a kind of mystical sublimity; between logical contradiction (or seeming contradiction) and certain forms of religious feeling there is a close relation, of which the historic manifestations have never been sufficiently studied. And for writers whose purpose, like Milton's, was a religious interpretation of the entire history of man, the paradox served, even better than the simple belief in a future millennium or celestial bliss, to give to that history as a whole the character, not of tragedy, but of a divine comedy.[3] Not only should the drama have (for the elect – and about the unredeemed the elect were not wont to be greatly concerned) a happy ending, but the happy ending had been implicit in the beginning and been made possible by it. The Paradox of the Fortunate Fall has consequently found recurrent expression in the history of Christian religious thought; the idea was no invention, or discovery, of Milton's. In the present paper I shall note a few earlier phrasings of the same idea, which it is of interest to compare with Milton's. They may or may not be 'sources' of *Paradise Lost*, XII, 469–78; they are in any case illustrations of a long tradition lying behind that passage.

To Milton specialists the occurrence of a similar passage in Du Bartas is, of course, well known, but to facilitate comparison it seems worth while to cite the lines here. In the section of the *Seconde Semaine* entitled 'The Imposture', after the Creator has pronounced sentence upon Adam, the poet interrupts his narrative to introduce a disquisition of his own, designed to answer the usual complaints against the justice of God in his dealings with Adam and his descendants:

> Here I conceive that flesh and blood will brangle,
> And murmuring reason with th' almighty wrangle.[4]

The ensuing essay in theodicy is apparently addressed primarily to mankind in general, though the poet sometimes rather confusedly seems, when he uses the second personal pronoun, to be thinking of those whose errors he is refuting, sometimes of Adam, sometimes of departed saints in general, sometimes of all the elect. The lines which concern us are the following:

> For thou complainest of God's grace, whose Still
> Extracts from dross of thine audacious ill,
> Three unexpected goods: praise for His name;
> Bliss for thyself; for Satan endless shame.
> Sith, but for sin, Justice and Mercy were
> But idle names; and but that thou didst erre,
> CHRIST had not come to conquer and to quell
> Upon the Cross, Sin, Satan, Death, and Hell,
> Making thee blessed more since thine offence
> Than in thy primer happy innocence . . .
> In earth thou liv'dst then; now in heaven thou beest:
> Then thou didst hear God's word; it now thou seest.
> Then pleasant fruits; now CHRIST is thy repast;
> Then might'st thou fall, but now thou standest fast.[5]

Since, as we shall see, the thought was not original with Du Bartas, the passage in *Paradise Lost*, XII, is not one of those which can confidently be cited among the evidences of Milton's utilization of *La Semaine*. There is, however, a similarity in one detail which perhaps lends a slight probability to the supposition of a conscious or unconscious reminiscence by Milton of the corresponding passage in the French poet: the fact that both specify three 'greater goods' which sprang from the evil inherent in the Fall.[6] Of these, two are identical in both passages – greater 'glory' to God, greater benefits conferred by God upon man. The third is different; for the defeat and humiliation of Satan Milton substitutes, as the last happy consequence, the manifestation of the predominance of God's grace over his wrath – religiously a more moving and edifying conception, though less apposite to the plot of Milton's epic of the war between God and the rebel angels.[7] There are two other differences worth noting: (*a*) Milton gains greater dramatic effect by putting the paradox into the mouth of Adam himself – a ground for this being laid in the device of the preceding recital of the future history of man by the Archangel.[8] (*b*) In Milton, however, the paradox is not so sharply expressed. Du Bartas puts quite categorically the point that but for the Fall there *could* have been no Incarnation and Redemption and that, 'but for sin, Justice and Mercy were but idle names'; Milton's Adam is made to express merely a doubt whether he should repent his sin or 'rejoice much more' over its consequences. Yet the logic of the paradox remains clear enough in Milton's lines; Adam could have had no reason for his doubt except upon the assumption that the sin was truly prerequisite to the 'much more good' that was to follow – was, in Milton's own significant term, to 'spring' from it – and an intelligent reader could hardly have failed to conclude that the doubt was to be resolved in favour of the second alternative.

Du Bartas, however, was not the only poetic precursor of Milton in the use of the paradox. It was peculiarly adapted both to the theme and the style of Giles Fletcher in his most ambitious poem, *The Triumph of Christ*. It naturally occurred to a devout but reflective mind when it dwelt rapturously upon that theme; the more intense the feeling of the sublimity of the redemptive act and the magnitude of the good both inherent in it and resultant from it, the more apparent the impossibility of regarding as merely evil the sin which had evoked it. And to a writer whose poetic method consisted chiefly in the multiplication of conceits and rhetorical antitheses, even when dealing with the gravest articles of his faith, such a paradox naturally had a special attraction. Consequently in *Christ's Triumph over Death* (1610) Fletcher, descanting upon the Passion of Christ in a series of what may be called antithetic parallels between the Fall and the Redemption – the two trees (i.e. the forbidden tree and the cross), the two gardens (Eden and Gethsemane), etc. – introduces the paradox – and converts it into a play upon words.

> Such joy we gained by our parentalls,
> That good or bad, whether I cannot wiss,
> To call it a mishap, or happy miss,
> That fell from Eden and to heav'n did rise.[9]

Fletcher, however, while raising the question clearly, is, like Milton's Adam, ostensibly non-committal about the answer to it; yet it is so put that the reader could hardly remain in doubt about the answer. A fall from Eden which made the greater joys of heaven possible was plainly no 'mishap'.[10]

The last act of Andreini's *L'Adamo* (1613) has a good deal in common with the last book of *Paradise Lost*, including a long speech by Michael in which, after reproachfully reminding Eve of her guilt—

> Tu cagionera a l'huomo
> E di doglia et di pianto –[11]

he proceeds to a prophecy of the final triumph of grace and of the future bliss to be enjoyed by the first pair and their progeny, both on earth, which will then be like Paradise, and in heaven.[12] In their response to this archangelic discourse, Andreini's Adam and Eve, like Milton's Adam, expand with gratitude and wonder over the benignant power which can so 'unite' good with evil:

> Con la morte la vita,
> Con la guerra la pace,
> Col perder la Vittoria,
> Con l'error la salute
> E con l'Inferno il cielo
> Insieme unir, non è poter umano,
> Ma de l'eterno mano
> Omnipotenza summa. Ondè, Signore,
> Ch' Eva trafitta è sana,
> E perdendo trionfa, et vinta hà gloria.[13]

There is in these lines, especially in *'perdendo trionfa'*, an evident adumbration of the paradox, but they hardly give it unequivocal expression.

Some of Milton's precursors, then, in the century preceding *Paradise Lost*, had dwelt upon the idea that the Fall had not only been over-ruled for good by the divine beneficence, but had been the indispensable means to the attainment of far greater good for man and – if it may be so put – for God than would have been possible without it. Milton's eighteenth-century annotators and editors soon began to point out – though with a characteristic and exasperating neglect to give definite references – that the idea had already been expressed in the patristic period. The earliest suggestion of such a source seems to have been given in J. Richardson's *Explanatory Notes and Remarks on Milton* (1734), in which line 473 is annotated: '"*O felix culpa, quae talem ac tantum meruit habere Redemptorem!*" 'tis an exclamation of St Gregory.'[14] Newton and other annotators in the same century were, prudently, still more vague in citation: 'He seems to remember the rant of one of the Fathers, "*O felix culpa, etc.*"'[15] So far as I have observed, no modern editor has given any more precise reference for this yet more striking phrasing of the Paradox of the Fall. An extensive, though not exhaustive, search of the writings of St Gregory fails to disclose it. But it is to be found in a probably earlier, more noteworthy, and, at least to non-Protestants, more widely familiar source – a passage in the Roman Liturgy.[16] In the service for Easter Even (Holy Saturday) there is a hymn, sung by the deacon in the rite of blessing the paschal candle, which bears the title of *Praeconium* but is better known, from the word with which it opens, as the *Exultet* (*exultet iam angelica turba caelorum*); in it, a Catholic writer has remarked, 'the language of the liturgy rises into heights to which it is hard to find a parallel in Christian literature.'[17] In this rapturous exultation over the mystery of the Redemption the sentence already cited is preceded by another expressing the same paradox yet more pointedly: '*O certe necessarium Adae peccatum, quod Christi morte deletum est! O felix culpa, quae talem ac tantum meruit habere redemptorem!'* Adam's sin was not only a 'happy fault' but 'certainly necessary' – necessary to the very possibility of the redemptive act, which, it may be supposed, was by the author of the hymn conceived as itself a necessary, and the [central, event in the divine plan of terrestrial history.

The date of composition of the *Exultet* and that of its incorporation in the service of Easter Even can be determined only approximately.[18] It was originally no part of the Roman Liturgy, but appears first in the Gallican, which, as some liturgiologists hold, was probably in existence by the beginning of the fifth century;[19] but the earliest manuscript of this liturgy which includes the hymn in question is of the seventh century.[20] Certain conjectures concerning its authorship have been made, but none is supported by any substantial evidence;[21] in the words of the most careful modern study of the subject, 'in the present state of the sources, one must give up the attempt to determine the authorship and even the place of origin of this famous hymn.'[22] All that can be said, then, on the question of date, is that the passage which some of Milton's editors have regarded as the probable source of *Paradise Lost*, XII, 473 ff., was in liturgical use as early as the seventh and possibly as early as the fourth century, in the churches employing the Gallican sacramentary. It is, however, certain that the popularity of the hymn was so great that it presently drove out, even in the Roman Liturgy – apparently after some hesitancies on the part of the Popes – all rival formulas in the rite of blessing the Easter candle. It evidently 'owed its triumph', as a Catholic historian of the liturgy has said, 'to the fact that it was far superior to all these rivals both in expression and content.'[23] In certain medieval missals there are some interesting variations in the wording of the two sentences relevant to the theme of this paper,[24] and it is of interest to note that these sentences were considered by some ecclesiastical authorities as dangerous, and were omitted from the hymn – rather generally in German and not infrequently in French and Italian sacramentaries.[25] But with the establishment of liturgical uniformity since the late sixteenth century, both sentences found an accepted and permanent place in the Missal of the Roman Church.

That the Protestant religious poets of the sixteenth and seventeenth centuries who gave expression to the Paradox of the Fortunate Fall had heard or read the part of the Catholic liturgy containing the *Exultet* is, of course, possible; but there is no need to suppose them to have done so. It is rather more likely that they – or at all events the earliest of them, Du Bartas – became acquainted with the idea through the reading of one of the Fathers, whose writings still had among Protestant theologians much authority. St Ambrose, for example (fourth century), had flatly asserted that Adam's sin 'has brought more benefit to us than harm' (*amplius nobis profuit culpa quam nocuit*),[26] and had even permitted himself the more generalized and hazardous apophthegm that 'sin is more fruitful than innocence' (*fructuosior culpa quam innocentia*).[27] God 'knew that Adam would fall, *in order that* he might be redeemed by Christ [*ut redimeretur a Christo*]. *Felix ruina, quae reparatur in melius!*'[28] The identity of the thought and the approximation of the phrasing here to those of the two sentences quoted from the *Exultet* are evident; and it is probable that these Ambrosian passages are the primary source of the expressions of the paradox, alike in that hymn and in Du Bartas, Fletcher and Milton. To the last two the idea may or may not have been transmitted through Du Bartas;[29] or to any of them it is possible that the medium of transmission may have been some later patristic repetition or amplification of the theme. In the century after Ambrose his enunciation of it was echoed, with some weakening, by one of the greatest of the Popes, Leo I, in his *First Sermon on the Lord's Ascension*:

Today we [in contrast with the first of our race] are not only confirmed in the possession of Paradise, but have even penetrated to the higher things of Christ; we have gained more by the ineffable grace of Christ than we had lost by the envy of the Devil.[30]

And in the next century Gregory the Great expressed the paradox with all possible explicitness:

What greater fault than that by which we all die? And what greater goodness than that by which we are freed from death? And certainly, unless Adam had sinned, it would not have behooved our Redeemer to take on our flesh. Almighty God saw beforehand that from that evil because of which men were to die, He would bring about a good which would overcome that evil. How wonderfully the good surpasses the evil, what faithful believer can fail to see? Great, indeed, are the evils we deservedly suffer in consequence of the first sin; but who of the elect would not willingly endure still worse evils, rather than not have so great a Redeemer?[31]

In the foregoing examples, the writers who enunciated the paradox, it is evident, usually had chiefly in mind the relation of causal dependence between specific historical events, the Fall and the Redemption; and the argument was that the latter, or consequent, being preponderatingly a good, the former, as its necessary (though not sufficient) cause, must have been preponderatingly a good. Yet the Fall none the less remained, upon orthodox principles, a moral evil. These considerations, taken together, tended to suggest two larger and awkward questions. Was it true in general that the existence of moral evils is, from another and more comprehensive point of view, a good? And if, from such a point of view, the Fall was preponderatingly a good, was it not necessary to assume that its occurrence must after all have been in accordance with God's will? These questions, implicit in the notion of the *felix culpa*, were fairly explicitly raised and considered by Augustine; and his answers to both were, at least sometimes, in the affirmative; in other words, he not only accepted the paradox but gave it a more generalized form:

Although those things that are evil, in so far as they are evil, are not good; nevertheless, it is good that there should be not only goods but evils as well. For unless this – namely, that there be also evils – were a good, men would under no circumstances fall away from the omnipotent Good.[32]

i.e., neither Adam nor any man would ever have sinned. And again:

The works of God are so wisely and exquisitely contrived that, when an angelic and human creature sins, that is, does, not what God wished it to do, but what itself wishes, yet by that very will of the creature whereby it does what the Creator did not will, it fulfills what he willed – God, as supremely good, putting even evils to good use, for the damnation of those whom he has justly predestined to punishment and for the salvation of those whom he has benignantly predestined to grace.[33]

The greatest of the Latin Fathers was here manifestly skating on rather thin ice. It was always difficult for an acute-minded theologian with a strong sense of the divine sovereignty to admit that Adam's sin had really frustrated the will of God, and had compelled the deity to perform, unwillingly, acts which he would not otherwise have performed; it was, therefore, not easy, when dealing with these matters, always to avoid the thought that the Fall itself, with its consequences – so happy for the elect – was but a part of the eternal and ineluctable divine purpose for mankind. These passages of Augustine's thus reveal more clearly some of the moral difficulties and metaphysical pitfalls which lay behind the conception of the *felix culpa* – difficulties and pitfalls which Augustine himself cannot be said to have wholly escaped.[34]

The familiarity of the idea in the fourteenth century is shown by its occurrence both in *The Vision of Piers the Plowman*, *c.* 1378, and in Wyclif's *Sermons*. In the former it is put into the mouth of Repentance, after the Seven Deadly Sins have made their confessions: God created man 'most like to himself, and afterwards suffered him to sin'.

And al for the best, as I bileve · what euer the boke telleth,
  O felix culpa! o necessarium peccatum ade! etc.
For thourgh that synne thi sone · sent was to this erthe,
And bicam man of a mayde · mankind to save.[35]

Wyclif in a Christmas sermon preached, perhaps, to his rustic flock at Lutterworth in the early 1380s, did not shrink from the paradox, but on the contrary joined with it a still more sweeping optimism, of very dubious orthodoxy: all things, including sin, are for the best in the best of possible worlds, since all happens in accordance with God's will:

And so, as many men seien, alle thingis comen for the beste; for alle comen for Goddis ordenance, and so thei comen for God himsilf; and so alle thingis that comen fallen for the beste thing that mai be. Moreover to another witt men seien, that this world is betterid bi everything that fallith therinne, where that it be good or yvel ... and herfore seith Gregori, that it was a blesful synne that Adam synnede and his kynde, for bi this the world is beterid; but the ground of this goodnesse stondith in grace of Jesus Christ.[36]

An interesting late-medieval lyrical poem gives to the paradox a turn not found in any of the other examples here cited; it is presented in its relation to the cult of the Virgin. Since there would have been no Incarnation without the Fall, all that phase of Catholic piety and religious emotion which centres about the figure of the Virgin Mother manifestly owed its possibility to Adam's eating the forbidden fruit. There is also in the poem, if I am not mistaken, a touch of sly humour; the anonymous author hints that poor Adam, to whom not only mankind in general but the Queen of Heaven herself are so deeply indebted, has been rather badly treated. This further inference from the idea of the *felix culpa* would, one may suspect, hardly have been approved by St Ambrose and St Gregory. Adam, the poet recalls, lay bound for four thousand winters:

> And all was for an appil,
>   An appil that he tok . . .
> Ne hadde the appil take ben,
>   The appil taken ben,
> Ne hadde never our lady
>   A bene hevene quene.
> Blessed be the time
>   That appil take was.
> Therefore we moun singen
>   '*Deo gracias.*'[37]

A sixteenth-century illustration of the vogue of the concept of the *felix culpa* is to be found in the widely used Latin *Commentary on Genesis* of the Jesuit Benito Pereira (Pererius). The commentator is dilating, *à propos* of Genesis i, 31, upon the manner in which God transmutes evils – even moral evils *(mala culpae)* – into good.

A signal proof and example of this is exhibited to us in the sin of Adam. How grave this sin was, how far and wide it spread poison and destruction, how severely it was punished, is acknowledged by all men. Yet this so great sin, such is the goodness and power of God, has been wonderfully converted into the greatest good and the most glorious of God's works, namely, the incarnation, passion and death of the Son of God. So that Gregory not unadvisedly or rashly somewhere exclaims, '*O felix culpa, quae talem ac tantum meruit habere Redemptorem*.'[38]

Upon the crucial point of the paradox however – that God could not have performed this *praeclarissimum opus* if Adam had remained innocent – Pereira does not dwell.

For a final example, which will bring us back to Milton's century, I will cite one of the most famous and widely read of Catholic devotional works, the *Traité de l'amour de Dieu* of St Francis de Sales (1616).

The mercy of God [he writes] has been more salutary for the redemption of the race of men than the wretchedness of Adam has been poisonous for its destruction. And so far is it from being true that the sin of Adam has overcome the benevolence [*debonnaireté*] of God, that on the contrary it has served to excite and provoke it: so that, by a gentle and most loving antiperistasis[39] and opposition, that benevolence has been re-invigorated by the presence of its adversary: and, so to say, gathering together its forces in order to win the victory, it has caused grace 'to abound more exceedingly where sin abounded'.[40] Therefore the Church, in a holy excess of admiration, exclaims on the Eve of Easter: 'O sin of Adam, truly necessary' etc. [quotes the two sentences from the *Exultet*]. Of a truth, we can say with that man of ancient times: 'We should be lost [*perdus*] if we had not been lost'[41]; that is to say, our loss has been our gain, since human nature has received more gifts of grace [*plus de graces*] from its redemption by its Saviour than it would ever have received from the innocence of Adam, if he had persevered in it. . . . The redemption of our Lord, touching our miseries, renders them more useful and amiable than the original innocence would ever have been. The Angels, the Saviour tells us, 'have more joy over one sinner that repenteth than over ninety-and-nine just persons that need no repentance'; and in the same way, the state of redemption is one hundred times greater in value than the state of innocence.[42]

Here the strangest aspect of the paradox is even more pointedly brought out than by Du Bartas or Milton: not only did the Fall make possible more good for man, but God himself *needed* a fallen race to evoke fully the divine attributes and powers.

It is unlikely that the pre-Miltonic expressions of the Paradox of the Fortunate Fall which I have noted are the only ones to be found in Christian literature from the fourth to the seventeenth centuries, but they pretty certainly include the most important; all but one of them could have been known to Milton at first hand; and they are sufficient to place in its proper historical perspective the passage of the Twelfth Book of *Paradise Lost* cited at the beginning. In that perspective, the passage ceases to be surprising, or indicative of any originality or of any great boldness in Milton's thought. A paradox which had been embraced by Ambrose, Leo the Great, Gregory the Great, Francis de Sales, and Du Bartas; had for at least ten centuries had a place in many missals, and had finally been officially adopted by the Roman Church, was, obviously, sufficiently orthodox; and it had been put more sharply and boldly by at least two of the Doctors of the Church, by the composer of the *Exultet*, by the French mystic, and by the author of *La Semaine*, than by Milton. Though the hint of antinomianism latent in it had made many writers to whom it was probably familiar avoid expressing it, it had nevertheless a recognized and natural place in the treatment of the topic in Christian theology – that of the culmination of the redemptive process in human history – which was also for Milton the culminating theme in his poem. Yet it undeniably placed the story of the Fall, which was the subject of the poem announced at the outset, in a somewhat ambiguous light; when it was borne in mind, man's first disobedience could not seem the deplorable thing which, for the purposes of the poet – and of the theologian – it was important to make it appear. The only solution was to keep the two themes separate. In the part of the narrative dealing primarily with the Fall, the thought that it was after all a *felix culpa* must not be permitted explicitly to intrude; that was to be reserved for the conclusion, where it could heighten the happy final consummation by making the earlier and unhappy episodes in the story appear as instrumental to that consummation, and, indeed, as its necessary conditions.

NOTES

1. So Milton himself in *De doctrina christiana*, bk I, ch. 11. [For fuller documentation the reader should consult the original essay. – Ed.]

2. On this last point, however, there were, in the early Fathers and later theologians, differing opinions; the view that the primeval state was not that in which man was intended to remain, but merely a phase of immaturity to be transcended, had ancient and respectable supporters.

3. This application of the phrase is borrowed from Professor C. A. Moore, *Publications of the Modern Language Association of America*, XII (1921), 11.

4. Sylvester's translation, 1611 ed., p. 249.

5. *The Complete Works of Joshua Sylvester*, ed. A. Grossart (1880), p. 111; in 1611 ed., p. 249.

6. This detail is not found in other expressions of the paradox known to me.

7. This eventual consequence of the Incarnation and Resurrection had, however, been dwelt upon by Milton in *Paradise Lost*, III, 250–58. If in writing the passage in Book XII Milton was restating that of Du Bartas, the change of the third 'good' may be attributable to a desire to avoid repetition.

8. Du Bartas employs the same device of a prophetic recital of subsequent history (*Seconde Semaine*, 1611 ed., p. 293); but here the prophet is Adam himself, who tells the story of things to come to Seth, and his

prediction abruptly ends with the Deluge. If we were sure that Milton was, in Books XI–XII, consciously recasting Du Bartas, the comparison between his and the earlier poet's use of the same group of themes would significantly illuminate the working of Milton's mind in the construction of his poem.

9. *Christ's Triumph over Death*, stanza 12; in *Giles and Phineas Fletcher*, ed. F. S. Boas (1908), I, 61.

10. The second stanza following might be construed as a more affirmative expression of the paradox:

> Sweet Eden was the arbour of delight,
> Yet in his honey flowres our poyson blew,
> Sad Gethseman the bowre of baleful night
> Whear Christ a health of poyson for us drew;
> Yet all our honey in that poyson grewe.

If the 'poyson' in the last two lines is that referred to in the second – i.e., the forbidden fruit, or the consequences of eating it – the final line is a figurative way of asserting once more the dependence of the Redemption upon the Fall. But it is possible that the 'poyson' in the penultimate line signifies the Agony in the Garden and that the last line is merely a repetition of this.

11. *L'Adamo*, tercentenary ed. E. Allodoli (1913), Act V, sc. ii, p. 140, ll. 4122–3; cf. *'cagionera'* with Milton's 'occasioned' in XII, 475, apparently his only use of the word as a verb.

12. Ibid., p. 143, ll. 4235 ff.

13. Ibid., p. 141, ll. 4157 ff.

14. *Explanatory Notes and Remarks on Milton*, 521.

15. Fourth ed. (1757) of Thomas Newton's ed. of *Paradise Lost*, II, 429 (note). The parallel is not indicated in the earliest important commentary, Patrick Hume's *Annotations on Paradise Lost* (1695).

16. For my knowledge of this fact, and for other valued assistance in this section, I am indebted to Professor G. La Piana of Harvard University.

17. C. B. Walker, in *Catholic Encyclopaedia*, art. 'Exultet'.

18. For the text of the hymn (in its oldest known form) see Duchesne, *Christian Worship*, 5th ed. (1923), p. 254; Migne, *Patrologia Latina*, LXXII, col. 269 f. For its history cf. Duchesne, loc. cit.; A. Franz, *Die kirchliche Benediktionen im Mittelalter* (1909), I, 519–53; V. Thalhofer and L. Eisenhofer, *Handbuch der katholischen Liturgik* (1912), I, 643 ff.; A. Gastoué, *Les vigiles nocturnes* (1908), p. 18; C. B. Walker, loc. cit.; J. Braun, *Liturgisches Handlexicon* (1922), art. 'Praeconium paschale'. An English version of the entire hymn may be found in I. Schuster, *The Sacramentary* (1925), II, 293–5.

19. Duchesne, op. cit., p. 86, thinks the hymn may be as early as the middle of the fourth century.
20. Cf. the liturgiological authorities cited.
21. Some ancient manuscripts credit it to St Augustine 'when he was deacon', a highly improbable ascription (cf. Thalhofer and Eisenhofer, op. cit., p. 644; Franz, op. cit., I, 534). It is probably due to the fact that Augustine, as he himself records (*De civitate Dei*, XV, 22), once wrote a short *laus cerei* in verse; but this was not the *Exultet*.
22. Franz, op. cit., I, 534.
23. Thalholfer and Eisenhofer, op. cit., 644.
24. E.g., in the Missal of Westminster Abbey (ed. Lagg, 1893, II, 581) the words *et nostrum* follow *Adae peccatum*.
25. See Franz, op. cit., I, 540 f., for examples, of which I cite only one: Hugo, Abbot of Cluny (d. 1109), commanded that these sentences should be 'deleted and no longer read, *cum aliquando non bene haberetur "O felix culpa", et quod peccatum Adae necessarium esset'*.
26. *De institutione virginis*, ch. XVII, 104 (Migne, *Patr. Lat.*, XVI, 331).
27. *De Jacob*, VI, 21.
28. *Contra secundam Julianum*, I, 39 (Migne, *Patr. Lat.*, XIV, 1065).
29. That Du Bartas 'used Ambrose's *Hexaemeron*' is said by U. T. Holmes and his associates to be a certainty (*The Works of Du Bartas* (1935), I, 128); it is improbable that Du Bartas's reading in Ambrose was confined to this writing. Cf. Thibaut de Maisières, *Les poèmes inspirés du débute de la Genèse* (1931), p. 26. Milton, however, was acquainted with Ambrose at first hand.
30. Migne, *Patr. Lat.*, LIV, 396.
31. *In Primum Regum Expositiones*, IV, 7; Migne, *Patr. Lat.*, VII, 222. Richardson was perhaps not wholly wrong in indicating Gregory as a source of the passage in *Paradise Lost*, though in error in attributing the '*O felix culpa!*' to that saint.
32. *Enchiridion*, ch. XCVI (Migne, *Patr. Lat.*, XL, 276).
33. Ibid., ch. C (Migne, *Patr. Lat.*, XL, 279).
34. Donne in one of his sermons bases upon the authority of Augustine as well as of Scripture a similar remark that matters have been so ordered that sin in general – not specifically the sin of Adam – is made conducive to moral good: 'If I cannot find a foundation for my comfort in this subtility of the Schoole, that sin is nothing, . . . yet I can raise a second step for my consolation in this, that be sin what it will in the nature thereof, yet my sin shall conduce and cooperate to my good. So *Ioseph* saies to his Brethren, *You thought evill against me, but God meant it unto good*: which is not onely good to *Ioseph*, who was not partaker in the evill, but good even to them who meant nothing but evill.' What

Donne has in mind here at least in part, however, is the more special idea that, after many little sins, a good round sin may be a means of grace, by bringing the sinner to a realization of his own state. 'Though it be strangely said, yet I say it, That God's anger is good; so saies S. Augustine, *Audeo dicere*, Though it be boldly said yet must I say it, *Utile est cadere in aliquid manifestum peccatum*, Many sinners would not have been saved if they had not committed some greater sin at last, than before; for, the punishment of that sin, hath brought them to a remorse of all their other sins formerly neglected' (*LXXX Sermons* (1640), p. 171).

35. B. Ms., *Passus V*, 489 ff., in Skeat, *The Vision of William Concerning Piers the Plowman* (1869), 60.

36. *Select English Works of John Wyclif*, ed. Thomas Arnold (1869), Sermon XC, I, 320–21. There is no corresponding passage in the Latin sermon from the same text and for the same festival: *Ioannis Wyclif Sermones*, ed. Loserth (1888), II, 1 ff. Wyclif also apparently confused in his memory the *Exultet* and the passage of Gregory above cited, or else believed Gregory to have composed the hymn.

37. Professor Douglas Bush has kindly brought this poem to my notice. It is printed in Chambers's and Sidgwick's *Early English Lyrics* (1907), 102, and is believed to have been written in the early fifteenth century.

38. *Benedicti Pererii Valentini commentariorum et disputationum in Genesim tomus primus* (Leyden, 1594), 168. Pereira, like Wyclif, it will be observed, either attributes the *Exultet* to St Gregory or has confused the phrase from the hymn with the dictum of Gregory above cited. The passage is a highly probable source of Richardson's similar error previously noted; and it is a conceivable source of the *locus* in Milton. On the importance of this and similar Renaissance commentaries on Genesis for the background of *Paradise Lost*, see the article of Arnold Williams in *Studies in Philology*, April 1937, pp. 191–208. But it is to be borne in mind that Pereira's work and the others mentioned by Williams were later than Du Bartas's poem.

39. A technical term of the physics of the period, signifying a process by which a quality or force in a substance is increased or intensified by the action of an opposing quality or force. Milton expresses the same idea in the hymn of the celestial choirs, *Paradise Lost*, VII, 613 ff.:

> Who seeks
> To lessen thee, against his purpose serves
> To manifest the more thy might: his evil
> Thou usest, and from thence creat'st more good.

The 'more good' here, however, is the creation of 'this newly-made world' and of man, to 'repair that detriment' resulting from the defection of the rebel angels – not the Redemption and its consequences.

40. Romans v, 20. The Pauline text gave a seeming biblical sanction to the paradox, though it does not in fact express the essential point of it.

41. The reference is to a saying of Themistocles in Plutarch's *Life of Themistocles*, 39.

42. *Traité de l'amour de Dieu*, bk II, ch. 5.

A. J. A. Waldock

PARADISE LOST: THE FALL*

THE preparations for the crisis of the poem, the fall of Adam, go some way back, and I think if we examine them closely we may detect the beginnings of a slight uncertainty on Milton's part: faint premonitory hesitations and inconsistencies that tell of trouble ahead. I do not suggest that Milton was even yet, except vaguely, aware of trouble ahead; but it is now, in the presentation of Adam's fall, that those deep underlying ambiguities in the theme begin to make themselves really felt, like subterranean weaknesses that all at once start the earth cracking at the surface. Rifts begin to open, hair lines at first; then they become wider, and presently there is a chasm.

We may detect such symptoms and signals, I think, in one speech especially, the speech towards the end of Book VIII that Raphael delivers 'with contracted brow'. Raphael in what he says here is obviously Milton's spokesman: he, and Milton behind him, feel that they have some highly important principles to lay down. The principles are, in fact, to serve as foundation for what ensues; their function is to support the poem across its most critical phase. But Raphael does his work rather clumsily and gives us little confidence that his props will hold.

Adam has been telling how in Taste, Sight, Smell he finds pleasure indeed, but pleasure not comparable to the 'commotion strange' that the presence of Eve has power to awaken. His own speech is a curious mixture. At one moment he merely mouths his author's theories of woman's place and function:

> For well I understand in the prime end
> Of Nature her th' inferiour, in the mind
> And inward Faculties, which most excell. (VIII, 540)

* From 'Paradise Lost' and its Critics (1947), ch. III, pp. 42–53, 53–7, 61–4.

At another, his tribute is so deep and moving that one can hardly relate it to the tone with which he seemed to begin – the tone of one who is

> in all enjoyments else
> Superiour and unmov'd, here onely weake
> Against the charm of Beauties powerful glance.
>
> (VIII, 532)

'Beauties powerful glance': the phrase is oddly discordant with the final lines of the passage in which Adam, speaking from the heart, tells us what he really feels:

> when I approach
> Her loveliness, so absolute she seems
> And in her self compleat, so well to know
> Her own, that what she wills to do or say,
> Seems wisest, vertuousest, discreetest, best;
> All higher knowledge in her presence falls
> Degraded; Wisdom in discourse with her
> Looses dicount'nanc't, and like folly shewes;
> Authoritie and Reason on her waite,
> As one intended first, not after made
> Occasionally; and to consummate all,
> Greatness of mind and nobleness thir seat
> Build in her loveliest, and create an awe
> About her, as a guard Angelic plac't.   (VIII, 546)

If the first half of Adam's testimony – in which he speaks of his nature's one 'weakness' – expresses Milton, so also of course does this half, and profoundly. But then Milton checks himself and makes the angel contract his brow.

Raphael's is an unpleasant speech; more than that, it is an untruthful one. It begins:

> Accuse not Nature, she hath don her part;
> Do thou but thine, and be not diffident
> Of Wisdom, she deserts thee not, if thou
> Dismiss not her, when most thou needst her nigh,
> By attributing overmuch to things
> Less excellent, as thou thy self perceav'st.

And then:

> For what admir'st thou, what transports thee so,
> An outside? fair no doubt, and worthy well
> Thy cherishing, thy honouring, and thy love,
> Not thy subjection: weigh with her thy self;
> Then value: Oft times nothing profits more
> Then self-esteem, grounded on just and right
> Well manag'd; of that skill the more thou know'st,
> The more she will acknowledge thee her Head,
> And to realities yeild all her shows.   (VIII, 561)

Raphael's technique, that is to say, is to ignore everything in what Adam has just said that is at all inconvenient for his own particular purpose. Having suppressed all that, he then takes what is left of Adam's speech and replies to it.

> For what admir'st thou, what transports thee so,
> An outside?

All Adam's qualifications have gone for naught: the whole of that extremely important *supplement* which ended his speech has fallen on deaf ears – or ears which have been deliberately deafened.

> And to realities yeild all her shows.

Once more Raphael wilfully misses the point. After which he proceeds to his homily on 'the sense of touch', still blandly assuming that there is no more in question, though the whole drift of Adam's confession has been to prove that there is a very great deal more in question. And then, having in this way completely reversed the proportions of Adam's speech he gives him permission to go on loving 'what higher' in Eve's society he finds, and concludes by explaining to him (as if there were need, for what has Adam been doing himself but giving the plainest possible exposition of this very thing?) 'wherein true love consists'.

Adam, 'half-abash't', though there is no reason why he should be, ventures on a reply. It is a good reply, and makes doubly clear what is already clear. Raphael has just said that

> love refines
> The thoughts, and heart enlarges.   (VIII, 589)

Listen to Adam:

> Neither her out-side formd so fair, nor aught
> In procreation common to all kindes
> (Though higher of the genial Bed by far,
> And with mysterious reverence I deem)
> So much delights me, as those graceful acts,
> Those thousand decencies that daily flow
> From all her words and actions, mixt with Love
> And sweet compliance, which declare unfeign'd
> Union of Mind, or in us both one Soule.   (VIII, 596)

May not one fairly suggest that a man who speaks like this has already had his thoughts refined and his heart enlarged – is already passing Raphael's tests tolerably well? Adam ends by protesting that he is not in 'subjection' – that that is not quite the right word for his state – and hints meekly that the angel's strictures may have been a little unfair.

Let us come now to the climax: the climax of the story of Adam and Eve, and of course also of the whole poem. Eve, running towards Adam excitedly and covering up her nervousness in a flow of rapid and eager speech, tells him what she has done.

It is, I think, of great importance to note *exactly* what happens now. Adam stands thunderstruck, 'amaz'd' and 'blank',

> while horror chill
> Ran through his veins, and all his joynts relax'd.
>   (IX, 890)

And then:

> First to himself he inward silence broke.   (IX, 895)

Before saying a word to Eve, that is, he communes with himself, and in doing so he accepts at once and completely two facts: first, she is lost; and second, he is lost with her. For he has decided on the instant, without thinking, without having to think, that that is how it is to be:

> And mee with thee hath ruind, for with thee
> Certain my resolution is to Die. (IX, 907)

It is to be observed that Eve has had no chance as yet to coax or persuade, within the first few appalled moments Adam has come uninfluenced to his resolve. I would suggest that the nine lines that complete this speech (the speech of self-communion) and the eight lines that complete the next (Adam's first speech to Eve after the shock of the news) are in many respects the two most important passages in *Paradise Lost*.

The first passage goes:

> How can I live without thee, how forgoe
> Thy sweet Converse and Love so dearly joyn'd
> To live again in these wilde Woods forlorn?
> Should God create another *Eve*, and I
> Another Rib afford, yet loss of thee
> Would never from my heart; no, no, I feel
> The Link of Nature draw me; Flesh of Flesh,
> Bone of my Bone thou art, and from thy State
> Mine never shall be parted, bliss or woe. (IX, 908)

How shall we interpret this? By what word shall we describe the feeling in the lines? There is apprehended loneliness in them, of course. In the several furious seconds that have passed since the disclosure the future has had time to flash on Adam in some of its implications. But dread of solitariness is only part of what these words convey. If Adam's words are permitted to have the meanings that words usually have in English, these lines mean *love*: I do not see how it is possible to withhold the word; and the lines that echo them a few seconds later mean the same.

In between comes what Mr Clarence Green has well called Adam's 'rationalizing' speech.[1] It is the speech in which, a little 'recomforted from sad dismay', he tries to persuade himself that things may not be as bad as they seem. He only half believes what he is saying even while he is saying it. Then (with the effect of putting aside these 'perhapses') comes the significant word 'however', and the transition to the second full avowal of purpose.

> However I with thee have fixt my Lot
> Certain to undergoe like doom, if Death
> Consort with thee, Death is to mee as Life;
> So forcible within my heart I feel
> The Bond of Nature draw me to my owne,
> My own in thee, for what thou art is mine;
> Our State cannot be severd, we are one,
> One Flesh; to loose thee were to loose my self.
>
> (IX, 952)

I would emphasize again the very great importance of these two passages. They demonstrate to us what Adam's feelings are as he takes his fateful decision – they are our prime, paramount evidence for those feelings – and I would suggest, therefore, that we should allow no one, *not even Milton*, to prise us loose from them or in any way to diminish for us their natural significance. Dr Tillyard says that Adam's first thought was of 'comradeship': that he cannot bear the thought of being alone, and that that is why he determines to die with Eve. 'Comradeship' and Dr Tillyard's companion word 'gregariousness' seem to me to hover timidly on the mere fringe of the truth. Adam wants company, that is certain; but he does not want the company of anyone, even the company of another Eve; it is *this* Eve he wants: he says so. 'Adam', says Mr Lewis, 'fell by uxoriousness.'[2] Is Adam uxorious? Perhaps. In his love, as in anyone's love, there are many strains. There is protectiveness in it, there is loyalty, there is (very pronounced) what Augustine called the 'drawing of kindred', and no doubt there is uxoriousness. His life with Eve up to this point has had the air of an extended honeymoon – which is very much, of course, what it really has been. To say that he is 'in love' with her is to use a mild expression. But at this supreme of moments, when life and death hang in the balance, the garland-weaving and all that it signifies are beside the point. When he decides, on his own impulse, at once and finally, to share her fate, are we to call *this* uxorious? The word (to me at least) seems fantastically trivial for a description of the deep movements of feeling that those two critical passages convey.

The second passage comes, as just noted, at the end of Adam's 'rationalizing' speech. I think that Dr Tillyard is less than fair to the impression of this speech when he says that it shows Adam falling into mental levity. Adam is serious enough underneath. The speech is a desperate attempt to put the best face on things. In a natural reaction from the horror of the first few moments Adam brightens a little; the decision that he has taken is in itself invigorating. But he has no real faith in what he is saying, as the transitional word 'however' sufficiently suggests.

And it will be observed (Dr Tillyard himself emphasizes the point) that not even yet has Eve had to say a word of persuasion: there has been no need. Of course now that she has heard from Adam's own lips what he means to do she is deeply moved and behaves as any woman would, embracing him and weeping tenderly and pouring out her gratitude in words. With a natural uprush of optimism she says that she is sure all will be well, and then offers him the fruit. But the grand, the controlling decision has already been taken.

Now comes a question that must be asked and answered. If all this is so, what then does Milton mean a line or two later when he tells us that Adam was 'fondly overcome with Femal charm'?

> She gave him of that fair enticing Fruit
> With liberal hand: he scrupl'd not to eat
> Against his better knowledge, not deceav'd,
> But fondly overcome with Femal charm.   (IX, 996)

Dr Tillyard notes the discrepancy: 'the last line is curiously inconsistent with what went before'.[3] I think it is: 'fondly overcome with Femal charm', take it as broadly as we will, *is* oddly out of harmony with what we have just been reading, and especially with the two key passages that have revealed to us the motions of Adam's heart. Dr Tillyard sees in the inconsistency a plain shift of motive: from his point of view the shift is one from 'gregariousness' to 'sensuality'; and his conclusion, therefore, is that Adam's 'final sin' is uxoriousness after all.

This, it seems to me, is to submit too meekly to Milton's leading, to abdicate far too many of our critical rights. That there is a shift of some sort is unquestionable, but it is not, I think, the kind of shift that Dr Tillyard has in mind. That would be to take the lines under discussion far too seriously, and the lines that have gone before not seriously enough. We have here, I would suggest, a perfect illustration of the principle noted at the beginning of the previous chapter, a perfect example of the sort of clash that we must sometimes expect in *Paradise Lost* between Milton's theory of a matter and the matter as he has actually presented it. This is, indeed, one of *the* moments in the poem for bringing that distinction to bear. 'Fondly overcome with Femal charm' is simply Milton's comment on the recent course of events: events the true nature of which he has just been demonstrating to us. And between a comment and a demonstration (though in the critical interpretation of *Paradise Lost* it has been nearly the rule, I suppose, to accord them equal rights) there can never be real question, surely, which has the higher validity. 'Femal charm' is merely Milton's way of inciting us to take a certain view of a matter that he has already presented with a quite different emphasis and to a quite different effect. What the comment really means is that Milton has begun to realize, if vaguely, that his material has been getting out of hand. He is rather like a steersman who, feeling the ship off her course and yawing, puts the helm hard over to bring her back: except that he is not quite as conscious of what is happening to his poem as a steersman would be of what was happening to his ship, and that his action is too late. For the 'harm' (if we like to look at it that way) is done. As long as those two key passages remain in the poem their effect cannot be neutralized (unless of course we permit ourselves to be levered out of all our critical rights). Adam's words ring so true that they *prove* to us his feelings, and against proof of that kind no comment can – or ought to – prevail. To accept Adam's final sin as uxoriousness, on the authority of this belated and tendentious summing up of his case, is merely, I would suggest, to allow Milton to lead us by the nose.

If anyone should feel that such a reading commits Milton to an improbable inconsistency let him consider merely the disagreements in the sequel. Adam presently is brought to book: he has to give an account of his deed to the Son. And it is very curious to note what happens at this interview. Adam is his own worst possible advocate. His testimony is unfair to himself and to Eve and amounts to a nearly total misrepresentation of what really occurred. He is silent about the extremely honourable motives that prompted him, and he puts Eve in a much worse light than is necessary by declaring that from her hand he could 'suspect no ill' – a flat lie, which at once lays additional discredit on her and deprives his own conduct of the nobility it possessed. Altogether, it is a miserable, hang-dog performance. It may be said that we are meant to see in this mean-spirited exhibition one of the earliest results of the Fall itself. But it is interesting to note that the Son accepts the account, takes Adam at his word so that the version becomes from now on, in a sense, the official view of the poem.

> To whom the sovran Presence thus repli'd.
> Was shee thy God, that her thou didst obey
> Before his voice, or was shee made thy guide ... (X, 144)

Adam did not 'obey' Eve, and she was not his 'guide'.

What then shall we say of the central event of *Paradise Lost*? Dr Tillyard points the paradox. On the one hand, 'the heart of any normal reader warms with sympathy at [those] exquisitely tender words of Adam refusing to forsake Eve in her extremity.' On the other, 'how can Milton at this of all places in the poem have given Adam his conscious approval?' And any other kind of 'approval', at such a crucial point as this, seems to Dr Tillyard difficult to accept. His conclusion is that we must make the best we can of what seems to be Milton's meaning, which is that 'ordinary man is far too weak to live alone.' Adam, owing to 'gregariousness', has sinned.[4]

I do not feel that this is quite the way out. Dr Tillyard, I think, is inclined to overestimate Milton's *awareness* of what is occurring. If one impression rather than another grows stronger with each reading of *Paradise Lost* it is (I would suggest again) that Milton is by no means always alive to the precise effect that his narrative is making and to the exact way in which parts of it interlock with other parts; and indeed, without going farther afield at the moment for examples, the glaring inconsistencies just noted are themselves ample proof. We have, I think, to remind ourselves that the presentation of the Fall was one of the severest tests for Milton in the poem; in many ways it was *the* test. The hidden difficulties of the theme can at this point remain hidden no longer; the lurking problems must now become apparent, even if they are still not faced. I do not think it can be said that Milton faces them: he is not, even here, in any proper sense aware of them. What he does is to yield himself, at the critical moments, to the full imaginative promptings of his subject. The treatment of the fall of Adam, in the passages I have so much emphasized, is a noble and generous treatment, and the whole account of the Fall is studded with true and memorable things. Only, there is the thesis in the background; he cannot forever neglect it; hence 'Femal charm'.

The matter then may be summed up quite bluntly by saying that Adam falls through love – not through sensuality, not through uxoriousness, not (above all) through gregariousness – but through love as human beings know it at its best, through true love, through the kind of love that Raphael has told Adam

> is the scale
> By which to heav'nly Love thou maist ascend.
>
> (VIII, 591)

This fact is not usually faced (one of the few who dare to speak of Adam's 'love' is Mr Green) but it is almost universally felt. It is difficult to find a critic of *Paradise Lost* who (however shattering to his scheme of the poem the admission may be) will not confess, as Dr Tillyard does, that his heart is warmed at Adam's act. M. Saurat, though the consequences of what he is saying do not, I think, quite strike him, concedes that Milton has a sense of chivalry: 'what greater instance in the whole world than that of Adam deliberately and clear-headedly joining Eve in her transgression, not to be parted from her in the punishment?' 'When Adam', writes Mr Williams, 'in the fullness of his passion for Eve, really does abandon heaven and his knowledge of God for her, Milton denounced his act. But it was, after all, Milton who imagined his passion so intensely as to make us almost wish it could be approved.'[5] Mr Williams will not quite say 'love', but 'fullness of passion' is a periphrasis for it. And even Mr Lewis, though somewhat frowningly, admits the 'half-nobility' of what Adam did. Everybody admits it; Milton himself by the sympathy and warmth of his presentment (not his comment) implicitly admits it. And yet this noble (or at the very least 'half-noble') act constitutes the Fall of Man.

What are we to say? Mr Lewis has his answer ready, and if this answer will not do, none will. 'If the reader', he says, 'finds it hard to look upon Adam's action as a sin at all, that is because he is not really granting Milton's premises.' He explains his point. 'If conjugal love were the highest value in Adam's world, then of course his resolve would have been the correct one. But if there are things that have an even higher claim on a man, if the universe is imagined to be such that, when the pinch comes, a man ought to reject wife and mother and his own life also, then the case is altered, and then Adam can do no good to Eve (as, in fact, he does no good) by becoming her accomplice.'[6]. . . .

Mr Lewis's argument, though it sounds plausible, will not, I think, stand up under examination. Let us imagine an extreme instance. Suppose we take, as a premise, that Might is Right, that it is proper for the weak to be pushed to the wall; and suppose that a writer, adopting this premise, concocts a short story about a lifeboat. In this story the men first fight amongst themselves, then the strongest, who are the ones left, grab the food and push the women and children overboard. We should not particularly enjoy such a story, and we should feel that the answer, 'Oh, but you must grant the premises', had overlooked something. I think that what it would have overlooked would have been an unbearable collision of values, for we could not concede *that* value without conceding virtually all – without anaesthetizing, temporarily, nine-tenths of our emotional nature. There are limits to what, in literature, can be conceded as premises. A simple instance is the beginning of *The Pilgrim's Progress*: we are near the danger line there, if indeed we have not crossed it. For Bunyan, theoretically, would not have us abandon our customary human values – his allegory, like every allegory, owes its very point to an acceptance of those human values – yet he comes very near in this passage to affronting some of the chief of them. Christian running across the plain, his fingers in his ears to shut out the cries of his wife and children, desperately bent on his own salvation, is not the kind of person for whom in normal circumstances we should have a strong regard. Though we understand perfectly what Bunyan is driving at we cannot very much enjoy the scene: we are forced, as we read it, to suspend a great many of our customary emotional responses. A child does not so easily do this and is likely to be taken aback, feeling in some vague way that the situation tugs against itself. It does; and so, on a much bigger scale, does the central situation of *Paradise Lost*.

Our predicament is this, that we are asked to set aside, to discount for the moment – not some trifling prejudice, not some new light modern fancy or custom – but one of the highest, and really one of the oldest, of all human values: selflessness in love. This is not merely one of *our* values: it is just as certainly one of Milton's values. And we must set this aside, keep it in abeyance while we read, suppress it – for what? It is by no means enough to set over against this powerful human value the mere doctrine that God must be obeyed: a mere doctrine can never counterbalance it, and Milton, theoretically, knows that as well as anyone. That, in fact, is precisely why he has written *Paradise Lost*: to *prove* the doctrine that God at all times and in all circumstances must be obeyed – to prove this in the only way in which a poet can prove anything, by bringing it home to our imaginations, by making us feel it, not in the abstract, but immediately, in the situation as shown, with all the conditions of that situation pressing strongly upon us. It is perfectly true, as Mr Lewis says, that 'pinches' come in life when a man ought to put his wife or family second, to leave them, perhaps, to death. The principle of the 'higher claim', from numberless treatments of it, is perfectly familiar to us. But the whole point surely is that we must be made to realize that there is a 'pinch'. Does any reader, responding naturally (as he ought to, for Milton has written his poem with the precise object of enlisting our natural responses) feel that such a pinch has arisen here? Adam seems to us – he seems to Milton, although Milton is not in a position to admit it – to be doing a worthy thing. Against the law, against what is theoretically good, against God, he deliberately asserts what is for him a higher good and pursues it.

It is not true, I think, to say (as is sometimes said) that we are here concerned with what is a normal thing after all in literature, the typical tragic conflict. The case seems very different. The conflict here is in us: it is we who are pulled in two ways, who are denied the full-hearted response that a great tragic theme allows and compels. For it is not as if the thesis of the poem were in the slightest degree in doubt. The poem thrusts on us a view, insists on an attitude. The assumption that Adam is to be condemned is basic: the whole of *Paradise Lost* rests on it. Yet, because of the nature of the presentation, we cannot condemn him: that is the kind of conflict in which we are caught. We should be watchful of apparent analogies. A woman in real life shelters her deserter husband; the court imposes the lightest of sentences, sympathizing with the woman and seeing that she could not have done otherwise. Here, in a sense, we both condemn and approve. But the conflict is nominal: we decide at once where the higher claim lies. The conflict in our response to *Paradise Lost* is far from nominal. If we push analysis to the limit we find, I think, that it comes to this: the poem asks from us, at one and the same time, two incompatible responses. It requires us, not tentatively, not half-heartedly (for there can be no place really for half-heartedness here) but with the full weight of our minds to believe that Adam did right, and simultaneously requires us with the full weight of our minds to believe that he did wrong. The dilemma is as critical as that, and there is no way of escape.

It does not help very much to imagine what Adam might have done; almost anything he might have done would have been less attractive than what he did. He might, for example (it is a suggestion of Mr Lewis's), have 'scolded or even chastised Eve and then interceded with God on her behalf'.[7] He might, though it seems hardly fair to blame him for taking God at his word. But if he had adopted this line, what then? Should we prefer even this Adam to the Adam we have? Would we rather that *he* had been our representative than the Adam who impulsively, uselessly, nobly stood by Eve and accepted, without further ado, her fate?

There is no way out. *Paradise Lost* cannot take the strain at its centre, it breaks there, the theme is too much for it. And it does not help very much to say that such a breakdown was unavoidable, though I suppose there is no question that it was. The myth of the Fall was dangerous, and the more intensely it was imagined the more dangerous it became. If Milton, in imagining it intensely and writing it large, succeeded only (as in a sense surely he did) in reaching a result the exact opposite of what he had intended: if the net effect of all his labour is to justify man's ways against God's ways: well, that was one of the risks, inherent in the venture, that he did not see . . . .

I add a few words on the aftermath. It would be profitless to raise again, I think, the logical difficulties. There was no way for Milton of making the transition from sinlessness to sin perfectly intelligible. It is obvious that Adam and Eve must already have contracted human weaknesses before they can start on the course of conduct that leads to their fall: to put it another way, they must already be fallen (technically) before they can begin to fall. Nor, again, is it possible to see just how the change from love to lust came about, or what it was in the act of disobedience that necessitated it. There is no help for these matters. Mr Lewis, it is true, makes a heroic effort to draw a distinction between fallen and unfallen sexuality, and suggests that Dante might have been able to portray the latter kind successfully. Even Milton, Mr Lewis thinks, if he had been less explicit – if he had been content to treat the loves of Adam and Eve 'remotely and mysteriously' – might have come near to succeeding. It may be so. It is perfectly obvious, of course, that nothing would have induced Milton to rest content with anything of the sort: he was not that kind of man – or poet. The poet who allowed Adam to turn the talk so neatly against Raphael with embarrassing questions about the love-life of angels was not likely to shy from the task of suggesting the innocent delights of Adam and Eve. It is perfectly evident, of course, that he very much enjoyed suggesting them. I cannot help thinking that Mr Lewis makes an unnecessary to-do about the provocativeness of Eve's sexual modesty. After the Fall a new self-consciousness enters, and we have sensuality itself. But how sensuality could have been absent from prelapsarian 'sex', if prelapsarian 'sex' be granted at all, is rather difficult to imagine. Milton, at any rate, could not imagine it and dismissed Augustine's efforts to square this particular circle (quite rightly) as nonsense.

Milton's triumph in what follows is, of course, the delineation of Eve. It is like watching some magic transformation; the

Fall transmutes her into a woman, a person; one by one the human lineaments are etched in before our eyes. She has not spoken a dozen lines before she is there, alive:

> other care perhaps
> May have diverted from continual watch
> Our great Forbidder, safe with all his Spies
> About him. (IX, 813)

Already, as Professor Stoll puts it, she is showing a 'defensive reaction',[8] dramatizing herself as in some obscure way injured: it makes her feel less guilty to reproach God, to suggest that it is all, in some indefinable sense, His fault. Do not let us be too hard on her for the jealous spasm that follows:

> but what if God have seen
> And Death ensue? then I shall be no more,
> And *Adam* wedded to another *Eve*,
> Shall live with her enjoying, I extinct;
> A death to think. Confirm'd then I resolve,
> *Adam* shall share with me in bliss or woe:
> So dear I love him, that with him all deaths
> I could endure, without him live no life. (IX, 826)

This, says Mr Lewis, is Murder. In a sense perhaps it is; and in a not dissimilar sense each of us commits murder five times a week; but we should not like to be called murderers. It is not as if she knew what death exactly was; nor is it quite fair, if we are to come down with a heavy hand on her jealous and possessive impulse here, to ignore (as Mr Lewis does) those other impulses – of love, heroism, self-sacrifice – that she shows in so many a later passage. Indeed we have only to move on forty lines to find one:

> Thou therefore also taste, that equal Lot
> May joyne us, equal Joy, as equal Love;
> Least thou not tasting, different degree
> Disjoyne us, and I then too late renounce
> Deitie for thee, when Fate will not permit. (IX, 881)

She means this, and who does not feel that she would be capable
of it, that if Adam were to be left she would tear herself away
from deity, if she could, to go back to him! She fibs sometimes.
Carried away by Adam's loyalty, which so enhances her own
value, she says:

> Were it I thought Death menac't would ensue
> This my attempt, I would sustain alone
> The worst, and not perswade thee, rather die
> Deserted. (IX, 977)

She is a liar, but who cares? She has found the right 'objective
correlative' for her feelings.

The picture of the 'distemper' of Adam and Eve is itself a
minor masterpiece, all the better for the glint of sardonic humour that Milton allows to intrude. Adam eats and is enrap-
tured:

> if such pleasure be
> In things to us forbidden, it might be wish'd,
> For this one Tree had bin forbidden ten. (IX, 1024)

'We can hear Eve's hectic, infatuate giggles at Adam's words',
says Dr Tillyard; and so we can.

From now on, indeed, as far as Eve is concerned, Milton's
bonds are fairly untied. The problem was somewhat different
with Adam. He must remain stilted. He has so much still to
exemplify, so much of the burden of the doctrine still to carry,
that he can never win through to complete freedom as a man.
But Eve's humanity only deepens as the poem moves towards
its end. In the debates in Book X hers are the words that reach
our hearts:

> While yet we live, scarse one short hour perhaps,
> Between us two let there be peace, both joyning.
>
> (X, 924)

And again:

> both have sin'd, but thou
> Against God onely, I against God and thee,

And to the place of judgement will return,
There with my cries importune Heaven, that all
The sentence from thy head remov'd may light
On me, sole cause to thee of all this woe,
Mee mee onely just object of his ire.   (X, 930)

Impetuous though the offer is, she is not pretending, and
Adam, though he makes what she has said the text for another
little lecture, scolds gently. On their joint problems she brings
her realistic, ruthless woman's sense to bear. If the future of
their 'descent' is what chiefly perplexes, then she advises: let
there be no 'descent', prevent the race unblest. If that involves
too hard an abstention, then she suggests the suicide pact. Both
are eminently practical, drastic, knot-cutting proposals. Again
she receives a slight scolding. But to our minds she has the
better of it, and it is pleasant that the last words spoken in the
poem should be hers. She regrets Eden, but Adam, after all, is
her world. She links arms with him and faces the future.

NOTES

1. ['The Paradox of the Fall in *Paradise Lost*', *Modern Language Notes*,
   LIII (1938), 562 f.]
2. [E. M. W. Tillyard, *Milton* (1930), p. 261, and C. S. Lewis, *A Preface to
   'Paradise Lost'* (1942), p. 122.]
3. Tillyard, p. 263.
4. Tillyard, p. 262.
5. [Denis Saurat, *Milton, Man and Thinker* (1925), p. 169, and Charles
   Williams, 'Introduction' to *The English Poems of John Milton*, World's
   Classics ed. (1940), p. xv.]
6. Lewis, p. 123.
7. Ibid.
8. *Poets and Playwrights* (1930), p. 261.

Arnold Stein

ANSWERABLE STYLE*

WHEN the Creator viewed the six days' work and saw 'all was
entirely good', He returned to behold

> how it shew'd
> In prospect from his Throne, how good, how faire,
> Answering his great Idea.   (VII, 555 ff.)

The poet-creator, entirely human in 'long choosing, and beginning late', has 'this Subject for Heroic Song', and he has
'the highth of this great Argument'. On a humbler plane he
may no doubt have his own 'great Idea', to which the whole
poem must be answerable. But even the divine Creator will
want to view in prospect the answerability of work to Idea;
and whether to poet-creator Idea is exactly knowable before
being expressed by the work – that is a problem the critic may
wisely be busy not to engage. To Milton speculating in prose
the poet is a virtuous man and true eloquence, like all noble
creation, will return to the pure source which it then will express. One may well think that for a poet with Milton's metaphysical commitments creation would not be conceivable
without an Idea, to which the completed poem refers, is potential, and is therefore in some sense subsequent. But having
said this, one has not eliminated the fine problems of relationship that remain to trouble metaphysical systems, and for
which theology like criticism tends to provide answers from a
different order of reasoning. So Milton, in the third chapter of
the *Christian Doctrine*, says that 'prescience can have no influence on the object foreknown, inasmuch as it is only an intransitive action.'

My own critical premises make me unwilling to consider
seriously Milton's Idea except as it is fully embodied by the com-

* From *Answerable Style: Essays on 'Paradise Lost'* (1953), pp. 119–62.
Condensed with the author's permission.

pleted poem – and then with a consciousness that my consideration is limited and partial. For the poem is itself a created world,
an object for contemplation and love, but refusing to yield its final
secrets; expressing its great Idea and answerable to reason and
love, but supporting the full complexity of creation. The world
of the poem requires of the ambitious understanding speculation
and recognition of a metaphysical final cause, though that recognition fall short of full understanding of the pure source and its
great relationship with every individual but answerable detail.
The world of the poem may also be thought of as requiring
action of the understanding, in the form of critical statement.
I prefer not trying to solve this problem of the creation and the
Idea, nor do I wish to insist on my own critical premises any
further than may serve to explain my critical deportment.

That Milton himself is aware of the problem is perhaps most
evident from his attitude toward the Muse. The poet's Idea can
be no pure thought thinking itself; its transcendence expresses
itself, according to the truth of its nature, in immanence; as
love may be thought to bridge the gap between God and man,
the Muse may be thought to bridge the gap between Idea and
poet. His Idea must *realize* itself through rising to Subject and
Argument, and by the intermediary of Muse. The song is ad-
venturous, what is low in the poet must be raised, what is dark
illumined; the verse is easy and unpremeditated, the Muse
comes unimplored; but without her aid the poet would be ex-
posed to the harsh influences of time and place. In a practical,
'efficient', sense the great Argument is prior to the poet's Idea;
though in stricter Platonic terms it is more correct to say that
the Idea has prior existence and has been recovered for the
individual poet by the Argument. But whatever its exact causal
relationship to the Idea, the Argument is also related inextric-
ably to the answerable style:

> If answerable style I can obtaine
> Of my Celestial Patroness.   (IX, 20 f.)

Milton's style is answerable to the Renaissance concept of

93

epic, which links this poem to classic literature, most particularly perhaps to Virgil. The style must therefore accept the requirements and justify the great privileges of *genus grande*. It must expect to be measured against noble examples, and yet so lofty is the undertaking that any appearance of direct contest will exhibit the personal and flirt with the ridiculous. It must satisfy the expectations of decorum. First of all, an elevation capable of variety must be sustained. In a negative sense this elevation means the purging of the personal, the trivial, the local – yet without exclusion of the natural and simple, or even the purified human voice of the poet himself. In a positive sense this means raising the feelings, mind, and spirit toward a superhuman loftiness beyond any merely immediate and individual passion into a higher unity of experience that can comprehend in its great simplicity of vision, in its terrible yet loving perspective of time and space, all that is various. For variety is also needed; variety of passion, local but not pausing to savour itself; variety of tension, seriousness, even of elevation; variety to make the ultimate unity bearable and true. These requirements, though my exposition may be too personal, were well understood by Milton's contemporaries, and, though there may be differences in emphasis, are, I think, largely accepted by modern scholars. In my approach to Milton's style I shall not try to isolate the Renaissance concept but shall take much of what I have just said for granted.

Milton's style is also answerable to the Renaissance concept of a Christian epic, which links this poem to Scripture, to doctrine, to concepts of biblical style and inspired Christian eloquence held by readers (and non-readers) of the classics from at least Augustine on. The tradition is a complicated one and I am even less competent to interpret and apply it to Milton than I am the classical concept. So I pass on to my third category, which includes the other two but insists less on competence in advance than on the aspiration to competence. Milton's style is also answerable to the as yet *unattempted*, to the poem this proves to be.

I shall begin with some of the immediate problems that Milton must have had to solve in order to solve his larger problem of building styles into style, variety into unity. It is toward the larger problem that I hope to work.

First there is the question of the dramatic in a poem which presents a large action and many smaller actions, which presents characters in a drama whose scope extends from the domestic to the cosmic. It is plain that the immediate, the local, and the individual cannot be allowed to dominate this epic situation. The stage is too vast – the panorama of hell, heaven, and earth, and their constant relationship. The events are too remote – the climax is on the threshold of time, and only at the end of the poem does the action move in a direct line into our time. (And these considerations must dominate, though there is a vision of history, and there are the frequent intrusive pressures of time, the echoes of the future that reverberate significantly on their source.)

The terms of the drama require that even Satan must realize himself as a public personality; it is not as a person but as a state of mind (however complex and far-reaching in significance) that he must express himself, less in speech than in speeches, and these never delivered without the audible overtones of God's providence. (The diminished Satan of *Paradise Regained* is more nearly individual.) Yet Satan is always interesting as a character; his public personality and his speeches have a liveliness of surface and a richness of depth; he has a history which is always bringing pressure upon the moment, and though the full dramatic illusion would violate the governing principles of this epic, at least there is an immediacy in the *impact* he makes. But if Satan must be presented under these controlling limitations, what of the human pair who are at the centre of the drama? Intimations of personality there must be, but shadowed and requiring translation, for only as Adam and Eve approach the Fall can they begin to assume full human personality.

It may seem perverse to apply the term 'dramatic' to a situation thus described – especially since visual imagery, colloquial language, and immediacy have usually been regarded by modern critics as indispensable to the 'dramatic'; and hostile criticism of Milton has tended to emphasize his lack of these indispensables. Yet Milton plainly conceived of his epic as a great drama; and not merely because he first planned the material as a play; but because as an artist, and indeed as a man, he saw the most significant human experience and human destiny itself as a kind of drama. What the critic must do is obvious – accept Milton's terms and not insist on his own at least if he wishes to see what Milton has done. And in Milton's kind of dramatic, which would ruin many other fine poems as their kind of dramatic would ruin his, the natural, the familiar, the sharply focused, the completely individual, and all aspects of the immediate must be subordinated to the larger considerations of context, perspective, and to the great order of dynamic interplay which is the total structure.

For instance, in *Paradise Lost* there is a constant and cumulative pressure of local context and its relationship to larger contexts, of local perspective and its relationship to the unfolding perspective which tests, purges, and unites parts into whole. In Milton's art the immediate, however striking it may be, is as likely to contradict as confirm. If it is Satan speaking, for example, there will be the immediate projection of his will, the rhetoric of his present intention; but there will also be a rich interplay of conflicting tensions which connect the most local context (which may be within Satan's own self-contradicting consciousness) with the chain of contexts leading ultimately to God's will. In such an art the elevation of perspective does not inhibit but rather creates variety and interior movement and counter-movement, which in turn test and prove the rightness of the perspective.

Most of these generalizations I have been making are based upon analyses of passages in *Paradise Lost* which I have previously used as arguments for interpretation. I assume that a kind of case for Milton's dramatic style has already been presented; but the issue is important enough to justify some fresh examples directly to the point, in order to illustrate more specifically the way this dramatic style works.

I take Satan's opening speech to Beelzebub, which is introduced by the specific reference to Satan's torment and to the bold words that break the horrid silence – bold in themselves, presumably, and bold because they express a will that can rise above the real terror of the numbing silence. The speech is followed by the choral commentary, 'Vaunting aloud, but rackt with deep despare'. Introduction and conclusion frame the speech and impose a formal perspective. This may seem to be a blemish and evidence of artistic inadequacy to the critic who regards commentary as the artist's personal intrusion on material that ideally should be able to speak for itself. But such a critical attitude, whatever its merits in other literary situations, can only be misleading here. For one thing, the formal perspective does not force itself upon Satan's speech, does not label and editorialize the impressive wilfulness out of existence; but rather sets up a dramatic conflict between the local context of the immediate utterance and the larger context of which the formal perspective is expression. This conflict marks, with a literal accuracy and precision that are dazzling, the tormented relationship between the external boast and the internal despair. (Before he is through with the poem, Milton will have wrung all the rich possibilities for action out of his concept of despair.)

Dramatically, the immediate impact of Satan's great wilfulness is more striking than the formal perspective, and this is as it should be; for then if there are small revelations that the external perspective is also expressed *within* the speech, that the despair does betray the boast, we shall have a tension within the speech as well, and the small quiet effects will clash advantageously with the large and loud effects. That is what does happen, and it is no mean dramatic accomplishment. The famous brassy effects come toward the middle of the speech, after Satan has pulled himself together. The opening lines keep trying for Satan's characteristic orchestration and assertiveness of rhythm, but lose their way and falter in a dazed and confused syntax. Mention of the good old cause almost regains him his voice, but memory of past and present interferes too violently and shakes loose the stunned surprise that must have been the shaping force of his first articulation, now finally stumbling its way into form:

> If thou beest he; But O how fall'n! how chang'd
> From him, who in the happy Realms of Light
> Cloth'd with transcendent brightnes didst outshine
> Myriads though bright: If he whom mutual league,
> United thoughts and counsels, equal hope,
> And hazard in the Glorious Enterprize,
> Joynd with me once, now misery hath joynd
> In equal ruin: into what Pit thou seest
> From what highth fal'n, so much the stronger provd
> He with his Thunder: and till then who knew
> The force of those dire Arms?   (I, 84 ff.)

In the lines that follow Satan assumes his characteristic style, which weaves a fine tissue of ironies between Satan's perspective and God's providence. The boast of 'that fixt mind' and 'the unconquerable Will' glitter most and reflect most, but only the full evolving of the drama under the process of time will reveal all the particular meanings of the bright refractions. As he concludes his speech, though, the formal perspective which has been looking over his shoulder, as it were, becomes part of his own expressed perspective. The movement is subtle, like the skilful merging of two themes in music; one of them dominating the other, whether tenderly or gently or patronizingly or harshly, but with a fine sureness of its own identity. Only here the shaping skill which is the management of the inner logic of form is not in Satan's control; he and his consciousness, whatever it may divine of what is happening, act out the drama of the immediate context without knowing the full relationship of immediate perspective to the whole dramatic plan. Nor do we as readers, but we see enough to realize that it is drama.

The last two lines of the speech defiantly but ignorantly transfer Satan's own defeated hopes to his description of God, now triumphantly holding the 'Tyranny of Heav'n' alone, and 'in th' excess of joy'. The approach to that ending is less defiant, a somewhat sobered letdown after the earlier largeness of statement. It is presented in the form of causal reasoning, a kind of scrambled syllogism. Since 'by Fate' – the metaphysical source which Satan nominates and to which he nominates himself as casual prophet – the 'strength' and the 'substance' of gods cannot fail; and since, 'through experience of this great event', we have lost nothing in arms and have gained in 'foresight':

> We may with more successful hope resolve
> To wage by force or guile eternal Warr
> Irreconcileable, to our grand Foe.   (I, 120 ff.)

It even has a nice internal cross-bolstering: the strength, arms, force lining up to demonstrate the series of unfailing continuance – the argument from soul or will, one might say; and then the more elevated and positive metaphysical argument, presumably from intelligence, the chain of substance, foresight, and guile. This latter series is itself a delicious metaphysical joke, one that comments with independent mischief on the argument, as substance humbly accepts the being of foresight and guile.

There is a rhetorical mischief too, in the disparity between the immediate thundering emphasis of the 'eternal' and the 'irreconcilable', and the remarkably shy string of hesitant advances toward the positive committal, which even then still remains governed by the carefully laid down 'may': 'We may ... with more ... successful ... hope ... resolve'. The formal perspective of despair has permeated the formal logic of the syllogism and acted out the drama of resolved hopelessness founding its hope on the irreconcilable maintenance of that state. The grand defiance of eternal war has quietly excluded the question of possible victory, and Satan has embraced despair as if he were no unwilling victim but an eager lover seeking to prove himself and to learn the nature of the beloved.

This example, though it is especially useful in demonstrating that familiar canons of the dramatic cannot arbitrarily be applied to Milton's style, is by no means unusual. The same basic control of materials, however varied, occurs time and again. Satan, of course, by nature of his role provides Milton with the best opportunities; the unfallen and still untainted creatures are too nearly in harmony with the great perspective to admit much conflict. Adam's first speech (Book IV), for instance, is dignified and simple, securely removed from the individual and the immediate. It is pure of internal conflict and yet does not lack external conflict; for it expresses the simplicity of unfallen nature in the great conflict that is shaping, and it follows immediately after Satan's fertile demonstration of internal conflict in the 'melting' soliloquy that 'wonders' at Paradise and man, and dances love and pity and duty into hatred and self-pity and evasive compulsion.

But Adam's speeches do not remain so simple, nor do Eve's, and the style – the voice – of each is successfully differentiated from the other. That is one kind of variety Milton skilfully maintains within his elevation. The most virtuoso display is, I suppose, that by the speakers in the Parliament of Hell. There we find stylistic characterization with broad and heavy strokes – the energetic stolidity of the die-hard general, the flat language and rhythms of the business executive. But there are subtly drawn differences too – as between the rhythms and sensuousness of Satan's first public speech and those of Belial's oration. Satan puts the pressure of his personality and feeling and will on every word and rhythm; Belial starts, at least, by creating the illusion of cool distance, by the curve of his rhythms, by the graceful syntax of apparently objective contemplation, though he ends in a sensuousness of attitude and direction that has no object for contemplation but the deliciousness of self.

God's speeches have hardly aroused critical enthusiasm,

though Milton's skill in providing and adapting biblical
phrases has been admired. Perhaps it is no answer to say that
Milton's God is not presented as a dramatic character. Meta-
physically He would seem to be properly outside the universe
of action, though He is also the biblical God revealing Himself
in His chosen terms, however symbolically, to angelic and
human understanding. Milton certainly did not expect his fit
audience to read literally, and with no consciousness of the
literary problem of presenting God's words. (Language and
cadence are as unsensuous as if Milton were writing a model
for the Royal Society and attempting to speak purely to the
understanding.) There at the fountain of light, where there can
be no shadow and no reflection, the words themselves can have
no overtones or echoes; though after they have been heard and
interpreted one may become aware of reflections, less to eye or
ear than to understanding, reflections that are the images of the
words. The grand style would be presumptuous, and what
Milton aims at is a particular kind of bare language that will
rise above the familiar associations of such bareness with austerity and harshness. Much, not all, of God's speech is delivered in rhythms that are markedly shorter than usual with
Milton, and yet successfully avoid the effects of brokenness or
crabbedness. They are no mean achievement of Milton's ear,
which has too often received credit for near-perfection at the
expense of recognizing the range of its imaginative accomplish-
ments.

Poetry is human and metaphorical, and the Father's speeches
are intended to express divine Justice as if directly: to seem
without seeming: to create the illusion of no illusion. I pass the
problem of trying to judge them – and say only that in Milton's
plan it is necessary that God be present and speak; that Justice
reveal, however imperfectly in human words, its Idea; which
then can be translated perfectly, in the universe where poetry
is valid, by the words and actions of God's creatures. The Son
is the authorized Word and has the greatest range of speech:
He is the Logos creating, the interpreter and declared will of

God, He uses 'I' gently to Adam and Eve as creator, sternly as judge. He expresses the fullness of divine love, God's 'dearest mediation' between eternity and time, immortality and mortality, justice and love.

The scene where He chooses sacrifice in order to fulfil justice is one of Milton's great triumphs of style. Again, all the conflict is external, in what this untroubled simplicity of utterance represents in the whole drama – in the way it will echo when Satan, also 'freely', volunteers as individual sacrifice; when Eve chooses the ambitious death of putting off human 'to put on Gods' and resolves to share with Adam 'all deaths' or 'equal Joy, as equal Love'; when Adam chooses death with Eve, for 'Death is to mee as Life'; and when Eve, as the drama moves into the myth of redemption, prays that all the 'sentence' fall on her; and Adam, in the forgiveness of renewed love and the acceptance of justice, gently says that if prayers could alter high decrees he would, first and more loudly, pray 'That on my head all might be visited'. The Son's speech has no internal conflict, for it is above human drama. But it expresses the divine order against which conflict is free to try itself – the expression of justice in terms of the immortal love for the mortal. It speaks with grace and beauty and purity to human senses, as the sanctioned mediation between the human metaphor of poetry and reality:

> Father, thy word is past, man shall find grace;
> And shall grace not find means, that finds her way,
> The speediest of thy winged messengers,
> To visit all thy creatures, and to all
> Comes unprevented, unimplor'd, unsought,
> Happie for man, so coming; he her aide
> Can never seek, once dead in sins and lost;
> Attonement for himself or offering meet,
> Indebted and undon, hath none to bring:
> Behold mee then, mee for him, life for life
> I offer, on mee let thine anger fall;
> Account mee man; I for his sake will leave

> Thy bosom, and this glorie next to thee
> Freely put off, and for him lastly die
> Well pleas'd, on me let Death wreck all his rage . . . .
>
> (III, 227 ff.)

The narrative and descriptive, which must bulk large in an epic, are also capable of conveying patterns of movement and conflict, so we must consider some properties of style that exist independent of direct speech. Milton's diction, his imagery, and his management of structures of sound all present separate problems in the larger problem of describing his style. The separate problems are not confined to the single problem of the dramatic, though it is convenient to study them in this connection.

Milton's diction is both carefully elevated and sensitively graduated. Without the elevation – the abstract level which must be created by the poet, built up and concretely maintained – his range would be far smaller, and he would not be able to use the reader's expectation as a constant by which to secure some very precise effects. This management of the levels of diction is a great technical accomplishment that deserves more extensive study than the present approach permits; but like all details of Milton's technique the final justification, whatever the rich immediate rewards, lies in the answerability of the style. (If the rewards are rich they are also necessary – in accordance with the tangible terms of Milton's concept of the human drama: which concept accords well with the relationship between freedom and necessity within the world which any great work of art creates. This is at the moment perhaps too serious a point to make, but it is a reminder that our chief subject is the unity of Milton's style.) The management of the diction is in effect much like the management of perspective in speeches or in narrative and descriptive passages. As we have already noted, when Satan resolves 'eternal' and 'irreconcilable' war he has significantly shifted his diction from the less positive level of 'We may with more successful hope'.

Even the generalized and the remote, twentieth-century readers apparently need reminding, may be more than an empty ceremony of elevation. When Eve, on the fateful morning, drops her formal address and calls Adam by his plain name, she presages her shocking change in style and status – to the completely individualized diction, accents, and rhythm of the naturally human; one might say, of the merely human as recorded in scenes of stage comedy. After the reconciliation, but most signally in the very last lines of the poem, the diction (though not that alone of course) restores them to a human dignity that accepts (and is expressed in the verse) both what was *individual* in their error and *universal* in its consequences. They are naturally human but not merely so, for they are both fallen and raised; if they let drop some 'natural tears', it is not for long, since the whole world – remote, grand, terrible, exciting – lies before them; and their great new adventure, anticipated in vision but still to be experienced, is at once the loss of their old freedom and the gain of their new freedom, with Providence their guide and the harsh immediacies of time mitigated by the known promise of eternity.

We remember our first view:

> So passd they naked on, nor shund the sight
> Of God or Angel, for they thought no ill:
> So hand in hand they passd. (IV, 319 ff.)

That is the simple grandeur of unfallen dignity seen as a whole, without individualizing physical detail; as from an indeterminate distance in which they move with an absolute evenness of progression that forces us to see only their wholeness, and nothing more individual than the added 'hand in hand' as our mind returns, from having contemplated the intellectual-spiritual source of their physical dignity, to the view of the sustained progress our eyes have never left.

And our last view:

> They hand in hand with wandring steps and slow,
> Through *Eden* took thir solitarie way. (XII, 648 f.)

This view is also one of wholeness, of two figures viewed as one in the distance; now no longer indeterminate but located in the dimension of time between a past already realized and a future promised in vision; and located between the tragic drama of human experience already realized yet still to be realized again and again; and between part of the myth of God's providential order already realized by them in their redemption, but still to be finally realized beyond the invisibly lighted horizon toward which they move, as the eastern gate of Paradise becomes their west, now dreadfully illuminated in the sunset-dawn of human time. But to say that our final view is located is not to say that it is concretely immediate, or to say that the diction is not generalized and remote, not kept pure of active metaphor and specific association: all of which sounds like a twentieth-century recipe for bad poetry.

More of that in a moment and a little longer on these lines – since I am letting this example stand for a quality that is pure in very many of Milton's lines and a significant part of his whole style. The language is familiar and simple but not *natural*, though the action deliberately presented is breath-taking in its naturalness *and* in its deliberate presentation – *and* in the relationship established between the two. Neither language nor rhythm is based on the colloquial; the words are carefully chosen to avoid *freshness*; they are literary, made familiar by Milton's poem and now elevated by rhythm and context and by the accumulating weight of the experience behind them. Words and rhythms echo and recapitulate but stiffen and turn straight out with the 'took' that announces the new life of choosing; at 'solitary' the echoes reverberate for a moment until the firm line of the rhythm and the more recent memories assert themselves and make the pathos bearable, together and under hope; while the surroundings drop undistinguishably back from them.

What I intend now is a modest attempt to examine some of the relationship between Milton's sound and sense. I begin by saying, since I have recently published a similar study of Donne, that Milton's patterns of sound are more difficult to analyse than Donne's. Milton's basic rhythm is more horizontal; the emphasis corresponds less obviously to a rhetoric of sharply defined metrical stresses; there is a far greater sensuousness, for *copia*, for the flow and sweep of heightened bigness; and patterns of sound are used with great confidence to shape and modulate metaphorical meaning. As I have already suggested, the cause is no doubt to be traced to Milton's poetic metaphysics, to his refusal to make a ruinous division between verbal soul and matter. But this is the kind of problem better treated, though inadequately, by modest example than by ambitious statement.

There *is* some naturalistic imitation in *Paradise Lost*. It may convey, though perhaps by a use of language that Mr Eliot could not countenance, an immediacy of physical action. For instance, the crowd of angels who rush into completed Pandemonium and are discriminated only by whether they praise the work or the architect: 'The hasty multitude/Admiring enter'd.' Their jostling mass and their articulating blur of enthusiasm seem to precede their actual entrance, which is an illusion true to the nature of such a crowd. The trick is also deliberate illusion – the transfers of epithet and syntax, the extravagant mouthing necessary to read the words – and meant to be comic. I think it has not been noted how often Milton's naturalistic imitations deliberately transfer their excess to the immediate situation, as a kind of dramatic device by which an action or a situation is given a characterizing voice. It is a particularly useful device for giving the qualities of a spoken part to description; and since it almost always seems a little extravagant, it is best suited for humour, and is capable of rather subtle gradations. After Satan has been subjected to his first extended view of the beauties of Paradise and the human inhabitants, the narrative voice returns to him. The first line describes him as still fixed, which reminds one of the internal conflict that has apparently been continuing between the preceding soliloquy and the one about to begin. The line itself is not particularly emphatic in its expression of fixedness; but the rather mechanical sequence of stresses perhaps suggests a kind of numbness, and does underline the extraordinary near-collapse of rhythm as the second line mischievously imitates the shocked physical and psychological condition of Satan:

> When *Satan* still in gaze, as first he stood,
> Scarce thus at length faild speech recoverd sad. (IV, 356 f.)

The effect is most likely to be comic when the imitation attempts to be quite complete, and for the most part when Milton is using the device seriously he follows the sound rhetorical principle that the good metaphor comes limping. (In his prose, for satiric purposes, he sometimes deliberately pushes a metaphorical correspondence to ludicrous extremes – as unsuccessful metaphysical poets sometimes do unwittingly.) For instance, the following serious example, the echoed line which closes Book X: 'in sign / Of sorrow unfeign'd, and humiliation meek'. Neither action nor psychological state is exactly imitated. But the two parts of the line are sharply contrasted, in sound as well as meaning. The first part is more emphatic, physically open and demonstrative in effect. The climax is loudly upon 'unfeigned', which rings out its vowels unhindered by the consonants but rather assisted; while the consonants of 'sorrow' are quite unemphatic, leaving the first syllable open and not sharply formed and allowing the second syllable to elide into the next word. The second part of the line is sharply defined in its consonants and kept at a low, level, and unemphatic movement in its rhythm. This pattern of sound does not correspond with the action or psychological state, but with a moral concept of behaviour that lies behind the immediate texture of the line. For the sorrow of repentance must be unfeigned and expressive to be genuine and single, to thrust beyond the inner complexities of the personal, and to purge in an initial and general way. But the humiliation must be restrained and unexpressive, meek and externally undistinguished. To test negatively one may see what happens by making the sorrow meek and the humiliation unfeigned.

This kind of example seems to me far more important for understanding Milton's metrical style than the more brilliant virtuosity that opens gates jarringly or melodiously, and the like. The basic point to make, in any case, is that the pattern of sound does not reinforce an already established meaning so much as it helps shape and modulate that meaning.

Consider this purple passage that announces the decision of the great debate in Pandemonium:

> With Trumpets regal sound the great result:
> Toward the four winds four speedy Cherubim
> Put to thir mouths the sounding Alchymie
> By Haralds voice explain'd: the hollow Abyss
> Heard farr and wide, and all the host of Hell
> With deafning shout, return'd them loud acclaim.
>
> (II, 515 ff.)

The first line convincingly imitates the abrupt punctuation and the carrying blare of the trumpets – by rhythmic emphasis, by the vowel tones, and the consonantal clusters (*tr-t, r-g, gr-t, r-t*); and also the necessary spit of the *s*, the brassy gurgle of the *l*, and the tongued stop of the *the*. This brilliant display of sound effects marks with flourishes the disparity between the substance and the announcement of the result, and mocks the gaudy pomp with which hell imitates the *state* of heaven. The 'alchemy', which Raleigh strangely thought an epic circumlocution to avoid with a pretty word and sound the vulgar naming of an instrument, is both the actual metal made by alchemists for trumpets and the familiar fraud of the alchemists' unachieved result. The 'explained', as rhythm and sound, is propelled outward with great energy and then sustained in a widening sound one seems to hear carrying on during the interval, which seems relatively long, before one can rhythmically resume the line; and what follows ('the hollow abyss') is lower in pitch and rhythmic intensity: which allows the preceding climax to be heard yet, or at least felt as an unsilenced force, *over* the lower pitch and intensity. (The effect is more common in music, where it may also be a created illusion, but can as well be an actual effect of orchestration.)

With the next line we have resumed the sustained and widening sound. The impulse of sound we heard carrying outward is now heard, with a similar intensity of rhythm and high pitch, on the far extremities. First we seem to be at the source of hearing it, and then as the sound moves into the distance we follow, overtake, and anticipate, without having quite lost it from our ears during the transition. Then we hear, from the far distance, the sound come and spread and return to the angels standing in the middle distance, as it were. They, like the hollow abyss, collect the sound during an interval of lowered pitch and rhythmic intensity ('and all the host of hell'), and return it to the source. It is not quite the same sound, one should note; for the distance is much less and the mass of the volume greater, so that one hears the final sound only as a totally enveloping choral chord, with no sense of linear dimension. One should also note that the final vowel of 'acclaim' repeats that of 'explained' – and this vowel sound has been carefully omitted in all the circular development that carries through the low pitch of 'the hollow Abyss', the high pitch, but altered, of 'Heard farr and wide', the low pitch of 'and all the host of Hell', and the mounting tones of the last line. The fact of the initial and final *l*'s, the final *m*'s, and the connecting *h*'s I note but pass by.

Unless I have erred badly, the pattern of sound just described is no music of beautiful vagueness and does not, of its own nature, encourage a relaxed 'attentiveness to sense'. Nor does it convey only an 'immediate sensuous impression'. The sounds do not reinforce rhetorically an established image, nor do they merely make alive and persuasive an image that is in any satisfactory sense prior and defined. The pattern of sounds is largely responsible for the dramatic immediacy which is created; but to stop with that conclusion is to see the pattern again as a kind of rhetorical device used for a calculated aim. If one insists on seeing the full role of the sounds in the image, one must recognize that the sounds shape the image creatively. In this sense, the sounds may with no more accuracy be called naturalistic imitation than the image itself. For one thing, the familiar precedents of naturalistic imitation are all far simpler in effect – usually limited to the kind of state, or action, or aspect of an action that the sensuous can successfully imitate or caricaturize. Here the physical action is complex and involves psychological action as well. Part of the complexity and the precision of the image is dependent on details that are nonnaturalistic. Most obvious is the elaborate 'musical' structure from 'explained' to 'acclaim'.

But take the word 'explained'. The customary meaning would neither contradict nor justify, but could accommodate, the description of its effect as sound. What Milton has done here is release the original metaphor, with its physical and psychological action, upon which the derived meaning is based. Compared with the more primitive meaning, the derived meaning tends to be abstract, the accepted equivalent of the familiar result or even process of an action, but with no physical or imaginative sense of the very happening of that process. The sound of the word, as Milton uses it here, justifies and is thoroughly involved in the etymologically older meaning of flatten out and so make *plain*. But whatever naturalistic origin may be furnished for this word or other words, the poet returning to an older meaning, even when he re-creates that meaning sensuously in the context, still owes something to what has become an unnatural usage, though sanctioned by art and history. The poet who exploits the imitative potentialities of such a word can do so, whatever he owes to the relationship between the primitive and the poetic, only as a scholar of words writing to scholars of words. Perhaps this is where one should stop, or start, by recognizing the full involvement of sound and meaning. My speculation on this word leads me back to my starting point: the best way to understand the pattern of sound here is as a shaping and integral part of the created image.

But I must look back a moment longer. For all its intensive and extensive particularity of detail, the pattern of sound just examined has more in common with that of the line, 'Of sorrow unfeign'd and humiliation meek', than with the patterns in lines that intend to be more completely imitative – say, for example, the virtuoso effects that introduce the comic reduction in size, in the hall of Pandemonium, of the minor angels: 'Brusht with the hiss of russling wings'. Though the physical process of the 'explained' is conjured up with a loving accuracy of sensuousness, that accuracy does not exist entirely for its own sake, but it focuses the process and it limits – toward a structure of meaning that is embodied in the immediate texture but extends beyond. (Similarly, the less complex pattern of sound in 'Of sorrow unfeign'd and humiliation meek' corresponds to an underlying concept of behaviour.) And part of the effect of the limiting is to prevent any merely sensuous response by a reader relaxing to the soft focus of large swirls of undiscriminated feeling. The sensuous precision is here as considerable as the intellectual precision; and both demand a wide-awake apprehension of the context, the sounding alchemy and the great result, and of the whole process as a magnificent illusion – with the echo amplified by the physical and the psychological-political surfaces, returning in greater volume than the initial sound. It is an illusion that the fallen angels participate in, while we both participate and observe. So the structure of sound here corresponds both to an immediate structure of meaning and to a larger structure of meaning. It shapes the image, but it shapes it intellectually, just as the intellectually perceivable meaning of 'explained' shapes the structure of sound.

Milton writes with the conscious impersonality of a great artist performing under the auspices of Muse the demanding and elevating tasks of a great theme. He does not dwell in a finical way on any single poetic moment, but no moment is lost in the pattern of the whole. Milton's relations with his Muse must be accepted as a literal fact that is also a rich and finally inscrutable fact. He is not making empty ceremonial gestures of polite antiquarianism – though he may seem to be doing so both to those who split his poem into conscious and unconscious meanings, and to those who are inclined to speak of Milton's consciousness as if he were a carpenter following a blueprint which can be *exactly* recovered by research into the poem and his life. The true eloquence Milton aspires to requires getting beyond self, and this is as necessary to the poet for an imaginative return to the true sources of nature and self as to the great figures in this drama.

But the poet does not forget the state of his world, as it now is, and works through conflict, and the impurity of the negative, and the impurity of false eloquence and mixed eloquence – with the pressure of relationship and history upon every phrase. And still, if the imaginative return is possible and real, as to Milton it certainly is, it cannot be achieved naturally, as an un-indebted act of intelligence and will. There is the Muse, and the composition is at night, and (though we do not learn the fact from him) in the dying and dead times of the year: in the natural darkness of season and person, which requires and receives irradiation in order to see the invisible. (I speculate, not too seriously, that the darkness of the true poet bears some humble analogy with the apparent darkness of God's 'unapproached' light.)

But whatever his private and public rituals, and whatever his attitude toward these, Milton does construct a poem of extraordinary complexity that is at last most impressive for its clarity. I have laboured at the complexity and I do not apologize, for not to have done so would have meant for me becoming conscious of a limited clarity. I have not been satisfied with the descriptions of Milton's style that emphasize its simplicity and urge vigilant surrender on the reader. (In these matters history alone will not save us, for there is not a critic alive who can read as if the eighteenth, the nineteenth, and half of the twentieth centuries did not exist.) One does not have to practise surrender to Milton, he commands it; one has to practise vigilance.

To slight his complexity is to slight his precision, and it is the very exacting exactness of his complexity that creates the true clarity. It is a profound clarity which no age or man can master and exhaust. It is a clarity which never fails to carry *through* the complexity (and in this he radically differs from Donne), a clarity which is always the sure master, perhaps one might even say the source, of the complexity. This does not deprive his subtleties of their value, of their contributions in depth and breadth; a clear, known form is, like metre, a guide, but not an answer that can be substituted for process. Milton has a secure metaphysical grasp of the principle, the centre, which can admit all kinds of surface complexity, and indeed must, to prove his grasp; he justifies the great theme *in* the process of mastering idea and texture in the perspectives of the whole cumulative weight of the epic structure, and in the traditions of human understanding which give life to and draw life from their embodiment.

Milton's mastery of perspective is intellectual but it must, and does, express itself physically in the poem. We have already examined some cases of perspective controlled in the management of scene and character, in the relating of local context to larger context, in the management of texture and the management of structure, in the imagery, in the diction that achieves transparency through the masterpiece of decorum uniting immediate and total answerability. Examples could be multiplied and observations, I have no doubt, both extended and refined. But I intend only one further extension; it has been implied in much of the preceding treatment. Milton's imagination maintains a distinctive control of the perspective of distance and of space. In detail it is physical, remarkably so; in concept it is intellectual, with space, it seems to me, an aspect of time. He presents the immediacy of the moment in the conscious perspective of time.

Things are held at an epic distance; if they approach close they are nevertheless always seen in the perspective of that distance, in the dimension of God's announced Idea of time. By allusion, epic simile, the constant outward thrust of the imagery, by countless structural references – the events in the foreground which are the immediate dramatic medium are related to eternity. It is a poetic demonstration of the concept of time in the *Timaeus* – 'a moving likeness of eternity'. It is helpful by way of distinction to refer to a striking moment in one of Milton's early poems, *At a Solemn Musick*: 'That undisturbed song of pure concent'. It is an example of beautiful style 'presented', 'projected' – and believably possible from another context by a skilful master of words. This is not demonstrable in any way I know, and so I must merely assert that other poetic statements in Milton are different though as polished and as formal; they have less of the personal and they are less possible as the projection of a detachable moment. Part of the distinction, I imagine, is in the built-up quality that proves itself as a sustained thing, not needing to exploit the moment for effect, yet always appropriate to the moment in its place in the whole continuum. (I think of the cellist who has mastered a fine tone and can manage some extraordinary moments, but cannot manage and modulate the tone so that its mastered qualities will endure through a strenuous composition.)

In *Paradise Lost* there are many detachable moments that are projected with striking beauty. Time seems to stop, and the illusion grants the enclosed moment a great intensity, which is always modified significantly as the moment re-enters the continuum of time. An obvious example is the sudden illusion of magnification in Satan's encounters with Death and with Gabriel. Some more important examples, which occur most liberally in hell, are the beautiful military review of the fallen angels marching forward in the momentary unification of music and discipline, with the illusion of past and present and future boldly but despairingly fused into one; or the whole building of Pandemonium, and the sub-moment of Mulciber's fall; or the whole experience of Paradise as a beautiful but impossible moment in time, with sub-moments complete in their purity, and others, like Eve's dream or Adam's praise to Raphael of Eve's apparent absoluteness; or the creation by Sin and Death of the causeway between hell and earth; or the sustained moments of many of the epic similes which rise out of the narrative to furnish great adventures in perspective. All of these, and countless more, gain enormous intensity from being seen both as they immediately are and as they are in the unfolding perspectives which lead finally to God's Idea of time, which includes as a smaller circle man's creation, fall, and redemption. The great circle, which begins with the creation of the angels, and proceeds from God to God, is described as finally ending thus with the last judgement:

> Hell, her numbers full,
> Thenceforth shall be for ever shut. Mean while
> The World shall burn, and from her ashes spring
> New Heav'n and Earth, wherein the just shall dwell
> And after all thir tribulations long
> See golden days, fruitful of golden deeds,
> With Joy and Love triumphing, and fair Truth.
> Then thou thy regal Scepter shalt lay by,
> For regal Scepter then no more shall need,
> God shall be All in All. (III, 332 ff.)

Under this positive vision of the whole, the powerful play of Satan's immediacy is contained while given the full expression that dramatically demonstrates its opportunism, its essentially negative evil. He has no real place to go, as his syllogism of despair argues; he vacillates between an impossible stasis and a real retreat. The great assertions of individual will which, with their counterplay of conscious and unconscious inner conflict, endow him with the illusion of dramatic being, drive him inevitably to allegorical being. He is drawn gradually into the mechanical existence of his unwilled creations, Sin and Death. It is part of their structural role to show this, for their allegorical being constitutes a kind of stable measure; but their author changes, to become more like his images. When they first meet at the gate of hell Satan ungallantly declares that he has never seen 'Sight more detestable then him and thee'. But when he returns to find his success anticipated by their 'connatural' sympathy, he expresses unreserved admiration for their work, for their very selves, and for their relationship to him:

> Fair Daughter, and thou Son and Grandchild both,
> High proof ye now have giv'n to be the Race
> of *Satan*.   (X, 384 ff.)

He has been demonstrating the logic of sin, the thraldom of self, the progressive deaths of spirit and will; now he passes on to the final mechanistic demonstration, his role in the mass metamorphosis. At this point he equals the abstract grotesqueness of Sin and Death, and he is himself a monster illustrating an allegory. The infernal trinity do more than parody the supernal trinity and true creation (though I agree with Mr Tillyard's recent observation that they do this); they demonstrate another order of being, the crude mechanistic existence of allegorical being. Their career constitutes a negative proof that also has some bearing on Milton's attitude toward the imagination; for they oppose, in a mechanical metaphor cut off from true reality, the whole imaginative vision of true creation and the true poem, with its degrees of metaphor leading up to the great source which allows imaginative freedom, under love and order, to the human and natural.

The moments not detachable from time are less gorgeous and exciting, freed from the dramatic burden of intensity. I think of the Son's volunteering for sacrifice, of the contrasting forward march to music by the loyal angels in heaven, of the reconciliation between Adam and Eve, of Adam's final recital of his lesson:

> > with good
> Still overcoming evil, and by small
> Accomplishing great things, by things deemd weak
> Subverting wordly strong, and wordly wise
> By simply meek; that suffering for Truths sake
> Is fortitude to highest victorie,
> And to the faithful Death the Gate of Life.   (XII, 565 ff.)

The whole of Book VII is the great example. The Creation occurs as an authentic miracle which can take itself for granted. Everything is easy and natural and right. All the creatures do the typical things, which are interesting for themselves, but are loved because they express the order and harmony of the created world. There is no extravagance of image or diction or rhythm. By contrast the building of Pandemonium is a dazzling piece of self-conscious conjuring.

But there are two other moments that are perhaps more significant in their contrast. First, the intoxicated extravagance of image and diction that celebrates the infernal creation by Sin and Death; especially this:

> The aggregated Soyle
> Death with his Mace petrific, cold and dry,
> As with a Trident smote, and fix't as firm
> As *Delos* floating once; the rest his look
> Bound with *Gorgonian* rigor not to move,
> And with *Asphaltic* slime.   (X, 293 ff.)

And then, the beautiful and quiet moment of natural description presented by the simile which concludes the consultation in Pandemonium:

> Thus they thir doubtful consultations dark
> Ended rejoycing in thir matchless Chief:
> As when from mountain tops the dusky clouds
> Ascending, while the North wind sleeps, o'respread
> Heav'ns chearful face, the lowring Element
> Scowls ore the dark'nd lantskip Snow, or showre;
> If chance the radiant Sun with farewell sweet
> Extend his ev'ning beam, the fields revive,
> The birds thir notes renew, and bleating herds
> Attest thir joy, that hill and valley rings.   (II, 486 ff.)

The natural beauty is as innocent here as in Book VII, but packed down into this moment is the human consciousness of change, of the certainty of uncertainty. The intense moment that prolongs day is made intense by the knowledge that it is a moment; man responds joyously as a part of nature because he is in the moment, but it is a mixed joy because he knows about time. And so the reader shares fallen feelings with these angels;

he participates in the experience, which is his experience too, but he is also outside it by virtue of the controlled perspective and its comment on this illusion. He will marvel at Milton's imaginative sympathy, but he will remember other moments: and he may remember particularly the delayed morning of the night-foundered skiff, the long summer's day, which ends, of Mulciber's fall; and the image that concludes Mammon's speech, the true and false illusion of the echoes in the craggy bay after the tempest; and he may be reminded later by the images of false light; and by Satan's sea finding a shore in the dubious light on the border of chaos, and by evening and morning in Paradise; and by the unknown beauty of the fruit of Paradise described in an image drawn from the known beauty on the edge of the border of change:

> On which the Sun more glad impress'd his beams
> Then in fair Evening Cloud, or humid Bow,
> When God hath showred the earth.   (IV, 150 ff.)

And by the final sunset image that formally begins human time and the long day's dying.

The wealth and variety of the answerable style is a vision of the whole, a vision that can accommodate natural beauty, and the necessary discipline in heaven and on earth, and the extravagant hope for man (who is made *to delight*, 'and delight to Reason joyn'd') – it is an affirmation of hope in God's love for creation, and a sober realization of the now under the great promise of Time. The *poetic* authority for the great vision of time is also poetic authority for the answerable style. This may be seen in its most direct expression in the passage that follows the Son's free offer to die for man:

> His words here ended, but his meek aspect
> Silent yet spake, and breath'd immortal love
> To mortal men, above which only shon
> Filial obedience.   (III, 266 ff.)

The variety is unity through the sanction of the immortal love for the mortal under obedience: with the stage, the focus of the feelings, successfully human, allowing the full play of human interest in the drama of freedom, fall, and redemption under the sanctioned perspective of love fulfilling justice. It is a vision that demands love from the style, under an Idea that authorizes and encourages love for created things, and does not require love for the Idea to dry up all other love. It holds to a Platonic insistence on the responsibility of reason, but with no drawing back from the natural and material; man knows God because God has given man the true means, which have dignity.

In his style Milton can trust the springs of the natural, because the 'simple' end loves the sensuous and passionate means to it, and does not withdraw its love completely from the means that tend away. Beauty is not blotted out of evil: the fallen angels lie like autumnal leaves 'that strow the Brooks / In *Vallombrosa*'; and Mulciber's fall is neither an 'unconscious' beauty nor merely (as I have thought) a deliberate irony – there is a place for that beauty finally. Love is the solution of the insoluble. The vision that can contain the necessity and beauty of Eve, the certain but not necessary fall, through misdirected love, and the certain but not necessary redemption in love, can contain in true perspective the individual beauty of each created part in the harmony of the whole creation. Song and dance in heaven express the same harmonious relationship between part and whole:

> No voice exempt, no voice but well could joine
> Melodious part, such concord is in Heav'n.   (III, 370 f.)

> mazes intricate,
> Eccentric, intervolv'd, yet regular
> Then most, when most irregular they seem.   (V, 6220 ff.)

When Adam becomes conscious that he has been created, he feels with a knowledge as spontaneous as love that he is happier than he knows, and at the end of the poem he knows that he is happier than he knows. The last two books are not to be explained away historically, as the aesthetic result of the seventeenth century's being more interested in biblical history than is the twentieth century. These books fulfil the rhythm of the poem, and they satisfy two kinds of time; they allow Adam a necessary interval to convalesce as man and hero under the aspects of human history and eternity. During this time he becomes a conscious tragic hero (both actor and spectator) accepting, with all passion spent, fully man's condition, and he himself now a fully experienced man; and becomes a mythic hero reborn; and finally becomes man, with all his history behind and before him.

The complex is the dramatic, the dust and heat of the world trying truth in no simple contest. But the clarity shines through the complexity. The style returns through full complexity to a source beyond innocence, without losing any of the wisdom of the whole experience – or the knowledge that it must be lived through again and again.

Kingsley Widmer

THE
ICONOGRAPHY OF RENUNCIATION:
THE MILTONIC SIMILE*

T HE conception of John Milton as primarily a Renaissance or Christian humanist, a view perhaps inevitably associated with the skilful study of his historical and literary relationships, raises difficulties when applied to Milton's later poetry. Scholarly humanism's allegiance to the values of classical learning, ethical and religious moderation, and general reasonableness may not do justice either to Milton's absolutistic religious commitment or to some of the distinguishing qualities of his poetry. Part of the critical issue might be suggested by two related questions: Does the modality, the tone and texture, of Milton's longer poems emphasize the meliorative or the absolutistic? And does the Miltonic valuation of the human world provide existential affirmation or transcendentalist renunciation?

Milton's figurative language, particularly the similes, provides advantageous focus for such discussion, not only because of its felicity but because it reveals Milton's peculiar use of traditional humanistic materials. The similes have also provided many modern critics with a nexus for their narrowly adverse judgements of Milton's style. Some of these criticisms, I suggest, display a hyper-logical analysis which fails to recognize the order of the baroque; the critics do not see the principled peculiarity that organizes the seemingly decorative flourishes. The counter-argument holds that the similes express the full poetic logic and moral commitment of the Miltonic view.

A simile from *Paradise Regained* (IV, 562–71) may illustrate some of the relevant dialectic. Satan, falling from the pinnacle

* From the *Journal of English Literary History*, XXV (1958), 258–69. Revised for the present volume by the author.

upon which he has, as a final threat, placed Christ, is compared to the earth-empowered giant (Antaeus) defeated in physical combat by a herculean Christ (Alcides). Milton self-consciously helps define the function of the simile by a parenthetical comment: 'to compare / Small things with greatest'. It is, then, the disparity as much as the similitude of the comparison which we must recognize. Clearly, there is an ironic disproportion in the comparison of Christ with Hercules: the pagan hero's victory was an active assertion of the body whereas Christ's victory was a renunciation of all bodily action. The simile directs our attention to Milton's point that Christian renunciation is the 'greatest' heroism. Furthermore, in comparing 'Small things with greatest', we see that Milton presents the far-ranging Satan as much superior to the earthbound classical giant. The practice of the disparate simile expresses Milton's moral principle of disparaging classical virtue because of Christian renunciation.

The disparate simile's negative treatment of the classical mythos receives confirmation in the vehement attack on classical learning two hundred lines earlier in *Paradise Regained*. (Any other assumption, such as that the anti-classical arguments and the pagan-heroic materials contradict each other, presumes incoherence in a self-conscious and serious poet.) The emphasized disparity between the combat of Satan and Christ and the combat of the classical heroes provides another fillip against classical learning. This belittling of a traditional heroic comparison accords with the Miltonic insistence on the incommensurability of the Christian and classical, and applies to much of the treatment of heroism in Milton's poems.

Some such fuller perspective on the style of Milton's poetry, rather than an emphasis upon local scenic effects, seems necessary if we are to relate the particulars of Milton's verse to his commanding ideas and values. Most of Milton's similes thus require an awareness of ironic disparity as well as the obvious sense of comparison. Further illustrations might be provided by Milton's devaluative use of another literary tradition linked to the pagan – the pastoral. Satan in the Garden of Eden (*Paradise Lost*, IX, 455 ff.) appears 'as one who long in populous city pent'. Satan in *Paradise Regained* (II, 300 ff.), though a considerably lesser dramatic figure because of the more direct doctrinal focus, belongs to the same negatively sophisticated type – 'as one in City, or Court, or Palace bred'. Some critics direct attention here to the poet's distaste for urban sophistication, which is correct, but the problem goes beyond the biographical to Milton's dialectic about the struggle with evil as sophisticated civilization. The association of Satan with urban civility in these two scenes prepares for the mocking of the rustics, Eve and Christ, by the sophisticated gentleman. Milton then provides a dramatic reversal in which the natural goodness of the rustic overcomes the villainous gentleman: in *Paradise Lost* it is because of Eve's natural beauty that Satan remains 'stupidly good' for the moment (IX, 465); in *Paradise Regained* the sophisticate's stupidity consists of tempting a born ascetic with food (I, 337–56). But then the easy pastoral victory of natural virtue reverses in Eve's temptation and in Christ's forced revelation of divine nature. In *Paradise Lost*, Satan's sly success with the apple in the pastoral garden reveals itself as finally illusory with the ashen apples of a divine miracle in the infernal garden (X, 547–72). In *Paradise Regained*, Christ saves his fall by miraculous divinity, and the illusory success of violence ends in Satan's own fall (IV, 551–71). This recurrent ironic parallelism rests on a theological paradigm which reverses the significance of the pastoral similes. Natural goodness (the rustic figure) momentarily wins in the struggle with the slyness and force of sophisticated evil, then loses, and finally must be superseded and redeemed by the miraculous revelation of divine slyness and force.

The pastoral metaphor, of course, takes larger dimensions than the specific similes; for example, Milton may be understood as negatively using the classical idea of Elysium in the Garden of Eden when he emphasizes the pastoral as the opening and inadequate scene in the struggle for redemption, rather than its reward. The pastoral representation, with calculating power as urban, appears also in the wicked cities of Gaza and Pandemonium, and rests on such distinguishing Protestant moral divisions as the *contrast* between the reign over 'cities of men' and the 'reign within'. But generally in Milton the pastoral dramatizes the momentary adequacy, and final inadequacy, of natural goodness, and the necessity for all simple virtue to be redeemed by the power of Christian authority.

While Milton's literary epic has a potentially vast range of figurative possibilities, he most often follows traditional directions in the materials for his similes. The epic insect simile, which appears in Homer, Virgil and Tasso, is often used by Milton but in ways that may be distinctive to him (and to the later poetry so indebted to him). In *Samson Agonistes* we see traditional classical imagery when Samson's 'restless thoughts' are 'like a deadly swarm of hornets' (19–20). However, Milton compared to inward torments while his predecessors saw external torments. When Samson refuses to 'sit idle . . . a burdensome drone' (567–8), the use of the insect image does not seem to have an adequate parallel in the classical sources. Equally revealing of the Miltonic harsh tone is the simile by the Chorus in *Samsom Agonistes* in which the 'common rout' of men are condemned as they who 'grow up and perish, as the summer fly'. Has not Milton added a sense of Protestant vocation, including the righteous sanctification of work, to the traditional classical insect comparisons?

Another use of the fly simile appears in *Paradise Regained* (IV, 15–24) where Satan is compared to a 'swarm of flies' annoying a Christ likened to a 'wine press'. (While Satan ostensibly tempts Christ, the terms of the simile appropriately suggest an entrapment by the deity.) A connected simile transforms the swarming of the flies to a 'vain battery', like that of waves upon a rock. The narrowly logical critic might ask how the similes can provide a plausible picture: how puny flies can be powerful waves, how a wine press can also be a rock, how buzzing can also be battery, and how the single person of Satan can be a swarm of flies and a series of waves. Milton's similes, however, do not primarily elaborate the visual logic of scene or character but religious dialectics. Satan's parasitic and futile temptations – actually ordained self-temptings to further definitions of evil – properly compare to a swarm of flies in trivial plenitude but also the battery of waves in the threatening persistence through all natural time. The dualities of evil, quotidian yet immense, seasonal yet universal, are revealed by the linkage of disparate similes. Similarly, the apparently rich and seasonable quality of Christ (the wine press) always turns out to be the image of immutability (a rock). The similes for Satan and Christ help define the recurrent and central Miltonic dialectic of the eternal conflict of energy and immutability.

Puzzling qualities of Milton's style frequently reveal a deeper coherence if read as part of his theological polarity between a dynamic and plenitudinous evil and an unchanging and absolute good. Part of the refusal to recognize this may be due to the traditional theory of the simile (as in Quintilian, Samuel Johnson, and T. S. Eliot's criticism) which held the simile to be digressive, ornamental and not essentially related to the commitments of the poem. Milton's use of the simile, however, appears to diverge from the classical view as inevitably as the conception of rhetoric in a logos-believing Protestant would diverge from the classical precepts of persuasion. The Word of the simile must also be part of the truth. In this Protestant baroque style, as generally in baroque art's use of disparities which return to equilibrium, the poetic flourishes reinforce the underlying Protestant logic.

Generally in Milton the imagery moves towards the antithetical patterns of energy and immutability. Milton usually links Satan with movement: the waves beating futilely and the Port of Despair in *Paradise Regained*; the ship similes for Satan in Books I, II and IX of *Paradise Lost*; Satan's repeated sailing or swimming through liquid and chaotic materials as in the Lake of Hell, part of his journey through Chaos, and the river and mist by which he enters the Garden of Eden. Satan also draws the similitudes with water monsters and classical voyages and fluid variety. One might suggest that the 'boundless deep' of Satanic despair in *Paradise Lost* essentially relates to the 're-morseless deep' and 'perilous flood' of Milton's fearful anger in *Lycidas*. Fluidity and flood and change are mortal and evil. Voyaging is death – thus Dalila as a ship in *Samson Agonistes*. Adventure, polytheistic variety, and terrifying mutability characterize the devil and the existential world in contrast to absolute morality and the unmovable divine authority.

Milton's similes often suggest multiple relationships rather than single comparisons. The Satan–Leviathan simile of Book I of *Paradise Lost* not only suggests the apocalyptic sea-monster and his illusory promise but the confusing giganticism of the evil world in flux. The magnification of Satan in the following series of similes emphasizes the principle of evil as the very power of mutability which dominates all of its multitudinous forms, the other fallen angels. Where Satan is compared to a sea-monster and his spear to a Norway pine that will 'be the mast of some great ammiral' – ship and Leviathan being in essence one from the Miltonic rejection – the other fiends are compared to the traditional epic 'autumnal leaves' (the residue of change rather than its gigantic principle) 'that strow the brooks' (instead of seas). By further reduction, the lesser fiends are compared to 'scattered sedge' on the 'Red-Sea Coast'. In Milton's usual movement from the classical to the Christian – this time apparently associational (the flaming lake of Hell as a Red Sea) – we reach the biblical exodus from Egypt and then the comparison of the devils to Pharaoh's drowned cavalry. The expansion in association from fallen leaves to fallen legions, from seasonal death to divine retribution, also suggests the transformation of the classical fatalistic simile into the biblical moral simile.

The Egyptian abjectness of the devils fuses with the dramatic action in Satan's angry demand that they arise (310–30). The concluding comparison of the verse paragraph shows the contrast of the now lowly fiends to their former stature as

'Cherub and Seraph'. A chain of being, from vegetable to human to angelic – the residual medieval hierarchy – ends in the dramatic intellection of evil and Satan's awareness of his fallen anguish. The pathos appears in the repeated disparities called forth by the comparisons between the earlier and present status. The same mode of double view applies all through Books I and II in the alternating expansion and deflation of the fiends. Patently, this goes beyond pathos to the moral dialectic of evil as simultaneously trivial and immense, multitudinous and unified. The cycles of comparison, the traditional nature comparisons, the emphasis upon heroic combat and temporal fortunes, and the epic order, also provide evil with insistently classical characteristics. This achieves its fullest embodiment in Satan as the classical hero, not only as warrior but as reasoner (by parody in Book II, by simile in IX, 670–6, and by implicitly defending Greek wisdom in *Paradise Regained*). It is the most abjectly low who yet appealingly encompass so much and who must be understood in pagan, natural, cyclic and heroic terms alien to Christian redemption.

When the fallen angels heed Satan's command and rise from the lake (337–43) for a new cycle of fortune they appear as 'a pitchy cloud of locusts'. Although this is a traditional epic simile Milton declassicizes the comparison by relating it, yet again, to the biblical Red Sea story. The locusts, which in *Exodus* preceded the Red Sea defeat of Pharaoh, are not, therefore, the natural misfortune of classical epic but a divine scourge that appears and disappears at the command of God's chosen prophet and his 'potent rod'. Classical misfortune is but the disguise of biblical chastisement in Milton's technique of reversal. The dialectic of subtly subsuming the pagan mythology under the antithetical Christian mythology provides a major force in Milton's style – and the reversal of what might otherwise be taken as a humanistic fusion of classical and Christian materials. When appearing most classical and humanistic, Milton is really being most Protestant Christian.

From the hordes of insects, Milton's comparisons move to

the hordes of barbarians 'of Rhene or Danaw', and then to the 'godlike Shapes' of pagan deities. The progression in size still maintains the denigration of ravaging a land (locusts to barbarians to false gods) and repeats the pattern of the preceding series (fallen leaves to fallen men to fallen angels). The following catalogue of the fallen angels as pagan gods and the building of a pagan temple as the infernal capital elaborately suggests a renunciation of the classical and humanistic telos of the temple-polis civilization.

In the final verse paragraph of Book I of *Paradise Lost* (752 ff.) a rich compound of similes elaborates Milton's view of evil. The ironies should not be ignored. With the infernal gathering-place compared to the field for chivalric 'champions' who 'Defied the best of Paynim chivalry', we must also recognize the contrary elements: the fallen angels' formation in unchivalric seventeenth-century 'squared regiment' and the larger irony of the fiends as, for Milton, the very deities of pagan chivalry. Such is the perplexity of impressive appearances. Then, also surprisingly, appears another of the classical insect similes, 'As bees in springtime. . . .' The replacement of the earlier ravaging locusts by hardworking bees has partly been prepared for by the labour of the 'industrious crew' building Pandemonium. But the virtue of dutiful hard work for its own sake pervades Milton. He later comments that Belial is wrong in advising the fallen angels to 'ignoble ease and peaceful sloth' (II, 227). Thus, too, Samson labours for the enemy at Gaza, and righteously: 'labour / Honest and lawful to deserve my food' (1365–6). And Adam and Eve labour even in the Garden of Eden. The characteristic moral absolutism insists on the one ethos, the Protestant sanctification of labour, everywhere, from Paradise to Hell.

However, the Miltonic casuistry separates the results from the actions; the hard work in Hell shows three corruptions. The beehive, the golden 'Straw bilt citadel', shows the moral impermanence of the 'precious bane' from which Pandemonium has been built. Secondly, the end of the serial simile emphasizes the thickly swarming mass-insect quality (negative) rather than the industry (positive). And there is the satiric political touch of the insects engaged in 'state affairs'. In larger terms, the positive qualities given to the fallen angels reveal not the absence of virtue but the power of active evil, whether the constructed falsity of Pandemonium, discipline, hard work, or any other heroic or natural attractiveness not submitting to the one faith. For Milton, evil is less nasty sin than false virtue, as in Satan's 'Evil, be thou my Good'.

The various positive and heroic qualities linked with the fallen angels, such as work, discipline, learning, ambition, debate, bravery, energy, and others, are only partly undercut by irony. For they reveal the rich variety of evil and the single nature of goodness as faith in and submission to divine authority. Neither virtues nor good works reach towards redemption for Protestant Milton; any and all activity may be evil. The true antithesis of the infernal turns not to a different activity than that of Hell but to the will and the faith beyond all nature and activity: the refusal of heroism, the immutable Lord, the untemptable Christ, the renunciatory Samson, the poetic mind pervaded by the single revealed authority.

The bee simile also prepares the way for the fantastic reduction of the giant fiends to 'smallest dwarfs', 'Pigmean race' and 'Fairy Elves'. These similitudes partly reverse the heroic emphasis, thus maintaining the Miltonic dialectic about evil as both trivial and immense, and hence so pervasive. Nor should we take the elaboration of the fairy elves simile (781–8) as simply a light and fanciful touch. This identification of moonlight magic (and its dance and music) with the fiends displays also the consistent Miltonic denigration of paganism – this time Celtic. The reduction of fallen angels applies to the spacious scene as well, which now becomes a 'narrow room'. The penultimate reduction – 'incorporeal Spirits to smallest forms reduced' – reaches logical absurdity (the formless given smallest form) and hence prepares the reversal. Book I concludes with the Satanic crew in all their ominously heroic largeness:

the 'great Seraphic Lords and Cherubim', 'the thousand Demi-Gods' in 'their own dimensions like themselves'. That final simile is no simile, but, for Milton, the dominant and overpowering truth of the immense and self-defining nature of evil.

In the pattern of tropes that conclude this book, both dramatic commonsense and theological principle dictate that the proportions of evil must rise above all ironic reductions and must still retain not only the power and pleasure but much of the virtuous and heroic appearance which makes evil significant. Or as William Blake aptly noted, Milton's Satan is true desire and energy, and the very source of much imagination and life. The dialectic of the similes reinforces rather than obscures the Miltonic principle of the richly varied, multitudinous and desirable actuality of all that which is to be renounced.

If we may leave the discussion at this point of suggestiveness rather than exhaustiveness, several general evaluations of the style might be raised. A widely accepted critical view holds that the essential weakness of *Paradise Lost* was Milton's inability to make Heaven 'poetically preferable' to the richness of Hell because of a drably legalistic and authoritarian celestial style, including the absence of a single complex simile in the speeches in heaven. But this rejects the cohering dialectics of all the work. The more general judgement gets disguised in historical explanations. It is suggested that the epic tradition did not supply appropriate materials for a Christian Heaven. Or, we are learnedly advised, there appear to be inherent contradictions in seventeenth-century mythology and poetic sensibility. Or, we are directed to Milton's personal contradictions and those of his turbulent times as causes that produced antithetical lyrical, humanistic and theological styles. Perhaps, but why should we focus on literary antecedents, biographical genetics and historical conflicts as adequate explanations of the major and principled characteristics of Milton's poetry? The entire Miltonic view (as well as much of Protestant Christianity) depends on the stylistic antithesis between Heaven and Hell.

Milton's Heaven may have Reason and certain traditional images of hierarchy and order which expound the Revelation and the Word, but most other similitudes simply do not belong there. Immutable transcendent authority, the crux of Milton's commitment, is stark and harsh; it could not be otherwise.

The texture of reality and plentitudinous human actuality is not, for the later Milton, part of the divine. The similes, from that of the obscene smell of flesh to those of the great pagan heroes, draw most of their appropriateness to Satan. The rich range of natural and mythical comparisons express the infernal, not just as ornament, but in the deepest sense. Classical wisdom, the qualities of the natural world, sensory experience, the desires and mutabilities of time, pagan and secular codes of heroism, and even certain appearances of Christian work and virtue are, for Milton, far more appropriate to the fallen state than to the immutable absolute. Satan may be the hero, but the hero in a poetic commitment which rejects heroism for submission to transcendental authority.

The traditional question about the hero hardly seems adequate. Satan, as the style insists, comprises not a person but a multiplicity, a simile refraction of the iconography of the ultimately transitory values and vitalities which are worshipped in life but not in Heaven. It has often been noted that such Christian paradoxes as the *felix culpa* and the assertion of 'good from evil' crucially serve Milton's longer poems. Perhaps we can add to these paradoxes those of anti-heroic poetry and the anti-humanist inversion of a mythology of regeneration. But most important, an appropriate and dialectical reading of the Miltonic modality suggests a peculiar, and for some a shocking, master simile: evil is like the richly human world, and virtue is its renunciation.

J. B. Broadbent

MILTON'S HEAVEN*

T RYING to make it easier for us to palate the God of *Paradise Lost*, C. S. Lewis points out that 'In the religious life man faces God and God faces man. But in the epic it is feigned, for a moment, that we, as readers, can step aside and see the faces both of God and man in profile.'[1] This is to transcend the all-transcendent; however pious the motives may be it remains logically impossible to contemplate God – he ceases to be God as you do it. Therefore all objective discussions of God are absurd, and though they may be amusing their contact with reality is restricted to moments at which the listener may share a glimpse of the speaker's God. That is not a philosophical experience, but an aesthetic one. 'What is offered to man's apprehension in any specific Revelation is not truth concerning God but the living God Himself.'[2] This is the form taken by the most satisfactory literary revelations. This is not to say that devotional poems are the best or only possible religious litera-ture. Donne's holy sonnets, Herbert's descriptions of his struggles with God, Hopkins's 'terrible sonnets', are not images of God but of the relationship between the poet and his God. It is true though, that any presentation of God in narra-tive must be within the individual's vision of him. The poet must take responsibility for what he sees as God. Unless he does, the God he presents will be open to theological and philo-sophical objections, as well as to literary criticism.

In the Old Testament God is a person: 'Thus saith the Lord', 'And the word of the Lord came unto me saying'; even the hellenized parts of the New Testament claim to be records of the experience that the writers have had of the living God in the resurrected Son or in vision. But the tendency in the art of

* From *Some Graver Subject: An Essay on 'Paradise Lost'* (1960), ch. IV, §§ 1–3. Some minor changes have been made with the author's permission.

Christendom has been to present God either Platonically or Homerically, or as a mixture of the two. Spenser's God is Platonic. In the *Faerie Queene* he confessed that the Holy City was 'Too high a ditty for my simple song' of objective fiction (I, x, 55), so in the *Hymns* he described heaven and God in abstract patterns of rhetoric. Heavenly love, instead of being a present power in the universe, or a dramatic motive in the poem, is 'Th' idee of his pure glorie' (283) which we 'shall plainely see' some day in the eschatological future. Heavenly beauty is not the face of God but 'th' aspect of that felicitie, Which they haue written in their inward ey' (284). Giles Fletcher's God in *Christ's Triumph after Death* is also 'th' Idea Beatificall', the paradoxically eternal end and beginning of everything, eyeless all-seeing – a structure of the intellect alone. Yet the heaven he lives in is an aesthetic pattern of solids:

> About the holy Cittie rowles a flood
> Of moulten chrystall, like a sea of glasse,
> On which weake streame a strong foundation stood;
> Of living Diamounds the building was,
> That all things else, beside it selfe, did passe.
>   Her streetes, in stead of stones, the starres did pave,
>   And little pearles, for dust, it seem'd to have,
> On which soft-streaming Manna, like pure snowe, did wave.
>
>   (38

This wrapping of a concrete, aesthetically conceived heaven round an abstract God typifies the discordance of Hebrew myth and Greek metaphysics. The heaven comes from Revelation, almost word for word; yet the mystic of Revelation had no scruples about anthropomorphism:

> I was in the Spirit on the Lord's day, and heard behind me a great voice as of a trumpet, saying, I am Alpha and Omega. . . . And I turned to see the voice that spake with me. And being turned, I saw seven golden candlesticks; and in the midst of the seven candlesticks one like unto the Son of man, clothed with a garment down to the foot.

The importance of John's recording his vision so subjectively – 'It happened to me' – is demonstrated by Fletcher in another poem in his series, *Christ's Victory in Heaven*. There he uses the mythological method consistently, managing to dramatize the Trinity as well as the angels and heaven itself into some appearance of cosmic action and immortal personalities. But Fletcher himself is not involved at all, so the effect is merely Homeric; religion is obscured in myth.

The *Paradiso* is consummated by a vision of the Trinity which, though Platonically geometrical in outline, is infused with more than ideographical potency by Dante's own passion:

> la mia mente fu percossa
> da un fulgore in che sua voglia venne.

> All' alta fantasia qui mancò possa;
>   ma già volgeva il mio disiro e 'l velle,
>   sì come rota ch' egualmente è mossa,

> l'amor che move il sole e l' altre stelle.

(xxxiii, 140)

The poetry makes the *'tre giri di tre colori e d'una continenza'* (116) adequate as symbols for the divine love and will that the poem is about, and even for the world outside the poem. Dante's God is hot as well as bright, a rose as well as a circle. There are difficulties, however, even with the *Paradiso*. The chief aesthetic difficulty is that the journey is not an action. Parts of it anticipate the consummation – the light imagery, the poet's own sensations, the explanation in Canto iii of the state of the blessed which Dante is to achieve – *'è formale ad esto beato* esse *tenersi dentro alla divina voglia, per ch' una fansi nostre voglie stesse'* (79). But it is difficult to remain interested in the Platonic cosmographying, the Aristotelian metaphysics and the Thomist theology that Dante discusses with Beatrice and the saints on his way up through *'una ad una spiritali vita'* – what have these to do with *'l'amor che move il sole e l'altre stelle'*? The religious difficulty in the poem lies in its chief aesthetic excellence, that we reach God only at the end. This is where Dante differs from Revelation. His God is immensely powerful but puts not forth his power – we do not see him immanent in any act, of creation, redemption, judgement. Except for the reader already at peace on the circumference of his will, he is not the still point of the turning world but the final point of an individual mystic vision.

This is perhaps the basic difficulty of Christian theology, that it cannot be mediated to any who have not themselves seen its God, even through Christ; for Christ is of only ethical interest unless he be recognized as God's Son. As Milton says in *De doctrina*, 'the disciples of the doctrine of Christ may fairly be required to give assent to this truth [sc. that God exists] before all others, according to Heb. xi, 6, "he that cometh to God must believe that he is."' The only answer to the question, 'Who is the god of the Christians?' is Pothinus', 'If thou art worthy, thou shalt know.' The Reformation was partly an attempt to return to this position. It recognized the deficiencies in both the standard views of God: a Platonic theology can appeal only to men of intellect and education, an anthropomorphic one becomes in the hands of unmystical men a mythology; and neither is of much help in promoting individual morality or social justice. Yet though it strove to return to the simple ethical monotheism of the Hebrew prophets, the Reformation could not escape the contemporary influence of Greek metaphysics, Roman law and the Humanistic sense of history. It implicated the individual Christian in the divine process, but the process was as difficult to understand as ever. Thus Calvin, to us an iconoclast, saw himself as a practical anthropomorphist decrying intangible Catholic mysticisms:

As for those who proudly soar above the world to seek God in his unveiled essence, it is impossible but that at length they should entangle themselves in a multitude of absurd figments. For God – by other means invisible – (as we have already said) clothes himself, so to speak, with the image of the world, in which he would present himself to our contemplation. They who will not deign to behold him thus magnificently arrayed in the incomparable vesture of the heavens and the earth, afterwards suffer the just punishment of their proud contempt in their own ravings. Therefore, as soon as the name of God sounds in our ears, or the thought of him occurs to our minds, let us also clothe him with this most beautiful ornament; finally, let the world become our school if we desire rightly to know God.[3]

But theology of a concretely manifest God is probably more intractable than Dante's. In Protestantism each man his own priest, deprived of the vicarious faith of componence in the Church as the mystical Body of Christ, has to work out his own salvation face to face with God; and for men of intellect not given to personal mysticism this means working out something like a sum in arithmetic.

Milton, convinced of the ethical and political truth of Reformation Christianity, was only casually a visionary of God. Of John Smith's categories of the religious he had been in his Idealist days and still was occasionally something of 'the true metaphysical and contemplative man . . . who running and shooting up above his own logical or self-rational life, pierceth into the highest life'. But he was never able to reach the mystic's consummation of 'knitting his own centre . . . into the centre of Divine being'; at worst the Enthusiast's 'sense of his own virtue and knowledge', at best the Rationalist's 'glass . . . of reason and understanding',[4] as well as his Hebraic pragmatism, drew him back into the world of sense and argument. Typically of the English mixture of Jewish, Greek and Roman traditions, his normal approach to God was an attempt – like the Victorian doubters' – to get him down to his own level for a debate. Milton did not enjoy the spiritual serenity or the environing peace of the worldly success which variously enabled the Metaphysical poets and the Cambridge Platonists to ignore the chaos of theology and find heaven in a vision or in themselves. He could not know Sir Thomas Browne's Dantesque heaven, for instance:

where the Soul hath the full measure and complement of happiness; where the boundless appetite of that spirit remains compleatly satisfied, that it can neither desire addition nor alteration; that, I think, is truly Heaven: and this can onely be in the injoyment of that essence, whose infinite goodness is able to terminate the desires of it self, and the unsatiable wishes of ours.... Heaven, whose happiness consists in that part which is best able to comprehend it, that immortal essence, that translated divinity and colony of God, the Soul.   (*Religio Medici*, i, 49 and 51)

Of other hexameral poets, Grotius and Vondel had not presented God at all; most others just addressed him lyrically in invocations. Milton in this invocation approaches God in a mood which I think Sewell has caught:

The immediate and satisfying consciousness of God, resulting from a confidence in God's special providence for England and for himself, had gone. The experiential proofs of God's favour had been found wanting. Little was left except a deep habit of mind expressing itself in an inadequate logical framework.[5]

But because he was not God-happy, something of the interest of devotional poetry does attach to the theologizing of Book III.

The paean to light forces problems on us. In the *Nativity Ode* the Son had been presented as

> That glorious Form, that Light unsufferable,
> And that far-beaming blaze of Majesty.

The indicative *that's* and the epithet 'unsufferable' establish the 'Form' as genuinely Platonic, something more than an ideograph; but here in *Paradise Lost* the light that Milton hails, though it suggest the Son – 'ofspring of Heav'n first-born' – is coldly, even Scholastically presented. The analogue is Tasso's opening of *Le Sette Giornate del Mondo Creato*, a didactic document of the Counter-Reformation, not the Age of Faith. This kind of writing seems to belong to the third stage in Ruskin's outline of the development of the false ideal in religious art:

For a long time, when art was in its infancy, it remained unexposed to this danger [sc. of creating false images], because it could not, with any power, realize or create *any* thing. It consisted merely in simple outlines and pleasant colours; which were understood to be nothing more than signs of the thing thought of. . . . But as soon as art attained the power of realization, it obtained also that of *assertion*. . . . But a shadow of increasing darkness fell upon the human mind as art proceeded to still more perfect realization. These fantasies of the earlier painters, though they darkened faith, never hardened *feeling*. . . . In early times *art was employed for the display of religious facts;* now, *religious facts were employed for the display of art.* The transition, though imperceptible, was consummate; it involved the entire destiny of painting. It was passing from the paths of life to the paths of death.

And this change was all the more fatal, because at first veiled by an appearance of greater dignity and sincerity than were possessed by the older art.[6]

Yet Milton's lines are not assertive. The metaphysical terminology, the querying ('May I express thee unblam'd?'), the adduction of biblical authority ('since God is light'), the logic ('dwelt then in thee') invite us to share an intellectual effort to understand God in the world. It is, so far, very intellectual. Augustine's distinction between 'the light which is God and the other light which God has made' is confused. Milton's affinities are with more speculative theologians. Fludd had wondered whether 'light is increate or created by an increate light'. Plotinus used light to designate the creative, unifying energy that emanates from the One, the Father, the Good, the first person of the Neo-Platonic triad of hypostases. His authority, 'God is light', is 1 John. If this was meant literally in the epistle or by Milton, it introduces Zoroastrianism, a Persian religion close to Judeo-Christianity in its mythology yet heretically Dualistic: the cosmic battle is between light and dark as equally divine aspects of Deity. So the learned reader is forced to ask, Is the God of *Paradise Lost* Ahura Mazdah, who is also Satan? or the One of primitive Neo-Platonism? or the Good of Plato? or the Johannine 'light of the world'? or light as Newton saw it? The lines alone would merely stir inchoate lumber of the mind like this, but Milton passes swiftly enough to more orthodox suggestions for them to serve only as a gesture of fellowship to the intellectual, whose worship must always be uncomfortable because his God, if he means anything at all, must mean so many complicated things. The 'pure ethereal stream' which light may prefer to be called comes from Psalm xxxvi:

> the children of men . . . shall be watered with the fatness of thy house; and thou shalt make them drink of the river of thy pleasures. For with thee is the fountain of life: in thy light shall we see light.

This has its difficulties too. The river, a fairly homely oriental metaphor, becomes the symbol of light as created life. But it is also a symbol for intellectual clarity, as in Psalm cxviii, 'God is Yahveh, which hath shewed us light' (27). Bacon had brought the two together on the basis of the third verse of Genesis, saying that light as the first thing to be created was to nature and the material as knowledge is to supernature and the abstract or spiritual. But Milton descends lower, into his own soul. This passage is rendered liturgical and choric by the undulating rhythms ('The dark descent, and up to reascend' is typical). The reader is offered identity with Tiresias, Thamyris, Homer, Phineus, the nightingale and Milton himself as seers singing in the dark, striving to apprehend the unknowable and understand its unsearchable decrees. It is possible to grope and 'feel thy sovran lamp' but not to see it, though profane and sacred poetry assist, the natural theology of the world, man's divinity, the regularity of the seasons, testify to the Creator's glory. A formalized version of Wordsworth's and Coleridge's *ichabod* odes, it is curiously penitential for an epic invocation. 'Celestial light Shine inward' is a prayer for vision whereas Dante's corresponding prayer is for power to manifest the vision he has had:

> O divina virtù, se mi ti presti
> tanto che l' ombra del beato regno
> segnata nel mio capo io manifesti . . . .   (*Par.*, i, 22)

The arrogantly intellectualized light of the first lines has been reduced through the splendid symbolic light of the Psalms to something indefinite, an only hope, as in the third collect, 'for aid against all perils', at evensong: 'Lighten our darkness, we beseech thee, O Lord'. Even the dynamics of Platonism have gone: the biblical mystics being caught up into heaven, Plotinus being drawn up by ἔρως, Dante by Beatrice, the medieval mystics somehow achieving the beatific vision for its own sake, have collapsed into the quiet ethical approach to God of Whichcote:

> The mind diverted from God wanders in darkness and confusion. But being directed to Him, soon finds its way, and doth receive from Him in a way that is abstracted from the noise of the world, and withdrawn from the call of the body; having shut the doors of our senses, to recommend ourselves to the Divine light, which readily enters into the eye of the mind that is prepared to receive it.[7]

In some ways this makes the transition to heroic narrative extra difficult. Not only will there always be a difference between what you see 'Of things invisible to mortal sight' and what you manage to tell, but the suggestions of Platonism in whatever form dissipate the idea of an immanently active and personal God. Neither the 'serene and lovely God' of John Smith nor its Deistic and Pantheistic derivatives – Newton's providential *primum mobile*, Wordsworth's impellent 'motion and a spirit', Shaw's *élan vital* – has any more personality than a God who 'is light'; and a God who can only be sensed intuitively cannot be justified in discourse. On the other hand the invocation which admits this confusion – and it is a confusion we all share – has set the episode in the framework of personal experience which is essential to the representation of God in literature.

The transition is conducted cautiously. It abolishes temporal sequence – 'Now had the Almighty Father ... where he sits ... bent down his eye ... past present future he beholds, Thus ... spake' – for 'in Eternity there is no distinction of

Tenses.'[8] The Father is steadfastly enthroned; then there is a vertiginous glance at 'His own works and their works'; a glance back at the angels, abstract as 'Sanctities', concrete as stars; then the Son, 'radiant image of his Glory', a description which evokes his transfiguration and our experience of sunlight radiating from a mirror. The view goes down again to Earth, the distant 'blissful solitude' suggesting the atmosphere of dream; then Satan in the present as he was at the end of Book II, his winged and footed scrabbling, his base mortality (weighed verbally in 'the *dun* air') assuring the spirituality of Heaven; and finally 'thus to his onely Son foreseeing spake'. The crushing of language into this expressionless line is an attempt to amalgamate in one mould the vision and the word, past and future, Father and Son. It is the key to the celestial dialogue.

The Father's speeches accord only too well with the Argument; he 'clears his own Justice and Wisdom from all imputation, having created Man free and able enough to have withstood his Tempter'. It is more important to condemn this than to make allowances for Milton's difficulties or the historical conditions of theology. Dramatically, the argument is ineffectual – so far as the poem is concerned, man has not yet been created, has not sinned, and has not imputed injustice or folly to God; so that the speeches are a work of supererogation. From the religious point of view it is vicious: the poet's rationalizings purport to be the expression of Divine reason. The Father speaks as judge, counsel and plaintiff in one. The plaintiveness offends most – 'So will fall, Hee and his faithless Progenie; whose fault? Whose but his own?' (95). The figures of debate, and the literally meant forensic metaphors, are symptoms of a legalism indigenous to Judeo-Christianity. Apart from its psychological origins, legalism will inhere in any primitivistic movement of the Church for practical reasons. The movement, being towards ideal apostolic conditions, will take for its authority the Paul who had to justify Christianity to Jews and Romans; it will wish to strengthen its case against the accusation of anarchy by an appearance of lawfulness; and against the sneer of upstart modernity it will try to root itself in the Old Testament. Hence 'the language of the Covenant' in the seventeenth century, legal and sheik-like, which is Milton's language here.

But beneath all this lie intricate schemes of logical rhetoric:

> As if Predestination over-rul'd
> Thir will, dispos'd by absolute Decree
> Or high foreknowledge; they themselves decreed
> Thir own revolt, not I: if I foreknew,
> Foreknowledge had no influence on their fault,
> Which had no less prov'd certain unforeknown.   (114)

This is the most concise statement of the problem and one of its 'solutions' ever written. Milton has acquired factitious control over the concepts by control of the language that designates them. That control was needed. Compare Chaucer's translation of Boethius on providence with Hooker's redaction of the same commonplace:

> The engendrynge of alle thinges . . . and all the progressiouns of muable nature, and al that moeveth in any manere, taketh his causes, his ordre, and his formes, of the stablenesse of the devyne thought. And thilke devyne thought that is iset and put in the tour (*that is to seyn, in the heighte*) of the simplicitie of God, stablissith many maner gises to things that ben to done; the which manere whan that men looken it in thilke pure clennesse of the devyne intelligence, it is ycleped purveyaunce; but whanne thilke manere is referred by men to things that it moeveth and disponyth, than of olde men it was clepyd destyne.   (Bk III, Prosa 6)

> The natural generation and process of all things receiveth order of proceeding from the settled stability of divine understanding. This appointeth unto them their kinds of working; the disposition whereof in the purity of God's own knowledge and will is rightly termed by the name of Providence. The same being referred unto the things themselves here disposed by it, was wont by the ancients to be called natural Destiny.   (*Ecclesiastical Polity*, I, iii, 4).

Obviously the clarity of syntactical rhetoric and the stability of a uniform vocabulary had to be achieved before a native philosophy or science could start work (hence the Johnsonianism of Bacon). In the seventeenth century rhetoric of this kind was still exercised chiefly in sermons. The Puritans objected to the tropal rhetoric of High Church preachers such as Donne: they wanted to strip away conceits, images, decoration, to suit the plainness of their preferred ecclesiastism. Their preachers developed a schematic rhetoric that would carve Scripture and feed the congregation with marrow of divinity. They were not seeking emotive devices, or intellectual appeal – metaphysical conceits savoured of curious speculation; they wished to know the 'truth'. There is a stolid honesty about this that carries over into the Father's sermon – at least we know, what we don't usually from an Anglican pulpit, precisely what he is saying. We can see the way it will go: already the Puritan sermon had affinities with the rationalist's discourse and the academic exercise. After the Commonwealth the sermon moved away from rhetoric into the form recommended by Bossuet, '*renfermant toute son éloquence dans le cercle d'une grande vérité réligieuse*', while philosophical dialectic, its fortifying rhetorical regimen having worked, was able to soften into the sure-of-being-understood elegance of Shaftesburian dialogue. By the time *Paradise Lost* was published, the Father's speech was antiquated. That Milton should have made him speak so skeletally implies anxiety, as if he were trying to authorize the dogma by solidification; or perhaps, by making it so unequivocal, to abandon his own responsibility for it. For all his querulousness, the Father does not speak with a human tongue: he juggles with a limited number of arbitrary words, meanings and syntactical shapes. 'They themselves decreed Their own revolt' is followed twelve lines later by 'they themselves ordain'd thir fall', and 'I made him just and right' by 'for so I formd them free'. Every sentence sets a balance: 'what praise could they receive? What pleasure I from such obedience paid?', 'of freedom both despoild, Made passive both', 'Both what they judge and what they choose', and so on. An extra-ordinary pattern of alliteration, prosonomasia and traductio on the words 'free-freely-all-fall-fault-failed-fell' runs through the Father's whole speech and into his next: lines 95, 96, 99, 101, 102, 118, 122, 128, 129 actually end with parts of this series, forming a subdued rhyme-scheme. Within the sentences argument depends on traductio of the 'foreknowledge-foreknew-un-foreknown' type. The words accelerate into a continuous single sound. This effect is appropriate in a way for it represents the Father's speech as Logos, Alpha and Omega, I AM. Milton has got the better of language – 'Only by the form, the pattern, Can words or music reach the stillness' – but by desecrating its nature. Ultimately his triumph is vain for he leads us into a corridor of verbal mirrors in which unbodied concepts are defined by their antitheses so all we can do is mark time with our lips. It had been done much better, in the Bible and by the Metaphysicals, and has been since, usually by relying on Dantesque imagery and human experience:

Inside the room was a great steadiness, a core of living eternity. Only far outside, at the rim, went on the noise and the destruction. Here at the centre the great wheel was motionless, centred upon itself. Here was a poised, unflawed stillness that was beyond time, because it remained the same, inexhaustible, unchanging, unexhausted.[9]

That succeeds not merely because it uses the human reflection instead of the divine source, but because it is enclosed in an experiential context more immediate than Milton's.

Some details in the Father's first speech suggest that it was not originally designed as the theological mainspring of the poem's action but as a bastion against the intellectual assaults of Milton-in-Satan. I suspect a suture about line 95 between two versions, the first treating the angels' rebellion only, the second adapting it to the Fall of Adam (as Milton himself had been, politically, a Satan in the forties, a self-justifying God in the fifties, and perforce a submissive Adam after 1660). 'Hee and his faithless Progenie' seems to refer to 'man' two lines before; but the Father has just been looking down to view 'His own works and their works' (59): 'their works' can hardly be Adam and Eve's 'Reaping immortal fruits of joy and love . . . In blissful solitude'; it must be the counter-creative activity of Hell. 'Progeny' looks human, but it is used of devils (II, 430) and angels (V, 600) as well as mankind (XI, 107). The subsequent 'his . . . he . . . him' probably refers to Adam, but the sentence runs on into 'all th' Ethereal Powers', who can only be angelic. The terminology of 'allegiance', and later on 'fealtie' (or 'realtie') and 'Treason' (204, 207), is more political than one would expect if it referred to Adam. The Father's reference to the 'sole Command' that pledges man's obedience (94) presupposes the explanation of the Tree of Knowledge to be given at IV, 420. There is the familiar confusion between the 'begetting' of the Son in V, which causes Satan's rebellion, and his glorification here which is the result of his sacrificial offer. The angels' hymn here makes more of the Son's victory over the rebels than one might expect at this stage, when the event has not occurred in the poem, and it is verbally very close to the description in VI. The theology of Book III is repeated in X and XI, where it is more immediately relevant to man. The eschatology is duplicated twice, in Book XII (451–65, 544–51). There are many small inconsistencies in the poem,[10] due to the overlapping of dramatic and epical versions, and to its having been written in anachronological order, as well as to mere absentmindedness. But what seems to have happened in the case of Heaven is that, having in the first three books conducted his quarrel with God through Satan, Milton found he could finish it on the right side only by bringing himself up against the impregnable rhetoric of dogma, and the historical fact of Christ's death. The preliminary speeches in Heaven represent submission to the intolerable fact that God should universally exercise both the monarchic absolutism Milton rebelled against on earth, and the omnipotence, freedom and incontrovertible rightness that he aspired to.

The Son's rhetoric is more flexible. His first reply picks up the Father's decree, 'Man therefore shall find grace', and weaves lyrical patterns with it as if to beautify brutality:

> Oh Father, gracious was that word which clos'd
> Thy sovran sentence, that Man should find grace;
>
> For should Man finally be lost, should Man
>
> > that be from thee farr,
> That farr be from thee, Father,

The dancing turns and repetitions suggest 'the still point'. The Father modifies his rhetoric into them:

> Man shall not quite be lost, but sav'd who will,
> Yet not of will in him, but grace in me
>
> Upheld by me, yet once more he shall stand
> On even ground against his mortal foe,
> By me upheld,
>
> To pray, repent, and bring obedience due.
> To prayer, repentance, and obedience due.

But this lyric note is interrupted by eschatological crunchings:

> > Thou at the sight
> Pleas'd, out of Heaven shalt look down and smile,
> While by thee rais'd I ruin all my Foes,
> Death last, and with his Carcass glut the Grave: (256)

The poem's parody-scheme backfires for the Son's manner of speaking about Death is the same as Death's manner of behaving: 'Grinnd horrible a ghastly smile to hear His famine should be fill'd, and blest his mawe Destin'd to that good hour' (II, 845). The derisive laughter of the Lord will not carry over from Psalm ii into the Heaven of *Paradise Lost* without debasement of both poems. Masson thought it 'worthy of remark that Milton . . . should have been thus careful to support his own invention absolutely, and to keep close to the words of the Bible' in this scene. But many such lines in *Paradise Lost* confirm Arnold's complaint in *Literature and Dogma* that so long as literary criticism of the Bible lags behind linguistic, archaeological and bibliographical scholarship, Bibliolatry will go on usurping faith and excusing brutality. Thus, the comparatively sensitive epilogue to the Son's eschatological prophecy –

> Thou wilt not leave me in the loathsome grave
> His prey, nor suffer my unspotted Soule
> For ever in corruption there to dwell

– is a paraphrase of Psalm xvi, 10. But that psalm is superior as poetry, and its subject, prayer for more abundant life – 'in thy presence is fulness of joy' – is not Milton's. The most elaborate piece of eschatology is the Father's about the last judgement, final conflagration and new creation:

> Mean while
> The World shall burn, and from her ashes spring
> New Heav'n and Earth, (333)

We receive no sense of cleansing fire or new birth: the phoenix imagery, which comes alive at the end of *Samson Agonistes*, is here quite dead. The Son's lyricism is finally ruptured in the Father's summary of his plan:

> So Man, as is most just,
> Shall satisfie for Man, be judg'd and die,
> And dying rise, and rising with him raise
> His Brethren, ransomd with his own dear life.
> So Heav'nly love shal outdoo Hellish hate,
> Giving to death, and dying to redeeme,
> So dearly to redeem what Hellish hate
> So easily destroy'd and still destroyes
> In those who, when they may, accept not grace. (294)

This is one of the most rhetorical passages in the poem, and the schemes are potentially lyrical. But there is no poetic grace in their handling, therefore no sense in the reader of theological grace. The theology is orthodox, but the coagulation of language makes 'Heav'nly love' feel so much the same as 'Hellish hate' that again the Father might be Ahura Mazdah.

It is sometimes remarked that the devils in Pandemonium, God in Heaven and Adam in Paradise use rhetoric of differing kinds which distinguish between the speakers' dramatic and moral position in the poem. The devils use rhetoric persuasively to put their own points of view, without regard for truth, as condemned in the *Gorgias*; the Father uses it to make a truism of the truth; Adam uses it to celebrate creation, including his own divinely rational power over language. But the least successful contrast is between the Father's rhetoric in Book III and Satan's. At the temptation Satan asks:

> Of good, how just? of evil, if what is evil
> Be real, why not known, since easier shunnd?
> God therefore cannot hurt ye, and be just;
> Not just, not God; not feard then, nor obeyd:
> Your feare it self of Death removes the fears.   (IX, 698)

The superficial similarities to the Father's speech are obvious. The only distinction is that Satan's rhetoric is forensically superior:

> One fatal Tree there stands of Knowledge call'd,
> Forbidden them to taste: Knowledge forbidd'n?
> Suspicious, reasonless. Why should thir Lord
> Envie them that? Can it be sin to know,
> Can it be death? and do they onely stand
> By Ignorance, is that thir happie state,
> The proof of thir obedience and thir faith?   (IV, 514)

This is neater as sheer rhetoric – the epanalepsis and erotema of the second line, for example – and more dramatic: 'Can it be sin to know, Can it be death?' is a real spoken doubt, not a rhetorical question; and the tone is morally preferable to the querulousness of the Father when he speaks with a real voice. We are left with only two distinctions of rhetoric that support the thesis of the poem, that God is better than Satan: Satan is never lyrical, and rarely schematic. His rhetoric is Pandemoniac not Heavenly: forensic, flickering through ploce and traductio and erotema with suspicious speed; pragmatic, lacking the ceremoniousness that in places gives to what the Father (and especially Adam) says an aesthetic value. This is not enough to mark the vast gap that the poem supposes to exist between the minds of God and Satan. The fault seems to lie in rhetoric itself. For all its elaborations as a system it is not a flexible enough instrument for the dramatic function of distinguishing between characters. If it be argued that this is not drama but epic, the reply is, I suppose, that we have in *Paradise Lost* a demonstration of the unsuitability of the epic form, with its assumption of a consistent epic style, for the representation of moral distinctions.

What rhetoric can do in epic, though, is to relate the actions of morally similar characters to each other or to a common source by choric echo. The Son's speeches do this:

> Behold mee then, mee for him, life for life
> I offer, on mee let thine anger fall;
> Account mee man;

> on me let Death wreak all his rage.   (III, 236)

This is the spring of self-sacrifice which Adam and Eve draw on after the Fall to recover sanity and love. The central ploce on 'me' is repeated on an even larger scale by Adam, and then by Eve: 'first and last On mee, mee onely, all the blame lights due . . . on me, sole cause to thee of all this woe, Mee mee onely just object of his ire' (X, 831 . . . 933; cf. 738, 817, 824 ff.).

The circular structure of the scene in Heaven, the angels' encirclement of the throne, their circling dances, the reciprocating dialectic of the divine will, as well as the details of rhetoric and the abstract language, make the episode essentially theoretical, a chorus on the poem's action. Milton seems to have modelled it on his conception of Revelation as

the majestic image of a high and stately tragedy, shutting up and intermingling her solemn scenes and acts with a sevenfold chorus of hallelujahs and harping symphonies

(*The Reason of Church Government*, ii, 479)

– God the central protagonist, the angels in the orchestra. But the Heaven of *Paradise Lost* differs from that of Revelation as Dante's does. Instead of enacting the divine comedy the Father postulates it. This presentation of the Father as Platonic Mind 'Consulting on the sum of things' (VI, 673) while second causes work its bidding is typical of a rationalistic age which has rejected a personal, interventional Deity; and of an age (such as the post-apostolic) or a man (Milton) whose expectation of divine intervention has been disappointed. We sympathize with the seventeenth-century distaste for anthropomorphism; better Milton's providential Father than the capricious Jove of *Gerusalemme Liberata* (e.g. ix, 57) with all his rhetorical virtuosity. But 'Eternal Providence' is alien to the Hebraic mannerisms of Milton's God; and it is as safe a refuge for complacent atheism as for disappointed faith. The Deistical result of seventeenth-century rationalism, obvious in Milton, is to deny the distinctive tenet of Christianity, that God is perpetually incarnate in man. The doctrine of incarnation is itself a poetic expression of faith; to versify the *Quicunque vult* and the Thirty-nine Articles is absurd. It is proper that confidence should be established in the immunity of God and the ultimate triumph of his will; but he should participate in the plot he controls. This can be done dramatically. Prospero, although acting as the providence of his island through a demiurge, is more deeply involved in the action than Ariel:

> *Ariel:*　　　　Your charm so strongly works 'em
> 　　That if you now beheld them your affections
> 　　Would become tender.
> *Prospero:*　　　　　　Dost thou think so, spirit?
> *Ariel:* Mine would, sir, were I human.
> *Prospero:*　　　　　　　　　And mine shall.
> 　　Hast thou, which art but air, a touch, a feeling
> 　　Of their afflictions, and shall not myself,
> 　　One of their kind, that relish all as sharply,
> 　　Passion as they, be kindlier mov'd than thou art?

> Though with their high wrongs I am struck to th' quick,
> Yet with my nobler reason 'gainst my fury
> Do I take part; the rarer action is
> In virtue than in vengeance; they being penitent,
> The sole drift of my purpose doth extend
> Not a frown further. Go release them, Ariel;
> My charms I'll break, their senses I'll restore,
> And they shall be themselves.   (V, i, 17)

He claims through the echoes of his verse the priestly 'power, and commandment . . . to declare and pronounce to his people, being penitent, the Absolution and Remission of their sins'; the power derives from Christ who was 'not an high priest which cannot be touched with the feeling of our infirmities; but was in all points tempted like as we are, yet without sin' (Heb. iv, 15). It is now that Prospero drowns 'this rough magic', the theory of his books, and becomes a man among men.

The descriptions that intersperse the Father-Son colloquy present a more incarnational Godhead, but still fail to reveal the heart of the doctrine. The Son's rhetorical modulations of the Father's theme of grace are realized visually between the speeches:

> Beyond compare the Son of God was seen
> Most glorious, in him all his Father shon
> Substantially express'd, and in his face
> Divine compassion visibly appeerd,
> Love without end, and without measure Grace,
> Which uttering thus he to his Father spake.   (138)

Rhetoric, whether its expertise appeal to contemporary taste or subsequently studied interest, demands theological training for its interpretation. But this imagery, ranging from intellectual to sensuous, asks only an experience of human love. It is the purest, most impressive anthropomorphism. The Son isn't really 'Beyond compare': we are reminded of a painting, or a living face such as occasionally seen, having in it a compassionate sanctity which we call 'radiance' because it is extrovert and warm. A Dantesque effect, it serves characterization and action by making the Son come alive. In Book VI where he is commanded to drive out the rebel angels the Paternal light strikes on his face like a blow:

> He said, and on his Son with Rayes direct
> Shon full, he all his Father full exprest
> Ineffably into his face receiv'd, (719)

so that he replies as if with effort: 'And thus the filial Godhead answering spake'. When he is sent to judge Adam and Eve,

> So spake the Father, and unfoulding bright
> Toward the right hand his Glorie, on the Son
> Blaz'd forth unclouded Deitie; he full
> Resplendent all his Father manifest
> Express'd, and thus divinely answer'd milde. (X, 64)

The enargia gives us a finer impression of spiritual power, and understanding of the atonement, than we get from all the theoretical exposition of Book III. Yet the Son remains God. He is not the Jesus-of-history but the Christ of the transfiguration in the synoptic gospels, 'the fashion of whose countenance was altered' (Luke ix, 29, etc.), the Johannine Christ who is pre-eminently the Son of the Father, the Christus Victor of Aulén's 'classic' theory of atonement.[11] Such attention to the godhead of the Son at the expense of the manhood of Jesus may be a mode of vicarious self-deification, or the Christian's substitute for Nietzschean hero-worship; but it helps in this context because the claim of Christianity to be more than an ethic rests on the dogma that the Jesus of history was the Son of God, and that the atonement takes place continuously in eternity. Any objection to the Son is not therefore that he is inhuman; but it might be that he is not sufficiently divine. Like Origen and Plotinus, Milton was privately, in *De doctrina*, a subordinationist. He is tactful about this in the poem, but does present the Son as secondary to the Father, dependent on him as a reflection to its light-source. In the speeches the theological result of this becomes clear, that the divine sacrifice is vicarious, not a self-sacrifice of the Father-in-the-Son. It is easy to see from this dramatization of theology why the Church has so fiercely opposed Arianism. All the psycho-mythic power of the gospel depends on its being God who suffers and rises again from the penalty of death that his own justice requires. Without this identity of judicial with suffering God, the Father is no more remarkable than Abraham offering Isaac, and the Son no more than a martyr. For the scene in Heaven to become 'a high and stately tragedy', God must act Oedipus to himself. Even the angels' final paean to the Son, with which Milton identifies himself, strains after acceptance. Subordinationism is confirmed: 'the strife of Mercy and Justice' is resolved outside the Father in him who 'sat / Second to thee'. The mistake is analysed in *Measure for Measure* (as in *Antigone*):

> *Angelo:* Your brother is a forfeit of the law,
>   And you but waste your words.
> *Isabella:*   Alas! alas!
>   Why, all the souls that were were forfeit once;
>   And He that might the vantage best have took
>   Found out the remedy. How would you be,
>   If He, which is the top of judgment, should
>   But judge you as you are? O, think on that;
>   And mercy then will breathe within your lips,
>   Like man new made.
> *Angelo:*   Be you content, fair maid.
>   It is the law, not I condemn your brother.   (II, ii, 71)

Angelo's excuse is Satanic, 'necessitie, The Tyrants plea'. Hooker makes the same mistake in theological discourse. Like Milton, he must find a rationale in the acts of God and therefore postulates something like the divine dialectic of *Paradise Lost*:

> They err therefore who think that of the will of God to do this or that there is no reason besides his will . . . he worketh all things κατὰ τὴν βουλὴν τοῦ θελήματος αὐτοῦ, not only according to his own will, but 'the counsel of his own will'. And whatsoever is done with counsel or wise resolution hath of necessity some reason why it should be done . . .   (*Ecclesiastical Polity*, I, ii, 5)

Hooker insists on legalizing all the divine operations by calling the rule of action, the self-imposed pattern of behaviour which God follows in order to achieve his ends, a law. This suggests that for him, as for Milton, even the salvific action of God was in accordance with law, rather than a passing beyond the bounds of law into mercy:

> O more exceeding love or law more just?
> Just law indeed, but more exceeding love!

Here in the Circumcision ode Milton, like the angels in *Paradise Lost*, acclaims the victory of ἀγάπη over law; but the carefully balanced rhetoric puts them back into an equation. Behind this and our objection lie two historical ideals of fatherhood: one in which the father is utterly reliable in his justice, but calculating even in his love; the other in which he is less predictable, but warm. The perfect father would be spontaneous and reliable; Milton's lacks a spontaneity equal to his reliability and it is because we are bound to see him – poetically and theologically – as an ideal parent that we object and cannot be soothed by theory.

The angels' hymn is a choric reiteration of what has passed. The Father is presented first as a negative abstraction – 'Immutable, Immortal, Infinite' (373) – but in the following lines he is astonishingly brought to life:

> Fountain of Light, thy self invisible
> Amidst the glorious brightness where thou sit'st
> Thron'd inaccessible, but when thou shad'st
> The full blaze of thy beams, and through a cloud
> Drawn round about thee like a radiant Shrine,
> Dark with excessive bright thy skirts appear,
> Yet dazle Heav'n, that brightest Seraphim
> Approach not, but with both wings veil thir eyes.   (375)

Reverently abstaining from an explicit simile for God, Milton implies it in this glimpse of the sun-bright edges of a cloud, as used in painting. But he keeps it supramundane by transferring our attention to the angels, and through their dazzlement makes

God not an abstract celestial light but a power active in his own creation. In the description of the Son light again becomes tangible: 'on thee Impresst the effulgence of his Glorie abides' (387). The chorus ends with a contrast between the 'Son of the Fathers might' whose actions are those of an epic hero, and 'thy dear and onely Son' who 'offered himself to die For mans offence'. With the change the verse drops into a lament, with lyrical repetition of 'thou didst not doome So strictly, but much more to pitie encline', and a final paean, 'O unexampl'd love', in which the poet chorically identifies himself with the choric angels, and brings the episode in a circle from 'Hail holy light' to 'Hail Son of God, Saviour of Men'.

The moments of reflected glory are the most valuable experiences in the episode. They link the invocation to the angels' hymn so that we have at least a framework of devotion. This mollifies the dogma of the speeches, placing it as the record of every believer's weary struggle to reconcile letter with spirit. As a struggle it models the whole poem, Milton *agonistes* on behalf of Christian doctrine. He achieves no mystical insight, but manages to recognize his own need for one to 'come a light into the world, that whosoever believeth on me should not abide in darkness'.

NOTES

1. *A Preface to 'Paradise Lost'* (1942), p. 128. With my counter-argument cf. Kierkegaard: 'A religious poet . . . will seek to establish a relation to the religious through the imagination; but for this very reason he succeeds only in establishing an aesthetic relationship to something aesthetic.'
2. William Temple, *Nature, Man and God* (1934), p. 322.
3. *Commentaries on Genesis,* trans. J. King (Edinburgh, 1847), I, 60.
4. F. M. Powicke, *The Cambridge Platonists* (1926), pp. 98–9.
5. *A Study in Milton's Christian Doctrine* (1939), p. 111.
6. *Modern Painters*, pt IV, ch. iv, sect. 5 (Everyman ed., 1907).
7. Powicke, p. 83.
8. Browne, *Religio Medici*, i, 11.
9. Lawrence, *The Rainbow*, ch. VI.

10. See A. H. Gilbert, *On the Composition of 'Paradise Lost'* (1947). Sewell and Waldock agree, for aesthetic reasons, about the split in the poem here.

11. *Christus Victor: An Historical Study of the . . . Idea of the Atonement*, trans. A. G. Hebert (1931).

William Empson

EVE*

A POST-GRADUATE student at Peking National University, when I went back there shortly after the war, was examining the Fall of Eve with growing indignation on her behalf, and seemed to me to have made an important discovery; I took his essay to the Summer School at Kenyon College, Ohio, in 1948, but failed to place it with a magazine, and he was unlikely to follow it up in later years. So when I at last got round to reading M. Morand (*De Comus à Satan*, 1939) I was relieved from an old sense of guilt; Mr King Fa-Shui would in any case not have had the priority. Rather little of this book is my own invention. These two critics are very unlike, except in their sense of justice and a certain independence of current critical fashion; and what occurred to both of them, not to me, was that Adam and Eve would not have fallen unless God had sent Raphael to talk to them, supposedly to strengthen their resistance to temptation. Merely cheating his own troops to get Satan into Paradise would not have been enough.

They are both hard to tempt; Eve at least wants to get to Heaven, and this is the point which is exploited, but Adam is so free from ambition as to be almost impenetrable. Even so, when Satan first tempts Eve, whispering ill dreams disguised as a toad, she wakes up determined to resist. I cannot sympathize with the view of Dr Tillyard, that her flushing and her anxiety show her already not quite innocent before her Fall; if it is lack of innocence to want to go to Heaven, and to find a need to distinguish between different methods of getting there, our fallen minds seem unable to distinguish innocence from imbecility. I expect Milton would have considered it a sin not to want to go to Heaven, and he makes her able to resist a

* From *Milton's God* (1961; rev. ed., 1965), ch. IV, pp. 147–74. Some paragraphs have been omitted with the author's permission.

temptation to use a wrong method till she had been subjected to the discourse of Raphael. She imagines herself in the dream as consenting, but Milton regards it as within the powers of Satan to give her such a dream. Hypnotists have long been saying, as I understand, that one cannot make people do by 'suggestion' anything they deeply resist, a random murder for example, but can put any ideas into their heads; thus agreeing with Milton on both points. In the dream Satan appeared to her as an angel, ate the apple, told her it was the food of angels and the way to get to Heaven, and suggested that she positively ought to acquire knowledge and become divine:

> Taste this, and be henceforth among the gods
> Thyself a goddess; not to earth confin'd
> But sometimes in the air, as we, sometimes
> Ascend to Heav'n, by merit thine, and see
> What life the Gods live there, and so live thou.   (V, 80)

The Bible says she was tempted by the savour (the smell, as she had not yet tasted it); Milton ascribes this mainly to the dream he has invented, which helps to make the real temptation less trivial. She is given a space-flight, and 'wonders' at it, but

> O how glad I wak'd
> To find this but a dream!

The comforting Adam remarks that the shock of an imaginary acceptance is more likely to strengthen her resistance than otherwise (120), and this view seems as plausible as Dr Tillyard's. We need not assume that the reason why she acts on the same arguments later is that they have been working underground upon her passions; Milton does not decide for us; they have also been rationally supported by the discourse of Raphael.

It occurs rather often to Raphael that he is not sure how much God will allow him to tell (V, 570; VII, 120; VIII, 175); this is to be expected from the emissary of a tyrant, and we need not blame him if the effect is to tempt them to speculate about God's intentions. But he has no doubt that he can give them a more practical piece of information at the start, while moralizing over his need and capacity to eat the fruit and nuts which Eve has provided. By the way, I do not know that anyone has answered the comment of Bentley on the passage: 'If the devils need feeding, our author has made poor provision for them in his Second Book, where they have nothing to eat but Hell Fire, and no danger of their dinner cooling.' One can't deny that Milton is careless on the point, but a reader who is troubled by it may conclude that God sustains the rebels by miracle, and thus deludes them into believing they have gained magical power. Otherwise the details about food are consistent with the Great Chain of Being; indeed we learn around XI, 50, when God is remarking innocently that Nature herself now compels Adam and Eve to leave Paradise, that before the Fall they had a less crude metabolism, and were perhaps actually better fitted to eat with Raphael than with ourselves. In any case, Raphael says:

> time may come when men
> With angels may participate, and find
> No inconvenient Diet, nor too light Fare:
> And from these corporal nutriments perhaps
> Your bodies may at last turn all to Spirit,
> Improv'd by tract of time, and wingd ascend
> Ethereal, as wee, or may at choice
> Here or in Heav'nly Paradises dwell;
> If ye be found obedient . . .   (V, 495)

The subject has been exhaustively discussed, but I think I am the first to point out the startling repetition of 'as wee', again surrounded by commas and given Milton's double *e* for emphasis, only four hundred lines later. Eve is meant to prick up her ears at this, and so are we (a flashback would be needed in the film version); the voice of the mysterious dream and the spokesman of God are not merely saying the same thing (that God expects them to manage to get to Heaven, and that what they eat has something to do with it) but even using the same tricks of speech. We may be sure that Raphael does not know what Satan has whispered, because he is not wicked enough to cheat Eve in such a way; but it is merely a matter of theology that Milton's God has arranged the correspondence – all such accidents lie within his Providence. He has thus made it baffling for her to gauge his intentions.

Dr Tillyard, who was the first I think to point out that Milton scrutinizes the approach to the Fall like a novelist, remarked very fairly that the reason why she says she wants to 'work' apart from her husband is that she feels the need to flap her wings a bit; after hearing Raphael on her future expected début, she may well want to obtain a tiny change in her experience, and indeed could hardly be admired if she had no impulse to react at all. This then is why Satan can catch her alone. The critics who blame Adam for letting her go, after giving her every warning, seem to me to preach an immoral moral; certainly, Milton thought that men ought to control women, but that would make him feel all the more outraged when Eve turns round and blames Adam for having let her go. Adam merely behaves well there, as Dr Tillyard I think proves without quite meaning to.

Before following the story further, I must consider a point about Milton's intentions. He remarks in the 'argument' to Book V (my italics):

God *to render man inexcusable* sends Raphael to admonish him of his obedience, of his free estate, of his enemy near at hand; who he is, and why his enemy, and whatever else may avail Adam to know.

This sounds like an exasperated confession that he has failed to justify God, and that M. Morand is right; but one needs to look for some other explanation. Perhaps the sentence feels harsh merely because of its order; after the first phrase it offers a rather liberal programme, but the tone has already been set as by the foreknowledge of God. The programme indeed is not fully carried out; Raphael does once let drop, in his lengthy discourses, that Satan 'now is plotting how he may seduce' Adam (VI, 900), but he never once says the practical thing which would be really likely to prevent the Fall, that Satan is known to have reached the Garden and spoken to Eve in her sleep, and will probably soon address them again in disguise. God tells Raphael that Satan has already 'disturb'd / This night the human pair', but does not tell him to tell them so (V, 230). We are told that God felt pity for them before giving this instruction to Raphael, and he reaffirms their free will in it; at the end of the speech he treats the visit as merely a legal precaution, but this order of presentation does not strike one as presuming throughout that they will fall:

> this let him know,
> Lest wilfully transgressing he pretend
> Surprisal, unadmonisht, unforewarnd.   (245)

Thus the 'argument' only gives a wrong summary in the words 'near at hand', which is not why it feels shocking. These prefaces were added a year after first publication, which meant some years after composing the poem (I see no reason to believe the theory that they were directives for the author composed beforehand); Milton might by then be regarding our parents more severely, with some forgetfulness of his poetic balance of judgement, or simply wanting to put more emphasis on the severity of God. Also he might want to insist that in giving a long reported narrative he had not merely imitated the epic formula but made it serve an important function. Even so, the brutal phrase is liable to excite the doubts of the justice of God with which he had so long wrestled, and might fairly be called a Freudian slip of the tongue.

Ever since the development of monotheism Eve has been blamed for wanting to become a God, and Milton accepts that accusation against her from the text of Genesis, but his language is not arranged to vilify her for it much. We are told that Raphael has 'divine effulgence' just before he encourages Eve to try to get to Heaven; and God himself has called the angels Gods, though perhaps only to encourage them to become so in a special sense. Eve was not taught like us about the classical gods at school, and Milton affects to believe they were devils in disguise; thus, one way and another, he feels free to use the noun and adjective with the looseness natural to a linguist and historian. What Eve means by becoming a God, on the other hand, is quite specific; she means becoming able to do space-travel, like the modest angels whom she habitually hears singing (IV, 680); thus she says she wondered in the dream at 'my flight *and change* / To this high exaltation' (V, 90). Milton added topical interest to the space-travel inherent in the story by repeatedly suggesting that there may be life on other planets; for example III, 565, 670; V, 260; VII, 620; VIII, 145, 175 and 150, where he also envisages other solar systems with inhabited planets. Various critics, feeling they ought to blame Eve in any way they can, have scorned her as a social climber trying to angle an invite to Heaven. In any case, a Christian has no business to be too refined to try to go to Heaven; but also the reader is encouraged to feel, and Eve is twice positively told, that for her it is a straightforward matter of space-travel technique, rather like improving the ships till they could discover America. On the other hand, Professor Lewis finds it particularly bad of her to bow to the Tree after eating the apple:

> She who thought it beneath her dignity to bow to Adam or to God, now worships a vegetable. She has at last become 'primitive' in the popular sense.

But she bows 'as to the power / That dwelt therein' (IX, 835); and Milton himself has to argue that the tree was sacred, when he is struggling in Chapter XI of the *De doctrina* to justify God for punishing the whole of her posterity. We may be content, I think, to blame her for disobedience only.

Another echo of Satan by Raphael concerns the phrase 'thought himself impaired', which C. S. Lewis used as a kind of slogan to sum up the case against Satan. Raphael says it around V, 660, in his description of the angels' revolt, and does of course mean that Satan fell through pride and envy. But Satan had whispered to Eve in her dream, shortly before,

> And why not Gods of Men, since good, the more
> Communicated, more abundant grows;
> The Author not impair'd, but honourd more?   (V, 70)

When the accredited Raphael tells Eve that Satan is despised in Heaven for this grudging impulse, she may naturally conclude that it cannot also actuate God; the argument of the mysterious voice is again confirmed. But God does think himself impaired when she eats the apple, unless indeed he only pretends to, for some political motive. Milton insists ruthlessly throughout the poem, whenever he pronounces about the motives of God, even when the incidental effects might be described as good, that God acted for his own glory. Indeed, he gives Satan a powerful joke about this in *Paradise Regained*, after the Saviour has rejected glory out of contempt for mankind,

> Of whom to be dispraised were no small praise. (III, 55)

> Therein least
> Resembling thy great Father; he seeks glory   (III, 110)

and so on through a very damaging speech. It is an intelligible view that God cannot work except for his own glory, because he includes all value in himself; but this makes it hard to feel that both Eve and Satan deserved all their punishments because they too wanted glory. They had been taught in a hard school.

Among the possible influences on her mind we should also consider the refusal of Raphael to explain astronomy, early in Book VIII. It is true that she has left the table at the end of his narrative, before the males begin general discussion, but we are told she will hear about it from Adam (50) and she admits later to overhearing some of it (IX, 275). Dr Tillyard pointed out that the effect on the reader is splendidly architectural; he has been flying to Heaven and Hell, but now he finds himself confined to earth and the domestic drama of one couple. This is very fine, but Adam and Eve would feel it differently. At lunch the angel practically offered them their wings, and towards evening he sharply refuses to answer a question relevant to way-finding, which is asked by Adam as soon as the narrative is concluded. Adam accepts the snub with adroit good humour, but they are bound to feel it as another bit of calculated bafflement. Raphael then suggests that God made astronomy difficult so as to be able to jeer at astronomers. He describes the Copernican controversy, refusing to tell the answer, for another hundred lines.

Mr Grant McColley, in his survey of the sources ('*Paradise Lost*', *an Account of its Growth and Major Origins*, 1940), gives quotations to show that the speech echoes a book by Wilkins, expressing belief in life on other planets, and also a pious rebuttal by an Alexander Ross (*The New Planet No Planet*, 1646). Thus the material was more than twenty years old when Milton published. Mr McColley remarks that Wilkins, and other scientists such as Oldenburg, had been on good terms with Cromwell but readily made their peace with Charles at the Restoration; he deduces that Milton had wanted to attack the new astronomy earlier, on religious grounds, but had been afraid of irritating his master. Thus Milton felt liberated by the Restoration on this issue:

> he was a human being who now was untrammelled by considerations which not unfrequently have softened the utterances of mankind. (p. 322)

Milton appears very mean-minded in this account, but we should not deduce that Mr McColley is too. He may be a free-thinker who expects Puritans to be narrow, or a neo-Christian who thinks it a religious duty to prove that seventeenth-century poets hated and despised science, imputing bad motives for a high spiritual purpose. I have to admit that Milton ascribes almost all our technical skills to the devils – Mr Werblowsky (*Lucifer and Prometheus*, 1952) is very good on the psychological background of this tradition; but Milton may have found it useful for his poem without being obsessed by its psychology. The idea that he disapproved of believing in life on other planets, I think, is refuted by his repeated gratuitous suggestion of it – 'but who dwelt happy there / He stayd not to inquire' (III, 570) – every time he takes an interest in one of the space-trips required by his story. His theological position removed some of the reasons for disapproving of the belief; we know nothing else about his attitude except that he toys with it readily. What does seem peculiar about the discourse of Raphael is that he does not mention the halfway theory of Tycho Brahe, which still held the field, on the existing evidence, at the date of publication. But it was wrong, and Milton would deserve praise if he felt that no halfway theory could satisfy the mind, or at any rate his own very all-or-none mind. The subject was still in a muddle, and we need not blame Milton for sticking to the old sharp alternatives; we do not know that he had any narrow motive for it. All he required for his poem was a snub for presumption, and while supplying that he positively in-sinuated that there is more in the universe than we know.

It seems only fair to distinguish between Milton and his God; I readily agree that his God does appear mean-minded. Alexander Ross did not say that God would laugh, only that anybody would laugh, if he read the rival astronomers. The heroic labours of seventeenth-century astronomers were con-sidered often to blind them, chiefly because Galileo went blind when very old; and Milton considered that he too had been driven blind by devoted work in another field. A certain puckish humour is being aimed at all through Book VIII, but Milton must have been aware that even this echo of a joke by God carries the same Quilp-like malignity as his actual jokes in the poem. Also, the long description of the alternative theories is likely to drive the curiosity of our parents in the direction which Raphael forbids. Here again, a detached observer may blame Eve for not deducing that God must be very ungenerous, but Milton could hardly blame her for continuing to trust him. Her own generous mind would lead her to think that, though perhaps rather nasty, he cannot be quite so nasty as she is being persistently told; well then, he must be trailing his coat, and wanting her to display her courage. A bullfighter of course does praise a bull if it is brave, but he means to kill it anyhow.

I do not have to deny that she is confronted at the crisis with a variety of arguments, some of them less worthy than others. She is typically a woman in that her decision is intuitive; at least, Milton would hardly have said so, because it was angels who were intuitive, meaning that their minds worked too fast to need the discursive reason (not always, V, 490); but Eve is intuitive in the modern sense that she lumps the arguments together and cannot afterwards pick out the one that decided her. Nowadays a critic is expected to pick it out, thus defining his position; but probably Milton would have said that she did not know, any more than all we critics do. I think it was the following argument of the serpent:

> will God incense his ire
> For such a petty trespass, and not praise
> Rather your dauntless virtue, whom the pain
> Of Death denounc't, whatever thing Death be,
> Deterred not from achieving what might lead
> To happier life, knowledge of Good and Evil? (IX, 695)

That is, she feels the answer to this elaborate puzzle must be that God wants her to eat the apple, since what he is really testing is not her obedience but her courage, also whether her desire to get to Heaven is real enough to call all her courage out. I think this the most likely motive because it is the most sublime, thus again following the principle of Mr Rajan that the characteristic virtue of the poem is sublimity.

The thought, indeed, is not prominent in her soliloquy just before she eats; if it had been, Milton would have had to call her justified. Instead, she has moved on to feel a certain impatience with the God who has set her such a difficult puzzle about his intentions; but this is very understandable, once you admit that she recognizes them as a puzzle.

> In plain then, what forbids he but to know,
> Forbids us good, forbids us to be wise?
> Such prohibitions bind not. (760)

This means that you ought not to obey a God if your conscience tells you that his orders are wrong; and that, if your God then sends you to Hell for disobeying him, you were still right to have obeyed your conscience. Any Christian missionary might find himself saying this when wrestling for the soul of a pagan, and a critic who jeers at it seems to me simply immoral. Nor does Eve take the further step of deciding that her God must be bad; if she did that, she might fairly be blamed for impatience and perhaps for disloyalty, in jumping ahead of the evidence before her. As so often in human affairs, her problem is one of Inverse Probability. Thus a candidate in an Intelligence Test often has to think 'Which answer is the tester likely to have thought the intelligent one?', and this tends to make him irritated with the whole test. In this case, if God is good, that is, if he is the kind of teacher who wants to produce an independent-minded student, then he will love her for eating the apple; her solution of the problem will be correct because she has understood his intention. But if he didn't mean that, then he has behaved rather queerly, and it doesn't appear that he deserves to be obeyed; for one thing, he hasn't even behaved as generously as the Serpent, who might have been tempted to use his new powers to contrive equality with mankind (770). If one considers intermediate hypotheses about the character of God, the penalties he has threatened are at least extremely vague, or even unknown. Hence, on any hypothesis, considering that God himself admits that eating the apple would provide something they need (755), to eat it is probably the best thing to do.

C. S. Lewis said truly enough that the poem's moral of obedience has the 'desolating clarity' of what we were taught in the nursery, adding that he cannot understand why modern scholars have missed it; but he also insisted very finely that we are not to regard Adam and Eve as ignorant savages – nor, therefore, as children. I too think that children should be taught to obey, and consider that the fashion has swung rather too far against smacking them; but Milton knew very well that if he had punished his own children for a trivial act of disobedience as God proposes to do here he would be lucky if he were taken to jail, because that would protect him from the just anger of his neighbours. We keep being told nowadays about the deep belief of the seventeenth century in the natural hierarchy; but Milton had not got the legal power to kill his children held by an Ancient Roman, and even those famous aristocrats regarded torture as only applicable to slaves, so that they too would not be allowed by their fellows to torture their children indefinitely. One expects the morality of a God to be archaic, but this God seems to be wickeder than any recorded society. The myth might indeed be justified as a warning that Nature is unjust, for example when innocent actions give us shocking diseases; but Milton insists that there was no magic about the apple, and that it was chosen by God as a random test of obedience. A father may reasonably impose a random prohibition to test the character of his children, but anyone would agree that he should then judge an act of disobedience in the light of its intention. Still more is this true of adult and responsible characters, because they ought to be expected, indeed have to be expected, to interpret an order rationally. It is an intelligible view about kids, though a very wild one, that if they have been told to stay in bed they ought to do it even though the house is burning down; because somebody is always responsible for looking after them, and they are less bother in a crisis if they don't rush about. A similar view is often taken of soldiers, and the boy who stood on the burning deck satisfied both criteria. But this is evidently an unsuitable way to treat Adam and Eve, as they point out themselves; indeed Milton would feel he was restoring dignity to mankind, as he went on imagining their speeches, by showing how very marginal the original ground of our fall had been. I admit that Eve herself claims to be something like a child at the moment before she falls, that is, she claims a justification from her admitted ignorance of good and evil; but that powerful stroke from the mind of Milton is in a way a very adult thing for her to do. I cannot think it morally wise for pious critics to try to turn this against her:

> What fear I then? Rather, what know to fear
> Under this ignorance of good and evil,
> Of God or Death, of law or penalty?
> Here grows the cure of all, this fruit divine . . . .   (775)

That is, she does not know the moral sanction behind this law, or even the meaning of the repeated obscure threats of a penalty. You might think that nothing needed 'curing' in Paradise, but she has already protested that it is too miserable to live in such terror of the unknown that they dare not spend half an hour apart. 'Divine' need only mean 'teaching divinity'. It seems to me odd of Dr Tillyard, whom I greatly revere for his work on Milton, to have described this turn of thought as 'triviality of mind'. The effect of the speech is simply that she decides she *ought* to eat the apple, think God what he may.

One of the most difficult parts of the assignment Milton had set himself was to make it credible that she would eat the apple at all, after he had turned the figures of the briefly recorded myth into high-minded intelligent characters. Nothing happens in Eve's life except pleasure and being warned not to eat the apple, so how can she do it without appearing fatuous? The point was cleared accidentally by C. S. Lewis, while rebuking us for our modern notions; we ought not to think of her as 'primitive', he said, but as a great lady, the ambassadress of mankind. Yes indeed, but more; as a medieval great lady, for example Eleanor of Aquitaine who was Queen both of England and of a French Court of Love. A puritan disapproved of these powerful females, including the Queen of Heaven; but they were still felt to be staggeringly grand, and Milton was set to turn all human culture into an expression of the grandeur of the Fall. A modern reader tends to have the same mixed feelings as the author; we can understand well enough that he was not merely vilifying Eve when he depicted her so. She thinks: 'The reason why all the males keep on saying I mustn't eat the apple, in this nerve-racking way, is obviously that they are longing for me to do it; this is the kind of thing they need a queen to have the nerve to do'; so she does it. It is a splendid bit of invention by Milton; true to life, and the only way to make sense of her story; and he makes her later behaviour support it. In effect, she presumes that God will love her for eating the apple, at any rate later on, when he has realized that that was what he had wanted her to do at bottom. So he would have done if he had been better, but the story is that he gives nearly all her descendants eternal torture for it.

M. Morand, who first drew attention to the curious effect of the visit of Raphael, deserves all the more credit because he finds difficulty in imagining the lady his argument requires; indeed, he seems to have been written off by the English and Americans as a cynical Frenchman. He revolts at the phrase 'virgin majesty' for his honeymoon figure, and finds that *'le lecteur peut rester perplexe'* about the sexual pleasures of Paradise; these are *'fautes de goût'*, indeed *'nous sommes gênés par le côté didactique et toute une lourdeur bourgeoise dont le jeune poète etait bien loin.'* The young poet, he means, had been both celibate and untainted by Government propaganda. Cardinal Newman had felt the same, and perhaps Mr T. S. Eliot was echoing Newman on the point in his essay of 1936; so we need not think that M. Morand was being peculiarly French about the matter in 1939; it was just part of the anti-romantic movement. The praise of licit sex in the poem feels to me a splendid bit of nerve, so that I am only amused by critics who boast of being embarrassed there and call love bourgeois. Having been irritated in this way, M. Morand attacks her fiercely when she pleads to work alone *'C'est là une bien petite créature qui juge ainsi, une très petite femme banale, sans jugement'* (p. 187). But his sense of justice is all the more outraged at the intellectual difficulty of the problem with which God confronts this fool, so that his build-up of hissing contempt greatly adds to the drama when she wins him over. At the moment of the Fall he becomes convinced, having considered the alternatives before her, that she decides nobly like Prometheus for the ultimate benefit of mankind: *'il n'y a donc pas sottise ou vanité de sa part à accepter ce but.'* We should salute M. Morand, and respect his earlier hesitation, when he steps out and restores the natural dignity of the Mother of Mankind.

This praise is also deserved by Dr Tillyard. The most important gain for my own understanding of the poem from his work on it, and probably for many people though we should be ashamed at having needed to be told, is to recognize the central splendour of the speech of pleading by Eve (X, 920) which wins back Adam and secures the reproduction of mankind. Critics used to be fond of saying that Milton was gloating in the passage over how he had humiliated his first wife, when she begged to return to him, after it had become plain that her royalist family was on the losing side in the Civil War. The idea is probably not false, but then the drama of that scene might well grow afterwards in his mind; to think he was merely satisfying an old grudge ceases to be entertaining when you realize what the speech achieves in the story. It is true that Adam has just been expressing the most extravagant hatred of women in all Milton's work. He says 'It spoils everything to have women about, and why should God saddle *us* with them? Angels don't get distracted by females.' Milton had experienced such feelings, but he is dramatic when he puts the wildest tantrum just before the overwhelming answer. Compared to this victory through the generosity of a woman, all the nagging against women in Milton, though much the best reason why so many people dislike him, reduces to a family grumble.

To talk about Eve's dignity will not appease those who dislike Milton for unvarying pomposity, so I had better recall the purpose of writing an epic. The Greeks liked to say that they had learned all their virtues from Homer, and the Renaissance deduced that each modern nation needed an epic of its own to live nobly. Milton thought that the English no longer deserved a patriotic epic, but badly needed making nobler somehow. It was thus of the first importance not to let us think meanly of our first parents, or even of the hand by which they fell; they could be made to argue absurdly, but must always keep a certain rock-bottom splendour. This indeed was a practical reason why the epic had to treat the justice of God as hard to defend. On the other hand, the stock accusation of pomposity of style, too Latinized to be able to give body-feeling or a natural movement of thought, cannot be made at all against this appeal by Eve.

> Forsake me not thus, Adam, witness Heav'n
> What love sincere, and reverence in my heart
> I bear thee, and unweeting have offended,
> Unhappily deceiv'd; thy suppliant
> I beg, and clasp thy knees; bereave me not,
> Whereon I live, thy gentle looks, thy aid,
> Thy counsel in this uttermost distress,
> My only strength and stay: forlorn of thee,
> Whither shall I betake me, where subsist?
> While yet we live, scarce one short hour perhaps,
> Between us two let there be peace, both joining,
> As join'd in injuries, one enmity
> Against a Foe by doom express assign'd us,
> That cruel Serpent: On me exercise not
> Thy hatred for this misery befall'n,
> On me already lost, mee than thyself
> More miserable; both have sin'd, but thou
> Against God only, I against God and thee,
> And to the place of judgement will return,
> There with my cries importune Heaven, that all
> The sentence from thy head remov'd may light
> On me, sole cause to thee of all this woe,
> Mee mee only just object of his ire.

One might think it a tiny point in favour of Milton's God that he lets this count as repentance, though it contains nothing to gratify his vanity; but Adam, though his heart is melted, begins his answer by treating the speech as further ground for rebuke, and only gradually argues his way to the correct solution, which is prostration before God; so Milton intends it to be clear that God would not regard her as repentant until Adam had redirected her impulses. He begins:

> Unwary, and too desirous, as before
> So now of what thou knowst not, who desir'st
> The punishment all on thyself; alas,
> Bear thine own first, ill able to sustain
> His full wrath whose thou feelst as yet least part,
> And my displeasure bearst so ill. If Prayers
> Could alter high decrees, I to that place
> Would speed before thee, and be louder heard,
> That on my head all might be visited,
> Thy frailty and infirmer Sex forgiv'n,
> To me committed and by me expos'd. (950)

It was all right, as literary criticism goes, for C. S. Lewis to discover that Eve envisages murdering Adam as soon as she has eaten the apple, but the same searchlight ought also to be turned upon her husband. His immediate determination to beat her at the new game of generosity, despising her for not enduring his displeasure, even accusing her of greediness for trying to get ahead of him, and assuring her he can shout her down, is likeable of Adam but just as fit to be called satire by Milton as anything said by Eve. M. Saurat remarked, with so much depth that he too almost deserves the title of restoring the dignity of the Mother of Mankind:

> Here Milton happily forgets his theories of the predominance of reason, and the influence of 'female charm' on Adam is this time his salvation.

Very true, except that we have no reason to think Milton had forgotten. It is the high point of his structure that Adam and Eve recover sufficiently to decide to produce the race of man in spite of their Fall. Yet her first repentance is towards Adam only, and she regards God as someone she might badger till he let Adam off; it is all God's fault really because he assigned them the serpent by 'doom express', she remarks with much truth. Hence it is important to realize, as various critics have remarked, that there is a total absence of heavenly aid at this crucial point. Milton had come to insist, as against the Calvinists, that our nature was not totally corrupted by the Fall, but this did not mean (*De doctrina*, ch. 18) that we can ever do good except by Divine Grace. He makes the Son remark, while rejoicing over the repentance of Adam and Eve, that God's 'implanted Grace' in man is already producing fruit (XI, 25). It is thus presented as like a seed, presumed to grow by itself after being planted; both God's grace and his curse act in a kind of biological way. Indeed this may explain why the Son made the tactless remark that God sends his Grace to 'all his creatures', not only to mankind (III, 230). The belief has a decisively good effect on the literary technique. If the melting of Eve begins the solution of the whole drama, ordinary Christian sentimens would expect at least a Guardian Angel at work; and, from the point of view of imitating Homer, it is positively breach of epic formula to have no divine intervention. Eve is never more absolutely alone, and it seems clear that any other treatment would have been painfully unconvincing. Sir Walter Raleigh said that Milton could not have brought a child into *Paradise Lost*, because one sensible remark would have destroyed the whole crazy piece of engineering; and it is true that the thought of a mind like Milton's having anything to do with a child is rather painful. But he was enabled to get something near the effect by his conception of Woman.

This, I think, is also the way to understand his treatment of the innocence of both Eve and Adam. C. S. Lewis, in the course of maintaining that the poem is not heretical, gave a useful summary of the position of St Augustine about sex before the Fall. The saint decided that the erection of the male organ was then under direct control of the will, and therefore could have been performed sinlessly, although for other reasons it was not. Milton was thus not essentially wrong, though no doubt tactless and so forth, when he presented our parents as actually making love without sin. I think that, as God tells them to multiply before the Fall in Genesis i, 28, the Saint's insistence upon their chastity was a slanderous accusation of disobedience. But Augustine is in another much deeper heresy about the conditions of life, because the spontaneity of a sexual

174

emotion is like that of any other, love towards God for example. The sexual condition he considers holy is that of an acrobatic prostitute; naturally enough, because he believes his own salvation to depend on being able to turn on his love for God 'with a tap' (as the limerick says), however appalled he may become at the behaviour of this God. But to achieve that degree of saintliness would only make his love not worth having. The independence of our feelings from our will, which he regards as the essence of being fallen, is our basic protection against the lethal convictions which so often capture our brains. If Milton had presented Adam and Eve as 'self-controlled' to this extent they would have seemed like insects and been unable to fall. In any case, he could not have presented them so, because he accepted enlightened views of the relations of soul and body. The idea that he fakes the Fall a bit, by making our parents rather fallen from the start, may make readers think but underrates the depth of his treatment; or perhaps one need not call 'deep' what an Elizabethan playwright and a modern novelist take for granted, but Milton had theoretical support for it.

Adam and Eve had to be spontaneous even before their Fall, because a chain of partly rational 'spirits' with a partly independent life are always at work in mankind relating soul to body; and this was not an upsetting discovery, because matter was part of God from which God had willingly removed his will. The doctrine was part of the confused challenge of Paracelsus, which had made a great flutter, so that Milton had no need to search the *Zohar* for it. He treats this view of matter as basic to his whole position, and probably came to do so when he broke with Calvinism by denying that Total Depravity is entailed upon us by Original Sin.

A literary reader such as myself finds the love-poetry of Donne unique for its paradoxes about the relations of soul and body, and is rather unwilling to regard them as commonplaces of his time. Surely they were at least 'advanced', if not 'left-wing'. The young Donne is uneasy about his mystical doctrine, sure that it is an important truth somehow but also that it is hard to fit into respectable theology, and therefore needs witty paradoxes. But it was only the sexual implications of the doctrine which the love-poets felt might become embarrassing; Spenser has the same earnestness, together with the same uneasiness, about his 'sensuous idealism'. The mere belief that soul and body are related by a subtle hierarchy of 'spirits', so that their relations are complex, was one that Donne felt free to expound in sermons; as Grierson pointed out in his great edition (1912; vol. II, p. 45). The O.E.D. gives the first use of 'materialism' as Restoration, no doubt in opposition to Hobbes; the position of Milton had perhaps come to seem bolder than when he was young by the time he published *Paradise Lost*. Even so, it was not complained of till long afterwards.

Nowadays pious authors take for granted that materialism is the bad thing, whereas everything spiritual is good; thus any religion, Thuggee for example, would be better than none. But Marlowe in *Faustus* treats the word 'spirit' as meaning a devil; for example the tempter tells Faustus, 'Thou art a spirit; God cannot pity thee.' In the same way, a modern reader tends to feel that the confusion of matter and spirit in *Paradise Lost* is part of the general bogusness of Milton's style; but after you have defined spirit as a subtle form of matter, as at any rate Lucretius had done, it is not contradictory to continue to use the word with that meaning. The modern pious use of 'materialism' and 'spirituality', which involves such a gross distortion of human experience, would have been considered mere ignorance in the seventeenth century. I grant that if you translate this use of 'materialist' as 'selfish' the sentence usually makes sense, but then, it often tells a lie.

Dr Tillyard said in his *Milton* (1930) that, if Milton had been in the Garden, he would have eaten the apple at once and written a pamphlet to prove that it was his duty. This has always seemed to me very profound; but Dr Tillyard repented of it, and the chapter 'Adam and Eve in Paradise' of his *Studies in*

Milton (1952) gives the rather beautiful spectacle of a man trying to expunge his joke without making the tactical error of repeating it. His very thorough reading in Milton publications was perhaps what made him tired of such remarks; indeed, *Studies in Milton* gives the only reference I have found to the work of M. Morand, though with no reference to its thesis (I found the work itself because M. Morand presented it to Sheffield University, having taught there earlier). They were going to have children anyway, Dr Tillyard sensibly pointed out, and the spectacle of their honeymoon is no reason for supposing that if they hadn't fallen they would have become bored. Thus Raphael's first words to Eve are 'Hail, Mother of Mankind', and he tells her that her sons will fill the world (V, 385). Michael, while nagging Adam about the results of the Fall, says that he might have had all future generations coming to pay him their respects at his capital seat in Paradise (XI, 345). The generous imagination of C. S. Lewis was stirred by this picture of Adam as the reality of which our Kings and Popes are a pale shadow, reminded perhaps of the Chief Selenite in *The First Men in the Moon*; it is clear from the word 'generations' that the rest of us would still be dying, out of courtesy to our children, as we do now, whereas Adam could last on without public inconvenience. But surely, all we learn from these remarks is what use the two angels make of their briefing by God when they speak to mankind. Michael is a pig about it, whereas the affable Raphael is embarrassed; but both of them have heard God say beforehand (III, 95) that the Fall is certain, therefore no great weight need be attached to their estimates of the alternative. The third quotation given by Dr Tillyard is the operative one, from the speech by God to the loyal angels after the rebels have been evicted, in which he announces that he will at once create the world (VII, 150). This announcement (though reported to us later in the poem) was made about ten days earlier than the speech of God in Book III, when he sees Satan approaching the newly-created world and prophesies the Fall. Raphael, when he is sent to exhort Adam and Eve to stand firm, has just recently heard the speech of Book III, which made clear that his work can have no use except 'to render Man inexcusable'; no wonder he seems rather oddly anxious not to let drop anything he mustn't tell them, because it is an essential part of his assignment not to tell them that they are certain to fall. God has set him an extremely unpleasant bit of work here, which more than anything recalls the earlier loyal activities, presented in a flashback from before, his imprisonment, of the hero of *Darkness at Noon*.

Joseph H. Summers

PARADISE LOST: THE PATTERN AT
THE CENTRE*

W HEN, in preparation for the second edition of *Paradise Lost*,
Milton changed the original ten books to twelve, he did not
simply make the two halves of the poem more nearly equal in
bulk (and therefore make Book VII, line 21 more nearly
accurate: 'Half yet remains unsung'), nor did he merely make
the organization of his poem more nearly resemble Virgil's; he
made a major structural change. An artist as self-conscious as
Milton would not make such a change lightly. Yet never was a
major change made with so little fuss: the division of the
former Book VII into the final Books VII and VIII and the
former Book X into the final Books XI and XII required the
addition or revision of less than a dozen lines. The publication
of the poem in twelve books seems to have been the result of a
change in Milton's perception of what he had already made,
rather than of a decision to make something new. Among so
many signs of Milton's conscious control, his certainty and
consistency, this evidence of a kind of humility before his own
creation – larger and other than his conscious intention – may
strike us as oddly touching.

The earlier organization of the poem failed to distinguish
structurally between the magnificence of the Creation and
Adam's recollections and anxious questionings, and between
the 'world destroy'd' at the Flood and the 'world restor'd' in
the covenant with Noah. In the final version, those distinctions
are made. More significantly, I believe, in the original version
the actions of the angel Abdiel, bridging the end of Book V
and the beginning of Book VI, are at the centre of the poem.
Here is the pattern of the 'one just man', the individual saving

* From *The Muse's Method; an Introduction to 'Paradise Lost'* (1962),
ch. V.

remnant in the midst of evil, the angel who resists temptation and conquers trial, which serves as an exemplum both to Adam and the reader and looks forward to the whole series of such individual triumphs in the final books (Enoch, Noah, Abraham, etc.), with their promise of 'a paradise within thee happier far'. Abdiel remains of the utmost importance in the final version. The significance of his action remains, but the emphasis has changed; for in the final version the War in Heaven and the Creation of the world are clearly at the centre. Milton seems to have discovered that in the poem which he had written the true centre was not the angelic exemplum of man's ways at their most heroic, but the divine image of God's ways at their most providential.

The second edition of *Paradise Lost* gives formal emphasis to a fact that has seemed odd to many readers: in the middle of the story of the Fall of man as Milton wrote it there are extended narratives of events which occurred long before man was born. A number of readers have understood and even accepted Books VI and VII as digressions, as evidence of Milton's desire to be encyclopedic and to imitate the earlier epics. How could one write an epic without an epic battle? And how could one write a Christian epic without a bow to the large hexameral tradition? Milton knew and used the traditional materials; but I do not believe, in the seventeenth century any more than today, that a classical, biblical, medieval, or Renaissance allusion or tradition was in itself a guarantee of quality or a sufficient formal principle. If traditionalism and learned decoration were all, we should have to concede that Books VI and VII, however interesting or impressive we find them in isolation, are flaws, and major flaws in the total structure of the poem. We should have to agree with Mr Daiches, one of the most recent and able critics of the poem, that in these two books 'the poem is marking time, its true progress is halted'. But I do not agree with Mr Daiches on this point. I believe that these books are central in reality as well as in form.

To speak of the 'structure' of the poem is to invite misconceptions. The word is a metaphor for our sense (or, more ideally, Milton's sense) of the organization and articulation of the whole, and it may dangerously imply that there is *one* principle of organization which, once perceived, makes all the particulars fade into insignificance. But our sense of the whole of any work can be no better than our responses to the particulars from which we have constructed it. It is inevitably imperfect. It is thin or false or perverse in proportion to how much of the whole we have failed to take into account, have failed to respond to properly, or have misconstrued. Perhaps it would be preferable when discussing *Paradise Lost* to speak of the 'structures' rather than the 'structure', for the poem is complex rather than simple. There is the sequence of the major actions as they are presented to the reader, shaped to control the reader's acquisition of knowledge within time. There is the organization of those same events according to the time in which they occurred and according to cause and effect. There is the spatial organization of those events in Hell and Heaven and the world. After the appearance of the human participants in Book IV, there is the structure of events as they contribute to the experience and education of Adam and Eve – a dramatic structure made possible by Milton's use of internal narrative. There is the structure of ideas and concepts, of symbols and imagery embodied in that physical organization of the poem into books, speeches, paragraphs, sentences, lines, and words. These create and control those expected movements *within* the reader's senses and emotions and imagination, those varying kinds and degrees of responses to the physical body of the verse and to what it images for which the poet evokes and shapes our previous experience, our knowledge, and our imagination of our own time and space – our own sense of life with its expectations and denials, its anxieties and resolutions. As in life itself at its most intense and imaginative, multiple events and perspectives and significances are present in the poem at any one moment.

All these structures are present and they are real. The attempt to trace them out systematically, however interesting an exercise for the tracer, would be impossibly dull and long-winded for the follower; it would be less illuminating than an oral recitation of the poem by a reader of modest vocal gifts. For the poem is still immediately effective. Although at certain moments we may recognize that one structural principle clearly predominates, at the highest moments the several principles are inextricable. We must beware of making simple and schematic what Milton did not make simple, of flattening out a large part of the very life of the poem: our experience of simultaneity. We must beware of our own insensitivity. In the pages which follow I wish only to suggest some of the reasons for the presence and the success of the accounts of the War in Heaven and the Creation.

We are reminded constantly of the dramatic function of the two books. After Satan has tempted Eve in a dream, God sends Raphael to 'bring on', 'as friend with friend', 'such discourse' with Adam 'As may advise him of his happy state, / Happiness in his power left free to will' (V, 229–35). More specifically, Raphael is to

> warn him to beware
> He swerve not too secure: tell him withal
> His danger, and from whom, what enemy
> Late fall'n himself from Heaven, is plotting now
> The fall of others from like state of bliss. . . . (V, 237–41)

Raphael introduces his narration of Satan's apostasy and fall in explanation of his phrase to Adam, 'If ye be found obedient' (V, 501, 513–14). When Raphael finishes the story, he summarizes its import for Adam:

> Thus measuring things in Heav'n by things on Earth
> At thy request, and that thou mayst beware
> By what is past, to thee I have reveal'd
> What might have else to human Race been hid:
> The discord which befell, and War in Heav'n
> Among th' Angelic Powers, and the deep fall

> Of those too high aspiring, who rebell'd
> With *Satan*, hee who envies now thy state,
> Who now is plotting how he may seduce
> Thee also from obedience, that with him
> Bereav'd of happiness thou mayst partake
> His punishment, Eternal misery. . . .
> But listen not to his Temptations, warn
> Thy weaker; let it profit thee to have heard
> By terrible Example the reward
> Of disobedience; firm they might have stood,
> Yet fell; remember, and fear to transgress. (VI, 893–912)

The poet repeats the lesson as he introduces 'what ensu'd' after

> *Raphaël*,
> The affable Arch-angel, had forewarn'd
> *Adam* by dire example to beware
> Apostasy, by what befell in Heaven
> To those Apostates, lest the like befall
> In Paradise to *Adam* or his Race,
> Charg'd not to touch the interdicted Tree,
> If they transgress, and slight that sole command,
> So easily obey'd amid the choice
> Of all tastes else to please thir appetite,
> Though wand'ring.   (VII, 40–50)

Raphael relates the story of the Creation in response to Adam's request. With his expression of gratitude for the 'Great things' ('which human knowledge could not reach' (VII, 75)) that the Angel has revealed, Adam asks Raphael to add to these 'Things above Earthly thought', 'What may no less perhaps avail us known':

> How first began this Heav'n which we behold
> Distant so high, with moving Fires adorn'd
> Innumerable, and this which yields or fills
> All space, the ambient Air wide interfus'd
> Imbracing round this florid Earth, what cause
> Mov'd the Creator in his holy Rest
> Through all Eternity so late to build

> In *Chaos*, and the work begun, how soon
> Absolv'd, if unforbid thou mayst unfold
> What wee, not to explore the secrets ask
> Of his Eternal Empire, but the more
> To magnify his works, the more we know. (VII, 85–97)

The dramatic function of the War and the Creation involves also the relation of those two actions in temporal and causal sequence. After God declares his intention to create (we are reminded that 'Immediate are the Acts of God, more swift / Than time or motion, but to human ears / Cannot without process of speech be told' (VII, 176–8)), the angelic hosts sing:

> Glory they sung to the most High, good will
> To future men, and in thir dwellings peace:
> Glory to him whose just avenging ire
> Had driven out th' ungodly from his sight
> And th' habitations of the just; to him
> Glory and praise, whose wisdom had ordain'd
> Good out of evil to create, instead
> Of Spirits malign a better Race to bring
> Into thir vacant room, and thence diffuse
> His good to Worlds and Ages infinite.   (VII, 182–91)

The final angelic chorus on the first Sabbath summarizes the import of the two actions:

> Great are thy works, *Jehovah*, infinite
> Thy power; what thought can measure thee or tongue
> Relate thee; greater now in thy return
> Than from the Giant Angels; thee that day
> Thy Thunders magnifi'd; but to create
> Is greater than created to destroy.
> Who can impair thee, mighty King, or bound
> Thy Empire? easily the proud attempt
> Of Spirits apostate, and thir Counsels vain
> Thou has repell'd, while impiously they thought
> Thee to diminish, and from thee withdraw
> The number of thy worshippers. Who seeks
> To lessen thee, against his purpose serves

To manifest the more thy might: his evil
Thou usest, and from thence creat'st more good.
Witness this new-made World, another Heav'n. . . .

(VII, 602–17)

The account of the Creation is as necessary for Adam to be fully 'advised' of his 'happy state' as is the account of the War in Heaven for him to be warned of his danger. Milton insisted that Adam and Eve could not fairly fall through simple ignorance: they must be granted not only the perfection of human existence, intellectual, emotional, sensuous, but also all the knowledge of which they were capable – knowledge beyond the possible inference of unaided human reason or experience. All knowledge is granted except the disabling *experienced* knowledge of evil which, without a new creation, takes away more than it gives; which, in recompense for its insight into separateness and imperfection and guilt, takes away the immediate apprehension of wholeness and perfection and innocence.

But it is possible for a reader to recognize the inner dramatic necessity of events in literary works and still to be bored by them; however necessary they may be to the characters involved, the reader may feel they are not at all necessary for him. By placing Raphael's narration in the centre of the poem, Milton took, knowingly I believe, a daring chance. (Like Yeats, he seems to have relished 'the fascination of what's difficult'.) He interrupted the psychological drama by separating Eve's dream of evil from the enactment of evil by three and one-half books of angelic narration and conversation. For every reader who would expect or welcome an account of the War in Heaven and the Creation in and of themselves, he must have known that there would be at least one who would expect and desire that the major action should continue. Having involved the reader in a plot above the human as we know it (the fall of perfect man and woman), he deliberately shifted the perspective by the introduction of actions which had no human participants at all, and which were even farther removed from our own experience and reason than from Adam's. He refused to allow any suspense about the outcome of these actions: Raphael reminds us repeatedly of the absurdity of the hopeless War and of the inevitable glory of the Creation. Milton presents two actions which the angels themselves do not fully understand and in which, at the crucial moments, even they are not actors but simply spectators. (Cf. 'stand only and behold' (VI, 810), and 'him all his Train / Follow'd in bright procession to behold / Creation' (VII, 221–3).) The reader is deliberately removed from a sense of direct engagement: he must behold God's power and God's providence as if he were not immediately concerned with them; he must 'see' intellectually primary historical images of God's defeat of evil and His transformation of evil into good.

As Milton conceived it, Raphael's account must be either great or a great hiatus in the poem. Refusing most of the conventional aids, the poet must, to succeed, suspend the intensity of his plot and at the same time not dissipate the intensity of his poem. His success seems to me extraordinary. He resolved the problems by bravura performances in which his literary craftsmanship can be perhaps more easily perceived than in any other books of *Paradise Lost*. If there is no suspense about the ends, there is enormous suspense concerning both the means of God and the means of the poet. The reader of these books experiences the central, extended, mythic forms of the poem's continually repeated motifs of falling and rising; he experiences them as inevitably related to the providence and power of God and as paralleling and often reversing the experience of Adam, his own experience outside the poem, and his own experience of heroic literature.

Something of Milton's success can be inferred from the passages already cited. Adam's and Eve's relation to the two actions is not simple. The account of the War in Heaven identifies for them (they have not shared the reader's views of Satan in Hell) the nature of the enemy: his motives both for rebelling against God and for hating man, his 'reasoning', his characteristic ways of acting, and even his language. Satan, moreover, serves as an image of the internal as well as the external enemy:

he shows what revolt against God will mean and how it may end. The narrative provides a commentary in action on the relations between individual identity and freedom and God's absolute power and providence. Adam is granted moving images of matter and spirit, good and evil, and of the varying stations in the hierarchy of being; he cannot fail to observe the differences between the reasons and actions of man and angels and God. He perceives in Satan an individual, part of being, in the process of destroying himself as he attempts to assert himself, to make himself absolute by denying and opposing exactly the whole which sustains him. He sees the inevitable defeat of that attempt by reality, by divine affirmation, by the astonishing fertility of creation in eternal movement – the dance and the song of the whole. He perceives these things as related to his own joy and perfection in Paradise, to his perfect sexual love, and to one of his earliest memories – the sound of the triumphant music as the Son reascends on the Sixth Day:

> Up he rode
> Follow'd with acclamation and the sound
> Symphonious of ten thousand Harps that tun'd
> Angelic harmonies: the Earth, the Air
> Resounded, (thou remember'st, for thou heard'st)
> The Heav'ns and all the Constellations rung,
> The Planets in thir stations list'ning stood,
> While the bright Pomp ascended jubilant.   (VII, 557–64)

The reader shares in most of this: the dramatic and rhetorical functions of these books are parallel or, occasionally, almost identical. Yet there are important differences. Except imaginatively (and through our experience of the poem) we have not known Adam's happiness and his perfection; but in every other respect we know much more than Adam. When, at the prospect of Creation, the angels sang, 'Glory . . . to the most High, good will / To future men, and in thir dwellings peace', it is we, not Adam, who recognize the anticipation of the song of the Nativity. It is we who know the Fall and human history, the Bible with its account of the end of Adam's story and the evidence of providence in the Incarnation. We know already what Adam is not fully to know until the final visions of the poem.

The differences in knowledge make for differences in our literary responses to the narration. We share with Adam the images of the deeds themselves and Raphael's comments on them, but we imagine too Adam's responses to the narration, and our fallen (and redeemed) experience makes us conscious of realms of additional meaning. War itself is unknown, almost inconceivable, to Adam. When Raphael describes the march of the loyal angels, he uses for Adam a more natural simile to convey an idea of their 'Order';

> On they move
> Indissolubly firm; nor obvious Hill,
> Nor straitening Vale, nor Wood, nor Stream divides
> Thir perfect ranks; for high above the ground
> Thir march was, and the passive Air upbore
> Thir nimble tread; as when the total kind
> Of Birds in orderly array on wing
> Came summon'd over *Eden* to receive
> Thir names of thee; so over many a tract
> Of Heav'n they march'd. . . .   (VI, 68–77)

The passage marks the distance between Adam's and the narrated experiences, but it also emphasizes our own distance from both. We know war, as Adam does not; but the war we know is as far removed from the war the poem describes as is Adam's memory of the birds. The 'order' of our infantry follows the landscape; our foot-soldiers do not march in the air, they have fathers and mothers and sometimes wives and children, and they truly bleed and die. Nor do the battles we have known through past literature, different as they are from those we know directly, come much nearer to this one. Achilles and Hector, Aeneas and Turnus also have wills within bodies that can die. However much their actions are fated, however much divine intervention, their wounds do not immediately heal of themselves. War as we know it and have imagined it, at its highest and lowest, serves as a constant source of metaphor in Book VI, a measure for contrast even more than for comparison, a source of parody and burlesque as well as heroism and horror.

There is another warfare of which we know something and Adam does not, and it provides us with a closer perspective on the War in Heaven: the Christian Warfare. A spiritual warfare, it is often thought of as internal rather than external. But Milton insisted that it involved material action and that it also concerned the body. The issues were more fatal than in ordinary war, for they were the life or death of the soul – of all – rather than merely of the body. It was the warfare in which everyone was engaged, whether he realized it or not, and about which no one knew enough. It was also the warfare in which success promised participation in the creation of a new 'paradise within'.

The most striking thing about the War in Heaven is that, except for the Father and the Son, everyone is surprised at one moment or another, no one's expectations are perfectly fulfilled. The surprises are sometimes comic. Any reader of Book VI today owes a large debt to Arnold Stein for pointing out with such care the elements of comedy, the way in which the entire narrative may be considered a 'comic metaphor'. But, as with Milton's account of Satan, Sin, and Death, the comic seems to me only one of the perspectives here. From the divine point of view the entire devilish attempt is comic and absurd; from the point of view of the unfallen angels the action is truly heroic; from that of Satan and his crew it is ultimately tragic – the calamitous fall of princes from great places. The reader is invited to share all of these points of view at various moments.

Satan had evidently expected victory against the Almighty; he discovers that he cannot even defeat other angels. He had assumed his invulnerability, and he experiences wounds and pain. He thinks that, whatever its outcome, the battle is 'The strife of Glory' (290), and he loses all dignity. He accepts the fact that he and his hosts were not utterly annihilated on the first day of battle as proof of God's fallibility – '(And if one day, why not Eternal days?)' (424). He assumes that his nature has not changed since the revolt and that, 'while we can preserve / Unhurt our minds, and understanding sound' (443–4), victory is possible; he demonstrates both his inventiveness and the extent of the injury to his mind by his assumption that technological inventions (here, the cannon) can achieve victory against the universe and the spirit of life itself ('eternal might / To match with thir inventions they presum'd / So easy' (630–32)). He and Belial are transported at the initial success of their weapons to the height of pride and of punning in the poem – 'scoffing in ambiguous words' (568); after one volley, they see (and feel) all their 'Engines' and 'all thir confidence / Under the weight of Mountains buried deep' (651–2). At this moment Satan seems about to fulfil at least one of his hopes: he had earlier expressed to Michael his determinaton either 'to win, / Or turn this Heav'n itself into the Hell / Thou fabl'st' (291–3). But he and his crew witness the fearful re-ordering of all of Heaven at the command of the Son, the recreation of all that they have managed to destroy, before they are reduced to the similitude of 'a Herd / Of Goats or timorous flock together throng'd' (856–7). The farthest thing from Satan's expectation was that he and his crew should co-operate with the divine judgement against themselves, that they should acknowledge and, helpless for the moment, choose their own defeat:

> headlong themselves they threw
> Down from the verge of Heav'n, Eternal wrath
> Burn'd after them to the bottomless pit.   (864–6)

From the beginning of the poem we have become accustomed to Satan's inability to understand and to the frustration of his desires, but I believe we are held in suspense by a good deal of this.

At the end of Book V, Abdiel had experienced prophetic insight when he stated to Satan, 'I see thy fall / Determin'd'

(878–9). He had turned his back 'On those proud Tow'rs'
which he and the reader equally knew were 'to swift destruction doom'd' (906–7). But neither he nor we knew precisely
when or how that destruction will come. Despite Satan's deception of Uriel and the beginning of Raphael's narration, we are
surprised, I believe, by the evidence in the war of the angelic
limitations in knowledge and understanding. The unfallen
angels are perfect but not absolute. Their station is higher than
man's and their understandings are nearer to God's, but they
are not God: they do not possess absolute foreknowledge or
power; they can be deceived by appearances; they can deduce
incorrectly; they can entertain mistaken expectations. Like
man's, their perfection finds its source in the freedom of their
love.

Abdiel journeys all night to bring news of the Satanic rebellion. When he reaches the hosts of God he 'found / Already
known what he for news had thought / To have reported' (VI,
19–21). He is greeted with rejoicing (the reader remembers the
rejoicing over the lost sheep), led 'high applauded' 'On to the
sacred hill', and approved by the voice of God. In God's approval, the reader recognizes images both from St Paul's description of the Christian warfare and from the final Judgement;
but this approval is joined to a new commission to Abdiel and
the other angels:

> Servant of God, well done, well hast thou fought
> The better fight, who single hast maintain'd
> Against revolted multitudes the Cause
> Of Truth, in word mightier than they in Arms;
> And for the testimony of Truth hast borne
> Universal reproach, far worse to bear
> Than violence: for this was all thy care
> To stand approv'd in sight of God, though Worlds
> Judg'd thee perverse: the easier conquest now
> Remains thee, aided by this host of friends,
> Back on thy foes more glorious to return
> Than scorn'd thou didst depart, and to subdue

By force, who reason for thir Law refuse,
Right reason for thir Law, and for thir King
Messiah, who by right of merit Reigns.
Go *Michael* of Celestial Armies Prince,
And thou in Military prowess next,
Gabriel, lead forth to Battle these my Sons
Invincible, lead forth my armed Saints
By Thousands and by Millions rang'd for fight;
Equal in number to that Godless crew
Rebellious, them with Fire and hostile Arms
Fearless assault, and to the brow of Heav'n
Pursuing drive them out from God and bliss,
Into thir place of punishment, the Gulf
Of *Tartarus*, which ready opens wide
His fiery *Chaos* to receive thir fall.   (VI, 29–55)

Abdiel and the others may certainly be forgiven if they do not fully understand; God has not intended that they should. He orders them to attempt to accomplish what they *know* will be accomplished (the defeat of Satan and the rebellious angels), and they naturally assume that they have been chosen as the instruments to bring about that result. God outlines precisely the immediate aim which His angels must pursue; they cannot possibly know that it will not be granted them to 'drive them out from God and bliss, / Into thir place of punishment'. It is intrinsic to this War and to our response to it that they should not know. As with the 'Counsel of Perfection' for men, the imperative is all that really concerns them: it defines the objective and controls the action; its fulfilment, as both angels and men must learn, lies within the will of God. The angels' failure to drive Satan out, their exposure to Satanic derision and violence, will provide them with the fundamental trials of their heroic virtue – not simply their ability to resist the external power of evil but to sustain their trust in God despite appearances.

And yet, with our privileged hindsight as readers, we can see in the darkness of God's oracle that the angels' failure too was only apparent. At his return from his debate with Satan, Abdiel is congratulated on having *completed* 'the better fight', in having 'maintain'd / Against revolted multitudes the Cause / Of Truth'. He is 'in word mightier than they in Arms', and he is invited to the 'easier conquest', 'aided by this host of friends'. But his former 'conquest' had meant only that he was stronger in reason than Satan, that his reason and will were invulnerable to devilish sophistry, derision, threats, and violence – not that he 'converted' Satan and his crew or captured them or even caused them, lovelessly, to acknowledge his superior strength and their inevitable defeat. The second 'conquest' will be like the first, 'easier' because it is no longer fought alone. He is ordered 'more glorious to return / Than scorn'd thou didst depart', and he does exactly that. He is ordered 'to subdue / By force, who reason for thir Law refuse', and he does 'subdue' them in the sense that he 'lowers' them, reduces their force and intensity. Michael and Gabriel are ordered to 'lead forth to Battle these my Sons / Invincible', and they do so and prove themselves invincible. The voice of God was not really deceptive. It expressed the divine will and imperative to free creatures with limited perceptions; it called upon them to exert all their individual strength to attempt an action, the final accomplishment of which they discover is beyond their free, unaided abilities.

Yet the angels' perception, like their strength, is remarkable. They marvel at what God allows, but they are never anxious and they never doubt. When Abdiel first sees Satan 'in his Sun-bright Chariot', 'Idol of Majesty Divine, enclos'd / With Flaming Cherubim and golden Shields', he is for a moment shocked that appearance fails to reflect reality:

> O Heav'n! that such resemblance of the Highest
> Should yet remain, where faith and realty
> Remain not; wherefore should not strength and might
> There fail where Virtue fails, or weakest prove
> Where boldest; though to sight unconquerable?
> His puissance, trusting in th' Almighty's aid,

> I mean to try, whose Reason I have tri'd
> Unsound and false; nor is it aught but just,
> That he who in debate of Truth hath won,
> Should win in Arms, in both disputes alike
> Victor; though brutish that contest and foul,
> When Reason hath to deal with force, yet so
> Most reason is that Reason overcome.   (VI, 114–26)

We, who have known of occasions in our realm when winners in the 'debate of Truth' have not been winners 'in Arms', are moved by this. But about *this* warfare Abdiel is right. He proceeds to prove it with full recognition of how much larger is God's plan and power than his own strength or immediate appearances:

> fool, not to think how vain
> Against th' Omnipotent to rise in Arms;
> Who out of smallest things could without end
> Have rais'd incessant Armies to defeat
> Thy folly; or with solitary hand
> Reaching beyond all limit, at one blow
> Unaided could have finisht thee, and whelm'd
> Thy Legions under darkness. . . .   (135–42)

We are surely intended to remember Christ's reproach to Peter's violence at the betrayal in the Garden.

Abdiel's encounter with Satan is the first of this war. With the blow of his sword, Satan is 'overcome':

> ten paces huge
> He back recoil'd; the tenth on bended knee
> His massy Spear upstay'd. . . .   (193–5)

Later, Michael is glad when he sees Satan approach, since he hopes 'here to end / Intestine War in Heav'n' (258–9). Yet, he too is conscious of the larger context:

> Author of evil, unknown till thy revolt,
> Unnam'd in Heav'n, now plenteous, as thou seest
> These Acts of hateful strife, hateful to all,

Thou heaviest by just measure on thyself
And thy adherents: how hast thou disturb'd
Heav'n's blessed peace, and into Nature brought
Misery, uncreated till the crime
Of thy Rebellion? how hast thou instill'd
Thy malice into thousands, once upright
And faithful, now prov'd false. But think not here
To trouble Holy Rest; Heav'n casts thee out
From all her Confines. Heav'n the seat of bliss
Brooks not the works of violence and War.
Hence then, and evil go with thee along,
Thy offspring, to the place of evil, Hell,
Thou and thy wicked crew; there mingle broils,
Ere this avenging Sword begin thy doom,
Or some more sudden vengeance wing'd from God
Precipitate thee with augmented pain.   (VI, 262–80)

Michael 'hopes to end it', but his statements of alternative possibilities are both true: his sword does 'begin' Satan's doom (when it shears Satan's right side it brings to Satan his first knowledge of pain), and the 'sudden vengeance wing'd from God' will finally come in a way not known by Michael to 'Precipitate' Satan 'with augmented pain'.

At the end of the first day of battle, the angels discover that they are 'Invulnerable, impenetrably arm'd', although they are moved 'from thir place by violence' (400–405). When in the second day they are more spectacularly moved 'from thir place' by Satan's cannon, they are for a moment uncertain what to do.

Rage prompted them at length, and found them arms
Against such hellish mischief fit to oppose.
Forthwith (behold the excellence, the power
Which God hath in his mighty Angels plac'd)
Thir Arms away they threw, and to the Hills
(For Earth hath this variety from Heav'n
Of pleasure situate in Hill and Dale)
Light as the Lightning glimpse they ran, they flew,
From thir foundations loos'ning to and fro

> They pluckt the seated Hills with all thir load,
> Rocks, Waters, Woods, and by the shaggy tops
> Uplifting bore them in thir hands. . .   (635–46)

They cannot be injured. They cannot be defeated. But on the third day the Messiah commands them to 'Stand still':

> Stand still in bright array ye Saints, here stand
> Ye Angels arm'd, this day from Battle rest;
> Faithful hath been your Warfare, and of God
> Accepted, fearless in his righteous Cause,
> And as ye have receiv'd, so have ye done
> Invincibly: but of this cursed crew
> The punishment to other hand belongs;
> Vengeance is his or whose he sole appoints;
> Number to this day's work is not ordain'd
> Nor multitude, stand only and behold
> God's indignation on these Godless pour'd
> By mee. . . .   (801–12)

As they follow sympathetically the actions and words of the good angels, the readers and (they imagine) Adam share many of the angels' innocently mistaken or ambiguous expectations. But we have many more surprises than do Adam or the angels. Depending on their familiarity with various literary traditions, most readers have expected either an epic battle or an immediate and overpowering manifestation of God's will. But this battle is both above and below our expectations. We have expected detailed accounts of heroic deeds; we get very few of them: 'deeds of eternal fame / Were done, but infinite' (240–41). We have expected catalogues of heroes; again, we get few:

> I might relate of thousands, and thir names
> Eternize here on Earth; but those elect
> Angels contented with thir fame in Heav'n
> Seek not the praise of men; the other sort
> In might though wonderous and in Acts of War,
> Nor of Renown less eager, yet by doom
> Cancell'd from Heav'n and sacred memory,

> Nameless in dark oblivion let them dwell.
> For strength from Truth divided and from Just,
> Illaudable, naught merits but dispraise
> And ignominy, yet to glory aspires
> Vain-glorious, and through infamy seems fame:
> Therefore Eternal silence be thir doom.   (373–85)

In these lines we can recognize the destruction of the old heroic tradition. When 'deeds of eternal fame' are 'infinite', it is difficult to choose particular ones for heroic celebration. When the good do not desire such celebration among men and the evil do not deserve it, the rationale for poetry concerned primarily with heroic physical action has collapsed.

We have expected some glorification of the arms, whether we have been most conscious of classical or Renaissance traditions of epic or of the allegorical possibilities. (Since Michael's sword was given him 'from the Armory of God', for example, we might expect it to be described with some fullness and to be related to the 'sword of the spirit, which is the Word of God'.) We get a little, but not much. These weapons and struggles are so far above the human that they are described largely by comparisons with cataclysmic natural forces: 'two broad Suns thir Shields / Blaz'd opposite' (305–6):

> all Heav'n
> Resounded, and had Earth been then, all Earth
> Had to her Centre shook. What wonder? when
> Millions of fierce encount'ring Angels fought
> On either side, the least of whom could wield
> These Elements, and arm him with the force
> Of all thir Regions. . . .   (217–23)

We are reminded that, in contrast to the similes of earlier heroic literature, these comparisons do not raise but lower the actions: the angelic forces are larger and stronger than the second terms used to describe them. When Michael and Satan 'wav'd thir fiery Swords', they are compared 'to set forth / Great things by small', to the actions resulting if

> Two Planets rushing from aspect malign
> Of fiercest opposition in mid Sky,
> Should combat, and thir jarring Spheres confound.
>
> (313–15)

We had not expected the cannon, those modern instruments of war which reduce for us individual physical prowess to insignificance or absurdity. We had particularly not expected the arms to be reduced to worse than 'tilting Furniture', to actual encumbrances. Faced with Satan's technological innovation, the good angels are momentarily discomfited:

> down they fell
> By thousands, Angel on Arch-Angel roll'd;
> The sooner for thir Arms; unarm'd they might
> Have easily as Spirits evaded swift
> By quick contraction or remove. . . .   (593–7)

They are strongest when they throw away their arms and, using mountains and 'Promontories', inflict a worse discomfort on the rebels – even more dependent on their arms:

> Thir armor help'd thir harm, crush't in and bruis'd
> Into thir substance pent, which wrought them pain
> Implacable, and many a dolorous groan,
> Long struggling underneath, ere they could wind
> Out of such prison, though Spirits of purest light,
> Purest at first, now gross by sinning grown.   (656–61)

However efficient and even inevitable the traditional means of warfare in the traditional wars, the trust in the material means in *this* warfare inevitably limits power.

We had expected the contests in boasts and threats between traditional literary warriors, but we had not expected such irony, so much 'derision'. We had expected violence, but surely not such a cosmic upheaval in which the good too, with the underground warfare and 'Infernal noise', deface the landscape and the beauty of Heaven:

> War seem'd a civil Game
> To this uproar; horrid confusion heapt

198

> Upon confusion rose: and now all Heav'n
> Had gone to wrack, with ruin overspread,
> Had not th' Almighty Father where he sits
> Shrin'd in his Sanctuary of Heav'n secure,
> Consulting on the sum of things, foreseen
> This tumult, and permitted all, advis'd:
> That his great purpose he might so fulfil,
> To honour his Anointed Son aveng'd
> Upon his enemies, and to declare
> All power on him transferr'd. . . .   (667–78)

We have been told before that God had limited His forces to
a like number to the third which revolted: one half of the unfallen angels had not even been engaged in this battle. We have
been told that God, while not intervening to increase the
strength of army or angel, had limited the might of all. With
the revelation of God's plan and the intervention of the Son,
we are reminded more forcibly that this war has also been a
pageant – or a ritual:

> two days are past,
> Two days, as we compute the days of Heav'n,
> Since *Michael* and his Powers went forth to tame
> These disobedient; sore hath been thir fight,
> As likeliest was, when two such Foes met arm'd;
> For to themselves I left them, and thou know'st,
> Equal in thir Creation they were form'd,
> Save what sin hath impair'd, which yet hath wrought
> Insensibly, for I suspend thir doom;
> Whence in perpetual fight they needs must last
> Endless, and no solution will be found:
> War wearied hath perform'd what War can do,
> And to disorder'd rage let loose the reins. . . .   (684–96)

Milton has followed some of the heroic assumptions to their
ultimate conclusions: what *if* two heroic forces, equal in
numbers *and* in strength did meet? If one were 'impaired', the
other would have some advantage, but neither could finally
'win': neither could achieve the unconditional surrender of

the other. The alternative possibilities are, for human warriors, mutual destruction and death; for angelic ones, 'in perpetual fight they needs must last / Endless, and no solution will be found.' The analogy holds too, I believe, for the spiritual warfare without divine intervention. Human and angelic wars are absurd if one expects them alone really to resolve uncertain issues.

We have known that it will be the Son who finally resolves this warfare, for we have heard as much in Hell. But I do not believe that we fully anticipate the way in which that victory will be achieved. The Father commands the Son:

> Go then thou Mightiest in thy Father's might,
> Ascend my Chariot, guide the rapid Wheels
> That shake Heav'n's basis, bring forth all my War,
> My Bow and Thunder, my Almighty Arms
> Gird on, and Sword upon thy puissant Thigh. . . .
>
> (710–14)

But the Son never uses the sword, and His seemingly material arms work in mysterious ways. We see the 'Chariot of Paternal Deity',

> Flashing thick flames, Wheel within Wheel, undrawn,
> Itself instinct with Spirit, but convoy'd
> By four Cherubic shapes, four Faces each
> Had wondrous, as with Stars thir bodies all
> And Wings were set with Eyes, with Eyes the Wheels
> Of Beryl, and careering Fires between. . . .   (750–56)

It is the eyes (not emphasized to anything like this extent in Ezekiel) which strike us and which, we later learn, are primary weapons. The Son's arms are Lights, 'Celestial Panoply . . . / of radiant *Urim*' (760–61). His 'Sapphire Throne' is 'inlaid with pure / Amber, and colors of the show'ry Arch', colours which reflect the bow of God's covenant, a type of his future mercy. Like the Disciples in their recognition of Christ's Resurrection after the dark days, the embattled angels are 'surpris'd' by 'unexpected joy' when they see Him, 'When the

great Ensign of *Messiah* blaz'd | Aloft by Angels borne, his
Sign in Heav'n.' His first act of 'war' is recreation rather than
destruction, and it is accomplished merely by His word:

> At his command the uprooted Hills retir'd
> Each to his place, they heard his voice and went
> Obsequious, Heav'n his wonted face renew'd,
> And with fresh Flow'rets Hill and Valley smil'd. (781–4)

This manifestation of absolute power and goodness, of 'eternal
Providence', is presented as if it were a final appeal to the evil
ones for repentance. Any rational creature must perceive the
hopelessness, the folly, the evil of resistance to the divinity which
thus manifests itself. But Satan and his legions are no longer
responsive to reality; they have hardened themselves:

> This saw his hapless Foes, but stood obdur'd,
> And to rebellious fight rallied thir Powers
> Insensate, hope conceiving from despair.
> In heav'nly Spirits could such perverseness dwell?
> But to convince the proud what Signs avail,
> Or Wonders move th' obdúrate to relent?
> They hard'n'd more by what might most reclaim,
> Grieving to see his Glory, at the sight
> Took envy, and aspiring to his highth,
> Stood reimbattl'd fierce, by force or fraud
> Weening to prosper, and at length prevail
> Against God and *Messiah*, or to fall
> In universal ruin last, and now
> To final Battle drew, disdaining flight,
> Or faint retreat. . . .   (785–99)

When the Son actually begins the battle, he

> into terror chang'd
> His count'nance too severe to be beheld
> And full of wrath bent on his Enemies.
> At once the Four spread out thir Starry wings
> With dreadful shade contiguous, and the Orbs
> Of his fierce Chariot roll'd, as with the sound

> Of torrent Floods, or of a numerous Host.
> Hee on his impious Foes right onward drove,
> Gloomy as Night; under his burning Wheels
> The steadfast Empyrean shook throughout,
> All but the Throne itself of God.　　　　(824–34)

When he comes 'Among them', he grasps and sends 'Before him' 'ten thousand Thunders'; but as his weapons differ from those of the angels, so do the ways in which they work. These thunders do not merely inflict material and easily cured injuries in the angelic substances; they infix 'Plagues' in 'thir Souls':

> they astonisht all resistance lost,
> All courage; down thir idle weapons dropp'd. . . .
>
> 　　　　(838–9)

When he rode 'O'er Shields and Helms, and helmed heads' 'Of Thrones and mighty Seraphim prostrate', they wish, anticipating the damned at Judgement, that 'the Mountains now might be again / Thrown on them as a shelter from his ire' (840–43). And the Son's arrows come not from his hand but from the eyes of the chariot itself and its 'four Cherubic shapes':

> from the fourfold-visag'd Four,
> Distinct with eyes, and from the living Wheels,
> Distinct alike with multitude of eyes;
> One Spirit in them rul'd, and every eye
> Glar'd lightning, and shot forth pernicious fire
> Among th' accurst, that wither'd all thir strength,
> And of thir wonted vigor left them drain'd,
> Exhausted, spiritless, afflicted, fall'n.　　　　(845–52)

Satan and his legions hear and see the absolute power of God manifested in the Son. The sound and the sight are 'infixed' in their souls, where no subterfuges or stratagems are possible; they carry absolute conviction. And they see that they are seen; they perceive this absolute power as alien to them and as hostile. They know their state. In this moment of the manifestation of God's judgement, they know that they are damned, cut off forever from peace with that power by their own actions: they have hated it and wished to destroy it. 'The devils believe and tremble.' With such knowledge, they can no longer continue their war. They experience paralysis and horror.

This is not, however, the Last Judgement; it is an image and an anticipation of that. Although they desire their own destruction, they are not granted it:

> Yet half his strength he put not forth, but check'd
> His Thunder in mid Volley, for he meant
> Not to destroy, but root them out of Heav'n:
> The overthrown he rais'd, and as a Herd
> Of Goats or timorous flock together throng'd
> Drove them before him Thunder-struck, pursu'd
> With terrors and with furies to the bounds
> And Crystal wall of Heav'n. . . .   (853–60)

In their reduction to the herd (of goats or sheep or other animals – we remember the Gadarene swine), we recognize that they have lost the freedom of their wills. By opposing the source of will and energy and life and goodness, they must inevitably have done so. They throw themselves 'headlong', for neither Chaos nor Hell nor their own fall is so fearful as the wrath and sight of God.

Was then the War meaningless? Not in the least. All – Satan, the fallen and the unfallen angels, Adam and Eve, the reader – have learned, however soon they may forget, the inevitable results of 'warfare' against the Almighty and His Messiah. The unfallen angels have learned both the extent and the limitations of their power, the nature of their warfare. They have fought properly in response to God's command. They have had 'no thought of flight, / None of retreat'; they have done 'no unbecoming deed / That argu'd fear' (236–8). Although 'led in fight', each has seemed leader; in the struggle

> each on himself reli'd,
> As only in his arm the moment lay
> Of victory. . . .   (238–40)

And when they are told to 'Stand still', they are also told that their warfare has been 'Faithful' and 'of God / Accepted' (801–4). They have discovered that in this warfare they are invulnerable; they have also learned that the ultimate resolution of the war lies beyond them. They have known from the first the divine ends, but they have not known the means; that ignorance is a condition of their freedom. Each must act as if victory lay 'only in his arm', each must rely 'on himself', for God may have so determined it. But coupled with this self-reliance is the trust in the providence of God beyond appearances. While devoting all their energy and strength to the immediate battle, they are not anxious about the outcome, they do not fear for God; they are careful only of the divine pleasure. They perceive or come to perceive themselves as agents in an action beyond their anticipations or immediate comprehensions. The sign of the Messiah brings them 'unexpected joy'; they rejoice in the final victory in which the fact is manifested which they have never doubted: that the Messiah is 'Worthiest to Reign' (888), that God's decree has been both just and merciful.

We share in the angels' knowledge. In the application of that knowledge to our own realm, we find here, as throughout the poem, that we are forced to revise or to define more sharply our conceptions, personal and literary, of heroism and of ultimately significant action. Physical heroism is not enough. Knowledge and intelligence are not enough. Abandonment to action, patriotism, or even self-sacrifice is not enough. To oppose the universe by our wills or our technology, as to oppose the good, is not heroic but absurd. To claim that we can change the course of history, even when fighting on the side of God, is also absurd – although, without any claims, we must act as if our actions could do so, for we do not know their ultimate effects. Heroism in human terms implies such action coupled with such knowledge. Its most interesting and mysterious moments are those of decision and commitment, of trial, from which the actions spring. Those moments are dependent, of course, on perception and reason, but with the heroic we are supremely conscious of the gap which exists between perception and conviction, the leap which must be made between understanding and decision. These are the moments from which action and the rest of personal history flows, 'determined' unless we choose the right, the will of God, or unless we experience a new creation which frees us from the slavery we have made. It is impossible to imagine the truly heroic moments apart from love; Milton insists that it is impossible to imagine them apart from the love of God.

For his account of the War in Heaven, Milton took various traditions and made something new of them. The disappointment of our preconceptions and the shifting of our perspectives are essential to his achievement. We have also not expected the invocation of Urania which separates the War in Heaven from the account of the Creation, and which relates the themes of both books directly to the poet's experience and to our own. The poet contrasts his own 'presumption' in composing what we have read thus far with Satan's; but he faces the possibility that he may fall, to wander in madness like Bellerophon, if divine wisdom does not attend him in his descent to our 'Native Element'. We are reminded of our place, after the fall of Adam and Satan, by the ironical comfort of 'More safe I Sing with mortal voice' (24). The conditions of our warfare are suggested by the description of the poet's voice in the context of human history:

> unchang'd
> To hoarse or mute, though fall'n on evil days,
> On evil days though fall'n, and evil tongues;
> In darkness, and with dangers compast round,
> And solitude; yet not alone, while thou
> Visit'st my slumbers Nightly, or when Morn
> Purples the East: still govern thou my Song,
> *Urania*, and fit audience find, though few.   (24–31)

The poet acknowledges and denies human loneliness. From his

own 'evil days' will come, he trusts, a new creation. But his
success will depend upon divine intervention. As the stories of
Bellerophon and of Orpheus show, mastery of art is not enough.
The Muse could not 'defend / Her Son'. If the poem is to be
completed, if 'that wild Rout that tore the *Thracian* Bard' is
to be evaded, it must be through the protection of divine power
as well as the inspiration of divine knowledge.

The continuation of divine protection is proved, at least
literarily, by what follows. The change in subject, however, involves a change in method. The account of the Creation in
Genesis determines much more precisely the shape of Book
VII than do any of the traditions the events and organization of
Book VI, but that fact does not significantly restrict the poet's
'freedom'. The subject and its disposition mutually accepted by
the artist and his audience, the cartoon established, the poet is
free to create. The events of the Seven Days provide the clear
and rhythmical framework for the book. Our major energies,
like the poet's, are free for the verse itself, where we find the
celebration and the imitation of the origins of life. We are invited
with the angels to 'behold' and to respond to the actions of the
Creator as he puts 'forth' his 'goodness', as he creates and
imparts life to that disordered matter from which he had
previously 'uncircumscrib'd', 'retired' Himself (VII, 165–73.
The meaning which I find in the passage is almost exactly the
reverse of the meaning which Saurat found in it.) In the magical
transformations we find the material source of 'Grateful vicissi-
tude'.

Few if any of the details are new. The possible sources, classical and Christian, are almost endless, but Ovid seems the
poet most relevant to the extraordinary rhythms of sense and
sound which Milton creates. Yet Milton has largely reversed
Ovid's characteristic motif: Milton's 'metamorphoses' concern
movements from non-life to life, from the static to the mobile,
from lower to higher forms. The life of the verse resides largely
in the verbs and adverbs, the words of motion. The latinate
comes alive and moves:

> but on the wat'ry calm
> His brooding wings the Spirit of God outspread,
> And vital virtue infus'd. . . .   (234–6)

> then founded, then conglob'd
> Like things to like, the rest to several place
> Disparted, and between spun out the Air,
> And Earth self-balanc't on her Centre Hung.   (239–42)

After the limitation of the universe, the creation of light and the firmament, dry land appears with the herbs and trees. Here, as before, divine creation is related to procreation:

> The Earth was form'd, but in the Womb as yet
> Of Waters, Embryon immature involv'd,
> Appear'd not: over all the face of Earth
> Main Ocean flow'd, not idle, but with warm
> Prolific humor soft'ning all her Globe,
> Fermented the great Mother to conceive,
> Satiate with genial moisture. . . .   (276–82)

In the perception of the movements which follow, we are aided by the magnifying glass as well as the telescope, by our ordinary vision, and by the poet's rhythms:

> Immediately the Mountains huge appear
> Emergent, and thir broad bare backs upheave
> Into the Clouds, thir tops ascend the Sky. . . .   (285–7)

As the waters move towards their newly created 'Capacious bed',

> thither they
> Hasted with glad precipitance, uproll'd
> As drops on dust conglobing from the dry. . . .   (290–92)

Immediately thereafter, 'Part rise in crystal Wall, or ridge direct, / For haste.' Then their motions are compared to those of the armies we have seen in the previous book; then to the more natural waters we have observed:

> as Armies at the call
> Of Trumpet (for of Armies thou hast heard)

> Troop to thir Standard, so the wat'ry throng,
> Wave rolling after Wave, where way they found,
> If steep, with torrent rapture, if through Plain,
> Soft-ebbing; nor withstood them Rock or Hill,
> But they, or under ground, or circuit wide
> With Serpent error wand'ring, found thir way,
> And on the washy Ooze deep Channels wore. . . .
>
> (295–303)

The speed and order of the appearance of vegetable life is magical:

> He scarce had said, when the bare Earth, till then
> Desert and bare, unsightly, unadorn'd,
> Brought forth the tender Grass, whose verdure clad
> Her Universal Face with pleasant green,
> Then Herbs of every leaf, that sudden flow'r'd
> Op'ning thir various colors, and made gay
> Her bosom smelling sweet: and these scarce blown,
> Forth flourish'd thick the clust'ring Vine, forth crept
> The swelling Gourd, up stood the corny Reed
> Embattl'd in her field. . . .   (313–22)

The description of the trees makes explicit the image of the dance to which we have been responding:

>   last
> Rose as in Dance the stately Trees, and spread
> Thir branches hung with copious Fruit: or gemm'd
> Thir Blossoms. . . .   (323–6)

The movements continue with the creation of the sun and moon and stars on the fourth day. God created their forms, 'And sow'd with Stars the Heav'n thick as a field' (358). We see the sun, 'made porous to receive / And drink the liquid Light' (361–3), 'First in his East',

>   jocund to run
> His Longitude through Heav'n's high road: the gray
> Dawn, and the *Pleiades* before him danc'd
> Shedding sweet influence. . . .   (372–5)

The rhythm of those lines seems to me as lovely as any that Milton ever created. A supposedly decorative word such as 'spangling' receives its full verbal force and comes alive as Milton describes the 'thousand thousand Stars, that then appear'd / Spangling the Hemisphere' (383–4).

With the fifth day the emphasis is not primarily on the water's 'generating', but on the fishes' and the birds' fulfilling of the divine blessing and command:

> Be fruitful, multiply, and in the Seas
> And Lakes and running Streams the waters fill;
> And let the Fowl be multipli'd on the Earth.   (396–8)

The entire passage is a *tour de force*. As in the morning hymn, more motions are described and imitated than we would have thought possible, and it is all done with ease and delight. As an example of what can be done with onomatopoetic effects in English verse, Milton's description of the life in the waters should be at least as well known as Pope's illustration of the device:

> Forthwith the Sounds and Seas, each Creek and Bay
> With Fry innumerable swarm, and Shoals
> Of Fish that with thir Fins and shining Scales
> Glide under the green Wave, in Sculls that oft
> Bank the mid Sea: part single or with mate
> Graze the Seaweed thir pasture, and through Groves
> Of Coral stray, or sporting with quick glance
> Show to the Sun thir wav'd coats dropt with Gold,
> Or in thir Pearly shells at ease, attend
> Moist nutriment, or under Rocks thir food
> In jointed Armor watch: on smooth the Seal,
> And bended Dolphins play: part huge of bulk
> Wallowing unwieldly, enormous in thir Gait
> Tempest the Ocean. . . .   (399–412)

Even *attend* becomes active here. Any reader tempted to forget Milton's playfulness should remember, 'Wallowing unwieldly, enormous in thir Gait'.

With the birds, the verse soars:

> Meanwhile the tepid Caves, and Fens and shores
> Thir Brood as numerous hatch, from th' Egg that soon
> Bursting with kindly rupture forth disclos'd
> Thir callow young, but feather'd soon and fledge
> They summ'd thir Pens, and soaring th' air sublime
> With clang despis'd the ground, under a cloud
> In prospect. . . . (417–23)

The imaginative motions of the 'Bursting with kindly rupture' and the speeded-up fledging and flight are blended beautifully with the absolute realism of the 'clang' of the birds' despisal of the ground. (Surely the 'prospect' is the birds': the point of view from which they scorn the low.) We are, or should be, less concerned with contemporary beliefs about the warfare of the 'prudent Crane' than with the varying methods of flight. Milton brings to life the V-formations of migratory waterfowl in the single phrase, 'wedge thir way':

> Part loosely wing the Region, part more wise
> In common, rang'd in figure wedge thir way,
> Intelligent of seasons, and set forth
> Thir Aery Caravan high over Seas
> Flying, and over Lands with mutual wing
> Easing thir flight. . . . (425–30)

The verbs and verbals are again all important for the swan:

> the Swan with Arched neck
> Between her white wings mantling proudly, Rows
> Her state with Oary feet: yet oft they quit
> The Dank, and rising on stiff Pennons, tow'r
> The mid Aereal Sky. . . . (438–42)

The contrast between the 'state' with its actively 'mantling' wings and those 'Oary feet', rowing in workmanlike fashion, is fine. Both the 'state' and the feet are realistically observed, but it is what Milton does with realism that is impressive. The incipiently comic incongruity is resolved as they 'quit / The Dank', rise on 'stiff Pennons', and 'tow'r'.

Milton could have found (and probably did find) all the details for his portraits of the cock and the peacock in Sylvester's version of Du Bartas. But Sylvester is chiefly interesting for the glimpses he affords us of the way in which Milton could turn pedestrian detail into poetry. It took imagination to perceive any poetic possibilities in Sylvester's exhaustive and disorganized catalogue:

> There the fair *Peacock* beautifully brave,
> Proud, portly-strouting, stalking, stately-grave,
> Wheeling his starry Trayn, in pomp displayes
> His glorious eyes to Phoebus golden rayes.
> Close by his side stands the courageous *Cock*,
> Crest-peoples King, the Peasants trusty Clock,
> True Morning Watch, *Aurora's* Trumpeter,
> The Lyons terror, true Astronomer,
> Who daily riseth when the Sun doth rise;
> And when Sol setteth, then to roost he hies. . . .
>
> (*The First Week,* Day V)

Milton condenses drastically, omits distracting details, and creates sounds and rhythms which convey his meaning:

> Others on ground
> Walk'd firm; the crested Cock whose clarion sounds
> The silent hours, and th' other whose gay Train
> Adorns him, color'd with the Florid hue
> Of Rainbows and Starry Eyes. (442–6)

The sixth day is the climax. Earth, 'Op'ning her fertile Womb, teem'd at a Birth / Innumerous living Creatures, perfet forms, / Limb'd and full grown' (454–6). And everything rises:

> The grassy Clods now Calv'd, now half appear'd
> The Tawny Lion, pawing to get free
> His hinder parts, then springs as broke from Bonds,
> And Rampant shakes his Brinded mane; the Ounce,
> The Libbard, and the Tiger, as the Mole
> Rising, the crumbl'd Earth above them threw

> In Hillocks; the swift Stag from under ground
> Bore up his branching head: scarce from his mould
> *Behemoth* biggest born of Earth upheav'd
> His vastness: Fleec't the Flocks and bleating rose,
> As Plants. . . .   (463–73)

'Whatever creeps the ground' also comes forth, and the insects do more than 'creep':

> those wav'd thir limber fans
> For wings, and smallest Lineaments exact
> In all the Liveries deckt of Summer's pride
> With spots of Gold and Purple, azure and green. . . .
>
> (476–9)

The ant ('The Parsimonious Emmet') and the bee are inevitable here, and we should not allow them to distract us. Unlike most of his predecessors and contemporaries, Milton had his angelic narrator qualify with a 'perhaps' his description of the ants as the 'Pattern of just equality . . . join'd in her popular Tribes / Of Commonalty' (487–9); and there was reputable contemporary support for his mistake about the sex life of the bees. But, as he avoids the 'unnatural' image of the 'feminine monarchy' of the bees, he substitutes an image which neither he nor any other intelligent seventeenth-century man would accept as a natural analogy to the life of man and woman; and he does it with playful onomatopoeia:

> swarming next appear'd
> The Female Bee that feeds her Husband Drone
> Deliciously. . . .   (489–91)

> Air, Water, Earth,
> By Fowl, Fish, Beast, was flown, was swum, was walkt
> Frequent,   (502–4)

but the masterwork remains to be created, man, 'the end / Of all yet done' (505–6). Man, created 'in the Image of God' but from the 'Dust of the ground', is the knowing link between the life of earth and the life of Heaven, brother to all. Granted

dominion over 'every living thing that moves on the Earth',
he is also, alone among earthly creatures, granted that reason
which makes possible self-knowledge and the knowledge of
God. He is also granted the divine blessing, 'Be fruitful, multiply, and fill the Earth' (531). Adam hears of how God brought
him, still on the sixth day, into

> this delicious Grove,
> This Garden, planted with the Trees of God,
> Delectable both to behold and taste;
> And freely all thir pleasant fruit for food
> Gave thee, all sorts are here that all th' Earth yields,
> Variety without end. . . .   (537–42)

He hears again of the prohibition, the one sign of his allegiance,
the only fruit which can cause death instead of life, misery instead of joy.

We have noted the song of the angels as they reascend on that
day, when all is completed and they as well as God see 'how
it show'd', 'how good, how fair, / Answering his great Idea'
(555–7). The final day, the Sabbath of Rest, is, as we should by
this time expect, no day of grim prohibition but of rejoicing.
The Divine Power,

> from work
> Now resting, bless'd, and hallow'd the Sev'nth day,
> As resting on that day from all his work,
> But not in silence holy kept; the Harp
> Had work and rested not, the solemn Pipe,
> And Dulcimer, all Organs of sweet stop,
> All sounds on Fret by String or Golden Wire
> Temper'd soft Tunings, intermixt with Voice
> Choral or Unison; of incense Clouds
> Fuming from Golden Censers hid the Mount.
> Creation and the Six days' acts they sung. . . .   (591–601)

What else but 'Variety without end' of music could follow this
vital Creation? The angels have seen fully manifested God's
power and goodness; they could not, unfallen, refrain from

praise. Their song ends with their rejoicing in the condition of man:

> Thrice happy men,
> And sons of men, whom God hath thus advanc't,
> Created in his Image, there to dwell
> And worship him, and in reward to rule
> Over his Works, on Earth, in Sea, or Air,
> And multiply a Race of Worshippers
> Holy and just: thrice happy if they know
> Thir happiness, and persevere upright.   (625–32)

We have seen God's providence and we have seen man's relation to it. Man, a creature of earth but in the image of God, has been 'advanc't' to a place analogous to that of the fallen prince of angels; he has been granted Paradise as a place for dwelling and worship; he has been blessed with sovereignty over all creation and with divine fertility. He is and will be 'thrice happy' if he merely *knows*, no difficult or recondite knowledge, but his own condition, his own happiness. In the accounts of the War in Heaven and of the Creation, he has been granted precisely images of that condition and that happiness. The 'Christian Warfare' of Adam and Eve in the Garden will be primarily to sustain that knowledge.

One can imagine little distance between the first listeners' and the later readers' responses to the poem's account of the Creation. If Adam and Eve had sustained the visions of these two books, there could have been no Fall. While we sustain them, the Fall, despite our knowledge, seems almost unimaginable.

Albert R. *Cirillo*

NOON-MIDNIGHT AND THE TEMPORAL STRUCTURE OF *PARADISE LOST**

IT will be the argument of this reading to demonstrate how Milton has embodied in the very structure of his narration the paradox of eternity: the effect is that of a double time scheme whereby events that are being expressed in temporal terms – in sequential action – are simultaneously occurring in the eternal present which is the central setting of the poem. The temporal, in this view, is the metaphor for the eternal, and time in its dual aspect becomes a basis of structure. The fall of Satan is related to the elevation of Christ, to the creation of man and the world; the fall of man is related to the Crucifixion–Redemption, and the Crucifixion, in turn, is significant because it *is* the defeat of Satan. Each one of these events must be seen with the other as part of the image of eternal providence. Virtually every event of thematic importance in *Paradise Lost* occurs at either midnight or noon, polarities that are at once disparate and concordant: the action that apparently oscillates between the two poles really occurs at the single noon imaged in the Great Year.[1]

Our first acquaintance with something approaching a symbolic use of noon together with a hinted juxtaposition of it with midnight comes in the often quoted description of the fall of Mulciber. The related images of the falling star and setting sun consign him particularly to the thematic images that surround Satan.

> from Morn
> To Noon he fell, from Noon to dewy Eve,
> A Summers day; and with the setting Sun
> Dropt from the Zenith like a falling Star . . .
>
> (I, 742–5)

*From the *Journal of English Literary History*, XXIX (1962), 372–95.
Condensed for the present volume by the author.

The almost casual mention of 'noon' in this early descriptive passage assumes full importance in retrospect.

As the fall of Satan is related to the fall of man the noon image is deliberately intensified and the Mulciber pattern repeated. It is seen most vividly in Satan's final descent into Hell and his complementary serpentine metamorphosis in Book X. That descent starts paradoxically as an ascent moving north while going down, and reaches its nadir while the sun reaches its zenith, climaxing the symbolic noon-midnight time scheme of the poem.

This final descent is climactic; but Satan throughout the epic is always associated with images of eclipse which are intimately related to noon and to the falling star of his own decline. These images directed to the metaphoric high noon centre produce the pattern which gives the poem a temporal image for eternity. As a metaphoric structure, then, whether the account of the fall is taken as literal history or as Christian myth, *Paradise Lost* illustrates the eternal contemporaneity of the events of Christian history.

The concept of noon for the Renaissance was a richly ambiguous one having an apparent opposite, midnight, to which it was intimately related, but which was no real opposite at all. Noon, according to the history given by the O.E.D., was not only the mid-point of the day but also the time of night which corresponded to midday – i.e., midnight or the highest point of day or night. Thus, it was a term that figuratively subsumed the meaning of midnight and encompassed both extremes, with evocations of the darkness at noon which occurred at the Crucifixion. The ambiguity of noon extended even further to apply to the hour of creation, to the perfect balancing of mid-point between day and night.

John Swan in his popular *Speculum Mundi* suggests the Spring when the sun is in Aries as the time of creation. If time begins with the creation of the world, as it does for Augustine and the Church Fathers, and if it begins with the sun in Aries in the centre of the sky – that is, at noon – then noon becomes the perfect time of the day, the image of eternity.[2]

It is no accident that Milton has Satan, in the account of his rebellion related by Raphael, defect at midnight and move towards the north. His specific sin, of course, is the often cited one of pride:

> he of the first,
> If not the first Arch-Angel, great in Power,
> In favour and praeeminence, yet fraught
> With envie against the Son of God, that day
> Honourd by his great Father, and proclaimd
> *Messiah* King anointed, could not beare
> Through pride that sight, and thought himself impaird.
> Deep malice thence conceiving and disdain,
> Soon as midnight brought on the duskie houre
> Friendliest to sleep and silence, he resolv'd
> With all his Legions to dislodge, and leave
> Unworshipt, unobey'd the Throne supream
> Contemptuous, . . .   (V, 659–71)

Satan's sin, conceived at the very moment when he refuses to obey, is a prideful disobedience. The parallel situation in the very centre of the poem, 'Man's . . . Disobedience', in turn is a sin of pride committed at noon. The circular structure of the poem effects a thematic reconciliation of apparent opposites that transcends the narrative level in which noon and midnight are distinct times for human understanding. Eternity, which exists only for God, and which is a concept not completely understandable in human terms, is paradoxically expanded from its single present point by contracting it to the apparent opposites of midnight and noon. In this context, Satan's fall at midnight is simultaneous with the fall of man at high noon. The common centre of two concentric spheres, one of human life, the other, of angelic time, is the sin of disobedience motivated by pride at noon/midnight.

With the significant events in schematic order the whole pattern becomes clearer. On one hand, while Satan sins at midnight he is defeated in heaven by Christ at noon on the third day. The first unsuccessful temptation of Eve is at midnight, and grows to its successful fruition at noon. Satan thus defects at midnight and apparently succeeds at noon as, conversely, man apparently succeeds at midnight but fails at noon. The present-ness of all events in eternity brings an even richer imposition of patterns: as Satan sins at midnight in heaven, the beginning of his defeat in eternity is contained in the very same act. Satan's defeat is manifested in the birth of Christ at midnight, an in-carnation that is the true fruit of the triunal union parodied in the incarnation of Sin and Death. As man falls at high noon of the ninth day giving Satan an apparent triumph, man is also, in an eternal view, saved at high noon by the Crucifixion. Satan's de-feat, his true eclipse, begun at the midnight moment of his sin is consummated at the noon death of Christ in the eclipse dur-ing the Crucifixion. This is merely an intensification of another aspect of the eclipse initiated by Christ in heaven at the moment of Satan's midnight rebellion.

> Another now hath to himself ingross't
> All Power, and us eclipst under the name
> Of King anointed, for whom all this haste
> Of midnight march, and hurried meeting here . . .

(V, 775–8)

As Satan approaches earth and descends into Eden for the first time, his movement is carefully though unobtrusively located at noon. In a passage that is important in the perspective of later developments, the fallen Lucifer has his first confronta-tion with the sun which 'now sat high in his Meridian Towre' (IV, 30). Later in the same book, Uriel, who had been deceived by the great hypocrite in the form of a beautiful angel, tells Gabriel that the unknown spirit has passed his sphere (the sun) at 'highth of Noon' (IV, 564). After Satan's expulsion from the garden by the vigilant Gabriel, Raphael is sent by God to warn and instruct Adam. The coming of the warning angel is at the hour of noon (V, 298 ff.). Raphael's evening departure on a warning note (VIII, 630–43) makes way for the return of Satan who, having circled the earth for seven continued nights with the earth always between him and the light, re-enters the garden as a dewy mist at midnight of the eighth day. In contrast to previous tantalizingly muted references to noon, from here on the coming of the noon hour of the ninth day is prepared for with almost overwhelming insistence.

The focal scene in the poem is the temptation and fall of Adam and Eve. Consonant with the central importance of this scene, Milton makes the noon image most prominent. Only as the narrative approaches the actual temptation of Eve do the references to noon increase in number and intensity. It is as if Milton has been insinuating the image in order to bring it before the reader in its full significance at the appropriate narrative climax. Eve, for example, in her first plea to work alone, refers her cessation of labour to noon: 'while I / In yonder Spring of Roses intermixt / With Myrtle, find what to redress till Noon' (IX, 217–19). From this point on in the Ninth Book the approach of noon is repeatedly stressed.

Satan, a midnight figure, joins the light of noon within a framework in which the essence of midnight is the promise of light from the east, the positive light which midnight merely negates. This negative-positive union is apparent as Satan, now a midnight mist, possesses the serpent and waits for the light of morning.

> Like a black mist low creeping, he held on
> His midnight search, where soonest he might finde
> The Serpent: him fast sleeping he found
> In Labyrinth of many round self-rowld,
> His head the midst, well stor'd with suttle wiles:
> Not yet in horrid Shade or dismal Den,
> Nor nocent yet, but on the grassie Herbe
> Fearless unfeard he slept: in at his Mouth
> The Devil enterd, and his brutal sense,
> In heart or head, possessing soon inspir'd
> With act intelligential, but his sleep
> Disturbed not, waiting close th' approach of Morn.
>
> (IX, 180–91)

Complementary to this midnight figure from the north and illustrating the reconciliation of the opposites under one symbol, is the physical presence of the sun in Aries in the southern sky at midday. This latter conjunction gave rise to the ambiguity of the word *meridies* which was used equally to mean 'south' and/or 'noon'.[3]

Some of the most important elements in the noon-day temptation are to be found in the body of tradition which gathered around the 'noon-day devil', the *daemonio meridiano* of Psalm 90 (91, in English translations other than Douay).

In virtue of such tradition Milton is able to place the temptation and fall in *Paradise Lost* in clearer perspective. As the symbol for the moment when divine things are most perfectly understood noon may be taken *in bono* because of the eternity symbolized in its zenith of light. Raphael descends at the eternal noon to instruct Adam in his origin and destiny and to warn him of the dangers to which he is now susceptible. On the other hand, temptation too occurs in eternity simultaneously with the heavenly visitation, just as midnight and noon stand at opposite ends of the axis that makes them one.

Satan, in his first temptation of Eve during her midnight dream, is at her ear in the form of a toad; but the 'serenade', if I may use Howard Schultz's term, stirs her imagination to a depiction of him as an angel of light prompting her to eat of the forbidden fruit. The juxtaposition of Satan as a toad in outward reality with the inner illusion provides just the ambiguous contrast implied in the concept of the noon-day devil, and illustrates an important point about the noon-midnight polarity. Temptation occurs in the noon light of eternity, under the positive aspect of good rather than under the negative aspect of midnight evil, because it is of the nature of effective temptation to occur under the appearance of good. Eve's dream (V, 29 ff.) is a prophetic vision of her true temptation with an important symbolic difference: her dream temptation takes place in the deceptive light of the Satanic moon, the false light that must eventually yield to the sun:

> now reignes
> Full Orb'd the Moon, and with more pleasing light
> Shadowie sets off the face of things . . .   (V, 41–3)

Eve's final noon temptation (IX, 739–43) is a surrender to more than physical hunger. She participates in *luxuria*, an intemperate appetite for what is in excess of human good, while Adam is led into his sin through his inordinate fondness for her 'Femal charm' which anticipates his fall into concupiscence. Concurrently, however, he is guilty of the same prideful aspiration that toppled Satan and Eve.

By deliberately seeking the 'test' of temptation, Eve is of her own free will submitting to the dangerous hour of noon and the fraud of the noon-day devil (IX, 399–403). As if to emphasize the danger that lies in store particularly at noon, Adam sets that hour as the limit by which she must return to the security of the Bower.

> Oft he to her his charge of quick returne
> Repeated, shee to him as oft engag'd
> To be returnd by Noon amid the Bowre,
> And all things in best order to invite
> Noontide repast, or Afternoons repose. (IX, 399–403)

Transcending the narrative level, the descent of Satan at noon and his subsequent tempting of Eve is the figurative device for a more universal meaning: the descent of midnight at noon is the descent of evil into the soul. Noon and midnight are then one – a symbolic darkening of the light of grace. Adam and Eve's temptation and fall places them into the context of the results of sin described in Isaiah lix, 10:

We grope for the wall like the blinde, and we grope as if we had no eyes: we stumble at noone day as in the night, we are in desolate places as dead men.   (A.V.)

The noon darkness of their sin and temptation is thus a darkness in the midst of light which is balanced by the act of salvation at noon performed by Satan's conqueror, Christ.

An ideal traditional context is set for the noon-day temptation within which the association of Satan with the cold north and the obverse association of noon with the warm south, with goodness and light, is illustrated in the first noon-day descent of Satan into the garden. The north wind of sin comes in a meeting of midnight and noon, north and south, darkness and light. This union of opposites is a symbolic preparation for the evil that is to come out of the good of creation; contrariwise, at the moment of his apparent noon-day triumph after the fall, the symbol is inverted to display the good that comes out of evil.[4]

And it is with the approach of the very hour of noon, a symbolic temporal occasion that by now has been woven into the texture of the entire temptation, that Satan makes his final entreaty as the serpentine noon-day devil, the temptation of Eve's prideful ambition to be like God. The appetite aroused at noon does not demand the satisfaction of physical hunger, but the fulfilment of pride and vanity in order to elevate oneself to the level of God:

> he knows that in the day
> Ye Eate thereof, your Eyes that seem so cleere,
> Yet are but dim, shall perfetly be then
> Op'nd and cleerd, and ye shall be as Gods,
> Knowing both Good and Evil as they know.
>
> (IX, 705–9)

Beguiled, in a strong sense metaphorically misled by the fraudulent and specious arguments, Eve finds the conjunction of all of these elements too strong to withstand, and at the precise moment when Eve plucks and eats of the fruit Milton returns directly to the noon theme so ominously anticipated a few lines earlier: 'Mean while the hour of Noon drew on' (IX, 739). At that time Eve's ears were still ringing with the sound of Satan's persuasive, seemingly reasonable and truthful words. Now the moment is emphatically underscored – 'in evil hour / Forth reaching to the Fruit, she pluck'd, she eat' (IX, 780–81). Adam's fall is essentially the same as Eve's, differing only in degree. He readily yields to Eve's own temptation in full knowledge of his error, not trying to justify it in Satanic rhetoric as Eve had done, but yielding to her illusory charms.

With the breaking of the stillness and balance of noon imaged in the unleashing of the passions in Adam and Eve (IX, 1121–31) the serpent has completed the work of the noon-day devil. In completing his midnight evil at noon in what he regards as his moment of greatest triumph, Satan begins his return to Hell. He has led Adam and Eve into his own sin, a symbolic meeting of his midnight fall with theirs at noon. As his fall through pride contains theirs, so midnight and noon are joined in one temporal image for eternity.

Paralleling this tradition that makes noon most important in the temporal structure is a tributary symbolic aspect of noon which illustrates in another way the circular structure of the action. At the moment of Adam's fall the earth trembles again as it had done when Eve sinned. When the earth shifts from its axis, reflecting the internal disruption of the passions in Adam and Eve, time and its accompanying decay begin:

> Earth trembl'd from her entrails, as again
> In pangs, and Nature gave a second groan,
> Skie lowr'd and muttering Thunder, som sad drops
> Wept at compleating of the mortal Sin
> Original . . .   (IX, 1000–1004; see also X, 668–95)

The cycle of the Great Year, the *magnus annus* of Plato's *Timaeus*, was also associated with noon when the sun was in Aries. Satan's first confrontation with the sun is at noon (Book IV). This meeting, at one and the same time the confrontation of midnight and noon (Satan and Christ as the moon and the sun), coincides with the complex of noon images and presents the same alignment for eclipse and for the Great Year, an alignment that began at the creation. At the fall the Great Year ends only to return again when, in Book X, the sun returns to Aries at noon and Satan is once more in alignment at the opposite pole.[5] Metaphorically, with the renewal of the

Great Year at the moment of the Crucifixion time begins anew
for the Christian soul.

The finest indication that the Great Year is of importance as
a temporal symbol in the poem may be seen in connexion with
Raphael. At his noon descent his resemblance to the Phoenix is
made quite explicit:

> Down thither prone in flight
> He speeds, and through the vast Ethereal Skie
> Sailes between worlds, with steddie wing
> Now on the polar windes, then with quick Fann
> Winnows the buxom Air; till within soare
> Of Towring Eagles, to all the Fowles he seems
> A *Phoenix*, gaz'd by all, as that sole Bird
> When to enshrine his reliques in the Sun's
> Bright Temple, to *Ægyptian Theb's* he flies.
> At once on th'Eastern cliff of Paradise
> He lights . . .
>
> Like *Maia's* son he stood,
> And shook his Plumes, that Heav'nly fragrance filld
> The circuit wide. Strait knew him all the Bands
> Of Angels under watch; and to his state,
> And to his message high in honour rise . . .
>
> (V, 266–76; 285–9)

The most important connexion between Raphael's phoenix-
like descent and the Great Year is made by Pliny:

. . . *Manilius* affirmeth, that the reuolution of the great yeare so much
spoken of, agreeth just with the life of this bird: in which yeare the
stars returne againe to their first points, and giue significations of
times and seasons, as at the beginning and withall, that this yeare
should begin at high noone that very day when the sun entreth the
signe *Aries*.[6]

It is not difficult to reconstruct the metaphoric texture of the
poem: the central temporal locale of noon represents the moment of creation with the sun in mid-heaven in Aries while all
of the planets are in alignment for the Great Year.[7] The Great
Year is the metaphoric perpetual noon that is the image of

eternity. Raphael himself tells us that it is the image of heavenly time; on the metaphoric 'Day' of the Great Year, Christ (the sun) was elevated in heaven; the rising of the sun in Aries is clearly a cosmological image of this elevation.

> As yet this world was not, and *Chaos* wilde
> Reignd where these Heav'ns now rowl, where Earth now rests
> Upon her Center pois'd, when on a day
> (For time, though in Eternitie, appli'd
> To motion, measures all things durable
> By present, past, and future) on such day
> As Heav'ns great Year brings forth, th'Empyreal Host
> Of Angels by Imperial summons call'd . . . (V, 577–84)

As a symbol of harmony before the fall in *Paradise Lost*, the Great Year ends with the fall at noon, and is renewed with the defeat of Satan in eternity on his return to Hell when he is in line with the sun in Aries. The circular, or cyclic, movement is thus a structural element of the poem as it was for Plato's conception of time and the Great Year.[8] This is what makes the temporal locale of all of the action of *Paradise Lost* part of the eternal present under the central image of noon around which all of the tangential referents form a cluster that always leads back to the noon axis and hence to eternity. The periodic reconstruction of the universe that was an essential element of the theory of the Great Year may be seen as the regeneration of the soul through the coming of grace when, with the eclipse at the Crucifixion, the Great Year returns.[9]

Like 'noon' itself the image of eclipse has been carefully patterned throughout the poem so that it works into the alignment of sun and moon imagery climaxed in the scene of Satan's return to Hell. Satan's association with the moon and with eclipse appears first in the description of his shield:

> his ponderous shield
> Ethereal temper, massy, large and round,
> Behind him cast; the broad circumference
> Hung on his shoulders like the Moon . . .
>
> (I, 284–7)

Satan here is the original brilliant Lucifer whose light is dimmed by the interposition of the moon. This image is reinforced later in the same book by two passages – one concerned with the meteor and another with eclipse proper. It is of considerable symbolic importance that the Satanic banner is likened to a meteor, a flashing falling phenomenon:

> Who forthwith from the glittering Staff unfurld
> Th' Imperial Ensign, which full advanc't
> Shon like a Meteor streaming to the Wind . . .
>
> (I, 535–7)

This emblematic ensign is closely followed by a description of Satan under the gradual diminution of his glory and light, like an eclipse or a meteor:

> his form had yet not lost
> All her Original brightness, nor appear'd
> Less then Arch Angel ruind, and th' excess
> Of Glory obscur'd: As when the Sun new ris'n
> Looks through the Horizontal misty Air
> Shorn of his Beams, or from behind the Moon
> In dim Eclips disastrous twilight sheds
> On half the Nations, and with fear of change
> Perplexes Monarchs. Dark'n'd so, yet shon
> Above them all th' Arch Angel . . .   (I, 591–600)

From the moment of his defection at midnight when he is eclipsed for the first time by Christ (V, 776), the course of Satan as he descends the scale of nature is that of the meteor or moon going into gradual eclipse. Satan's midnight movement is that of defection from God resonating thematically the synonymous value of the terms 'eclipse' and 'defectum'.[10] Satan's gradual descent down the scale of being is imaged in this 'defectum', or gradual eclipse. His association with the descending dragon of the Apocalypse at the beginning of Book IV coincides with the astronomical phenomenon which accompanied comets and which the Renaissance knew as the 'dragon'.

According to William Fulke, whose *A Most Pleasant Prospect into the Garden of Natural Contemplation*[11] was one of the standard Renaissance handbooks on comets, these 'dragons' are a combination of damp vapours and cold air; the 'dragon', he says, has often been associated with the Devil himself.[12] The metaphoric possibility opened up by this belief is evident: coming from the north, where comets were customarily located, Satan partakes of the cold air and vapour of the 'dragon', and transforms himself into a mist to enter the garden. Further, the phenomenon of the falling dragon was concomitant with the eclipse of both sun and moon, a point made in Sacrobosco's account of a lunar eclipse.[13] The texture of the continued symbolism of eclipse and falling star is consistent with the narrative.

It is in this context that we must view the most important scene in the poem, Satan's return to Hell after the fall; this scene represents the culmination of his evil, the height of his splendour and, at the same time, his eternal defeat in the climax of his eclipse. His defeat occurs when the sun is at noon in Aries, the final indication of the juxtaposition of events in the simultaneous present of eternity.

At the moment of his return the symbols of noon – the Great Year, the eclipse – are revealed in their fullest implications. The scene is a repetition of Satan's earlier noon *approach* to earth in Book IV. At that time he had paused to fix his sight on the sun:

> Sometimes towards *Eden* which now in his view
> Lay pleasant, his grievd look he fixes sad,
> Sometimes towards Heav'n and the full-blazing Sun,
> Which now sat high in his Meridian Towre . . . .
>
> (IV, 27–30)

Now, returning to Hell, the midnight figure of the north has an even more explicit confrontation with the image of Christ, the noon figure of the south. Christ sees Satan's fall which fulfils the prophecy of Genesis iii, 15, that the seed of the woman will stamp on the serpent:

> So spake this Oracle, then verifi'd
> When *Jesus* son of *Mary* second *Eve*,
> Saw Satan fall like Lightning down from Heav'n,
> Prince of the Aire; then rising from his Grave
> Spoild Principalities and Powers, triumpht
> In open shew, and with ascension bright
> Captivity led captive through the Aire,
> The Realm it self of Satan long usurpt,
> Whom he shall tread at last under our feet . . .
>
> (X, 182–90)

As Sin and Death build their bridge to the world, they behold Satan returning:

> when behold
> *Satan* in likeness of an Angel bright
> Bewixt the *Centaure* and the *Scorpion* stearing
> His *Zenith*, while the Sun in *Aries* rose . . . .
>
> (X, 326–9)

Not only does this scene illustrate the complete undoing of all of Satan's actions by Christ, but within these few lines and the succeeding narrative is contained the ultimate concentration of the temporal simultaneity of the noon action. The eternal framework contains all of the action and justifies the ways of God to man showing, from God's standpoint, how the ambiguity of noon/midnight is resolved under the single unambiguous noon of the Crucifixion, the symbol of the noon of eternal life.

Satan's descending movement in this scene, from the world to Hell, is along the ecliptic of the now shifted world. In terms of the poetic structure he is travelling both north and west in the traditional directions of evil, between the Scorpion and Sagittarius, while at the same time the sun is rising directly opposite in Aries properly consigned to the east and the coming of light. The sun, once more at its meridian height in Aries (significantly the sign of the Ram) was in mid-sky in the south. For both Batman and Ficino the sun in the sign of Aries was an indication of the hope of life, of the coming fortune of the whole world.[14] This promise of rebirth, of the hope of life, occurs for the Christian with Christ's suffering and death as Picinello points out in connecting the ascent of the sun in Aries with the time of Crucifixion and with spiritual rebirth through Christ's merits.[15] Just as the original sin of Adam and Eve had cosmic effects, shifting the earth from its axis and causing a rumble in the universe, so nature responds at the Crucifixion with an answering cosmic effect – an earthquake and eclipse – restoring, on the level of grace, the balance broken in both grace and nature at the original fall.

What this scene presents, then, is one of the basic paradoxes of the poem under the noon aspect of eternal presentness. At the same time as Satan is returning north towards his midnight sin, he is reaching *his* meridian height, a nadir which is, for him, a noon at midnight; his height of splendour is a descent into darkness, to a midnight meridian. At the other pole, the sun is rising in Aries to its meridian height at noon: Christ, through his elevation on the cross at noon, is completing the eclipse of Satan begun at the midnight fall in heaven. Satan's triumph is thus a defeat in eternity wherein the ambiguity of the apparent polarity of noon and midnight is resolved in a *single* eternal noon. Further, the scene fulfils Christ's prophecy to Satan articulated in *Paradise Regained*: 'Know'st thou not that my rising is thy fall,/And my promotion will be thy destruction?' (III, 201–2).

Satan returns to Hell in the form of the noon-day devil, that is, as an angel of light (X, 327). His eclipse occurs ironically in the symbolic form of his triumph. This resolves a further ambiguity in which Satan as the moon is also an angel of light, and is thus the false sun eclipsed at the Crucifixion. At the same time the astronomical symbolism remains valid, for he is opposite the sun in position of lunar eclipse. As Christ is crucified, the ultimate eclipse of Satan is fully realized not only in his descent toward midnight but in his actual and final unwilling transformation into the serpent. His full glory, earlier obscured by his moon-like shield, by his aspect of a falling star and eclipsed sun, has now degenerated to that of the hissing serpent:

> till supplanted down he fell
> A monstrous Serpent on his Belly prone,
> Reluctant, but in vaine, a greater power
> Now rul'd him, punisht in the shape he sin'd,
> According to his doom . . .   (X, 513–17)

With the approach of the sun into Aries all of the noon references converge in order that time may be seen as the metaphor for eternity. At creation the sun was in the middle of the sky in Aries making noon the first and most perfect time; it is in Aries at the fall of man; it is in Aries at the Crucifixion, the beginning of the time of grace, and this is the metaphoric renewal of the Great Year. To an age which could see Christ's Crucifixion as taking place in the same spot where the tree from which Adam and Eve ate the forbidden fruit stood, and at the same time of day as Adam sinned,[16] the scene of Satan's return to Hell would be an ideal image of the eternity of fall and redemption, of the opposition between Satan and Christ which is in effect, no real opposition at all. Satan, imitating good, has attempted a deceptive parody of the divine. The result of his successful temptation has been only his own final eclipse.

In a poetic incarnation Milton creates his poem to justify God's eternal providence. He must submit eternity to time in an imitation of the Incarnation, the central fact of eternal providence; and in an imitation of that history which is both sacred and profane, he must demonstrate that midnight and noon are polarities only for man, the temporal being who must understand the eternal through temporal symbols. This divine providence presented in temporal terms reflects the Christian universality at the heart of Milton's poetic myth. If the fall happened at a moment in history, it is perpetually present in Christian lives; if the Incarnation was a historical event, it is co-present with the redemption which it implies. Time, developed through the basic transcendent symbol of noon, significantly contributes to structure the whole poem and is the basic metaphor, making the poem through its depiction of physical battle, of ascent and

Albert R. *Cirillo*

descent, a temporal image of the eternal epic of good versus
evil. It is an exemplum of the divine lesson that what is given in
time be healing for eternity.

NOTES

1. See Plato, *Timaeus*, The Loeb Classical Library (1929), pp. 75–83.
Proclus' relevant commentary on the Great Year as 'all time' is
discussed by F. M. Cornford, *Plato's Cosmology* (New York, 1957), p.
104. For fuller documentation the reader should consult the original
version of this essay.

2. Swan, *Speculum Mundi*, 3rd ed. (London, 1665), pp. 8–12, 319.

3. See M. A. Orr, *Dante and the Early Astronomers*, rev. ed. (London,
1956), pp. 29–30.

4. For the association of the east and south with light, heat, and life;
north and west with dark, cold, and death, see A. B. Chambers,
'Goodfriday, 1613. Riding Westward: The Poem and the Tradition',
Journal of English Literary History, XXVIII (1961), 45–6.

5. This alignment was much commented on in connexion with Virgil's
famous Eclogue IV. See the commentary by Carolus Ruaeus, *P.
Virgilii Maronis Opera*, 4th ed. (The Hague, 1723), p. 24.

6. Pliny, *The Historie of the World*, tr. Philemon Holland (London, 1634),
p. 271.

7. Pierre Duhem, *Le Système du Monde* (Paris, 1913–59), I, 67, notes that in
the theory of the Great Year the planets have the same position that
they had at creation. See also the commentary of Chalcidius, *Platonis
Timaeus interprete Chalcidio*, ed. Ion Wrobel (Lipsius, 1877), pp. 183–4.

8. Cornford, op. cit., p. 103.

9. For the association of the eclipse with the beginning of the Great Year
see Duhem, I, 283, which cites Cicero's *Dream of Scipio*. It is also well to
remember Pliny's conjunction of the sign of Aries with the Phoenix in
the light of the traditional identification of the Phoenix with Christ.
Another adumbration of the temporal pattern of the poem can be seen
in the fact that the Phoenix was believed to have made its last appearance
at the time of the Crucifixion.

10. See Laurentio Beyerlinck, *Magnum Theatrum Vitae Humanae* (Leyden,
1678), III, 46.

11. William Fulke, *A Most Pleasant Prospect into the Garden of Natural
Contemplation*, 3rd ed. (London, 1640).

12. Fulke, op. cit., p. 10 recto and verso.

13. Sacrobosco, *The Sphere*, trans. Lynn Thorndike (Chicago, 1949), pp. 141–2. For the position of the sun and moon on the ecliptic paralleling the position of Satan and the Sun, see p. 125.

14. Ficino, *Liber de Sole* in *Opera Omnia*, ed. M. Sancipriano (Turin, 1959), I, 2, fol. 966. D. Philippo Picinello, *Mundus Symbolicus* (Cologne, 1688), I, 29, col. 1, associates Christ with the divine sun and rebirth. On 27, col. 2, Picinello draws an analogy between the Incarnation and the entrance of the sun into Aries.

15. Picinello, op. cit., I, 27, col. 2; 28, col. 1.

16. The whole question of the time of the Crucifixion was the subject of some discussion. See Matthew xxvii, 45, Mark xv, 25, and Cornelius à Lapide, *Commentarius in Quatuor Evangelia* (Antwerp, 1695), pp. 535, col. 2 – 536, col. 1; John Diodati, *Pious Annotations upon the Holy Bible* 2nd ed. (London, 1648), pp. 45, 52, 119.

F. T. Prince

ON THE LAST TWO BOOKS OF
*PARADISE LOST**

PARADISE LOST is perhaps the only long poem in English in which every part contributes to the whole. There is no waste or loose matter: unity of design and execution is sustained from beginning to end. It is all the more remarkable that much modern criticism of the poem tends to weigh the effect of some books against that of others. There is a common delusion, soon dissipated by reading further, that the first two books are superior to the rest; and one can trace the growth of a further mis-judgement, less easy to dispose of, that Milton's imagination flags, not after Book II, but after Book X: that Books XI and XII are disappointing.[1] My present purpose is to consider the place of these two books in the poem, and to give reasons for thinking that they make a full contribution to the whole effect.

Everyone acknowledges that Milton's scheme required what Books XI and XII give us. But a brief account of their context and contents is necessary to give substance to this view; it may also reveal more of their quality by the way.

Book X gives the immediate consequences of the Fall. Adam and Eve receive their sentence: the Son of God declares that, being sinful, they are now subject to death; Adam must earn his bread by the sweat of his brow, Eve must bring forth her children in pain. With these pronouncements from the Book of Genesis we have also the prophecy that the seed of the Woman shall bruise the head of the Serpent. While these judgements are announced, Satan and his followers rejoice, but receive their own punishment, and are transformed into serpents;

* From *Essays and Studies* by Members of The English Association, n.s., XI, 38-52 (1958). This paper was given as a Public Lecture in the University of Southampton in November 1956.

Sin and Death enter the world and begin to lay it waste. God ordains that now Nature must also fall from perfection, and the earth begins to know extremes of heat and cold and other evils. These changes take us back to Adam and Eve: Adam, perceiving the alterations in Nature, laments that Earth and he must now endure such miseries, only to be ended by death. Eve approaches him seeking forgiveness; he at first repels her, but their love soon brings them together. At last Adam proposes that they should throw themselves on God's mercy, asking what help He can give them to face life in their fallen state. With their repentance and prayer the book closes; Milton emphasizes the solemn dramatic meaning of the moment by one of his few Homeric repetitions. Adam asks:

> What better can we do, than to the place
> Repairing where he judg'd us, prostrate fall
> Before him reverent, and there confess
> Humbly our faults, and pardon beg, with teares
> Watering the ground, and with our sighs the Air
> Frequenting, sent from hearts contrite, in sign
> Of sorrow unfeignd and humiliation meek.   (1086–92)

These seven lines are repeated, with the needful changes, to bring the book to a close with a kind of double chord, denoting a shift of mood and situation:

> So spake our Father penitent, nor *Eve*
> Felt less remorse: they forthwith to the place
> Repairing where he judg'd them, prostrate fell
> Before him reverent, and both confessd
> Humbly thir faults, and pardon beggd, with teares
> Watering the ground, and with thir sighs the Air
> Frequenting, sent from hearts contrite, in sign
> Of sorrow unfeignd, and humiliation meek. (1097–1104)

This pregnant pause introduces the last phase or 'act' of the poem, the last two books (which in the First Edition formed one book). At the beginning of Book XI Adam and Eve are still in the posture in which we left them. God accepts their prayers, which he had inspired. The angels are summoned, and the Archangel Michael is sent down to see that Adam and Eve leave Paradise, but also to reveal to Adam God's intentions for the future of mankind: the revelation will support and comfort Adam and Eve in their new way of life. Such is the main substance of the rest of the poem, about a thousand lines; it presents the whole 'scheme of salvation' implied in Christian dogma, the outline of the Old and the New Testaments. Adam is shown in vision the death of Abel, the growth of civilization before the Flood, the Flood itself, Noah's survival and the covenant between God and man. Here ends Book XI, 'betwixt the world destroyd and world restor'd'; and the method of presentation changes from vision to narration. Michael describes the building of the Tower of Babel, God's promise to Abraham, the history of the Israelites in Egypt and in Palestine. Finally he tells of the coming of Christ, His preaching, His death and resurrection, and His promise to come again to judge the living and the dead and to establish 'new Heavens, new Earth'.

It is easy to see how this vision of futurity is necessary to Milton's plan to 'justifie the wayes of God to Men'. *Paradise Lost* is prophetic as well as 'historical'; it takes us from eternity to eternity, from the eternity before the universe was created to the eternity after it will be dissolved. The story which began with the revolt of the angels will end only with the Last Judgement, the end of the world as we know it.

However, in a poem which is founded throughout on Christian dogma, Books XI and XII are the most direct and sustained statement of dogma which we get; and this may well be why readers and critics encounter some difficulty here. Dr Johnson said of *Paradise Lost* that 'the substance of the narrative is truth'; Sir Walter Raleigh 150 years later could call the poem 'a monument to dead ideas'. Neither of these statements would have found universal assent in its own time, and surely we need not follow the impulse which led to their being made.

Of course Milton's epic is a poem with a religious content, with a Christian dogmatic purpose; but our function as critics should be to assess its qualities as a poem, to explore the poetic results which Milton has obtained from his material. In doing this we should of course be ready to respond in imagination to the religious beliefs in question; but we need not commit ourselves to any decision upon their truth or untruth, their lost or eternal validity. What matters to us as literary critics is what Milton has done with them, whether he has given them intellectual coherence, emotional depth, poetic force.

These may indeed be among the qualities which some critics have denied to Milton's last two books. I must now examine them from the point of view of their poetic effect, both within their own limits and in their relation to the rest of the epic.

One of the objections which I have heard expressed is that at this point in the poem the principal actors take ringside seats, turn their backs to the audience and become themselves spectators of an action remote both from them and from us. Yet Milton has followed his usual method of dramatization. These books are not merely historical or theological statement; they are what is revealed to Adam; and in Adam's reactions to the knowledge given him, Milton seeks to renew our vision of human life and of the Christian faith. Thus, when Adam sees Abel murdered by Cain, he sees for the first time the death of a human being, and is overcome by horror:

> But have I now seen Death? Is this the way
> I must return to native dust? O sight
> Of terror, foul and ugly to behold,
> Horrid to think, how horrible to feel! (XI, 462–5)

Michael has to explain that there are many other 'shapes of Death' and shows the dreadful pageant of all the diseases that will afflict mankind; to which Adam again reacts intensely with 'a virgin mind':

F. T. Prince

O miserable Mankind, to what fall
Degraded, to what wretched state reserv'd!
Better end here unborn. . . .
                              Can thus
Th' Image of God in man created once
So goodly and erect, though faultie since,
To such unsightly sufferings be debas't
Under inhuman pains?   (XI, 500–502; 506–11)

So too Adam responds fully in joy at the climax of the Christian
revelation, the redemption which Christ brings and promises:

O goodness infinite, goodness immense!
              . . . full of doubt I stand,
Whether I should repent me now of sin
By mee done and occasiond, or rejoice
Much more, that much more good thereof shall spring,
To God more glory, more good will to Men
From God, and over wrauth grace shall abound.
                              (XI, 469; 473–8)

Everything in *Paradise Lost* is presented dramatically, that is, as
it affects one or other of the characters (the method is not very
different from that of Henry James). In Milton's purpose of re-
newing our vision, the characters of Adam and Eve have been
particularly useful as 'registers' of consciousness: so we have
Adam's description of his first impressions of Paradise and of
his feelings for Eve, and Eve's corresponding account of her
first sensations, her first sight of Adam, and her love for him.
The method of presenting various states of consciousness or
awareness goes together with Milton's tendency to *allegorize*
throughout the poem: Adam is in some sort the human consciousness itself, luxuriating in faith and innocence, falling into
guilt and self-hatred, struggling toward penitence, glowing
once more in faith and hope. (If we look back at the poem as a
whole, Satan represents the soul in damnation; the repeated
descriptions of Paradise and of created beauty convey the paradisal consciousness of Adam and Eve: and everything can be
taken in a similarly 'spiritual' sense). Looked at in this way,

Books XI and XII are certainly a part of Adam's story, of the evolution of his consciousness.

To paraphrase T. S. Eliot's remark on his own Tiresias, 'what Adam *sees*, in fact, is the substance of the poem'. The selection of what he is to see from the reaches of future history is thus determined: he must be given an outline of the spiritual history of mankind, with the emphasis on those points which will give him the right attitude of hope, patience and effort. In so selective an account of the Old and the New Testaments, and of the history of the Church which follows, it is inevitable that there should be little room for poetic elaboration of the kind which people take for granted as characteristic of *Paradise Lost*; the imaginative intensity is to be found rather in the vibration of the story in Adam's reacting consciousness. Yet it cannot be denied that within the limits he has here set himself Milton has compressed some of his most 'Miltonic' effects: the vision of humanity's future is one which only he would have so conceived and projected. There are many characteristic details of substance and of presentation, and there is a prevailing sweep and force that only Milton could have given.

In the first place one may point to a characteristic device in the 'staging'; Michael takes Adam up to a mountain-top to view the pageant of the future:

> So both ascend
> In the Visions of God: It was a Hill
> Of Paradise the highest, from whose top
> The hemisphere of Earth in clearest Ken
> Stretcht out to th' amplest reach of prospect lay.
>
> (XI, 376–80)

This mountain is at once compared to that from which Satan showed Christ 'the kingdoms of this world', and we are reminded how much Milton made of that hint in *Paradise Regained*. In the present passage he indeed anticipates the immense prospects unfolded in the later poem, giving a typically sonorous catalogue of the lands and cities which Adam might have seen from this point:

> from the destind Walls
> Of *Cambalu*, seat of *Cathaian Can*
> And *Samarchand* by *Oxus, Temirs* Throne,
> To *Paquin* of *Sinaean* Kings, and thence
> To *Agra* and *Lahor* of great *Mogul* . . .
> . . . in Spirit perhaps he also saw
> Rich *Mexico* the seat of *Motezume*,
> And *Cusco* in *Peru*, the richer seat
> Of *Atabalipa*, and yet unspoild
> *Guiana*, whose great Citie *Geryons* Sons
> Call *El Dorado*.   (XI, 386–91; 406–11)

This outburst of high-sounding harmonies has been condemned as frivolous, as 'a solemn game', by T. S. Eliot. But this is of course to attack the very basis of Milton's style – employment for a *bel esprit* rather than a critic; if we accept his poetic instrument for the magnificent thing it is, and for the magnificent uses to which he puts it, we can see that this prelude sets the scene for a series of far-sweeping visions, of men and nations moving across mountains and plains, of civilizations rising and flourishing, fighting and falling; visions of 'the giant-race before the Flood',

> that sober Race of Men, whose lives
> Religious titl'd them the Sons of God,   (XI, 621–2)

of the Flood itself overwhelming civilization, of Nimrod and his conquests, of the Tower of Babel; and then of the wanderings of Abraham and of his descendants the Chosen People. Milton loves to set himself or his characters on a high place, from which they can see the world or history spread out below: this habit of thought or vision appears intermittently in the early poems, from the *Nativity Ode* to *Lycidas*, in the prose and in the Sonnets, until it reaches its utmost development in the two great epics. Here it contributes powerfully to our impression of the heroism and the pathos of history, the struggles and sufferings of humanity.

And with this vision of repeated struggle and failure, of

repeated lapses and renewals of effort, goes the characteristically Miltonic conception of the 'one just man' (XI, 890). This archetypal figure first appears before the Flood:

> Of middle Age one rising, eminent
> In wise deport, spake much of Right and Wrong,
> Of Justice, of Religion, Truth and Peace,
> And Judgement from above: him old and young
> Exploded, and had seiz'd with violent hands,
> Had not a Cloud descending snatcht him thence. . . .
>
> (XI, 665–70)

Soon it is Noah, vainly trying to warn his fellow-men of the doom they are calling down upon themselves (XI, 719–26); it is Abraham, who is summoned by God to leave the lands of idol-worship (XII, 114–51), or Moses, leading the Israelites out of Egypt, governing them and granting them laws in the wilderness (XII, 169–260). Lastly, after the Judges and Kings of Israel, comes the greatest of all, the Saviour, Christ himself (XII, 359–71). Yet Michael, questioned by Adam, makes clear that the succession of lonely just men must continue for ever, that Christ's coming has not changed the nature of things, and that the Church He leaves will suffer persecution both from within and from without:

> Whence heavie persecution shall arise
> On all who in the worship persevere
> Of Spirit and Truth; the rest, farr greater part,
> Will deem in outward Rites and specious formes
> Religion satisfi'd;   (XII, 531–5)

The prophecy then rises to its conclusion with the most emphatic repetition that justice will be for ever persecuted and yet finally triumphant:

> so shall the World goe on,
> To good malignant, to bad men benign,
> Under her own weight groaning, till the day
> Appear of respiration to the just,

And vengeance to the wicked, at return
Of him so lately promis'd to thy aid,
The Woman's seed, obscurely then foretold,
Now amplier known thy Saviour, and thy Lord,
Last in the Clouds from Heav'n to be reveal'd
In glory of the Father, to dissolve
Satan with his perverted World, then raise
From the conflagrant mass, purg'd and refin'd,
New Heav'ns, new Earth, Ages of endless date
Founded in righteousness and peace and love,
To bring forth fruits, Joy and eternal Bliss.

(XII, 537–51)

It is strange, if it is true, that modern readers should not be able to respond to the heroic faith of these passages.

Before passing to a more general consideration of the effect of these books, I must relate the 'dogmatic' content to the one passage which even hostile critics must acknowledge to be equal to anything else in the poem: that is, the conclusion, describing the expulsion of Adam and Eve from Paradise. Fortified by what Michael has revealed to him, Adam descends from the hill and returns to Eve; she wakes from her sleep and declares that she too has been comforted in her dreams by glimpses of the future that he has seen. But they can delay no longer; they must now go out into the world and take their first steps toward the life of fallen man, the life of faith and suffering and effort, which they can now understand:

whereat
In either hand the hastning Angel caught
Our lingring Parents, and to th' Eastern Gate
Led them direct, and down the Cliff as fast
To the subjected Plain; then disappear'd.
They looking back, all th' Eastern side beheld
Of Paradise, so late thir happie seat,
Wav'd over by that flaming Brand, the Gate
With dreadful Faces throngd and fierie Arms:
Som natural tears they dropd, but wip'd them soon;

241

> The World was all before them, where to choose
> Thir place of rest, and Providence thir guide:
> They hand in hand with wandring steps and slow,
> Through *Eden* took thir solitarie way.   (XII, 636–49)

The epic ends with the image of the wide plain, the 'subjected plain' below the mountain of Paradise, and the two small human figures making their way across it into the distance. But one must ask if this picture would have its full significance if it had not been preceded by the vision of world history in the previous thousand lines: Milton's methods of construction never served him better.

It remains to face the most interesting question of all, and that is, what poetic effect results from the place of these two books in Milton's poem as a whole. It is here that modern methods of criticism are liable to fail us, based as they often are on minute verbal analysis and on the search for implied ironies or ambiguities, for subtle correspondences between images and 'themes'. It would be ungrateful to deny that the 'New Criticism' has contributed much to our appreciation of at any rate some kinds of literature. But even those who are most convinced of its merits are sometimes prepared to admit that it is not very successful with long poems, or with any imaginative works, drama or novels, on a really big scale. The fact that Milton's poetry does not respond to this kind of analysis and appreciation, and that his work has therefore always been ranked low by the founders and followers of this school, suggests that we must find other methods of analysing the total effect of such a poem as *Paradise Lost*. It is plain that a work on such a scale, based on the traditional epic procedures derived from Homer and Virgil, produces an effect which goes far beyond its strictly linguistic qualities, even if we take into account all the echoes and associations of Milton's style. Only if we compare the conclusion of *Paradise Lost* with the conclusions of other great epics can we measure Milton's achievement.

One of the chief objects of the classical epics is to give us the sense of human destiny working itself out through history, of disaster and adversity repeated and sustained and foreseen for yet longer periods to come. The *Iliad* covers a period of some weeks toward the end of the ten-year siege of Troy. At the beginning of the poem Achilles has withdrawn from the fighting; toward the end, enraged by the death of Patroclus, he returns to the battle and slays Hector. The poem ends with the games at the funeral of Patroclus, and with the funeral of Hector. But the fall of Troy, which has been foreseen throughout the poem, we now know to be imminent; and we know too, as Achilles has always known, that Achilles himself is to die. The *Iliad* therefore ends at a pause in the long-drawn-out misery of the Trojan War. With a very different story and purpose – 'Ilion falling, Rome arising' – Virgil has nevertheless achieved a not dissimilar effect at the end of the *Aeneid*. The *Aeneid* is an historical and prophetic poem, relating the foundation of Rome and prophesying her future greatness. Since it is the will of the Gods that Rome should come into existence, it might be said that the success of Aeneas is a foregone conclusion. Yet throughout the poem we see Aeneas struggling to fulfil his task; the prophecies of Rome's greatness become explicit as he toils on, yet the last stretch of the poem is devoted to the fiercest of the conflicts he has to face, the war against Turnus. The poem ends with Aeneas slaying Turnus in single combat, and the way is open to the future. The task of Aeneas is in one sense accomplished; in another it is just begun. World-history stretches away through the centuries to Imperial Rome, to Virgil himself, and to the vision of Roman civilization spreading through the world for the benefit of mankind.[2]

One of the rules of an epic poem, much emphasized by Renaissance theorists, is that it should deal with an action complete in itself; yet the conclusions of the *Iliad* and the *Aeneid* suggest that this action should be set against what is to follow as well as what precedes. We all know, if we know little else about epic form, that an epic is supposed to begin *in medias res*; is it possible that Homer and Virgil saw the end of an epic as a mirror-image of the beginning – a conclusion which deliberately implied much more to come? These great poems certainly leave us vibrating or composed, perhaps chastened, on the brink of great impending events. The sense of looking back on the past, yet taking farewell of it and turning to the future, is most powerful in Virgil. Milton has given a variation upon it, which is in some ways more charged with meaning. Virgil felt himself to be concerned with the destiny of mankind; Milton, by virtue of his religious beliefs, makes the claim more explicit: his epic is that of the human race, in its relations with God. If the claim to religious assent is an obstacle to any reader, let him endeavour to 'get round it' by allegorizing, or 'psychologizing', what Milton gives us (and I have already suggested that Milton constantly points in the direction of allegory). The conclusion of the poem might then recall Proust's dictum that '*les vrais Paradis sont toujours les Paradis qui sont perdus*'; or it might be held to crystallize something which is inherent in man's experience of time, his feeling for past, present and future; or the expulsion from Paradise, with the preceding view of world-history, might be seen as a vehicle for Blake's 'two contrary states of the human soul', innocence and experience.

Not only, however, the adaptation of epic conventions in the close, but something in the total architecture of Milton's poem, reinforces the relatively subdued poetic tone of the last two books and gives them a heightened meaning. One comes here to the consideration of our experience of a long poem or novel, and to the analysis of elements in it which are very often overlooked, for reasons which will be obvious. I mean the fact that, as we read a lengthy work, the nature of our interest changes, our interest itself must in some degree flag, perhaps intermittently, but certainly in some degree as we enter the later reaches. It seems to me that this inevitable change in the degree of our interest enters into the effect of Books XI and XII of *Paradise Lost*, and is provided for, consciously or unconsciously, by Milton's plan. At the end of Book X we must have quite strongly the feeling that 'all the great things are over', as a character says toward the end of one of Mr E. M. Forster's novels. We have seen enacted the tragedy of the Fall, the 'subject' of the poem; and leading up to that climax we have seen and felt so much else – Satan's heroic villainy, the horrors of Hell, the splendours of Heaven, the luxuriant loveliness of Paradise: Adam and Eve and the wealth of poetry with which Milton surrounds their happiness – the almost demoniac misery into which they fall. If we reflect on what the poem has already given us up to this point, we may well feel that we have seen the full exhibition of Milton's genius, that he can scarcely do more, or do better, than he has done already. Here, in fact, is a moment at which we must become aware of a feeling of imagination satisfied: a feeling which is hardly distinguishable from a loss of interest, a slight weariness, almost a sense of disappointment. Now my contention is that this feeling enters the poem precisely at the point where it becomes of positive value, where it can set the mood for what Milton still has to say.

Literary critics, and particularly those who are also teachers of literature, may be forgiven if they have not much stressed that side of a reader's experience which I have in mind. Yet, if we are allowed to refer to natural human limitations in the criticism of drama, discussing for example the problems a dramatist has to face in his fourth or fifth act, I do not see why we should not take into account the fluctuation of our interest in long poems: the poets themselves must surely have done so. For we have here a very common, practically universal, psychological experience. How often do we find that the later phases, or the last stretch, of a long work is less 'interesting' than the first, or even positively disappointing? If we consider even briefly, we see that it is almost bound to be so. If we take our evidence from novels (the only long works of which most modern readers have much experience), it is clear that the kind of interest which carries us to the end of the story must necessarily lack the freshness, the keenness, with which we make the acquaintance of the characters, grasp their situation, follow the statement of the author's intentions, and so on. Even in reading less great works, we can indeed derive a special pleasure from this autumnal atmosphere, the mood of languor, of curiosity appeased, which prevails toward the close of the story. Such impressions should certainly be counted among the rewards of reading, even if it would be difficult to make them the grounds of our appeal to those who have not yet acquired the reading habit.

It would be a fascinating exercise in the analysis of one's aesthetic experience to try to determine at which point in various great works the atmosphere I have indicated becomes important. It is traceable in *Hamlet*, after Hamlet's return from England; where would one place it in *War and Peace*, in *The Ambassadors* or *The Golden Bowl*, in *Troilus and Criseyde*? However, *Paradise Lost* is perhaps the only long poem in English in which it can be found closely integrated with the subject-matter, and announced plainly in musical and constructional effects: it enters in the latter part of Book X and is sealed by the conclusion of the book, with its solemn double chord of penitence. The feeling that 'all the great things are over' coincides with the change in the nature of Adam and Eve, the change from unfallen to fallen man which makes them at last human beings like ourselves. Here for the first time in the poem we have man as we know him, with his divided will, his passions and aspirations and his sense of guilt and discouragement. Here too the poem for the first time begins to deal with the world as we know it, with history, with our own past (which to Adam is the future). These shifts of interest must make the poem more obviously serious, if less obviously exciting. Finally I would claim that the mood of chastened interest, of more sober concentration, which I have been trying to define, is peculiarly appropriate to the new matter which occupies Books XI and XII, the vision of the future. That vision is based upon the Christian view of life, that it is to be suffered in faith, hope and charity. It is perhaps a little frivolous to suggest that the reader's reflection 'I have now read ten books, and have only two left', is not inappropriate as a preparation for this survey of the fate of mankind. I would rather maintain in all seriousness that Milton has shown an instinctive grasp of the ebb and flow of interest in a long poem, and that at this point he has utilized the inevitable shift in our attention, to coincide with the mood of the last phase.

One certain conclusion I have already mentioned – that the last twenty-five lines of the poem would not act on us as they do if we had not read through the previous thousand. To see 'our first parents' setting out into the world is to see them consciously entering on the long and patient work of human history, which we have had presented to us. And one detail in this last passage shows that Milton could make use for his purpose, not only of the conventions of classical epic which we have considered, but also, occasionally, of the subtler and smaller devices which are the business of the 'New Criticism'. When the angels who are waiting to exclude Adam and Eve from Paradise move at length to the final positions they must take up, Milton compares their movement to that of a gliding mist:

> for now too nigh
> Th'Archangel stood, and from the other hill
> To thir fixt station, all in bright array
> The Cherubim descended; on the ground
> Gliding meteorous, as Ev'ning Mist
> Ris'n from a River ore the marish glides,
> And gathers ground fast at the Labourer's heel
> Homeward returning.   (XII, 625–32)

The brief image of the labourer returning home after a day's work in the fields is a very simple allusion to the contents of Books XI and XII: it looks back and it looks forward, and in this context of 'dreadful Faces' and 'fierie Arms' it is especially effective, a moving evocation of the life of toil and poverty and weariness, and also of homely satisfactions – all the common experience of humanity – which Adam and Eve must now undertake.

NOTES

1. Professor Kenneth Muir wrote recently: 'The last two books are poetically on a much lower level' than the rest, though he added that 'they are essential to the scheme of the poem' (*John Milton*, London, 1955, p. 160).
2. Both Ariosto and Tasso imitate, in different ways, the conclusion of the *Aeneid*.

Christopher Ricks

MILTON'S GRAND STYLE:
ENHANCING SUGGESTIONS*

FOR Bagehot, *Paradise Lost* was distinguished not only by 'a manly strength', but also by its 'haunting atmosphere of enhancing suggestions'.[1] And these suggestions are not just a matter of the great vistas of Milton's themes, but also of delicate and subtle life in the verse. This chapter tries to show how Milton, without abandoning epic grandeur, draws on the infinite suggestiveness of word-order and words.

The eighteenth-century critics were quick to spot these effects. So Addison, talking of such rhetorical patterning, says that 'several passages in Milton . . . have as excellent turns of this nature as any of our English poets whatsoever; but [I] shall only mention that which follows, in which he describes the fallen angels engaged in the intricate disputes of predestination, free-will, and foreknowledge; and to humour the perplexity, makes a kind of labyrinth in the very words that describe it':[2]

> reason'd high
> Of Providence, Foreknowledge, Will, and Fate,
> Fixt Fate, free will, foreknowledge absolute,
> And found no end, in wandring mazes lost.   (II, 558–61)

Similarly Richardson commented on the lines in which Satan looks into Chaos before leaping into it: ''tis Observable the Poet Himself seems to be Doing what he Describes, for the Period begins at 910. Then he goes not On Directly, but Lingers, giving an Idea of *Chaos* before he Enters into it':[3]

> Into this wilde Abyss,
> The Womb of nature and perhaps her Grave,
> Of neither Sea, nor Shore, nor Air, nor Fire,

* From *Milton's Grand Style* (1963), pp. 78–102. Some slight changes have been made with the author's permission.

> But all these in thir pregnant causes mixt
> Confus'dly, and which thus must ever fight,
> Unless th' Almighty Maker them ordain
> His dark materials to create more Worlds,
> Into this wild Abyss the warie fiend
> Stood on the brink of Hell and look'd a while,
> Pondering his Voyage .... (II, 910–19)

In the same spirit, Newton too noticed how 'the Poet Himself seems to be Doing what he Describes' in praising the lines

> Thir song was partial, but the harmony
> (What could it less when Spirits immortal sing?)
> Suspended Hell, and took with ravishment
> The thronging audience. (II, 552–5)

'*The harmony suspended Hell*; but is it not much better with the parenthesis coming between? which suspends as it were the event, raises the reader's attention, and gives a greater force to the sentence.'[4] What makes the sentence delicate as well as forceful is the way the syntactical effect echoes the play on 'suspend' – suspension as a technical harmonic term.

Newton also quoted an excellent comment by William Benson:

> Thus at thir shadie Lodge arriv'd, both stood,
> Both turnd, and under op'n Skie ador'd
> The God .... (IV, 720–22)

'This artful Manner of writing makes the Reader see them *Stop* and *Turn* to worship God before they went into their Bower. If this Manner was alter'd, much of the Effect of the Painting would be lost.

> And now arriving at their shady Lodge
> *Both stopt, both turn'd* and under open Sky
> Ador'd the God, etc.'[5]

Plainly there will always be differences of opinion about such effects, but Benson does seem to be pointing to a genuine function of the line-ending: the verse wheels, just as Adam and Eve wheel.

Presumably it was rhetorical training as well as confidence in Milton's exactitude which made the eighteenth-century critics take his syntax seriously. They assumed that it meant what it said, even if this sometimes necessitated supposing that he was a subtle poet. So Richardson drew attention to Eve's leaving Adam:

> Thus saying, from her Husbands hand her hand
> Soft she withdrew . . . .   (IX, 385–6)

"'Tis Pity any Reader should Overlook the Beauty and Force of This Passage. Impatient to Compleat her Conquest, while she was yet speaking what did not really Convince Herself, she was Going; His Forc'd Consent is finely Mark'd, she Drew away Her Hand from His, yet Wishing to Detain her, Loath, Dreading to Part. In vain! 'tis a Master-Touch of Tenderness in Few Words.'[6] And Richardson is as sensitive in his comment on the syntax when Eve

> as oft engag'd
> To be returnd by Noon amid the Bowre.
>
> (IX, 400–401)

'*Return'd*, as if Already done; very Elegant and New, and full of Energy.'[7]

Such syntactical mirroring is of a rather obvious kind, as were most of the instances pointed out in the eighteenth century. But it provides solid reason for thinking that Milton had a real interest in expressive syntax, and so it justifies an investigation into subtler effects. Sometimes such subtlety closely resembles that of eighteenth-century poetry. When Pope tells us that Atticus manages to ' Just hint a fault, and hesitate dislike', his adaptation of 'hesitate' to a transitive instead of an intransitive verb carries a weight of condemnation: other people just hesitate, Atticus's hesitation is active, a tool that he uses.[8] So in Milton a lowring sky does not merely scowl – it scowls snow:

> the lowring Element
> Scowls ore the dark'nd lantskip Snow, or showre.
>
> (II, 490–91)

The eighteenth-century editors were well aware of, though often exasperated by, the fluidity of Milton's syntax – the hesitations as to which are main verbs, the clustering of dependent clauses, and the indivisible or variously divisible flow. Pearce enjoyed 'for the sake of Perspicuity inserting the Note of a Parenthesis'.[9] Mr Empson dryly observes that at one point Bentley 'let in a couple of main verbs, like ferrets'.[10]

But in the eighteenth century they were also clear about the advantages of such a style: its combination of a wide suggestiveness with the momentum of statement. So Richardson commented on the lines describing Adam's first view of Paradise:

> all things smil'd,
> With fragrance and with joy my heart oreflow'd.
> (VIII, 265–6)

Richardson saw that it would make a difference to move the comma to after 'fragrance': 'The Difference is only in the Placing of a Comma, but That Vary's the Sence considerably. In the One *Adam* says, All things Smiling, his Heart overflow'd with Fragrance and Joy; in the Other, that All things Smil'd with Fragrance, and his Heart o'erflow'd with Joy: Both are Beautyful ... but This Sense [the former] is the Best; it takes in the other, and with an Additional, and more Noble Idea. All things Smile, not with Fragrance Only, but in Every respect. That Universal Balmy, Cordial, Exhilarating Air which He breath'd continually whilst he Beheld the General Lovelyness around him is also Express'd, together with the Overflowing Joy Arising from All.'[11]

That is excellently said, and finely brings out the merits of the flowing syntax, its terminations no more than hints:

> So evenings die, in their green going,
> A wave, interminably flowing.

Milton's line and a half can be divided in many ways, the sense varying minutely each time:

1. All things smil'd.
    With fragrance and with joy my heart oreflow'd.

2. All things smil'd with fragrance,
    And with joy my heart oreflow'd.

3. All things smil'd with fragrance and with joy,
    My heart oreflow'd.

4. All things smil'd,
    With fragrance and with joy,
    My heart oreflow'd.

In the last case, the fragrance and the joy would fit Pearce's description of a phrase elsewhere in Milton, 'so plac'd between the two Sentences as equally to relate to both'.[12] The fragrance and the joy would be poised between both Nature and Adam, just as Adam himself is poised: fragrance without, and joy within. Not that we need to break the verse down like this in reading – its flow keeps us moving. But to do so is instructive, and confirms Richardson's understanding of the syntax. And the word 'oreflow'd' alerts us to the function of the syntax, itself overflowing. Everything smiles, is fragrant, is joyful, overflows; the harmony of Eden, in itself and between man and nature, is once again beautifully captured.

The overflowing is itself a tribute to the Creator. Comus perverted the truthful tribute, and tried (like Satan) 'out of good still to find means of evil'; but Rilke restored the truth in speaking to God:

> Thus every superabundance flows to you.
> And as a fountain's upper basin stands
> for ever overstreaming, as with strands
> of loosened hair, into the lowest bowl,
> into your valleys will their fullness roll
> whenever things and thoughts are overflowing.[13]

Nor is this an isolated syntactical effect. Milton's first commentator drew attention to it in his note on 'transported I behold, transported touch' (VIII, 529–30): 'Pleas'd to excess, I find my Feeling pleasant to excess: Raised above my self, I perceive my Feeling raised as far above it self: Or carried beyond my self I perceive my sense of Touching carried too beyond what's usual.'[14]

After the Fall, Adam cries out to the trees to shelter him from seeing God and his angels. It is a very simple cry:

> Cover me ye Pines,
> Ye Cedars, with innumerable boughs
> Hide me . . . .   (IX, 1088–90)

The cry is not made less simple if one points out that here too the syntax is curiously fluid, that one may divide it at all sorts of places:

1. Cover me ye Pines,
   Ye Cedars, with innumerable boughs hide me.

2. Cover me
   Ye Pines, ye Cedars,
   With innumerable boughs hide me.

3. Cover me ye Pines, ye Cedars,
   With innumerable boughs hide me.

4. Cover me ye Pines, ye Cedars, with innumerable boughs
   Hide me.

All these cries are equally simple, but all are slightly different. The punctuation selects from among them, of course, just as it did in the other examples. But the effect of the two lines is as of innumerable cries, as of innumerable boughs, to innumerable trees – all of which telescope into one terrifying simple cry. And just as 'oreflow'd' was a signal in Richardson's example, so here is 'innumerable'.

Perhaps such a comment on the syntax may seem less far-fetched if we notice how it is analogous to the patterns of rhyme which Mr Prince has traced in *Lycidas*, 'a type of rhyme which looks both back and forward'.[15]

The effect is similar to that which Hopkins gains in the phrase 'My lament is cries countless', where he brilliantly uses what always seems the mysterious construction of single subject, single verb, plural complement. One lament, countless cries; and the 'is' acts as a funnel from which they pour. Milton, the poet who wrote with splendid liberty that 'Both Death and I am found eternal' (tersely thrusting home the single nature of death and Adam) – Milton is in many ways not so different a poet from Hopkins as some believe.

Taking his cue from the eighteenth century, Mr Empson brought out more fully what Milton gained. Bentley had disapproved of the phrase 'words or tongue':

> to recount Almightie works
> What words or tongue of Seraph can suffice,
> Or heart of man suffice to comprehend?
>
> (VII, 112–14)

Bentley's emendation to *words from tongue*, as Mr Empson says, 'loses the completeness of the statement; "How can any stage in the production of the speech of seraphs be adequate; how can they find words, and if they could how could their tongues pronounce them?" But besides this, the merit of *or* is its fluidity; the way it allows "words from tongue" to be suggested without pausing for analysis, without holding up the single movement of the line.'[16]

If we want 'the completeness of the statement' in words other than Milton's (and, in particular, in different syntax), expressing it is a lengthy matter. See, for instance, the censorious attempts to rephrase that magnificent compression, 'Yet Virgin of Proserpina from Jove'. And one can support Mr Empson's comment on 'words or tongue' by referring to another use of 'or', where Milton, as often, shows the classical virtue of being original with the minimum of alteration. Satan laments among the beauties of Paradise:

> I in none of these
> Find place or refuge.   (IX, 118–19)

Bentley[17] wanted to alter this to 'place of refuge', but just as 'words or tongue' suggested 'words from tongue' while making a more complete statement, so here does 'place or refuge' suggest 'place of refuge' – while also saying something stronger: Satan not only cannot find 'place of refuge', he cannot find *place* in Paradise. Newton provided the paraphrase '*I in none of these find place* to dwell in *or refuge* from divine vengeance. And this sense seems to be confirm'd by what follows. "But neither here seek I, no nor in Heaven / *To dwell*".'[18] The 'Heaven on Earth' offers no more place to Satan than does Heaven itself. That is no country for Satan – the young 'imparadis't in one anothers arms', birds in the trees. . . .

Mr Empson adds a valuable insight into the reason for Milton's fluid syntax: 'Milton aims both at a compact and weighty style, which requires short clauses, and a sustained style with the weight of momentum, which requires long clauses.'[19] Furthermore, another of his examples shows that Milton can use the fluidity of his syntax both for an immediately dramatic reason and also to establish an important link. In Eve's dream, the false angel tempts her to be

> not to Earth confind,
> But somtimes in the Air, as wee, somtimes
> Ascend to Heav'n. (V, 78–80)

'The Words *as we*', remarked Pearce, 'are so plac'd between the two Sentences as equally to relate to both, and in the first Sentence the Verb *be* is understood. Dr Bentley has alter'd this Passage thus, "*But sometimes* RANGE *in Air, sometimes, as we, etc.*" But in this reading of the Doctor's are not the Angels excluded from ranging in the Air?'[20]

Mr Empson adds with characteristic subtlety, and with characteristic respect for Milton's subtlety, 'Surely there is a dramatic reason for the gawkiness of the line here; the doubt implied as to whether he could go to Heaven himself shows a natural embarrassment in the disguised Satan.'[21] But the more important point – and it is stressed in *Milton's God*[22] – is that the syntax throws heavy stress on the words 'as wee'. We can't help noticing them, they hook themselves on to our memory,

and it is they as much as the other diction which make manifest
the grim coincidence later in the same Book when Raphael tells
Adam and Eve that they may, because of what they eat,

> wingd ascend
> Ethereal, as wee, or may at choice
> Here or in Heav'nly Paradises dwell.
>
> (V, 498–500)

Eve perversely misunderstands that 'choice', and it is a detail
of syntax that helps to make the point.

Mr C. S. Lewis is not on the whole sympathetic to Mr Empson's kind of criticism, but he too adds some excellent amplifi-
cations of the eighteenth-century view of Milton's syntax. Let
me quote one of the best pieces of stylistic comment in *A
Preface to 'Paradise Lost'* (it is a great pity that there are not
more pages about the style): 'A fixed order of words is the
price – an all but ruinous price – which English pays for being
uninflected. The Milton constructions enable the poet to depart, in some degree, from this fixed order and thus to drop the
ideas into his sentence in any order he chooses. Thus, for example,

> soft oppression seis'd
> My droused sense, untroubl'd, though I thought
> I then was passing to my former state
> Insensible, and forthwith to dissolve.   (VIII, 291)

The syntax is so artificial that it is ambiguous. I do not know
whether "untroubled" qualifies *me* understood, or "sense", and
similar doubts arise about "insensible" and the construction of
"to dissolve". But then I don't need to know. The sequence
"drowsed – untroubled – my former state – insensible – dissolve" is exactly right; the very crumbling of consciousness is
before us and the fringe of syntactical mystery helps rather than
hinders the effect.'[23]

That is an excellent point, even though the wording of it is at
times rather bluffly casual. 'Any order he chooses' sounds a bit

light-hearted or wilful for the sort of choice to which a great poet is impelled; and 'I don't need to know' sounds almost like relief or Terror of the Cognitive, and would be liable to invite a sharp riposte from the anti-Miltonists. Nevertheless, they would be wrong, and Mr Lewis is right.

Milton's magnificent lines on the creation of Light are a noble comment on his own poetry and its light:

> Of Light by farr the greater part he took,
> Transplanted from her cloudie Shrine, and plac'd
> In the Suns Orb, made porous to receive
> And drink the liquid Light, firm to retaine
> Her gather'd beams, great Palace now of Light.
> Hither as to thir Fountain other Starrs
> Repairing, in thir gold'n Urns draw Light,
> And hence the Morning Planet guilds his horns;
> By tincture or reflection they augment
> Thir small peculiar, though from human sight
> So farr remote, with diminution seen . . . .
>
> (VII, 359–69)

By far the greater part of the light of Milton's poetry acts with the noble directness of the sun itself. The Grand Style is a 'great Palace now of Light'. That directness ensures that we receive the rays of the sun – the sun which is like poetry in that its

> vertue on it self works no effect,
> But in the fruitful Earth; there first receavd
> His beams, unactive else, thir vigor find.
>
> (VIII, 95–7)

But not all the radiance of Milton's poetry is shed in this way. Like the light, it too is liquid; and it too is both porous and firm. And just as the stars receive and transmit light by 'tincture or reflection', so too do Milton's words. If we are to see not merely the greater part of the light, but all of it, we must receive the tinctures and reflections which gild his liquid verse.

Richardson offers a good example of what I mean. He drew

attention to the suggestiveness of the placing of 'retir'd' in the lines

> Others apart sat on a Hill retir'd,
> In thoughts more elevate, and reason'd high . . . .

(II, 557–8)

'Though the Text does not Say it, the Reader will from the Words naturally be led to imagine Some were Retir'd, in Thought, as well as from the Company, and Reason'd and Debated, Discours'd within Themselves, on these Perplexing, but Important Suttleties: This gives a very Proper Image here, a very Melancholly and Touching One.'[24] Richardson's tone, tentative yet precise, is admirable – and so is his insistence that many of Milton's images depend on what is suggested as well as on what is explicitly said. The modern critic is often accused of reading too much into works of the past, and certainly he ought to point precisely to what it is that suggested his comments. But it is interesting to find the eighteenth-century critics responding to Milton in so supple a way.

An interchange between Bentley and Pearce brings out that flexible syntax in Milton can be mistaken for careless syntax. Bentley objected to the description of Satan,

> His count'nance, as the Morning Starr that guides
> The starrie flock, allur'd them, and with lyes
> Drew after him the third part of Heav'ns Host.

(V, 705–7)

'In this Reading the Construction will be, *His countenance allured and drew them with Lies*. He is the *Father of Lies* indeed, if not his Tongue, but his Countenance spoke them.'[25] Of course this is a quibble – such a shift is easy enough, and the main meaning offers no real difficulty. But as often with a quibble by Bentley, he fastens on a boldly suggestive metaphor: 'He is the *Father of Lies* indeed, if not his Tongue, but his Countenance spoke them.' And Pearce's reply brings out very well both the straightforward sense and the metaphorical suggestion: 'By the expression *His Countenance* is meant He himself. . . . But if this will not be allow'd to be *Milton's* meaning, yet it may be said that *Satan's Countenance* seducing his followers by disguising the foul intentions of his heart, may be very properly said to *seduce with Lyes.*'[26] That Pearce's suggestion is plausible may be seen from the innumerable occasions when Milton makes profound and subtle use of Satan's countenance.

At any rate, the fact that the solid and respectable eighteenth-century editors were aware of suggestive niceties of syntax gives one some right to proceed.

After long argument, Eve leaves Adam to go gardening on her own:

> Thus saying, from her Husbands hand her hand
> Soft she withdrew. (IX, 385–6)

If we had to paraphrase the lines, we would say that 'soft' was an adverb, not an adjective: she softly withdrew her hand. This makes admirably grim sense; 'soft' ought to include 'yielding', but Eve is firmly and unshakeably insisting on her own way. She is stubborn but sweet:

> Eve, who thought
> Less attributed to her Faith sincere,
> Thus her reply with accent sweet renewd.
>
> (IX, 319–21)

Persistent, but meek:

> but Eve
> Persisted, yet submiss, though last, repli'd.
>
> (IX, 376–7)

And she is obdurate but soft. So much for the main sense: she softly withdrew her hand. But Milton didn't exactly say that; and since 'soft' is the adjectival form as well, and since Milton so often puts his adjectives after his nouns, the word 'soft' gets attracted into Eve's hand, delicately and as it were by reflection. So that the total effect is 'her soft hand softly she withdrew', with *soft* sounded much more quietly than *softly*.

And with a delicate fusion of two points of view, since the adverb has the neutrality of an onlooker, while the adjective puts us in the place of Adam as he feels Eve's hand. E. E. Cummings might achieve such effects through typography and punctuation – Milton uses syntax. Mr Lewis's remark about Milton's network is applicable to his syntax too: 'Nearly every sentence in Milton has that power which physicists sometimes think we shall have to attribute to matter – the power of action at a distance.'[27]

This is obviously open to the charge of over-ingenuity, and substantiation is scarce. (It would be likely to be, with so delicate an effect.) But, first, one might point to softness as pre-eminently the characteristic for which Eve was created:

> For contemplation hee and valour formd,
> For softness shee and sweet attractive Grace.
>
> (IV, 297–8)

Her 'soft imbraces' and 'her Heav'nly forme Angelic, but more soft, and Feminine' are contrasted elsewhere with Adam, 'Less winning soft, less amiablie milde'.[28]

And, second, one might support this with the lines when Adam awakens Eve, which interestingly give us the 'hand' again:

> then with voice
> Milde, as when Zephyrus on Flora breathes,
> Her hand soft touching, whispered thus . . . .
>
> (V, 15–17

In the eighteenth century this was seen to be ambiguous, and was tidied up with a hyphen: *soft-touching*. And again if we had to choose, the paraphrase would obviously be 'softly touching'. But the close parallel with the other line reinforces for me the idea that 'soft' once again affects our sense of Eve's hand, a tincture that is quietly beautiful, and that would certainly deserve Bagehot's praise of Milton's 'haunting atmosphere of enhancing suggestions'.

To combine clarity of stated sense with such suggestiveness is the mark of those poets who rise above divisions into Classical and Romantic. Milton's use of syntax for such purposes is often supported by alliteration, which – like rhyme – can tie together suggestively things which are not tied together in the plain statement. This was perhaps one of the many effects which Hopkins developed from Milton. Take, for instance, the alliteration in the line from 'I wake and feel the fell of dark, not day', when Hopkins says that the heart must endure more before it reaches God's peace: 'And more must, in yet longer light's delay.' Obviously a simple paraphrase would say 'While light delays even longer', but that is not what Hopkins wrote. The compression of the syntax, itself Miltonic, brings 'longer' up against 'light', which furthermore alliterates. And the alliteration is stressed by the opening of the line ('and more must . . .'). So that although logically, and primarily, 'longer' goes with 'delay', and not with 'light', the effect of the syntax and alliteration is to suggest that it is light which is longer. So that it is as if, thinking apparently only of the fact that it will be a long time before God's peace comes, Hopkins also remembers that when the light of eternity does come, it will be 'longer' than the darkness of this life. The phrase has just that combination of strong present despair and quiet distant hope which is characteristic of his best poetry.

Milton uses syntax and alliteration in just the same way – they allow him to suggest things which he doesn't actually say. In the account of Mulciber's fall, for example, we move through 'he fell . . . he fell. . . dropt' to

> He with this rebellious rout
> Fell long before; nor aught avail'd him now
> To have built in Heav'n high Towrs; nor did he scape
> By all his Engins, but was headlong sent . . . . (I, 747–50)

Alliteration and word-order tie 'Heav'n' and 'high' together, though the plain sense is 'high Towrs', enforced as it is by the rhythm as well as by the earlier reference to 'a Towred

structure high'. But Milton is not satisfied with the plain sense
alone. The feeling of *high Heav'n* is important to the sense of
Mulciber's fall from that height, Mulciber who fell headlong
down to Hell. To say that Heaven is high would be to risk
cliché; but to suggest it while saying something else is another
matter.

The support for this comes in the way Milton uses 'high'
elsewhere. It is used more than a hundred times; and he uses
it in the immediate context of 'Heaven' more than twenty
times, without actually applying it, with dull predictability, to
'Heaven'. Only twice does he say that Heaven is high – but the
one is tinged with a moral meaning, stressed by 'lowly':

> Heav'n is for thee too high
> To know what passes there; be lowlie wise.
>
> (VIII, 172–3)

And the other is Eve's silly hopefulness:

> Heav'n is high,
> High and remote to see from thence distinct
> Each thing on Earth. (IX, 811–13)

But most worth noticing is that Milton is very fond of using
this same pattern elsewhere to bring 'Heaven' and 'high' together while stating something else: 'Heav'n's high jurisdic-
tion', or 'Heav'ns high behest'.[29] Perhaps the closest to the
pattern of 'in Heav'n high Towrs' is this sequence:

> Had not th' Eternal King Omnipotent
> From his strong hold of Heav'n high over-rul'd
> And limited thir might. (VI, 227–9)

'High' there is an adverb, but how finely the syntax and alliteration merge it with 'Heav'n'. (Or conversely, if it is taken as an
adjective, how finely it suggests the moral power of the adverb.)

Yet one can bring out the point of such a merging only by
leaving syntax for a moment in order to stress the crucial
importance to Milton of the word 'high', partly reflected in

its great frequency. Just as 'stand' is clashed against 'fall', so is 'high' clashed against 'deep': 'the deep fall of those too high aspiring' (VI, 898–9).[30] Insisting on 'the highth of this great Argument', a height that must be worthy of Him who sits 'High Thron'd above all highth', Milton simply but powerfully plays the literal against the abstract:

> nor ever thence
> Had ris'n or heav'd his head, but that the will
> And high permission of all-ruling Heaven . . . .

(I, 210–12)

The play is in earnest because the physical fact about Heaven has a moral significance:

> Strait knew him all the Bands
> Of Angels under watch; and to his state,
> And to his message high in honour rise.   (V, 287–9)

And Milton even makes the word receive the full weight of his sardonic condemnation. Pandaemonium, 'the high Capital of Satan and his Peers', is down in Hell. There 'highly they rag'd against the Highest'. And there we hear of Dagon, who 'fell flat, and sham'd his Worshipers', and yet 'had his Temple high'.[31]

Milton uses such fluidity of syntax so that it both makes clear sense and also is suggestive. Sometimes the suggestion is of a hyperbolical beauty which it would be indecorous to state as fact – particularly in the epic. To show this at work, it is best to take one of the most powerful and consistent of the Paradisal images: the mingled beauties of sight and of scent (and of sound too). The image itself is a lovely one, but it is the mingling syntax which brings it to life, which both suggests the magically pre-lapsarian and states the matter of fact. The syntax combines the charmed subjectivity of the lyric with the grave objectivity of the epic. Macaulay thought that poetry and science were the ends of a see-saw: 'We cannot unite the incompatible advantages of reality and deception, the clear discernment of truth and the exquisite enjoyment of fiction.'[32] Milton often did, as Richardson insisted: 'When the Imagination is Rais'd as much as Possible, let it still know More is Un-conceiv'd; Let the Lark Sing after he is Lost in Air.'[33]

When we see Eve as she

> strews the ground
> With Rose and Odours from the shrub unfum'd,
>
> (V, 348–9)

we know perfectly well what is meant and find no unseemly violence of syntax. But the actual sequence – 'strews the ground with odours' – makes the scents magically visible and physical. So, too, does the superb word-order in these lines:

> So to the Silvan Lodge
> They came, that like Pomona's Arbour smil'd
> With flourets deck't and fragrant smells; but Eve
> Undeckt . . . .   (V, 377–80)

If we want simple sense, then 'deck't' goes only with 'flourets' and not with 'smells' – 'deck't with smells' might be too boldly metaphorical if baldly stated. But the lines do obliquely state it, and the encircling of 'fragrant smells' by 'deck't' and 'undeckt' ensures that the metaphor is not so obliquely presented as to be itself invisible. The imagination once again treats scents as if they were as solid and visible as flowers. And there is also a perfectly intelligible non-metaphorical syntax ('smil'd with fragrant smells and deck't with flourets'). The lines combine the virtues of both poetry and prose. Moreover, they achieve through syntax the mingling of the senses which Keats achieves through diction: 'Nor what soft incense hangs upon the boughs'.

This particular image for the beauty of Paradise can take simpler forms. There is the syntactical stroke of describing 'Cassia, Nard, and Balme' not – as we would expect – as 'odorous flowers', but as 'flouring Odours'. Bentley found the phrase 'Affectation extravagant'; Pearce paltered; and it was

left to Richardson to maintain that the phrase was a fine one.[34]
And the beautifully unexpected substantiality of the scents here
is skilfully introduced by 'field' and 'Groves':

> and now is come
> Into the blissful field, through Groves of Myrrhe,
> And flouring Odours, Cassia, Nard, and Balme.
>
> (V, 291–3)

Or the syntactical imagination can juxtapose 'Rose' and
'Odours' as if they were of equal substantiality, and then apply
to them both a verb that, in its vigour, insists on the substantial:

> fresh Gales and gentle Aires
> Whisper'd it to the Woods, and from thir wings
> Flung Rose, flung Odours from the spicie Shrub.
>
> (VIII, 515–17)

The close parallel there with the first passage quoted above
(V, 348–9) brings out how important to Milton is this image
of Paradise. (The biographical critic would justifiably make at
once for Milton's blindness.) And the poet invests Eve with this
image as Satan fatally finds her:

> Eve separate he spies,
> Veil'd in a Cloud of Fragrance, where she stood,
> Half spi'd .... (IX, 424–6)

The veil and the cloud make the roses' scent beautifully visible
– does 'Half spi'd' even perhaps suggest that the scent was so
thick that it almost hid her? Not really, because I have cut short
the sentence:

> Half spi'd, so thick the Roses bushing round
> About her glowd.

Reasonably, it is not the scent but the roses which hide her.
But the other instances of Milton's seeing a scent, and the
general fluidity of his syntax, persuade me that we are meant
for a moment to believe that 'Half spi'd' follows the 'Fra-

grance', just as it follows 'he spies'. Of course it in fact anticipates the roses, but the deliberate 'flicker of hesitation' which
Dr Davie[35] finds elsewhere in Milton is perhaps being used
here with characteristic subtlety. Like a skilful advocate,
Milton says something which would be impermissibly far-
fetched, and then has it struck from the record. But his skill
has lodged it in our minds or feelings.

Obviously such a device, to offer and then to deny (which
has much in common with the rhetorical figure *occupatio*), is
very common in Milton, above all in the allusions but also in
the syntax. Bentley objected to the line 'The fellows of his
crime, the followers rather': 'This RATHER, this correction of
what he had said before, has something little and low in it. For
if the Word wanted correcting, why was it put down here.'[36]
But Bentley ought to allow that unsaying is not the same as
never having said – and Milton makes fine use of the difference.
It is on this that the poignant aptness of the classical allusions
depends: Mulciber fell, but no – 'Thus they relate, erring.'

The 'flicker of hesitation' which Dr Davie so well defined,
and which he so well illustrated in its effects, is not as uncom-
mon in Milton as might be suggested by Dr Davie's deploring
of the average run of the syntax. Milton uses the slightly surprising compression of a double syntax to carry the weightiest
suggestions. The syntax is not usually double in that it actually
takes two paths – that would defeat narrative and sequence. But
it stands for a moment uncertain which of two paths to take,
and deliberately exploiting the uncertainty. Later, when we
look back, we feel not only the relief of having chosen, but also
a powerful sense of what the other path led to.

> Footfalls echo in the memory
> Down the passage which we did not take
> Towards the door we never opened
> Into the rose-garden. My words echo
> Thus, in your mind.

Milton can combine, through the hesitations of his syntax,

the suggestiveness of vistas with the progressions of ordered narrative.

This is so when Milton tragically exclaims

> O much deceav'd, much failing, hapless Eve,
> Of thy presum'd return! event perverse!
> Thou never from that houre in Paradise
> Foundst either sweet repast, or sound repose . . . .
>
> (IX, 404–7)

At first, one takes 'deceav'd' and 'failing' as absolute in their application to Eve – the poet's imagination is absorbing the full bitterness of the imminent Fall. But then the next line – 'Of thy presum'd return!' – declares that she is *deceived in* the one present circumstance: her presumed return. So the lines are both tragically prophetic and dramatically momentary. And the hesitation, as to whether 'deceav'd' and 'failing' are absolute or particular, is resolved here by our realizing that there are not in fact two paths at all, but only one. For Eve to be wrong about anything (even that she would soon be back) is for her to be wrong about everything. Before the Fall, the distinction of absolute or particular failing does not exist. Once deception and failure have arrived, then they have arrived absolutely. It is the hesitating syntax which makes the point, and resolves itself.

Mr Stein has drawn attention to the delicate balance of present innocence with potential danger when Eve leaves Raphael and Adam:

> With Goddess-like demeanour forth she went;
> Not unattended, for on her as Queen
> A pomp of winning Graces waited still,
> And from about her shot Darts of desire
> Into all Eyes to wish her still in sight.   (VIII, 59–63)

'She leaves', says Mr Stein, 'under circumstances that emphasize (and create the opportunity for emphasizing) at once her genuine charms, her potentially dangerous charms (the "darts of desire"), and her relations (according to the scale of creation) with Adam.'[37]

It is true that the 'Darts of desire' are potentially dangerous.[38] But the point about the delicate balance of danger and innocence could best be made by reference, first, to the rhythm (which emphatically juxtaposes 'shot Darts'), and, second, to the syntax:

> And from about her shot Darts of desire
> Into all Eyes to wish her still in sight.

The balance is in the hesitation. At first, 'desire' seems absolute, and as such potentially dangerous and prophetic of the Fall:

> Carnal desire enflaming, hee on Eve
> Began to cast lascivious Eyes, she him
> As wantonly repaid.　　　　　　　　(IX, 1013–15)

And the hesitation is maintained by the delaying phrase 'into all Eyes' – after which, and only after which, is the 'desire' defined as still innocent: 'to wish her still in sight'. Richardson noticed the ambivalence of the syntax, and hurried to protect Eve's honour: 'This passage must be pointed Thus, as in *Milton's* Editions; as Some have done it, it makes Wild work. Darts of desire but Only to Wish her Stay.'[39]

The potential danger, then, is expressed in the potential syntax. We are shown a path which Adam and Eve might take (and which tragically we know they will take), but they have not yet taken it. Potential danger, but still actual innocence. So the syntax is resolved into innocence, with justice to Eve. But the hesitation about 'desire' is essential to the effect – if it is equivocal, that is because it thereby provides a perfect mirror for the equivocal position of Adam and Eve before the Fall (if they could fall, were they not already in some sense fallen?). The lines admirably fulfil Dr Davie's wishes for poetic syntax: 'a movement of syntax can render, immediately present, the curve of destiny through a life or the path of an energy through the mind.'[40]

How, and how admirably, the lines do so, is clear if we

substitute a more usual word-order, one that does not deliberately delay:

> And from about her shot into all Eyes
> Darts of desire to wish her still in sight.

The innocence of 'desire' is there established too quickly. The subtle effect depended on subtle syntax, and also on the opportunity for legitimate surprise that is offered by the line-endings. Dr Davie finds that the line-endings are poorly used. Just how effective they really are is shown by William Forde's *The True Spirit of Milton's Versification* (1831), which quaintly rearranges the verse into sense-units: 'The *Lines* will now represent the natural division of every sentence into its component Members', so that 'the reader may attend solely to the sense and the harmonious order of the words, without feeling any embarrassment from the contrariety between the linear division, and the meaning of the language'.[41] But it is exactly this 'contrariety' which Milton uses to enforce his meaning, and when this 'embarrassment' disappears, so does the precision and the emphasis. A neat modern example is Mr Whaler's observation that at one point Milton's lines may be slid along into a different iambic pattern, and with very different effect. Thus Milton wrote:

> But wherefore thou alone? wherefore with thee
> Came not all Hell broke loose? is pain to them
> Less pain, less to be fled, or thou then they
> Less hardie to endure? courageous Chief,
> The first in flight from pain, had'st thou alleg'd
> To thy deserted host this cause of flight,
> Thou surely hadst not come sole fugitive.   (IV, 917–23)

Mr Whaler[42] slides the pattern along, and the result is fascinating, not so much numerologically (Mr Whaler's concern) as critically:

> But wherefore thou alone?
> Wherefore with thee came not all Hell broke loose?
> Is pain to them less pain, less to be fled,
> Or thou then they less hardie to endure?

> Courageous Chief, the first in flight from pain,
> Had'st thou alleg'd to thy deserted host
> This cause of flight, thou surely hadst not come
> Sole fugitive.

Milton's lines have become eighteenth-century Miltonics. The surge of the verse has gone, and been replaced by the dullness of three questions that fall neatly at the ends of the lines. The playing of the syntax against the metre has disappeared, and with it has gone the emphatic placing of 'Less pain' and 'Less hardie' at the opening of the lines, and above all the great weight which the last line of the speech received by being the only one where the sense-unit met and clinched the metre.

Let me return from the 'hesitations', and their dependence on the skilful use of line-endings, to the point at which it was necessary to explain them: the suggestive mingling of the senses in the harmony of Paradise. An eighteenth-century editor might well have objected to Eve's lines:

> Not distant far from thence a murmuring sound
> Of waters issu'd from a Cave and spread
> Into a liquid Plain, then stood unmov'd
> Pure as th' expanse of Heav'n . . .   (IV, 453–6)

We all know what this means, but it does say that the '*sound* . . . spread into a liquid Plain . . . .' Is this just carelessness? Or is there a reason why Milton treats the water as sound?

First, we must remember Milton's recurring insistence that sound is a movement of the air, that an air is the air. We sense how all the different movements of the air, including sounds, blend together in Paradise:

> for his sleep
> Was Aerie light, from pure digestion bred,
> And temperat vapors bland, which th'only sound
> Of leaves and fuming rills, Aurora's fan,
> Lightly dispers'd, and the shrill Matin Song
> Of Birds on every bough.   (V, 3–8)

'Sound' as 'air', then, in the lines of Eve under discussion. But what is there in the context that explains the further mingling of the air with water?

Eve awakes, and gazes like Narcissus into the lake, which is 'pure as th' expanse of Heav'n',

> the cleer
> Smooth Lake, that to me seemd another Skie.
>
> (IV, 458–9)

Upon this mirroring of the airy sky in the lake depends the whole important episode. But perhaps 'mirroring' judges the situation more knowledgeably than Eve could – say rather, indistinguishability: 'Uncertain which, in Ocean or in Air' (III, 76). Milton insists on the indistinguishable commingling not only by the explicit comparisons, but also by the syntactical mingling in a 'sound . . . spread into a liquid Plain'. It is not entirely accidental that we might talk of the 'fluidity' of such syntax.

That this is Milton's creation rather than mine is made clear if we notice how he does not rely upon the syntax and the explicit comparisons alone, but uses for the water the diction with which he elsewhere presents the creation of the airy sky – 'liquid', 'pure', and 'expanse':

> and God made
> The Firmament, expanse of liquid, pure,
> Transparent, Elemental Air.   (VII, 263–5)[43]

Of course 'the liquid air' is a commonplace,[44] but it is one of great use and importance when Eve as it were regards herself as Narcissus – one of the most poignantly significant of her appearances before the Fall. Milton brings this commonplace to life by blurring the distinction between air and water in his syntax.

Bentley was shocked by the lines which I have just quoted from the opening of Book V, describing Adam waking to the vapours and sounds of Paradise. He took exception to the phrase 'th'only sound of leaves and fuming rills': 'What's that which follows, *The sound of fuming Rills?*' Newton followed Pearce and said sensibly: 'They do not make a noise as *fuming*, but only as *rills*.'[45] True enough. But it is not necessary to believe that Milton was unaware of the strangely lovely suggestion which Bentley noticed.

To handle syntax with such various control is not what one would expect from a poet who was callous to the intrinsic nature of English. The syntax moves between the quiet poles of the power that can launch an 'adventrous Song', and the delicacy that augments the song by tincture and reflection. 'Milton', said Hopkins, 'is the great master of sequence of phrase'; and R. W. Dixon, agreeing, offered an apt image in describing the Miltonic style as 'a deliberate unrolling as if of some vast material'.[46] The more one looks closely at Milton's word-order, the less truth there seems to be in Mr Eliot's remark[47] that 'the syntax is determined by the musical significance, by the auditory imagination, rather than by the attempt to follow actual speech or thought'.

NOTES

1. 1859. *Literary Studies* (1905), II, 217.
2. *The Tatler*, No. 114, 31 December 1709. Cf. William Smith: 'the very Structure of the Words expresses the Intricacy of the Discourse; and the Repetition of some of the Words, with Epithets of slow Pronunciation, shews the Difficulty of making Advancements, in such unfathomable Points' (*Longinus on the Sublime*, 2nd ed., 1742, p. 185).
3. Jonathan Richardson, Father and Son, *Explanatory Notes on 'Paradise Lost'* (1734), p. 81.
4. Thomas Newton, *Paradise Lost* (1749), I, 118.
5. William Benson, *Letters Concerning Poetical Translations* (1739), p. 48.
6. Richardson, p. 410.
7. Richardson, p. 412 (misnumbered 421).
8. *O.E.D.* 3. '*trans*. To express or say with hesitation' – the first example is Pope.
9. Zachary Pearce, *A Review of the Text of Paradise Lost* (1733), p. 58; also pp. 35, 92, 99. And Matthias Mull, a bizarre latter-day Bentley who edited *Paradise Lost* (1884), has three pages listing necessary parentheses.

10. William Empson, *Some Versions of Pastoral* (1935), p. 160.
11. Richardson, p. 367.
12. Pearce, pp. 154–5.
13. *The Book of Hours*, trans. J. B. Leishman.
14. Patrick Hume, *Poetical Works of Milton* (1695), p. 239.
15. F. T. Prince, *The Italian Element in Milton's Verse* (1954), p. 86.
16. Empson, p. 161.
17. Richard Bentley, *Paradise Lost* (1732), p. 270.
18. Newton, II, 132.
19. Empson, p. 161.
20. Pearce, pp. 154–5.
21. Empson, p. 163.
22. *Milton's God* (1961), p. 150 [above, p. 159].
23. *A Preface to 'Paradise Lost'* (1942), pp. 45–6.
24. Richardson, p. 63.
25. Bentley, p. 172.
26. Pearce, p. 185.
27. *A Preface,* p. 42. J. H. Hanford has two particularly interesting pages on the beauty of Milton's ambiguous syntax in *A Milton Handbook* (4th ed., 1946, pp. 300–301). And John Wain, discussing Hopkins, has deftly pointed out the suggestiveness of a verb 'that radiates both ways' (*Proceedings of the British Academy*, 1959, XLV, 194).
28. IV, 471; IX, 457–8; IV, 479.
29. This is the pattern at II, 62, 319, 359; V, 220, 467; VII, 373; XI, 251.
30. Mrs I. G. MacCaffrey writes interestingly on this in chs. III and IV of *Paradise Lost as 'Myth'* (1959). Jackson I. Cope goes through all the examples in ch. IV of *The Metaphoric Structure of Paradise Lost* (1962).
31. I, 756, 666, 461–3.
32. T. B. Macaulay, *Literary and Historical Essays* (1934), pp. 7–8.
33. Richardson, p. 41.
34. Bentley, p. 157; Pearce, p. 169; and Richardson, p. 218.
35. 'Syntax and Music in *Paradise Lost*', in *The Living Milton*, ed. Frank Kermode (1960).
36. Bentley, p. 27.
37. *Answerable Style* (1953), p. 91.
38. Adam was 'here onely weake / Against the charm of Beauties powerful glance' (VIII, 532–3).
39. Richardson, p. 356.
40. *Articulate Energy* (1955), p. 157.
41. *The True Spirit of Milton's Versification* (1831), pp. xxix, xxxiii.
42. *Counterpoint and Symbol* (1956), pp. 20–21.
43. Cf. 'Nor in thir liquid texture mortal wound
    Receive, no more then can the fluid Aire'. (VI, 348–9)

44. John Arthos quotes thirty-eight examples from Empedocles to Genest
(*The Language of Natural Description in 18th Century Poetry*, 1949, pp.
237–40).
45. Bentley, p. 146; Newton, I, 311.
46. Letters of 13 June and 25 September 1878.
47. *On Poetry and Poets* (1957), p. 142.

B. Rajan

THE STYLE OF *PARADISE LOST**

THE term 'world-picture' must be used with caution in referring to *Paradise Lost*. Its implications are static and what the
poem conveys is not simply a system but a process, an account
of reality that is sufficiently comprehensive for every fact to find
its location and valuation within it. If this is understood and if
we speak of the 'order' of *Paradise Lost* as part of this 'process'
we can also speak of the cosmography of the poem as the diagram of that 'order'. Like any diagram in such a context it is
moral and symbolic as well as spatial. The location of hell outside the created universe for example, is not simply because
'Heaven and Earth may be suppos'd as yet not made, certainly
not yet accurst' but also because the placing of the world between Heaven and Hell makes it the middle ground as well as
the inevitable battleground in the struggle between the forces
of good and evil. Man is the central link in the Scale of Nature;
he is also at the spatial centre of the cosmos and at the dramatic centre of the action. The cosmography moreover places
Hell at the maximum distance from Heaven and the distance is
clearly spiritual as well as spatial; 'darkness visible' conveys a
moral reality within a physical paradox. Even in speaking of
Hell as a place of 'utter darkness', Milton probably uses the
adjective in the double sense of 'utter' and 'outer' and so inte-
grates in a single word the different levels on which the cosmography functions.

The created universe bespeaks the power, providence and
protection of the divine. It is demarcated from chaos by God's
golden compasses and hung from heaven by a golden chain.
When evil enters its all but hermetically sealed perfection, Sin
and Death build a causeway connecting the world to Hell. The

* From the 'Introduction' to *'Paradise Lost'*, *Books I and II* (1964), pp.
xix–xxxviii. Some minor changes have been made by the author.

physical links have of course a symbolic function; both ways lie open and it is for man to choose.

The outer shell of the universe separates it from 'chaos and th' inroad of darkness old'. On its 'backside' is Limbo the 'Paradise of Fools' and the home of the 'unaccomplisht works of Natures hand'. Within it is the Primum Mobile which imparted motion to the spheres within, either directly or (according to some accounts) in conjunction with the opposite movement of the sphere of the fixed stars. Then follows the crystalline sphere added by Arabian commentators upon Ptolemy, in order to account for the apparent retrogradation of the fixed stars. Its existence was denied among others by Marlowe and Raleigh. Within the crystalline sphere are the sphere of the fixed stars, separate spheres for the seven planets (Saturn, Jupiter, Mars, the Sun, Venus, Mercury and the Moon), a sphere of fire, a sphere of air (divided into upper, lower and middle regions) and finally the earth.

Within the outer shell the cosmos is Ptolemaic; outside it, it can only be called Miltonic. It is homocentric rather than geocentric (VIII, 98–9). The celestial bodies serve man and so declare his dignity; but the complexity of their motions and the vastness of the space in which they move, declare man's limitations against the background of God's glory. The book of nature is an aesthetic and a moral rather than a scientific treatise. When celestial motions are interpreted mathematically (VIII, 75 ff.) they lead to 'quaint opinions' and to laborious attempts to save appearances 'With centric and eccentric scribbled o'er'. When they are understood imaginatively (V, 618–27) they resemble the mystical dance of the angels. Significantly the dialogue on astronomy comes to life most vividly in the metaphors of dancing (VIII, 122 ff.; VIII, 160 ff.). The world is created perfect but it is a perfection fulfilled in motion rather than one memorialized in stillness.

It is tempting to see the movement of *Paradise Lost* in terms of conflict between massed polarities, Christ and Satan on the dramatic level, darkness and light on the physical, order and disorder on the metaphysical, good and evil on the moral, reason and passion on the psychological, chaos and creation on the cosmic, and being and non-being on the ontological. One must recognize however, that these oppositions are only an abstract recognition of what the epic has achieved and created and that in the poem itself there are no compasses to mark these spheres out and to prescribe their music. On the contrary the richness of the poetry depends on the ease with which it can move from one sphere to another and on the extent to which it can take for granted the presence of the whole order behind the effect of any detail. Hell for example, is a state of mind as well as a place. Its 'darkness visible' is moral and spiritual and is in calculated contrast to the 'holy light' which in the invocation to Book III is identified with God and with the force of creation. Similarly, Hell's 'silent valley' where 'heroic deeds' are sung and its 'hill' where philosophy is discussed belong to an inward rather than a physical geography. On the other hand, Satan's declaration of evil as Hell's controlling principle (I, 159–65), is objectified in a physical world 'Where all life dies, death lives and Nature breeds/Perverse, all monstrous, all prodigious things.' The chaos through which Satan journeys is reflected in the 'hateful siege/Of contraries' by which his mind is tormented (IX, 121–2), while his state of mind in turn, finds embodiment in his 'outward lustre' and in the 'original brightness' which his form is losing. Sin begins in Satan's thoughts and is then exteriorized; Paradise can be external but the 'happier' Paradise is restored within man.

To say that any detail in *Paradise Lost* requires all that has preceded it as its context is eventually only to say that *Paradise Lost* succeeds in being a poem. If the remark is considerably more than a platitude it is because the dimensions of *Paradise Lost* obscure its unity or tempt one to seek its character in the local achievements of language rather than in the poem's total structure and growth. In fact as will be suggested later, the style of *Paradise Lost* enacts its unity but it is not the only integrative force in the poem and may not even be the most important.

The totality which is shaped by *Paradise Lost* is, as has already been made clear, invented as well as inherited. It is indeed a striking example of tradition transformed by the individual talent or rather reorganized so as to reveal its nature. Yet Milton's originality should not blind us to the fact that a certain awareness of tradition, a certain 'given' structure of values and responses are taken for granted by the movement of the poem. Though *Paradise Lost* to a surprising extent, creates or rather revalidates its own terms, it is not a poem which can be read without commitments and one necessary assumption is that Satan is evil. In fact Satan himself declares his commitment to evil (I, 156–62) in a passage of singular poetic force, but both this and other indications are sometimes set aside as dishonest stage directions which are contrary to the real trend of the poetry. The idea that Milton's imagination was busy writing a certain kind of poem, while his intellect looked apprehensively over the result and from time to time advised the reader how to misread it, is of course, based on a theory of composition that only needs to be stated to be recognized as farcical. However the idea still controls popular and even scholarly conceptions of Satan, such as the view that Satan's degeneration in the later books is a mere moral assertion which Milton fails to make poetically valid and that it is in fact, inconsistent with the poetic effect of the first books. For these reasons it is not irrelevant to look at Satan's first speech and to see how far the facts support the theory of his 'sublimity' for which the evidence here ought surely to be at its strongest.

Before Satan's first words are spoken the frame in which we are to judge them has been defined. Satan has been charged with guile, envy and revenge with 'obdurat pride and stedfast hate' and with aspiring to 'set himself in Glory above his Peers' and seeking to equal 'the most High'. The 'Ethereal skie' from which he was 'Hurld headlong' has been contrasted with the 'bottomless perdition' which is now his element. Lost happiness has been set against lasting pain; the word-play dramatizes the nature of the reality. The reference in the

Argument to the 'utter darkness' of hell which is 'fitliest call'd *chaos*' has set in motion the traditional association of light with order and of darkness with anarchy; 'darkness visible' has added to these associations the recognition of evil as the shaping and illuminating principle of Hell. Hell we are also told, is 'As farr remov'd from God and light of Heav'n/As from the Centre thrice to th' utmost Pole' and the spiritual spatial distance is thus established in terms of the dominant antitheses of the poem. As Satan begins to speak we must remember that he has already been characterized as 'Th' infernal Serpent' and 'th' Arch-Enemy' and that Bëëlzebub his partner, has been described as 'One next himself in power, and next in crime'; the coupling should remind the alert reader that the purpose of power is not crime but justice.

This is hardly the best of frameworks for 'sublimity' and in fact what Satan says strengthens rather than undermines the framework. When he refers to his assault upon God as a 'Glorious Enterprize' we are surely to remember that it has already been referred to as 'impious Warr in Heav'n and Battel proud'. When he speaks of the 'happy Realms of Light' he fundamentally misconceives the nature of happiness, seeing God's rule as tyranny and finding in tyranny 'th' excess of joy'. His statement that he 'shook' the throne of God in 'dubious Battle' has already been valued in the description of his downfall. His 'High disdain, from sense of injur'd merit' is by no means the noblest of motivations and his scorning of repentance ought to be regarded as further evidence of his 'obdurat pride'. As for 'th' unconquerable Will, / And study of revenge, immortal hate', these qualities establish ironically the content of Satanic glory, a glory that is more specifically valued in 570–72 (where it is coupled with pride and the sinner's hardened heart), and in II, 427–9, where 'transcendent glory' becomes a restoration, diabolically perverted, of the 'transcendent brightness' that Satan and Bëëlzebub once possessed. In this context Satan's 'fixt mind' is an obsessed mind; the change in his 'outward lustre' is the proof of an inner abandonment of goodness and indeed his first words to Bëëlzebub ('If thou beest he; But O how fall'n! how chang'd') tie together the physical and the moral transformation. Even Satan's scornful reference to God's 'thunder' as embodying only superior force (the point is made again in 257–8) is taken up dramatically in 600–602 where the 'scars of Thunder' on Satan's face become a spiritual as well as a heroic disfigurement.

The conclusions which have emerged from this analysis are latent in the other speeches of Satan and his followers and are also carried forward by the imagery. The comparison of the angels to a plague of locusts and a barbarian invasion, to fallen leaves, scattered sedge and to trees blasted by lightning, create an awareness of evil both as the scourge of God and as a decaying of life, destined eventually for the death which it inflicts. The comparison of Satan to Briareos, Typhon and Leviathan clothes him in associations of rebellion, deception and monstrosity. When he is described as a 'great Sultan', the tyranny of which he accuses God surrounds him and we are prepared for his subsequent exaltation to the 'bad eminence' of his 'throne of royal state'. When he is likened to a tower, it is a tower of pride, meant to be contrasted (as Professor Cope points out) with the traditional image of Christ as a tower of safety and salvation.

What has been said above is part, and an important part of the truth; but it is not the whole truth as any sensitive reader of *Paradise Lost* must recognize. The surface of grandeur is preserved, whatever may be the qualifications in depth. The angels are not simply a plague of locusts but a disciplined army marching to the Dorian mode. Their courage may have 'fainted' but it revives into 'Deliberat valour'. Their glory may have 'wither'd' but their loyalty is unshaken. They sing of their own 'Heroic deeds' with 'notes Angelical'. They are armed with 'stubborn patience' though the patience is described as 'pleasing sorcerie', and is valued in retrospect by the 'better fortitude' which Michael teaches Adam. Their 'firm concord' is contrasted with human disagreements and we are reminded explicitly that 'Spirits damnd' do not lose all their virtue. The infernal army is made to dwarf the accumulated armies of legend and history. Pandemonium may be a mockery of creation but it is a mockery which surpasses Babylon and Alcairo.

The basic complexities of Milton's approach are focussed in the description of Satan about to address his troops to which reference has already been made:

> Dark'nd so, yet shon
> Above them all th' Arch-Angel: but his face
> Deep scarrs of Thunder had intrencht, and care
> Sat on his faded cheek, but under Browes
> Of dauntless courage, and considerat Pride
> Waiting revenge: cruel his eye, but cast
> Signs of remorse and passion to behold
> The fellows of his crime, the followers rather . . . .

Here Satan's 'Deep scarrs of Thunder' are contrasted with the lustre (however darkened) of his person and eminence. 'Care' sitting on his 'faded cheek' suggests the elder statesman and the responsibilities of high office but the evocation is surely more than ironic. The tone of the description looks forward to the later description of Bëëlzebub 'Majestick though in ruin' and 'faded', by developing the associations of 'Dark'nd', deepens the impression of glory in decline. Satan's 'dauntless courage' is given due weight; but it is qualified by its connexion with pride and cruelty. Cruelty in its turn is qualified by remorse but remorse is significantly coupled to 'passion' and one is meant to remember that the usurpation of reason by the passions is a characteristic of Satan's and Adam's fall. The success of the passage lies in its preserving the impact of grandeur while obliging us to remain conscious of how that impact ought to be valued. This is in fact the quality of Milton's achievement in the first two books; whether valuation takes place on the surface as in this example, or in depth, through the poem's structure and the perspective it creates, the process of valuation is unremitting and yet does not impair the effect of what it judges; the grand and the heroic are 'placed' rather than undermined.

On this basis the argument can be carried a stage further. In the universe of Hell, God's rule is felt in terms of superior force, 'Whether upheld by Strength or Chance or Fate'. God is the thunderer, the torturer, the great enemy, the supreme foe, the conqueror, the potent victor, and in Mammon's sarcasm 'Heavn's all ruling Sire'. The epithets are many but the implication is one: God is a dictator and the fallen angels the only true democrats. The reader is of course not expected to accept these illusions at their face value, but rather while seeing them as illusions, to be aware also of the logic which they generate. If the divine rule is experienced as tyranny and worse still as omnipotent tyranny the only possible response is 'th' unconquerable will'. Within the limited circle of their vision the inhabitants of Hell are heroic and tragic and if Hell makes so profound an impression on us it is because it is consistent on its own terms. In addition, the terms are part of ourselves. Since we are fallen, we live partially in Hell and our response to it therefore, must be one of recognition as well as of animosity. But living in it, we must also learn to judge it; the growth of the poem is the growth of that learning.

Thus to understand Satan is to understand the limitations of heroism and to recognize that the war between good and evil is necessarily unlike any other war. In bringing about this understanding Milton's methods are original enough to elude conventional labels. When Professor Summers speaks of the first two books of *Paradise Lost* as one of the most successful examples of the 'serious mock-heroic' in English literature, both the words he chooses and the slight uneasiness with which one accepts them are evidence of the extent to which *Paradise Lost* resists accepted classifications and indeed creates a classification of its own. Too educated an acquaintance with Milton's sources can sometimes blind us to this fact by persuading us to read the inherited content in the inherited manner. What one is required to recognize instead is not simply the balance of

precedent and originality, but originality underlined by the
author's use of precedent, by the manner in which the literary
past is taken into and transformed by the poem's aesthetic
design. It has been argued for example that the infernal council
in Book II shows in its details the possible influence of no less
than eight Renaissance poems: Mantuan's *Georgius*, Vida's
Christiados, Tasso's *Gerusalemme Liberata,* Valvasone's *L'Ange-*
leida, Marini's *La Strage degli Innocenti*, Phineas Fletcher's
Locustae Vel Pietas Jesuitica and *The Locusts or Appollyonists,* and
Cowley's *Davideis*. One need not deny that resemblances of detail exist but one ought to add that they are limited to details;
the whole which Milton creates is securely his own. There is
about the debate a prearranged quality lacking in other versions, which connects it immediately to the reality of the con-
ference room. The participants too are acutely differentiated so
that their speeches stand neatly on platforms of party and
principle. Moloch is the militarist, Belial the intellectual and
Mammon combines the spirit of capitalism with something of
the Protestant ethic. Each proposal reveals the characteristic
virtues of its advocate – courage in Moloch, clarity in Belial,
and self-reliance in Mammon's plan for Hell's economic development. But each speech is also embroiled in contradictions.
Moloch begins by proposing to mix God's throne with '*Tar-*
tarean Sulfur' and ends by admitting that the throne is 'in-
accessible'. Belial sees God as 'Not more Almighty to resist our
might/Then wise to frustrate all our plots and wiles'. Nevertheless he hopes that a policy of 'not offending' will bring about
the abatement of God's wrath. One is expected to apply to
Belial's arguments, not only his own remarks in II, 160–61, but
also the stark and traditional truth of I, 65–7, against which all
delusions of escape must founder. As for Mammon, his contribution to the debate is to debase into materialistic terms,
Satan's proposition that the mind is its own place and can
make a Heaven of Hell. His programme receives angelic
applause but the reader is expected not to overlook the perversity of 'as hee our Darkness, cannot wee his Light/Imitate

when we please.' In addition the optimism of 'This Desart soile/Wants not her hidd'n lustre' needs to be set against II, 618–25, with its overwhelming sense of Hell's sterile perversity. Hell whatever it is, is also a place of self-deception. This is one of the facts connecting Hell to humanity but it obliges us not to identify ourselves with Hell, but rather in seeing it, to see ourselves more clearly.

To some extent the stratagems of the fallen angels can be said to be futile but the critic appraising them must beware of slipping into fallacies. I would be mistaken to call the fallen angels absurd when the human race is the victim of their absurdity. It would also be insufficient to call them tragic since the tragedy of damnation takes root in an area of choice and ultimate evil has no choice but itself. Repentance is a possibility excluded from Hell's concave and Satan is not Dr Faustus but something inexorably grimmer. Indeed the quality of the debate depends on its being consistent, plausible and even realistic on its own terms while at the same time calling on the reader to recognize the extent to which those terms are self-defeating. It is no accident that the debate opens with a misstatement of the *felix culpa* by Satan and ends with a reminder of the true nature of the paradox after Bëëlzebub's decisive intervention. 'Thir spite still serves/His glory to augment' is the poem's restorative judgement and the implicit contempt in 'spite', the shrinkage of the word by its juxtaposition with 'glory', places the plan in its true setting. At the same time, the consequence of that 'spite' is 'to confound the race / Of mankind in one root and Earth with Hell / To mingle and involve' so that the reader is not simply invited but obliged to respond to the event in two perspectives. None of these subtleties can be found in Milton's sources and it is these subtleties which give creative significance to commonplaces which might otherwise have petrified into clichés.

The same cautions apply to Milton's Hell. 'Myself am Hell' besides being existentially more valid than Sartre's proposition that Hell is other people, is part of the tradition of seventeenth-century thinking. But Milton gives life to the view that Hell is a state of mind as well as a place by his accurate fitting of the mind to the place. The freedom with which the poetry moves from the exterior to the inner landscape obliges us to give each word in it a continuous extension of significance. Other poets have elaborated conventionally on the torments of Hell but not everyone has been able to give their descriptions an inner as well as an architectural meaning.

Hell's concave encloses its 'nether Empire', the world of an ultimate and permanent opposition, if one may use the word 'permanent' within the permissive limits of God's providence. It is a life-negating world but still a world; Chaos which lies outside Hell, is not so much superhuman as pre-human. Because it is without form it is peopled by abstractions, while Hell is alive with forces which man can relate to his nature. On the boundary between Hell and Chaos are two creatures who do not belong completely to either kingdom. It is perhaps more than a nicety that the poetic manner in which they are approached is also intermediate, reflecting as it were, their spatial-symbolic position. Sin and Death have the customary Miltonic ancestry – they are compounded out of biblical texts, patristic commentary, classical myth and contemporary poetry. In the last analysis however, they are shockingly unlike any of their possible parents. Milton's originality here is inescapable but it is also disconcerting enough to make one ask whether the originality is more than the poem can accommodate. The answer has to start from the basis that what seems surprising is in reality logical. That Satan, Sin and Death should make up an infernal Trinity is a natural consequence of the correspondences and contrasts that dominate the poem and establish its structural irony; and that Milton thought this particular contrast important enough to drive it virtually to the edge of blasphemy shows how vital a part this 'structure' is intended to play in controlling and shaping our response to the poem. In the preface to *Samson Agonistes* Milton deplores 'the Poets error of intermixing Comic Stuff with Tragic sadness and gravity'; yet the truth is that the closest approach to his treatment of Sin and Death is in those Elizabethan dramas where the sub-plot distorts and comments upon the main plot. Moreover this is not the only link with the drama. Satan's confrontation of Sin and Death is a recognition scene to end all recognition scenes and the recognition even makes possible a *peripeteia* of sorts. This unexpected use of Aristotle's precepts is in keeping with the quality of the episode. To say this is not to argue that the 'stuff' of Sin and Death is essentially comic. Perhaps it is best to describe the total effect as an alliance of grim levity and horrifying seriousness. The result is not of course metaphysical wit but it has its own individual and highly charged complexity.

The discussion of Milton's 'style' has been left to the last because style, whatever else it is, is not the man but the poem. Some may feel that this means that the poem can only be approached through its language, but the fact is that the language of *Paradise Lost* works in conjunction with its structure and it is the union of the two which we ought to be discussing when we use that misleading label 'style'. Of this 'style' we still lack a satisfactory description. This may seem strange after the long course of the Milton controversy, which should at least have shown us where to agree to disagree; but in reading criticism of Milton one is conscious of as much disagreement about what the facts are, as of disagreement about how to judge the facts. Thus one notes Dr Leavis's view that there is 'no pressure' in Milton's verse, 'no suggestion of any complex and varying currents of feeling and sensation; the words have little substance or muscular quality.' As against this, Richardson observes (in a passage which Coleridge thought well enough of to make his own) that 'A reader of Milton must be always on duty; he is surrounded with sense; it rises in every line, every word is to the purpose. There are no lazy intervals: all has been considered, and demands and merits observation . . . Milton's words are all substance and weight'. Mr Eliot complains that Milton's syntax is determined 'by the musical significance, by the auditory imagination, rather than by the attempt to follow actual speech or thought'. This objection might be more telling if Mr Eliot had not elsewhere defined the auditory imagination (in taxing Arnold with the lack of it) as 'the feeling for syllable and rhythm, penetrating far below the conscious levels of thought and feeling, invigorating every word; sinking to the most primitive and forgotten, returning to the origin and bringing something back, seeking the beginning and the end'. An excess of these abilities hardly strikes one as a grave defect but that does not prevent Mr Eliot from concluding that there is a fundamental disunity of effect in *Paradise Lost* and that to extract everything possible from the poem, 'it would seem necessary to read it in two different ways, first solely for the sound, and second for the sense.' Against this, let us set Hazlitt's conclusion that, Shakespeare apart, 'there are more perfect examples in Milton of musical expression, i.e. of an adaptation of the sound and movement of the verse to the meaning of the passage, than in all our other writers, whether of rhyme or blank verse, put together. . . . The sound of his lines is moulded into the expression of the sentiment, almost of the very image.' Helen Darbishire in her meticulous edition of Milton's poems reaches the same conclusion: 'To Milton . . . every sound and syllable counted, every pause or silence between sounds. Never has poet known better than he that sound expresses sense.'

Differences regarding the facts arise even when one is discussing the stuff of Milton's language. Richardson and Addison for instance, note and commend Milton's power of assimilating Greek, Latin and Hebraic elements into English. But Johnson accuses Milton (as Ben Jonson accused Spenser) of writing no language but 'a *Babylonish Dialect*, in itself harsh and barbarous'. Dr Leavis develops Johnson's view of the facts: 'the mind that invented Milton's Grand Style had renounced the English language.' But Professor F. T. Prince's view is altogether different: 'Milton's diction and verse made an obvious effort to emulate certain features of Greek, Latin and Italian poetry; but he succeeded in this emulation only because he had an incomparable instinct for English.'

We have therefore not quite reached the stage of simplicity which Professor C. S. Lewis implies when he says: 'Dr Leavis does not differ from me about the properties of Milton's epic verse. He describes them very accurately – and understands them better, in my opinion, than Dr Pearsall Smith. It is not that he and I see different things when we look at *Paradise Lost*. He sees and hates the very same that I see and love.' Similarly Mr Bergonzi admits that the objections of Dr Leavis and his followers are 'unanswerable within the terms of reference in which they are made'. He then goes on to suggest that the terms of reference themselves are insufficient. Mr Bergonzi's view ignores the testimony of a number of critics who have found the verse of *Paradise Lost* alive with complexity, irony, ambiguity, paradox and the other qualities which make poetry respectable in our time. The present editor in the notes* has impartially added to the evidence though he does not agree with the conclusions which are drawn from it.

It is evident that some confusion remains regarding the facts of Milton's verse and that no fully acceptable description of it exists. Analyses (sometimes statistical) of its mechanics are frequent, but these are no substitute for the living body and are possibly not even a substitute for its skeleton. A just description of the verse is obviously beyond the compass of this essay but some suggestions will be made in what it is hoped, is not the wrong direction. At the outset it is well to remember Aristotle's view that the 'perfection of Diction is for it to be at once clear and not mean'. Diction becomes 'distinguished and non-prosaic by the use of unfamiliar terms, i.e. strange words, metaphors, lengthened forms, and everything which deviates from the ordinary modes of speech'. On the other hand the 'ordinary words' in diction 'will secure the requisite clearness'. In the epic form, which is characterized by its grandeur, the metre, which is 'the gravest and weightiest of metres', is also 'more tolerant than the rest of strange words and metaphors, that

* [The reference is to Professor Rajan's edition of *Paradise Lost* for which the present essay serves as general introduction. – Ed.]

also being a point in which the narrative form of poetry goes beyond all others'. Aristotle's precepts are fully endorsed by Addison: 'It is requisite that the language of an heroic poem should be both perspicuous and sublime. In proportion as either of these two qualities are wanting the language is imperfect.' In the quest for sublimity 'a poet should take particular care to guard himself against idiomatic ways of speaking' and must 'deviate from the common forms and ordinary phrases of speech.'

These quotations are not made to seek approval for Aristotle's somewhat mechanistic view of poetic diction but rather to suggest that sublimity and a certain deliberate 'distancing' from the ordinary, are controlling qualities of Milton's style. The language of *Paradise Lost* of course can only be justified by what it does and if the style is what it is, it is not because Aristotle says so but because the poem requires these specific characteristics in order to bring itself into being. When one considers the facts that Milton's epic endeavours to bring into poetic life it should be evident that no 'natural' language can express a range of reality that is beyond and prior to nature, particularly in a form that is not reflective but objective. The very nature of the aesthetic problem calls for a language that is held away from and yet connected to nature, a language that is artificial if one uses the word as it should be used, in an analytical, not a pejorative sense. When one considers further the design of *Paradise Lost*, its interconnections and contrasts, its rhythm of light out of darkness and good out of evil, it should become clear that the style which realizes these attributes, must be charged with momentum and propulsive power. The 'enormous onward pressure' which Professor C. S. Lewis finds characteristic of the language is thus one of the ways in which the poem becomes alive. The suspension, retardation and controlled advance of the verse, the play of the paragraph against the metre, manifestly purposeful yet not immediately obvious, recreate and repeat the poem's design in its texture. The language enacts the reality it expresses.

Paradise Lost has not one style but several, as Pope was among the first to recognize. There is at the simplest level of discrimination, an infernal style, a celestial style, and styles for Paradise before and after the fall. But the infernal style itself differs both mechanically and actually, in the heroic preparations of the first book, in the 'great consult' in Pandemonium and in Satan's encounter with Sin and Death. The other styles reveal similar and substantial differences of application. In these circumstances it may seem irrelevant to talk of the poem's style at all, but the word though deceptive, is not wholly beside the point. With all its variations, the language of the poem has a basic homogeneity and in fact one of the pleasures of reading *Paradise Lost* is to discover the wide differences the language can accommodate, without imperilling its unitive power. In this sense also the poem makes alive a basic quality of the reality which it celebrates.

Sublimity is a quality usually conceded to *Paradise Lost*, though it is argued that the sublimity is monolithic, that its price is petrification and that the style marches on irrespective of what is inside it. But perspicuity is not ordinarily associated with the poem, the general impression being that its syntax, its erudition and its latinized usages combine to invest it with a pervasive obscurity. Mr Eliot is typical in observing that 'the complication of a Miltonic sentence is an active complication, a complication deliberately introduced into what was a previously simplified and abstract thought.' Although this is from the 1936 essay we also find Mr Eliot in his 1947 recantation, still proclaiming that Milton's style is personal rather than classic, that its elevation is not the elevation of a common style, that in Milton 'there is always the maximal never the minimal, alteration of ordinary language' and that as a poet, Milton is 'probably the greatest of all eccentrics'. Similarly, Dr Leavis observes: 'So complete, and so mechanically habitual, is Milton's departure from the English order, structure and accentuation that he often produces passages that have to be read through several times before one can see how they go, though the

Miltonic mind has nothing to offer that could justify obscurity –
no obscurity was intended: it is merely that Milton has forgotten the English language.' Quite apart from these contemporary
strictures, there is the fact that Renaissance theorists were not
wholly behind Aristotle's requirement of clarity in epic diction. Mr Prince notes for example that 'all the devices of language and versification described by Tasso are intended to produce
a certain difficulty, even an obscurity, in the sense, and an
equivalent difficulty, even a roughness in the sound.' Milton
mentions Tasso in the same breath with Homer and Virgil as a
poet and in the same breath with Aristotle and Castelvetro as a
critic. One cannot easily discount the likelihood that his own
use of language was influenced vitally by Tasso's practices.

Fortunately all generalizations about *Paradise Lost* (including
those that offer themselves as truisms) have to encounter and
survive the text. The following lines from the Ninth Book are
quoted not only because the syntax is uniformly unorthodox,
but also because the unorthodoxy is maintained at a crisis in the
action, in other words, under conditions of potentially maximum irrelevance:

> From his slack hand the Garland wreath'd for *Eve*
> Down dropd, and all the faded Roses shed:
> Speechless he stood and pale, till thus at length
> First to himself he inward silence broke.

It should not be necessary to point out how the first inversion
sets in motion the succession of linked *a*'s that makes 'slack' a
reality in the sound and pace of the verse, or how the wreathing
of the *e* sound in 'wreath'd for *Eve*' is made more vivid by the
placing of '*Eve*' at the climax of the line. The plummeting force
of 'Down dropd' is created both by the inversion and by its
dramatic positioning (which the previous inversion has made
possible). These departures from the normal word-order indicate how the syntax is being manoeuvred to create a pattern of
impact rather than a logical or grammatical sequence. In this
context 'all the faded Roses shed' is surprising only in analysis.

Within the poetry itself, it spreads out of the numbness of
'Down dropd', so that Adam's paralysis seems to be measured
by the manner in which it passes into nature, withering the roses
with the same shock that withers him. The image succeeds precisely by not calling attention to itself, by being shaped into the
situation, into the inert downward movement. The next inversion places 'Speechless' at the beginning of the line; both the
stressed position and its anchoring by 'stood' (the alliteration is
of course purposive) charge the word with the surrounding
sense of deadness. We are made aware that Adam's speechless-
ness is not ordinary consternation but the mental surface of his
'inward silence'. The separation of 'speechless' and 'pale' by
'stood' (a favourite Miltonic device) is similarly functional; both
in the syntax and in the reality being enacted, the inner condition is precedent and decisive. 'Pale' we must also remember,
was a stronger word to Milton's contemporaries than it is to us.
The suggestion here is of the pallor of death. One recalls the
'shuddring horror pale' of the fallen angels and the 'pale and
dreadful' light of their damnation. In this context, 'till thus at
length' is creatively ambiguous; the grammatical coupling
with 'he inward silence broke' is deliberately weakened by the
inversion of the fourth line and this enables the emotional
link with 'Speechless he stood' to become active in the total
movement. 'First to himself' delays and defines the climax.
Adam is not soliloquizing. Rather, he is seeking to achieve a
response out of the momentary paralysis of his being, to create
out of inward silence a ground for interior debate. The movement and tension of the poetry, charged with meaning beneath
the lucid surface shape and intensify this reality. Diction, syntax, sound and imagery contribute purposefully to the poetic
result.

This analysis has been pursued in some detail to indicate that
the poetry of *Paradise Lost* can bear and will respond to a far
greater pressure of interpretation than it normally receives. It
also suggests that 'the complication of a Miltonic sentence' is a
creative rather than an 'active complication' if indeed it is a

complication at all; the true aim seems to be the playing of metrical against grammatical forces to form and embolden the emotional line. This conclusion is not limited to the 'simpler' kind of writing that has been analysed; the following lines present a characteristically different surface but are modelled by essentially similar forces. The quotation is from one of those passages in the Third Book where God the Father turns a school divine, though according to some of our better scholars, he speaks more like a seventeenth-century rhetorician, an ideal student of Puttenham and Peacham.

> Man disobeying
> Disloyal breaks his fealtie, and sinns
> Against the high Supremacie of Heav'n,
> Affecting God-head and so loosing all,
> To expiate his Treason hath naught left,
> But to destruction sacred and devote,
> He with his whole posteritie must die:
> Die hee or Justice must; unless for him
> Som other able, and as willing, pay
> The rigid satisfaction, death for death.
> Say Heav'nly Powers, where shall we find such love,
> Which of ye will be mortal to redeem,
> Mans mortal crime, and just th' unjust to save?
> Dwels in all Heaven charitie so deare?

One is expected to note such touches as the manner in which 'high Supremacie' recalls I, 132, tying the human sin to the angelic. Less obvious, but equally part of the underlying network, is the exact premonition in 'But to destruction sacred and devote' of the truth which breaks into Adam's inward silence (IX, 901) as he faces the finality of Eve's sin. The irony of 'Affecting God-head and so loosing all' has a sardonic validity in itself but the punishment is also measured by the presumption and the legal matching of the two is part of the poem's concept of justice. Some may find the use of the images of kingship curious, but Milton's view that the only true monarchy is that of Heaven (XII, 67–71) is not only consistent

but republican. In any case the imagery with its legalistic under-
tone, makes possible the intensification of disobedience into
disloyalty and finally into treason, thus dictating the measured
and monolithic verdict: 'He with his whole posteritie must die.'
One notes how the quasi-rhymes bind the judgement together
and how the crucial words 'He' and 'die' stand dramatically
at the beginning and end of the line. Then comes the concentration, the sudden sweep of emphasis, as these terminal words
are driven and fused together, with the inversion, the emphatic 'hee' and the brief almost ferocious power of the movement, joining to assert the law in its angry finality. Everything
is to the purpose now. The semicolon after 'Die hee or Justice
must' reinforces the compulsive strength of 'must' and once
again the inversion strengthens the impact. At the same time
the strong medial pause coming after an auxiliary verb creates
a sense of expectation, of basic incompleteness; the movement
in its clenched decisiveness dictates the relaxation into the lines
that follow. The body of the verse begins to react to the awareness of a law transformed by charity. Though the language of
'Som other able, and as willing' remains legalistic, the fluent
movement of the verse, the suggestion of infinite love in
'willing' escapes from and redefines the merely legal. In the
next line, the two tendencies are forced into creative collision.
'Death for death' states the law in its sterile absoluteness, an
absoluteness reflected fully in the conclusive, hammer-like
movement. But in 'rigid satisfaction' the organic word plays
against and undermines the mechanical. The legal content of
'satisfaction' engages with 'rigid' and with 'death for death',
locking itself into the circle of crime and punishment. But the
overtones of life and growth in the word point securely to a
higher satisfaction, a reality beyond the exactions of the law.
The line is a fortress which only love can enter but the language in erecting it has also breached it. The relaxation of the
movement is now both logical and organic. One need only
note the way in which the two uses of 'mortal' preserve the
legal equivalence while opening the way into the wider paradox

of 'just th' unjust to save'. In terms of the 'rigid satisfaction' the balance is inequitable but the poetry has established a higher reality. It has created a world in which charity becomes an imaginative fact as well as a theological principle. This is an achievement of peculiar difficulty since sensuous imagery is forbidden by the circumstances, and the animating forces must therefore be those of syntax, and of word-play precisely and imaginatively controlled. Given these limited resources the result is a triumph of considerably more than craftsmanship.

These two widely different passages suggest both the variety of Milton's style and the criteria to which the style is answerable. That the verse will bear considerable scrutiny is evident and in fact the most difficult temptation to reject in modern criticism is that which seeks to establish complexity, irony, ambiguity and paradox as controlling qualities of Milton's writing. It is not merely convenient but reassuring to suggest that there is one right way of using poetic language and that Milton's poetry like all poetry, can be found true to that way. To deny the complexity of *Paradise Lost* would of course be perverse; but that does not mean that complexity should be regarded as a principle shaping the local life of the language. The complexity of Milton's epic is less one of surface than of reverberation. It arises not so much from the immediate context, as from the connexion of that context to other contexts and eventually to the context of the whole poem and of the cosmic order drawn into and recreated within it. Professor Svendsen is right in arguing that 'the basic mode of *Paradise Lost* is ambivalence' and paradox and irony are equally vital in its total effect. But these qualities operate through the poem's structure rather than its texture. The surface is not characteristically complex, and the resources of diction, syntax and imagery cooperate to clarify and intensify, rather than to qualify the main thrust of the poetry. Coleridge understood this when he observed that 'the connexion of the sentences and the position of the words are exquisitely artificial; but the position is rather according to the logic of passion or universal logic than to the logic of grammar.' A more recent critic, Professor Wright, describes Milton's style as 'unusually clear and forceful', while Mrs MacCaffrey begins a perceptive discussion by stating: 'elevation, not breadth is the principal dimension of epic. Unity and elevation demand that there should be a single – even, in a sense, a simple – effect produced in the reader, and this end is not to be accomplished by a style with a verbally complex surface.'

All this is clearly as it should be. If the style is to develop its primary (and symbolic) qualities of sublimity, of propulsive power, of designed and inexorable movement, it can only do so through a deliberate simplicity of surface. The other qualities which matter are not sacrificed and indeed are realized to a far greater extent than in any other poem of this magnitude. They live, however, not so much on the surface, as in the weight of qualification, connexion and commentary which the whole poem places behind every point on its surface. Milton's observation that poetry is more simple, sensuous and passionate than rhetoric is surely not meant as an attempt to confuse us about the predominant qualities of his verse. The style is capable of 'metaphysical' effects or more correctly, it can frequently draw the metaphysical into the heroic; but it remains heroic and not metaphysical. The distinction is important not only in terms of decorum, but as an indication of how to read the poem, of how to respond to its impact and its tactics. The present writer is frankly not appalled by the discovery that there is more than one way of using poetic language or that Milton is Milton because he is not Donne. The open society of poetry ought to have room for the excellences of both.

On *Paradise Regained*

Northrop Frye

THE TYPOLOGY OF *PARADISE REGAINED**

T H E second of three main episodes on the agon of Christ and Satan is presented in *Paradise Regained*. First is the original war in heaven recounted in *Paradise Lost*, and third is the final binding of Satan in the second coming of Christ, prophesied in the Book of Revelation. The defeat of Satan as tempter fulfils the prophecy in Genesis that the seed of Adam shall 'bruise the serpent's head'; the imagery suggests the romance theme of a knight-errant killing a dragon and is one of several such images in the Bible. Besides the serpent in Eden, the Old Testament speaks of a dragon or sea-monster, called 'leviathan' or 'Rahab', who was defeated once at the Creation and is to be destroyed or, in the metaphor of the sea-serpent, hooked and landed on the day of judgement. Isaiah refers both to the previous and to the future victories over this leviathan, and Ezekiel and Isaiah appear to identify him with Egypt as the symbolic land of bondage. In the Book of Revelation this figure becomes a dragon with seven heads and ten horns, whose tail draws a third of the stars from heaven, the basis of Milton's account of Satan's fall; and in the symbolism of the same book the Satan of Job and the Gospels, the serpent of the Eden story, and the leviathan of the prophecies are all identified.

From this is derived the conventional iconology of Christ as a dragon-killer, such as we have in medieval sculptures portraying him with a dragon or basilisk under his feet. In the first book of *The Faerie Queene*, the story of St George and the dragon is used as an allegory of the imitation of Christ by the church. St George's dragon in Spenser is clearly identified with the whole Satan-serpent-leviathan complex in the Bible, and as a result of St George's victory the parents of his lady Una, who

* From *Modern Philology*, LIII (1956), 227–38.

are Adam and Eve, are restored to their inheritance, the Garden of Eden, which is also the unfallen world. Milton's reference in *The Reason of Church Government* to the allegory of St George and 'the king's daughter, the Church' indicates his early absorption of this theme. Michael explains to Adam in *Paradise Lost*, however, that the agon of Christ and Satan will be not a physical but a spiritual and intellectual fight, the cutting weapons used being those of dialectic and the true dragon being a spiritual enemy.

Paradise Regained is clearly Milton's essay in the 'brief epic', mentioned in a famous passage of *The Reason of Church Government*, for which the model is there said to be the Book of Job. We should therefore expect *Paradise Regained* to have a particularly close relation to that book. In the Book of Job the contest of God and Satan takes the form of a wager on Job's virtue, and the scheme of *Paradise Regained* is not greatly different, with Christ occupying the place of Job. Satan soon disappears from the action of Job, however, and when Job's mind is finally enlightened by God, God's speech consists very largely of discourses on two monsters, behemoth and leviathan, the latter of whom, the more important, is finally said to be 'king over all the children of pride'. These monsters seem to represent an order of nature over which Satan is permitted some control, but, in a larger perspective, they are seen to be creatures of God. By pointing these beasts out to Job, God has, so to speak, put them under Job's feet and taken Job into his own protection; thus the Book of Job presents, in terms of this symbolism, a dialectical victory over both Satan and leviathan.

In the Incarnation the precise point of the agon of Christ and Satan is more usually located between Christ's death and his resurrection. It is then that he descends to hell, harrows hell, and achieves his final victory over hell and death. In medieval paintings of the harrowing of hell, hell is usually represented as leviathan, a huge, open-mouthed monster into which, or whom, Christ descends, like the Jonah whom Christ accepted as a prototype of his own Passion. For Milton, however, the scriptural evidence for the descent into hell was weak, and, besides, Milton believed that the whole of Christ's human nature died on the cross, with no surviving soul or spirit able to visit hell. The temptation in the Synoptic Gospels immediately follows the baptism, and Milton's view of baptism represents one of the rare exceptions to his general antisacramental attitude toward biblical symbolism: he is willing to see in it a symbol of the three-day crisis of Christian redemption, death, burial, and resurrection. Hence the temptation becomes for Milton the scripturally authorized version of the descent into hell, the passing into the domain of Satan, and the reconquest of everything in it that is redeemable. Certain features, such as the bewilderment of the forsaken disciples and the elegiac complaint of the Virgin Mary at the beginning of the second book, might belong more naturally to the period immediately following Christ's death. Christ's withdrawal from the world at this point is the opposite of a 'fugitive and cloistered virtue', as he is being led directly into the jaws of hell itself, and not yet as a conqueror.

In the typology of the Bible there are two parallel versions of the fall and redemption of man. Adam falls from a garden into a wilderness, losing the tree of life and the water of life; Christ, the second Adam, wins back the garden ('Eden raised in the waste wilderness') and restores to man the tree and river of life. Similarly, the fight between St George and the dragon in Spenser takes place at the boundary of Eden, St George being refreshed by the paradisal well of life and tree of life, which continue in the church as the sacraments of Baptism and Communion. And as the natural home of Christ on earth is a fertile garden, the Eden in which he walked in the cool of the day, so the natural home of devils is the wilderness, 'A pathless desert dusk with horrid shades', a blasted land like the country traversed in the *City of Dreadful Night* or by Browning's Childe Roland, the sort of scene one instinctively calls 'Godforsaken', where the panic inspired by hunger, lost direction, and loneliness would have unsettled the reason of most people in much less than forty days.

Inside the story of Adam is the story of Israel, who falls from the Promised Land into the bondage of Egypt and Babylon. Besides being a second Adam, Christ is also a second Israel, who wins back, in a spiritual form, the Promised Land and its capital city of Jerusalem. In this capacity the story of the Exodus, or deliverance of Israel from Egypt, prefigures his life in the Gospels. Israel is led to Egypt through a Joseph; Christ is taken to Egypt by a Joseph. Christ is saved from a wicked king who orders a massacre of infants; Israel is saved from the slaughter of Egyptian first-born. Moses organizes Israel into twelve tribes and separates it from Egypt at the crossing of the Red Sea; Christ gathers twelve followers and is marked out as the Redeemer at his baptism in the Jordan (which the Israelites also later cross). Israel wanders forty years in the wilderness; Christ forty days. The Israelites receive the law from Mount Sinai; the gospel is preached in the Sermon on the Mount, which in its structure is largely a commentary on the Decalogue. The Israelites are plagued by serpents and redeemed by a brazen serpent on a pole, also accepted as a prototype of the Crucifixion by Christ. The Israelites conquer the Promised Land under ' Joshua, whom the Gentiles Jesus call' (i.e., Joshua and Jesus are the same word), corresponding to Christ's victory over death and hell, as in the church's calendar Easter immediately follows the commemorating of the temptation in Lent.

Thus when the Angel Gabriel tells the Virgin Mary to call her child's name Jesus (Joshua), the typological meaning is that the reign of the law is now over and the assault on the Promised Land has begun. Similarly, the death of Moses just outside the Promised Land typifies the inability of the law alone to redeem mankind.[1] The difficulty of the temptation for Christ is complicated by the fact that he is still, at this stage of his career, within the law; his temptation is only a part of a much subtler process of separating, in his own mind, the law which is to be annihilated from the law which is to be fulfilled. Milton explicitly says that

Christ in the wilderness 'into himself descended' and employed his time in clarifying his own mind about the nature of his messianic mission. We see little of what is actually passing in Christ's mind; but as his refusal of one after another of Satan's temptations drives Satan to display his resources in a steadily rising scale of subtlety, the poetic effect is that of a negative clarification of Christ's own thoughts. The climax of the temptation corresponds to the death of Moses in the Exodus; it is the point at which Jesus passes from obedience to the law to works of faith, from the last Hebrew prophet to the founder of Christianity.

The typical Old Testament figures who represent the law and the prophets, respectively, are Moses and Elijah, who accompany Jesus in his transfiguration and are the two 'witnesses' to his teaching in the Book of Revelation. Both of them prefigured the forty-day retirement and fast of Jesus in their own lives. The Old Testament says that Elijah will come again before the Messiah, a prophecy fulfilled by John the Baptist, but in a sense Moses has to be reborn too, as the law is fulfilled in the gospel. The Bible suggests the possibility that Moses did not die but was, like Elijah, transported directly to Paradise – an early version of *Paradise Lost* was to have begun with some speculations on this point. In any case Eden, the Promised Land, and the inward Kingdom of Heaven proclaimed by Jesus are all the same place, and Jesus' victory as second Adam and Israel is identical with the central act of his ministry, the casting of devils out of the human mind.

Christ has fasted for forty days, and, as Luke remarks with some restraint, 'he afterward hungered.' He has a Freudian wish-fulfilment dream, in which memories of Old Testament stories of prophets are mingled with food. In Milton, however, Christ is not hungry until after the first temptation to turn stones to bread, which consequently has nothing to do with hunger but is superficially an appeal to his charity, corresponding to the miraculous provision of manna in the Exodus. Jesus' answer that man shall not live by bread alone is a quotation from a passage in Deuteronomy that refers to the giving of manna. A contrast is thus involved between the material bread of the law and the bread of life of the gospel, distinguishing the gospel from what for Milton was the sacramental fallacy, the tendency to translate the Jewish ceremonial code into Christian terms, which produces the doctrine of transubstantiation. But Milton's interest is less in the temptation than in the tactical manoeuvre which Satan makes after his disguise is penetrated.

In Giles Fletcher's *Christ's Victory and Triumph*, Milton's most obvious source, the first temptation is primarily a temptation of despair and closely follows the episode of Despair in the first book of *The Faerie Queene*. Milton's Christ uses only the term 'distrust', but still Milton is here the poetic grandson of Spenser.[2] Despair's argument in Spenser is based on the logic of law without gospel: i.e., sin is inevitable, and the longer one lives, the more one sins. Satan's argument in Milton is a refinement of this: good and evil are inseparable in the fallen world, and, in a world where all instruments are corrupted, one must either use corrupt instruments or not act at all. The use of evil or Satanic means being inevitable, Satan himself must be a reluctant agent of the will of God – that is, as long as we can believe in the will of God. In terms of the law alone, which can discover but not remove sin, this argument is more difficult to refute than it looks – in fact, it could be a clever parody of the central argument of *Areopagitica*. Christ's answer, leading up as it does to a prophecy of the cessation of oracles and the coming of the Word of God to the human heart, is based on what is familiar to the reader as the gospel or spiritual view of Scripture. Satan has never met such a view before, however, and feels sufficiently baffled to retire and consult with his colleagues before going further.

The conflict in *Paradise Regained* is ultimately a spiritual one, but the basis of the human spirit is the physical body, and the body is the battlefield of the spirit. Phineas Fletcher's *The Purple Island* begins with a detailed allegory of the physical body and then expands into a psychomachia, in which the principals are Christ and the Dragon. This allegory is based on the defence of the House of Alma in the second book of *The Faerie Queene*, which presents the quest of Guyon, the knight of temperance or continence, the physical integrity which is not so much virtue as the prerequisite of virtue. The crucial ordeal of Guyon is the Bower of Bliss, where the tempting agent is female and the temptation itself primarily erotic. In Giles Fletcher's version of the temptation of Christ the final[3] temptation is modelled on the Bower of Bliss. Satan's rejection of Belial's proposal to tempt Christ with women indicates Milton's deliberate departure from his predecessors. Milton had already dealt with such themes in *Comus,* and *Comus* presents, so to speak, the temptation of innocence, in contrast to the temptation of experience, which is the theme of *Paradise Regained.*[4]

Nevertheless, the sequence of temptations, which now proceeds unbroken to the end of the poem, begins with an attack on Jesus' temperance or continence, the physical basis of his humanity. There are two of these temptations – a banquet and an offer of money; neither is biblical, and it is generally recognized that the temptations of 'Beautie and money' in the second book of *The Faerie Queene* are mainly responsible for them. They take place in a pleasant grove, one line, 'Nature's own work it seemed (Nature taught Art)', being a vestigial survival of the Bower of Bliss, with its triumph of artifice over nature. Attacks on temperance could be resisted by any genuine prophet or saint or even by a virtuous heathen. Satan is an imaginative oriental bargainer, and one has the feeling that, although, of course, he wishes to gain Christ as cheaply as possible, he is reconciled to seeing these temptations fail – his strategy, as we shall see, is cumulative, and individual temptations are expendable. The temptations of food and money continue the argument of the first temptation, in that they urge the necessary use of doubtful means for good ends. Their rejection establishes the principle, which is also in Spenser, that the moral status of the instrumental depends on the mental attitude toward it: if the initial attitude is one of passive dependence, the instrument will become an illusory end in itself. It is not immediately apparent, however, why Satan has so much higher an opinion of food than of women as a temptation, even granting that there is really only one temptation of food.

We should be careful not to take anything in Satan's reply to Belial, such as his remark that beauty stands 'In the admiration only of weak minds', at its face value. Nothing that Satan says in the poem is as trustworthy as that. He is, of course, right in thinking that Christ cannot be tempted to sins which are foreign to his nature; he can be tempted only to be some form of Antichrist, some physical or material counterpart of himself. But he is right for the wrong reasons.

The epic is traditionally a poem of heroic action, and a Christian poet must decide, before writing an epic, what in Christian terms a hero is and what an act is. For Milton all real acts are good and there are no real evil acts.[5] Christ in *Paradise Lost* illustrates the pattern of this positive or real act: all his acts are creative or re-creative (i.e. redemptive). Adam's fall was thus not an act but a failure to act, the sham act of disobedience. Satan's fall was the parody act of rebellion, which, unlike disobedience, involves an attempt at rivalry with God. In the fallen world (since Nimrod, who introduced political authority and with it the possibility of imitating the demonic), man naturally turns to the demonic pseudo-hero as the pattern of heroic action. The genuinely heroic act is found only in the imitation of Christ, in endurance and obedience, and its pattern is illustrated in Abdiel, the faithful angel. For Satan, of course, heroic action means his own type of aggressive and destructive parody-heroism. His assumption that the Messiah's heroism will be in some way of this type is genuine, and he is consequently willing to give Jesus credit for a heroic contempt of 'effeminate slackness'. His own contempt for the kind of heroism that Christ seems to prefer is also genuine, and for anyone else this would be itself a major temptation: Faithful in Bunyan, for example, remarks that 'Shame', the sense of worldly contempt, was his worst enemy. Satan, the accuser of

Israel, is what, since Milton's day, we have learned to call a Philistine. Both Satan and Christ divide the world into the material and the spiritual, but for Satan the material is real and the spiritual is imaginary or, as he says, 'allegoric'. It is only from Christ's point of view that he is an Archimago or master of illusion.

Hence, just as Comus puns on the word 'nature', so all the elements of the dialectical conflict are attached to a material context by Satan and to a spiritual one by Christ. By rejecting everything that Satan offers in Satan's sense, Christ gets it again in its true or spiritual form, just as Adam, if he had successfully resisted his temptation, would still have become as the gods (i.e. the true gods or angels), knowing good, and evil as the possible negation of good. In the *Christian Doctrine* Milton speaks of the virtue of urbanity and its opposing vice of obscenity, which, he says, consists of taking words in a double sense. He means, of course, what we mean by the *double entendre*; still, Christ is the source of urbanity and Satan of obscenity, and something of the *double entendre*, the great words 'the kingdom, the power, and the glory' 'profaned' to their worldly opposites, runs all through Satan's speeches. As in the previous conflict, Satan is 'scoffing in ambiguous words', and the opening colloquy between Satan and Christ in the first book is already a clash of oracular powers. Satan's dialectical instrument is the evasive or quibbling oracle; Christ's is the simplicity and plainness that Milton prizes so in Scripture, especially the Gospels. The climax of *Paradise Regained*, when Satan falls from the pinnacle and Christ stands on it, is marked by two very carefully placed classical allusions, almost the only mythological ones in the poem. One is to Hercules and Antaeus, of which more later; the other is to Oedipus and the Sphinx. Christ has not only overcome temptation, but, as the Word of God, he has solved the verbal riddle of human life, putting all the words which are properly attributes of God into their rightful context.

The temptations which follow are temptations to false heroic action and fall into three parts: the temptation of Parthia, or false power; the temptation of Rome, or false justice; and the temptation of Athens, or false wisdom. One problem of interpretation is raised by Milton's curious proportioning of emphasis. The temptation of Parthia seems much the crudest of the three, yet it takes up the entire third book, while the other two are huddled with the third temptation into the fourth.

In Jesus' day, with the memory of the Maccabees still vivid, the question of armed rebellion against Roman power was very insistent; it was the course that most Jews expected the Messiah to take and had already been in the mind of the youthful Christ:

> victorious deeds
> Flamed in my heart, heroic acts, one while
> To rescue Israel from the Roman yoke.

And, though even then Christ thought of putting down violence rather than of using violence, still Satan's arguments on this point are unanswerable: to defeat Roman power by arms requires princely virtues, and princely virtues, as Machiavelli demonstrated, are not moral virtues, far less spiritual ones; they are martial courage and cunning, both demonic gifts. What Satan unwittingly does for Christ in the temptations of Parthia and Rome is to dramatize the nature of that aspect of law that is to be annihilated by the gospel – law as a compelling external force in which spiritual authority is subject to and administered by temporal authority.

Satan is shrewd enough to throw in the suggestion that, by gaining the power of Parthia, Christ will be able to realize the patriotic dream of reuniting the lost ten tribes with the Jewish remnant. In rejecting this, Christ rejects also the legal conception of Israel as a chosen people and is ready to usher in the new Christian conception of Israel as the body of believers. There seems also to be some personal reference, however indirect, to the great blighted hope of Milton's political life. Some Milton scholars think that *Samson Agonistes* is earlier than *Paradise*

Regained: if so, the latter is Milton's final poetic testament, and his treatment of this theme takes on an additional intensity and pathos.

The final binding of Satan, the third phase of the agon, is prophesied in the Book of Revelation, where, in the twelfth chapter, we have again a wilderness, a symbolic female figure representing the church, and a threatening dragon beaten off by Michael, the angelic champion of Israel, in a repetition of the first encounter. Milton, like everyone else, took the Book of Revelation to be in part a prophecy of the troubles the church was to suffer after the apostolic period. In *The Reason of Church Government* he attacks the supporters of tradition on the ground that they do not understand that the Book of Revelation foretells an apostasy of the church and 'the Church's flight into the wilderness'. Several times in the prose pamphlets Milton refers to the rebellion against Charles I in terms of the Exodus from Egypt and expresses a hope that England will be a new chosen people, chosen this time for the gospel instead of the law, the rescued apocalyptic church coming out of the wilderness with Michael into a new Promised Land. In this role the English nation would represent the returning lost tribes, a new Israel taking up the cross that the Jews had rejected. By the time he wrote *Paradise Regained*, the English had chosen, in the terrible phrase of *The Ready and Easy Way*, 'a captain back for Egypt'. Yet even Milton cannot allow Christ to dismiss the unfaithful tribes, who have lost their birthright rather than their home, without adding a few wistful cadences in another key, too gentle in tone to be a direct reply to Satan and at most only overheard by him:

> Yet he at length, time to himself best known,
> Rememb'ring Abraham, by some wondrous call
> May bring them back, repentant and sincere,
> And at their passing cleave the Assyrian flood,
> As the Red Sea and Jordan once he cleft,
> When to the Promised Land their fathers passed;
> To his due time and providence I leave them.

The temptation of Parthia, to ally the Messiah with an anti-Roman power in order to overthrow Rome, had, in short, been a temptation of Milton as well as of Christ. It is a commonplace that if Milton had written his epic around the time he wrote *The Reason of Church Government*, it would have been more closely affiliated to the epic-romance convention established by Boiardo, Ariosto, and Spenser, in which Arthur would probably have represented a crusader or Christian warrior and some heroine an aspect of 'the king's daughter, the Church', like Spenser's Una. But the female figure over whom physical wars are fought is likely to be closer to the erotic conventions, 'Inductive mainly to the sin of Eve', to Courtly Love, uxoriousness, and lust. The rejected Romantic tradition appears in Milton's reference to 'The fairest of her sex, Angelica', where we might expect the more familiar Helen of Troy or Guinevere; one reason for his choice may be that Boiardo's landscape is more shadowy and insubstantial than Troy or Britain.

In *Paradise Regained* Satan displays all his kingdom; consequently, Christ must refuse all of it, including much that in other contexts he might handle fearlessly. Later in his career he shows no hesitation in providing miraculous food, sitting at table with sinners, or accepting money and other gifts. But he has not yet entered on his ministry: the teaching and healing Christ that we know, with his compassion and courtesy, his love of children, and his sense of humour, has no place in Satan's kingdom. The haughtiness and aloofness of Christ mean that, before Christ can work in the world, he must recognize and repudiate all worldliness. In *Paradise Regained* Christ is looking at the world as it is under the wrath, as the domain of Satan. Wrath is the reaction of goodness contemplating badness; it is disinterested and impersonal and is the opposite of anger or irritation. If God is capable of wrath, he is incapable of irritation. Milton goes to grotesque lengths in *Paradise Lost* in emphasizing this point: he transforms the Father into a monster of indifference, who merely smiles when he observes that a third of his angelic creation has revolted. The word 'unmoved', so often applied to Christ in *Paradise Regained*, refers to his emotions as well as his intellect: Satan is condemned but not railed at. Christ cannot exercise mercy until he has separated it from sentimentality, and his comments on the misery of man under wrath are part of this separation. Hence *dramatically* Christ becomes an increasingly unsympathetic figure, a pusillanimous quietist in the temptation of Parthia, an inhuman snob in the temptation of Rome, a peevish obscurantist in the temptation of Athens.

When Adam in *Paradise Lost* decides to die with Eve rather than live without her, the reader is expected to feel some sympathy for Adam, to feel that he might well have done the same thing in Adam's place, as, of course, he would. Conversely, one might almost say that the point at which the reader loses sympathy with Jesus in *Paradise Regained* is the point at which he himself would have collapsed under the temptation. All of us are, like Christ, in the world and, unlike him, partly of it, and whatever in us is of the world is bound to condemn Christ's rejection of the world at some point or other. This aspect of the temptation story is the theme of the other great literary treatment of it, the Grand Inquisitor episode in *The Brothers Karamazov*, but it is present in Milton too.[6]

In *Paradise Regained*, as to some extent in *Comus*, the dramatic and the dialectical aspects of the conflict are opposed and in a paradoxical relation to one another. Comus and Satan get our dramatic attention because they show such energy and resourcefulness; the tempted figures are either motionless or unmoved and have only the ungracious dramatic function of saying No. Yet, of course, the real relation is the opposite of the apparent one: the real source of life and freedom and energy is in the frigid figure at the centre. One would think that Milton had selected the temptation episode because it is, with the possible exception of the agony in the garden (on which Milton also meditated a 'Christus patiens'), the only episode in which suspense and the feeling of the possible awful consequences of failure are consistently present. But Christ's ability to reply 'Why art *thou* solicitous?'

to every temptation destroys all opportunity for narrative suspense. Yet it is essential to Milton's plan that Christ should be able to see every card in Satan's hand, for if he is once puzzled, he is lost. Narrative suspense and dramatic sympathy go together; we can have them in *Samson Agonistes*, but they must be renounced here.

The reader may feel that the effect is to make both Christ and Satan seem bored with their roles and that such boredom is infectious. Of course, in long poems there are two areas of criticism – the structure or design and the poetic realization of details – and value-judgements established in one area are not transferable to the other. It is quite possible for a poem to be, as *Paradise Regained* may be, a magnificent success in its structure and yet often tired and perfunctory in its execution. In structure, however, *Paradise Regained* is not only a success but a technical experiment that is practically *sui generis*. None of the ordinary literary categories apply to it; its poetic predecessors are nothing like it, and it has left no descendants. If it is a 'brief epic', it has little resemblance to the epyllion; its closest affinites are with the debate and with the dialectical colloquy of Plato and Boethius, to which most of the Book of Job also belongs. But these forms usually either incorporate one argument into another dialectically or build up two different cases rhetorically; Milton's feat of constructing a double argument on the same words, each highly plausible and yet as different as light from darkness, is, so far as I know, unique in English literature.

The rejecting of the temptation of Rome forces Satan to relinquish one of his trump cards, which is the appeal to opportunity, the panic inspired by the ticking clock. The aspect of temptation which suggests the temporal is an aspect with a particular significance for Milton himself, who for a great part of his life was torn between two contradictory, but equally powerful and valid, impulses – one to complete his epic, the other to postpone it until it was ready. This problem, in itself peculiar to Milton as a poet, was for him also a special case of the general principle that the Christian must learn to will to relax the will, to perform real acts in God's time and not pseudo-acts in his own. In the temptations of Adam and Samson, too, the same theme recurs of an action not so much wrong in itself as wrong at that time, a hasty snatching of a chance before the real time has fulfilled itself. Christ is older than Milton was at twenty-three when he wrote his famous sonnet, and Satan constantly urges him, from the first temptation on, to be his own providence, to release some of his own latent energies. The discipline of waiting is not only more difficult and inglorious but constantly subject to the danger of passing insensibly into procrastination.

The subtlest thing that Satan says in the poem is his remark that

> each act is rightliest done,
> Not when it must, but when it may be best.

The demonic hero judges the present by an intuitive sense of the immediate future. He is distinguished from other men by his capacity to take thought for the morrow, to be, in short, a diviner. In the classical epic, knowledge of the future is usually gained from a dark underworld, in contrast to the revelations of gods, which as a rule illuminate the present moment. Similarly in Dante the damned know the future but not the present, and in *Paradise Lost* Michael prophesies the future to Adam after he has gained his forbidden knowledge. Hence we are not surprised to find that Satan's oracular powers in *Paradise Regained* include a knowledge of Christ's future 'fate' gained by astrology. In contrast, all times are present to the Father, and the Father is manifested as a real present, or presence, by the Son. Christ's main scriptural ally on this point is Ecclesiastes, with its doctrine that there is time for all things, but the sense of strain in waiting for God's time comes out in several places, not least in the reference to the lost tribes, already quoted.

The temptation of Athens has, as its Antichrist core, the Stoic ideal, the 'apathy' of the invulnerable individual who feels that the wise man in a bad world can only do the best he can for himself. In rejecting it, Christ also rejects the contemplative life as an end: Christ's aim is to redeem the world, not to live a morally sinless life, which he might conceivably have done as a philosopher. In the temptation of Athens the clash of the two oracular traditions, the prophetic and the demonic, reaches its climax. Here again it is Greek philosophy in its context as part of Satan's kingdom that is being rejected. A Christian working outward from his faith might find the study of Plato and Aristotle profitable enough; but if he were to *exchange* the direct tradition of revelation for their doctrines, which is what Christ is tempted to do, he would find in them only the fine flower of a great speculative tree, with its roots in the demonic metaphysics and theology described in the second book of *Paradise Lost*.

The third temptation begins with a night of storm, not in itself a temptation but an indispensable preliminary to one. Its object is to impress Christ with Satan's power as prince of an indifferent and mindless order of nature, to suggest that his Father has either forsaken him or is unable to reach him in a fallen world. It is, in short, another suggestion of despair or distrust, but with the specific aim of making Christ feel lonely and deserted, hence isolated, hence the self-contained ego which is the form of pride. It demonstrates the fact that in a world of death and mutability the light of nature is surrounded by the darkness of nature; but as Christ has already rejected all arguments based on the analogy of natural and revealed wisdom, this fact comes as no great surprise. The placing of Christ on the pinnacle of the temple follows and is, as Satan makes clear, a temptation of Jesus purely in his capacity as Son of God, an ordeal that no simple human nature would be able to survive. Here, for once, we can cautiously accept what Satan says, although, of course, his motive in saying it is to drop a suggestion of arrogance into Christ's mind.

The temptation of the pinnacle is equally a bodily and a mental assault. Christ has been weakened by forty days of fasting and by the night of storm. Satan won over Eve by instilling

thoughts into her mind while her consciousness was pre-
occupied with the wonder of a talking snake; and Eve, when
she came to search her own mind, found Satan's thoughts there
and took them for her own. Christ is far more astute, but still
the sequence of blinding visions of earthly glory may have left
in his mind some faint trace of attachment, some unconscious
sense of exaltation. If so, he will feel dizzy on the pinnacle.
Mentally, then, Christ is being tested for *hybris*, or pride of
mind. He is in the position of a tragic hero, on top of the wheel
of fortune, subject to the fatal instant of distraction that will
bring him down.

Physically, Christ is being tested for exhaustion, for a slight
yielding to pressure that will make him stagger out of sheer
weariness. Satan quotes the Psalms to show that the Messiah
could fall, trusting in the support of angels; but Christ, though
led by the Spirit into the wilderness, is not being led by the
Spirit to fall off the pinnacle. That would be his own act, and
the Antichrist core of it would be a trust not in angels but in his
own fortune, and trusting to one's fortune is the same thing as
trusting to Satan. It would perhaps be a reasonable definition of
cowardice to say that a coward is a man whose instinct it is, in a
crisis, to do what his enemy wants him to do. Christ's ordeal is
one of fortitude as well as wisdom, and he has proved himself
no coward; but even brave men have had traitors lurking
within them, something that co-operated with an outward
attack. If there is the smallest trace either of pride in Christ's
mind or what we should now call the death-impulse in his
body – the impulse that would make any other man accept the
vinegar sponge on the cross – this final test will reveal it. If not,
Christ is ready to be God's sacrificial victim, a martyr who, so
far from being like some martyrs, half in love with easeful
death, dies as the implacable enemy of death.

Christ has been tempted *quasi homo*, purely as man. For
Milton what man can do for himself is negative and icono-
clastic: man does not save himself, but, by clearing his world of
idols, he can indicate his willingness to be saved. Christ has

resisted the whole of Satan's world; he has done what man can do, and the only possible next step is for God to indicate acceptance of what he has done. Thus the fact that Christ successfully stands on the pinnacle is miraculous, but not a miracle drawn from his own divine nature, not an ace hidden up his sleeve, which is what Satan is looking for. It means that his human will has been taken over by the omnipotent divine will at the necessary point and prefigures the commending of his spirit to the Father at the instant of his death on the cross.

Christ's answer, 'Tempt not the Lord thy God', is the only remark Christ makes in the poem which employs ambiguity.[7] Primarily, it means 'Do not put the Father to unnecessary tests', the meaning of the passage in Deuteronomy which Jesus is quoting. But here the Son carries the name and nature of the Father, and the statement bears the secondary meaning 'Do not continue the temptation of the Son of God.' At this point, probably, Satan for the first time recognizes in Jesus his old antagonist of the war in heaven. Earlier in the poem he had spoken of Christ as an opaque cloud which might be a cooling or shading screen between himself and the wrath of the Father. This is, of course, the direct opposite of Christ's true nature,

> In whose conspicuous countenance without cloud,
> Made visible, the Almighty Father shines.

So far from screening the fire of the Father, the Son is focusing it like a burning glass, the two natures of the Godhead united as closely as Milton's Christology will permit. And just as this last temptation was of Christ in his specific role as Son of God, so with his victory Satan is defeated in his own headquarters, the lower heaven or element of air which is the spatial limit of his conquest at the Fall. That is why Christ's victory is immediately followed by a reference to the struggle of Hercules and Antaeus, in which Hercules (a prototype of Christ also in the *Nativity Ode* and elsewhere) overcame the monstrous son of earth in the air.

There is a hidden irony in Satan's quotation from the Ninety-first Psalm. He quotes the eleventh and twelfth verses; the thirteenth reads, 'The lion and the adder, the young lion and the dragon shalt thou trample under foot.' In his fall Satan assumes the position of the dragon under Christ's feet, the only place for him after his failure to gain entrance to Christ's body or mind. At this point a new centre of gravity is established in the world, as the gospel is finally separated from the law. Judaism joins classical wisdom as part of the demonic illusion, as the centre of religion passes from the temple Christ is standing on into the true Christian temple, the body of Christ above it. The destruction of the Garden of Eden at the Flood showed that God 'attributes to place no sanctity', and the later destruction of the temple, prefigured at this point, illustrates the same principle. Christ's casting the devils out of heaven prefigured the cleansing of the temple, with which, according to John, his ministry began. Here, with the end of the temptation, Christ has chased the devils out of the temple of his own body and mind and is ready to repeat the process for each human soul.

The temptation of the pinnacle corresponds to the point in *Samson Agonistes* at which Samson, after beating off Manoah, Delilah, and Harapha, refuses to go to the Philistine festival. He is right in refusing but has come to the end of his own will. At that point he appears to change his mind, but what has happened is that God has accepted his efforts, taken over his will, and changed his mind for him. In *Samson Agonistes*, which is a tragedy, this point is the 'peripety': Samson is now certain to die, though also certain of redemption. Jesus has also made it impossible for himself to avoid death, as his prototypes Elijah and perhaps Moses did; but *Paradise Regained* is less a tragedy than an episode in a divine comedy, and we need another term for the crucial point of the action.

In the *Christian Doctrine* Milton distinguishes between the literal and what he calls the 'metaphorical' generation of the Son by the Father. By the latter he means what might more accurately be called 'epiphany', the manifesting of Christ in a divine capacity to others. The showing of Christ to the angels in *Paradise Lost* is a metaphorical or epiphanic generation of him: the Father's phrase 'This day have I begot' can hardly refer to literal generation. The same distinction recurs in the Incarnation. Two of the Gospels, Matthew and Luke, are nativity Gospels, beginning with Christ's infancy or physical generation in the world. The other two, Mark and John, are epiphanic Gospels and begin with his baptism, where he is pointed out to man as the Son of God. (In the Western churches epiphany means particularly the showing of the infant Christ to the Magi, but in the Eastern churches it means particularly the baptism, though the date of observance is the same.) Epiphany is the theological equivalent of what in literature is called 'anagnorisis' or 'recognition'. The Father recognizes Jesus as the Son at the baptism: Satan recognizes him on the pinnacle in a different, yet closely related, sense. That is, the action of *Paradise Regained* begins with the baptism, an epiphany which Satan sees but does not understand, and ends with an epiphany to Satan alone, the nature of which he can hardly fail to understand. Behind this is the still larger scheme in which *Paradise Regained* is the sequel of *Paradise Lost*. The epiphany of Christ to the angels, which caused the original revolt of Satan, was chronologically the first event in *Paradise Lost*, and, with the climax of *Paradise Regained*, the great wheel of the quest of Christ comes full circle, as far as Milton's treatment of it is concerned.

<h3 style="text-align:center">NOTES</h3>

1. *De doctrina christiana*, I, xxvi (Columbia ed., XVI, 110–11).
2. For the homiletic tradition behind Milton's and Fletcher's treatment see E. M. Pope, *'Paradise Regained': The Tradition and the Poem* (Baltimore, 1947). For Spenser's Despair see also E. Sirluck, 'A Note on the Rhetoric of Spenser's Despair', *Modern Philology*, XLVII (1949), 8 ff.
3. Giles Fletcher follows the Matthew order of temptations; Milton, of course, follows Luke.
4. This contrast is symbolized by the fact that the action of *Comus* moves up to the sprinkling of the Lady by Sabrina, an act with some analogies

to baptism, whereas the action of *Paradise Regained* follows baptism (cf. A. S. P. Woodhouse, '*Comus* Once More', *University of Toronto Quarterly*, XIX (1950), 218 ff.).

5. *De doctrina christiana*, I, xi (Columbia ed., XV, 198–9).
6. For an explicit assertion that Satan was right and Christ wrong see the passage from the nineteenth-century anarchist Proudhon quoted in Karl Löwith, *Meaning in History* (Chicago, 1949), p. 64.
7. A. S. P. Woodhouse, 'Theme and Pattern in *Paradise Regained*', *University of Toronto Quarterly*, XXV (1956), 181.

Barbara K. Lewalski

THEME AND ACTION IN *PARADISE REGAINED**

WITH consummate architectonic skill Milton has reworked the biblical story of Christ's temptation as a dramatic account of the hero's progress toward complete self-realization, and also as an epic treatment of his entire heroic/redemptive mission. The dramatic conflict between Christ and Satan develops in relation to the description of Christ's nature as 'Son of God', and of his threefold mediatorial office as prophet, king, and priest. This conflict takes on epic dimension by being shown in the double perspective of the past and the future, as indeed the turning point between past and future: in the course of the temptation episode Christ relates himself to and at length fulfils and subsumes various Old Testament and classical types of himself and his role, and he also assumes and exercises the three functions of his mediatorial office which are to continue throughout his life and throughout the entire history of his church. Accordingly, the temptation episode becomes the centre and epitome of all history – an appropriate subject for a brief epic.

The induction (I, 293) establishes the terms for such a reading of the poem. In the first place, it characterizes hero and antagonist before the duel begins. By juxtaposing a variety of epithets for Jesus – 'glorious Eremite', 'exalted man', 'man of men, attested Son of God', 'perfect Man, by merit call'd my [God's] Son' – the induction calls attention to the ambiguity of Christ's title, 'Son of God', which, as Satan later remarks, 'bears no single sense' (IV, 517). The induction shows, moreover, that the Son who is the hero of this poem is not coessential and coequal and coeternal with the Father as orthodox Trinitarians

* Based on 'Theme and Structure in *Paradise Regained*', *Studies in Philology*, LVII (1960), 186–220. Revised for the present volume by the author.

believe, but rather that he has the qualities Milton ascribes to the Son in his *Christian Doctrine*: radically inferior in essence to the Father; not eternal but generated 'within the limits of time' by the Father's deliberate decision; holding all his divine gifts and attributes by the Father's express donation; and made incarnate by a true *kenosis* or emptying out of these divine attributes, so that he might regain them again 'through the teaching of the Father'.[1] The dramatic advantages of such a hero for the poem are obvious: he is genuinely subject to temptation, able to fall, and capable of growth in understanding. The induction displays the incarnate Son emptied of divine understanding and will, and a puzzled Satan uncertain about Christ's divinity and role, beginning their duel at approximately the same level of knowledge: both are cognizant of the prophesies, both saw the signs at the recent Baptism, but both are ignorant of the identity between this Son and the 'first-begot'. Satan knows that Christ has been pronounced the Son of God in some sense, but he cannot imagine that this humble human being can be the divinely powerful first-begotten Son (I, 89–91). He saw the signs at Christ's baptism – a great prophet who 'Pretends to wash off sin', and 'a perfect Dove . . . whate'er it meant' (I, 73, 83) – but his descriptions indicate that he cannot interpret them. He understands that the prophecy about the seed of a woman bruising his head probably signifies the overthrow of his whole empire of earth and air, but he expects Christ to achieve this by military conquest. Christ's meditation as he enters the wilderness indicates that he has hitherto learned what he knows of himself from his Mother's testimony and from Scripture: he knows that he is 'Son of . . . th' Eternal King', 'King of *Israel* born', and 'Messiah', but he obviously does not yet understand what these prophetic metaphors really mean. He has no recollection of his previous celestial history, and he is led into the desert 'by some strong motion' without knowing why – 'to what intent / I learn not yet.' But remembering the testimonies at his baptism, he confidently expects that revelation from God will be available to him as needed – 'For what concerns my knowledge God reveals' (I, 290–93).

These characterizations, established in the induction, prepare for the debates of the temptation episode to be 'battles of wits' in which both hero and antagonist strive for the advantage which accompanies superior understanding. To succeed in perverting Christ Satan will have to understand him perfectly, but Satan is himself the victim of imperfect knowledge and naïveté regarding Christ's nature and mission. To withstand Satan's temptations Christ must refuse all inadequate, partial, or erroneous versions or parodies of himself and his mission, and must finally attain to full and perfect understanding. Satan's special advantage in the duel is his direct observation and knowledge of human motives and human weaknesses through all history, whereas Christ knows such things only at second hand, through his wide reading in the scriptural and historical records. But Christ's special advantage more than compensates: he may merit as he needs it the gift of divine illumination, whereas Satan can only rely upon his own mind – brilliant indeed but now warped and literalistic, unable to fathom God's metaphors. Yet Satan's very literalism constitutes an aspect of the dramatic situation and of Christ's temptation, for as long as Christ does not wholly understand himself and his role he can conceivably be deluded by the Satanic interpretation of his situation. These characteristics prepare also for the great central paradox in the dramatic movement of the poem whereby action and passion are virtually transmuted into each other. Satan appears to do all the acting: it is he who dances about Christ in a fever of motion, trying one scheme after another, one argument after another, while Christ remains impassive, immobile, unaffected by all of Satan's proposals. Yet it is in Christ's consciousness, not Satan's, that all real change takes place: Christ in responding to the challenges of the temptations progresses steadily toward full understanding of his nature and the various aspects of his role, evidencing this development by his increased certainty of tone and calmness of manner, whereas Satan, constantly failing to resolve the puzzle about Christ's sonship and mission, gives way to progressive frustration and loss of control over himself and over the course of the action.

Besides characterizing the combatants and thereby setting the terms of the conflict, the induction also establishes a typological perspective for that conflict. The thematic statement – 'I who erewhile the happy Garden sung, / By one man's disobedience lost, now sing / Recover'd Paradise to all mankind, / By one man's firm obedience fully tried /. . . And *Eden* rais'd in the waste Wilderness' (I, 1–7) – identifies Christ as re-living and reversing Adam's temptation experience. This motif, reinforced by other references to Adam in the induction and throughout the poem,[2] recalls the familiar typological identification of Christ as Second Adam, and especially the so-called Triple Equation which equated Christ's three temptations with those of Adam, interpreting them as temptations to carnal appetite, to avarice or ambition, and to vainglory or presumption.[3] The scarcely less familiar typological identification of Christ's temptation as a reprise and heightening of Job's victory over Satan[4] is also recalled explicitly in the induction: Satan comes forth again in his role as Adversary (the term by which he is known in the Book of Job); he has been to another assembly (Christ's baptism) where he has heard another 'exalted man' acclaimed by God; and he has been moved by such testimony to undertake another temptation (I, 33–7). The Father's comment reinforces the suggestion that Christ is a Second Job – 'he [Satan] might have learnt / Less overweening, since he fail'd in *Job*, /. . . He now shall know I can produce a man /. . . Far abler' (I, 146–51). Other Jobean echoes and allusions throughout the poem emphasize this relationship.[5] We are led to expect therefore that Christ will call upon the typological traditions attaching to Adam and to Job in defining his own mission, and we are also prepared for the extension (which I have elsewhere discussed in detail[6]) of this typological perspective to other notable Old Testament and classical personages who figure in the debate of

Christ and Satan: Moses, Elijah, David, Daniel, Judas Maccabaeus, Hercules, Socrates, and many others. Satan's temptation
strategy is to invite Christ to accept inferior images of his
redemptive action in place of those major types he has seized
upon, or else to identify with his types in their literal significa-
tion and thereby fail to fulfil them spiritually, as his mission
demands. Christ must solve the difficult intellectual problem of
how he ought to relate himself to history, how far the past is to
provide a model for his actions and wherein he must redefine
its terms in order to become himself the model for the future.
These typological allusions enhance the epic scope of the poem
by projecting the episode of Christ's temptation against the
panorama of history, with Christ becoming the summation, the
compendium, the completion of all the earlier heroes.

My special concern here, however, is with another perspective
upon the temptation episode, also established in the induction.
John's declaration of his readiness to resign to Christ 'his
Heavenly Office' at his baptism (I, 22), and Christ's musing as
he enters the desert about how to 'Publish his Godlike office
now mature' (I, 188), evoke the precise theological meanings
still attaching in the seventeenth century to the term 'Christ's
office'. In his *Christian Doctrine* Milton defined the three
functions of that office – those of prophet, king, and priest –
according to the standard Protestant formula:

HIS FUNCTION AS A PROPHET IS TO INSTRUCT HIS
CHURCH IN HEAVENLY TRUTH, AND TO DECLARE THE
WHOLE WILL OF HIS FATHER. . . .

His prophetical function consists of two parts; one external,
namely, the promulgation of divine truth; the other internal, to wit,
the illumination of the understanding. . . .

Christ's prophetical function began with the creation of the world,
and will continue till the end of all things. . . .

CHRIST'S SACERDOTAL FUNCTION is that whereby HE
ONCE OFFERED HIMSELF TO GOD THE FATHER AS A
SACRIFICE FOR SINNERS, AND HAS ALWAYS MADE, AND
STILL CONTINUES TO MAKE INTERCESSION FOR US. . . .

Barbara K. Lewalski

THE KINGLY FUNCTION of Christ is that whereby BEING
MADE KING BY GOD THE FATHER, HE GOVERNS AND
PRESERVES, CHIEFLY BY AN INWARD LAW AND SPIRITUAL
POWER, THE CHURCH WHICH HE HAS PURCHASED FOR
HIMSELF, AND CONQUERS AND SUBDUES ITS ENEMIES. . . .
[Christ] governs not the bodies of men alone, as the civil magistrate,
but their minds and consciences. . . . Hence external force ought
never to be employed in the administration of the kingdom of Christ,
which is the Church.[7]

Many Protestants regarded Christ's baptism and temptation in
the wilderness as the formal entry or initiation of Christ into his
office, some of them going so far as to interpret the three conventional temptations as tests of the three functions of that
office.[8] In the induction the explicit references to Christ's
office, Satan's frequent references to the kingly function,
Christ's partial definitions of all three roles in his opening
meditation, and the Father's characterization of the temptation
as Christ's exercise in the 'rudiments' of his everlasting warfare
against Satan, Sin and Death (I, 155–60), alert the reader to
expect issues relating to Christ's office to loom large in the
Christ/Satan debates. Indeed, I hope to demonstrate that Milton
structures the three conventional temptations to display a
precise and progressive development and testing of the three
functions of Christ's office, and that since these functions are
thought to continue forever in Christ's Church, Milton can
hereby subsume within the temptation episode the entire course
of Christ's life, the experience of his Church throughout
Christian history, and even the anagogic fulfilment of these
roles at the end of time.

As a test of the prophetic role the first temptation sets in
opposition truth and falsehood, using physical bread as metaphor. Christ identifies God's word as his proper spiritual food
(I, 349–51) and declares of Satan, 'lying is thy sustenance, thy
food' (I, 429). As founder of the New Law, Christ associates
himself on the basis of the common forty-day fast with two
recognized types of his prophetic office – Moses who established

327

the Old Law, and Elijah who reformed it (I, 351–4). At the outset of the temptation Satan disguises himself as a shepherd in quest of 'some stray Ewe' (I, 315), evidently in parody of the true Good Shepherd who seeks after the lost sheep, and thereby challenges Christ directly in his role of prophet and teacher. After an obscure offer of 'guidance' to Christ in the assertion that none have returned 'single' from this wilderness, Satan's overt proposal to change stones into bread invites Christ as prophet to imitate Moses in distributing bread to the starved desert dwellers: 'So shalt thou save thyself and us relieve / With Food, whereof we wretched seldom taste' (I, 344–5). The elimination of actual hunger from the first temptation (Christ's hunger is noted as a new sensation just prior to the banquet temptation, II, 243–4) makes this invitation an especially apt challenge to the prophetic role, for Christ is hereby urged to distrust God's support for that office and so to provide in advance for his own necessities and those of the other 'shepherds'. The episode thus alludes to the issue of ministerial tithes and clergy support which will continue to plague the Church throughout its history. Christ's answer, 'Man lives not by Bread only, but each Word / Proceeding from the mouth of God' (I, 349–50), decisively separates his prophetic role as exercised by himself and by the ministers of his Church from any necessary dependence upon such material support.

Christ's developing awareness of his role as prophet is evidenced by his unmasking of the false shepherd. But Satan's posturing is not limited to physical disguise. When Christ recognizes him he adopts the stance of a smooth-tongued, fawning, obsequious inferior, humbly admitting his identity but at the same time subtly insinuating his own claim to prophetic office: he has served as God's agent in the matters of tempting Job and deceiving Ahab's prophets, and he also aids mankind with his oracles and portents. The last claim intimates an offer of such aid to Christ, inviting him thereby to identify his own prophetic role with this inferior type of it. After Christ roundly denounces all the Satanic pretensions to prophecy, he then

affirms his own prophetic office with an authority which contrasts markedly with the uncertain tone of his initial meditation,
and which is perhaps the sign of a divine illumination granted
to Christ after he has withstood in all human vulnerability the
first tests posed by Satan. At this point, in terms closely paralleling the description of the prophetic role in Milton's *Christian
Doctrine*, the hero asserts unequivocally his claim to be the
living Oracle who will teach the final Word of God, causing
thereby the cessation of all lesser forms of prophecy:

> Nor more shalt thou by oracling abuse
> The Gentiles; henceforth Oracles are ceast,
> And thou no more with Pomp and Sacrifice
> Shalt be inquir'd at *Delphos* or elsewhere,
> At least in vain, for they shall find thee mute.
> God hath now sent his living Oracle
> Into the World to teach his final will,
> And sends his Spirit of Truth henceforth to dwell
> In pious Hearts, an inward Oracle
> To all truth requisite for man to know.   (I, 455–64)

Unable and unwilling to comprehend Christ's claim, Satan
adopts a new posture, that of the admitted liar and hypocrite
who yet loves truth, a Balaam-figure. Arguing that God himself
'vouchsaf'd his voice / To *Balaam* Reprobate, a Prophet yet /
Inspir'd' (I, 490–92), he seeks formal permission from Christ
for his return, and thereby invites Christ deliberately to link his
unique prophetic role with the inferior type of it that the venal
Balaam represents (and thereby to sanction a Church based upon
outward conformity rather than regeneration).[9] Christ avoids
this difficulty by stating simply that Satan will return or not, as
God wills.

The theme of the prophetic role extends into Book II, providing one level of meaning in the intricate banquet temptation.
Christ's new experience of hunger emphasizes again his human
vulnerability, manifested especially in a hunger dream in which
Christ sees himself sharing the food brought by the ravens and
the angel to Elijah, who wandered this same desert; but he

concludes upon waking that God is able to sustain him without food. Satan, however, taunts Christ with the fact that his types Moses and Elijah were not abandoned in the desert as he is, and he presents the lavish banquet as at once a diabolic parody of the heavenly manna and the temperate repasts offered to Elijah, and a literal fulfilment of the types: since God has not provided for Christ in the wilderness, the devil will. Moreover, Satan poses Christ with a dilemma by his false claim that the banquet in no way violates the dietary provisions of the Law, when in fact it contains forbidden shellfish and grisamber and probably also some forbidden flesh (II, 342–6).[10] If Christ refuses it because of the forbidden foods, he seems to subject himself (and his Church) to the dietary prohibitions of the Law which he has come to supersede, or to the scruple about eating food offered to idols. Indeed Satan's argument in offering the banquet – 'Hast thou not right to all Created things, / Owe not all Creatures by just right to thee / Duty and Service. . .?' (II, 324–5) – cleverly parodies the Pauline declaration of the Christian's liberty in such matters: 'The earth is the Lords and the fulnesse thereof' (I Corinthians x, 26). If on the other hand Christ accepts the banquet, he will participate in idolatry, eating at the devil's own table. The idolatrous banquet alludes also to the superstitious and idolatrous Roman Mass which throughout history will oppose the Church's true worship, and so in repudiating it Christ also repudiates false priesthood, in preparation for the definition in the tower temptation of his true sacrificial priesthood.

Christ escapes the theological dilemma posed by refusing the banquet simply on the basis of the giver. It is the Devil's table, the apex of idolatry which Paul shows to be forbidden in the New Law as in the Old: 'yee cannot be partakers of the Lord's Table, and of the table of devils' (I Corinthians x, 20–21). And the authoritative tones of Christ's final refusal of the banquet assert with new force his function as prophet of the New Testament fulfilling and superseding the Law and the Prophets:

> Shall I receive by gift what of my own,
> When and where likes me best, I can command?
> I can at will, doubt not, as soon as thou,
> Command a Table in this Wilderness.

(II, 381-4)

He is Lord of Nature, not subject to the ceremonial restrictions of the Law; his spiritual banquet will supersede the manna and the food supplied to Elijah; he is himself the provider (when and where likes him best) of the 'fat banquet' of Isaiah xxv, 6, which Christian exegetes took as a symbol of the Gentiles' call under the New Covenant.[11]

The structural complexity of the poem, achieved by setting various structural patterns against each other in an elaborate counterpoint, begins to be especially evident in Book II, which at once carries forward the motifs relating to the prophetic office (as has been seen) and also introduces those relating to Christ's kingship. According to one pattern the lures in the Kingdoms temptation, the great central movement of the poem, are arranged according to the standard ethical classifications of goods: *voluptaria* (Belial's proposal of women and the Banquet temptation), *activa* (wealth, glory, kingdoms), and *contemplativa* (poetry and philosophy). But the more basic division is two-fold: the temptations relating to the kingship over the self (the banquet-wealth-glory sequence), and those addressing the public, mediatorial kingly role (Parthia and Rome). Appropriately, Satan begins the Kingdoms sequence in a new guise 'As one in City, or Court, or Palace bred' (II, 300), that is, in his character as Prince of This World. He is no longer rustic, obsequious, and fawning, but a knowledgeable man of the world, affecting to condescend to a naïve and inexperienced Christ.

The banquet-wealth-glory sequence constitutes Milton's special version of the Triple Equation: in these temptations Christ overcomes just those temptations which defeated Adam, and thereby displays that kingship over the self which Milton saw as the basis for any kind of public rule or dominion. The

Satanic Council in Book II, a comic variation on the temptation pattern in which Belial (taking up Satan's role) proposes
the enticements of women, and Satan (playing Christ's role)
estimates the worthlessness of the lure, develops a parallel to
the specific weakness whereby Adam drew Eve's guilt upon
himself – undue susceptibility before women. Satan indeed
includes beautiful women, and also beautiful boys, in the
banquet scene, but transforms the crude enticement Belial
suggests into a subtle, understated addition to the whole
panorama of refined pleasure which he offers to Christ. The
banquet itself is an analogue to Eve's first temptation conceived
in the traditional manner as a temptation to carnal appetite: this
is evident from the narrator's comment, 'Alas how simple, to
these Cates compar'd, / Was the crude Apple that diverted *Eve*'
(II, 348–9). The parallel is further developed by the circumstance
that the banquet foods are 'forbidden' – unclean under the Law
and forbidden to Christians as the Devil's table. Also, with its
lavish abundance of natural goods the banquet is a kind of
mock Eden, a diabolic parody of Christ's own mission to raise
Eden 'in the waste Wilderness'. The second phase of the
Triple Equation traditionally involved avarice and ambition:
accordingly, after the banquet Satan seeks to stimulate Christ to
an inordinate desire of kingly dominion, and offers wealth as
the only means by which he might compass such an ambition.
Finally, the glory temptation serves as the analogue of Satan's
temptation of Eve to vainglory and pride in desiring to be 'as
Gods'. Answering this temptation Christ disparages the world
conquerors precisely because they seek to make themselves
Gods, and unlike Eve he vehemently refuses to imitate his
Father in seeking glory, 'which to God alone of right belongs'
(III, 141).

Besides proving himself in this sequence the true Second
Adam who directly reverses Adam's actions, Christ associates
himself with other, more positive types. One of the climactic
epic similes of the poem presents Hercules' victory over
Antaeus (often allegorized as sensual desire) as a type of Christ's

victory over Satan (IV, 562–71); this explicit identification reinforces elements in the banquet scene relating Christ's experience here to the initiation experience of the young Hercules in that notable Stoic parable of Temperance, the story of Hercules' choice. The young Hercules chose the path of arduous noble deeds pointed out to him by the Lady Virtue in place of the path of sensuous delights offered by the Lady Pleasure, and, significantly, many Renaissance representations of Hercules' choice made a banquet scene the primary symbol of the path of vice or sensual pleasure.[12] Hercules was allegorized by the Stoics and Cynics, and by many Renaissance writers and artists, as a notable example of temperance in regard to both sensual pleasures and worldly goods; moreover, because of this kingship over himself and because of his just ideals of kingship he became Jove's agent for restoring and ruling the earth.[13] After Christ has refused the banquet Satan appears to address him as a Second Hercules who has elected to follow that other path of 'high designs, / High actions' (II, 410–11); he therefore urges Christ to seek dominion as a means to glory as did Alexander, Caesar, and Scipio, all of them supposed progeny and/or successors of Hercules and imitators of his temperance.[14] These world conquerors were, however, heirs to a literal, militaristic version of the Hercules mission and as such were denounced by Stoics and Christians alike (much as Christ denounces them here) for their glorification of conquest and their blasphemous assumption of divine honours. Satan is again attempting to foist upon Christ a literal version of the type he ought to fulfil spiritually.

At the conclusion of this sequence Christ names Socrates, the teacher of mankind and willing sufferer for truth's sake, as the noblest classical type of himself, identifying thereby the source of many of the ethical principles he has been enunciating throughout this primarily ethical sequence. Christ's impressive definition of the kingship over self (II, 457–83) draws especially upon the ideal of the Socratic/Platonic philosopher or lover of wisdom, whose reason rules over the less noble parts of the soul (the appetitive principle which seeks sensual pleasure and money, and the passionate part which is concerned with ambition and honour) and who is accordingly 'most royal . . . and king over himself'.[15] Despite Christ's stern renunciations of the Satanic offers his ethical stance throughout this sequence derives not from the Stoic but from the Socratic/Platonic ideal. His self-conquest is not grounded upon Stoic self-sufficiency, but upon trust in God; he shows genuine concern, not Stoic impassivity, when he first experiences hunger; he is consoled not by the Stoic reflection that nothing external is necessary to him but by the thought that God can sustain his body without food if need be; he defines kingship over the self not as the elimination but as the rule over 'Passions, Desires, and Fears'. Moreover, Christ does not repudiate absolutely any of the goods offered, or deny them to be goods, but according to the Platonic principle he seeks to distinguish and order them. He does not shun pleasure as the Stoic urges but enters freely into the 'pleasant Grove,/ With chant of tuneful Birds' (II, 289–90); he shuns the lavish Satanic banquet but dreams of sharing a temperate meal with Elijah or Daniel; he deems wealth unnecessary because God can raise men up to greatness without it; he esteems kingly dominion over nations lightly because kingship over the self and rule by persuasion are yet higher forms of rule; and he despises the glory attending upon military conquest because true glory is only that given by God to such men as Socrates and Job, for 'deeds of peace, by wisdom eminent' (III, 91).

Christ's concluding statements in this sequence exalt Job even above Socrates as an exemplar of wisdom and moral virtue. Christ thereby associates himself most closely with that hero who had already defeated Satan by withstanding all of Adam's temptations, and who was often identified as the most complete of Christ's Old Testament types on the ground of his sinlessness, his suffering, his supposed prophecies of Christ's coming, and his exemplification of Christ's three offices of prophet, priest, and king.

By the statement, 'But to a Kingdom thou art born, ordain'd / To sit upon thy Father *David's* Throne' (III, 152–3), Satan shifts the discourse from the kingdom within to the public realm. The offers of Parthia and Rome accordingly challenge Christ's divinely ordained kingly role and the nature of his mediatorial kingdom, the Church. The exchange between Christ and Satan just prior to the Parthia temptation is an induction to this third segment of the poem, and also a temptation in its own right to false conceptions of 'Zeal' and 'Duty', to action at the wrong time. Satan urges Christ to take up arms at once, in imitation of his Old Testament type Judas Maccabaeus, in order to avenge new desecrations of the Law and the Temple, and to seize the throne of Israel. Christ's answer affirms that zeal and duty consist first of all in waiting upon God's time, avoiding both passivity and false zeal: 'All things are best fulfill'd in their due time, / And time there is for all things' (III, 182–3). Then, in a highly charged dramatic interchange, Christ challenges Satan to account for his implausible pose of solicitude about the kingdom (III, 198–202), and Satan, in what seems to be a moment of honesty and tragic insight, expresses his sense of weariness and futility, making a pathetic appeal to Christ for salvation. Yet such is Satan's corruption that he can make even this emotion, if it is genuine, serve his own ends: he cites his own haste to reach the 'Port of Worst' to urge Christ to hasten to his kingly best, and he invites Christ to pervert his kingly role by becoming Satan's king, protecting Satan rather than exercising his proper kingly function of conquering Satan and all his kingdom.

Satan's offer of Parthia builds upon Christ's identification of himself with David; it suggests that Christ become literally a second David, seeking after David's physical kingdom, Israel, by David's means – the use of armed force. After showing Christ the extensive Parthian territories and the splendid military formations of the Parthian horsemen, Satan argues with characteristic literalism that if Christ is to be the new

David and enjoy Israel's throne in its full extent he must control Parthia which now holds the ten lost tribes of Israel in servitude (III, 370–77) and must have command of Parthian military power to establish and maintain his own kingdom. Parthia appears to symbolize, therefore, the power of the civil state, the wrong means for the maintenance of Christ's spiritual kingdom, the Church. And in the typological perspective of the poem Satan's statement that Parthia has been 'of late / Found able by invasion to annoy / Thy country, and captive lead away her Kings' (III, 364–6) suggests the continuing persecution of the Church by the civil power throughout Christian history. But Christ, in terms recalling Milton's arguments for Church-State separation in the *Christian Doctrine*, decisively separates his kingly office and its exercise in his Church from any use of or league with civil power, denouncing the Parthian military display as 'Much ostentation vain of fleshly arm / And fragile arms, much instrument of war / . . . Plausible to the world, to mee worth naught' (III, 387–93). He is accordingly characterized by the narrator at the end of the Parthian temptation as 'Israel's true King', that is, as the true peaceful king of the new Israel, the invisible Church. And his harsh repudiation of the ten tribes as deserving their servitude under Parthia by their idolatry is softened by his vision of the final, peaceful restoration of the lost ones by God's providence, in his own time. In imagery drawn from Isaiah's eloquent description of the Millennial kingdom (Isaiah xi, 6–16), Christ asserts that the peaceful kingdom will ultimately prevail and transform the earth:

> Yet he at length, time to himself best known
> Rememb'ring *Abraham*, by some wondrous call
> May bring them back repentant and sincere,
> And at their passing cleave the Assyrian flood,
> While to their native land with joy they haste,
> As the Red Sea and *Jordan* once he cleft,
> When to the promis'd land thir Fathers pass'd.   (III, 433–9)

Barbara K. Lewalski

The Roman Empire is symbolically the great Antichrist – at once the Kingdom of This World and (as often in Protestant polemic and exegesis) the Roman Catholic Church. In offering Rome Satan tempts Christ with a substitute kingdom – 'Aim therefore at no less than all the world' (IV, 105) – in place of his own spiritual realm. The dazzling vision of Imperial Rome is displayed as an appropriate climax to the entire Kingdoms temptation, encompassing all the former lures in their most civilized manifestation – 'ample Territory, wealth and power / Civility of Manners, Arts, and Arms, / And long Renown' (IV, 82–4). Moreover, many details of the imperial palace and the embassies of the praetors and proconsuls in their robes of state suggest papal Rome. Satan's argument also subsumes former motifs: the time is now ripe for Christ to supplant the old, licentious, and childless emperor – literally Tiberius, but suggestive also of the papacy (IV, 90–102); Rome is a means for gaining Christ's own kingdom, as 'without the highest attain'd / Will be for thee no sitting, or not long / On David's Throne' (IV, 106–8); and charity and justice urge the liberation of the Roman people from the brutish emperor (IV, 96–102). With a nice irony Christ indicates his perception that Rome is indeed a compendium of all the previous worldly temptations by picking Satan up on his one omission, the 'sumptuous gluttonies, and gorgeous feasts' of the empire, which recall the banquet temptation and are also suggestive of the idolatrous mass (IV, 114–21). By declaring that there is no use in trying to make free men of 'inward slaves' and no use in expelling a brutish emperor without expelling 'a Devil who first made him such' (IV, 129), Christ further defines the work of his kingdom to be the expulsion of devils and the restoration of man's inner freedom. Thus he separates it entirely from worldliness as such and from the worldly Roman Church, as before he had separated it from any involvement with civil power.

At this point, having resisted all perversions of his kingly role, Christ seems to receive another special illumination, enabling him to state the far-reaching ramifications of that role with full understanding and certainty. He cites two metaphors from Daniel – the tree in the midst of the earth which grew 'unto heaven' (Daniel iv, 10–11) and the stone cut out of the mountain without hands which crushed the great image symbolizing the four empires of the world (Daniel ii, 34–44) – to express the power and universality of his wholly spiritual kingdom and its ultimate victory over all worldly kingdoms whatsoever:

> Know therefore when my season comes to sit
> On *David's* Throne, it shall be like a tree
> Spreading and overshadowing all the Earth,
> Or as a stone that shall to pieces dash
> All Monarchies besides throughout the world,
> And of my Kingdom there shall be no end:
> Means there shall be to this, but what the means,
> Is not for thee to know, nor me to tell.   (IV, 147–53)

Satan's rather astonishing restatement of his offer after this rebuff, this time on condition of idolatry of himself, should probably be seen as an attempt to salve his wounded pride. He now asserts the value of the gifts so summarily refused by brazenly revealing the high price always attaching to them, for to desire any of these worldly goods immoderately or to suppose them in any sense needful for the establishment of Christ's kingdom is an idolatry of the things of this world and therefore of its Prince. After this unwitting self-revelation by Satan, Christ asserts with finality that all the realms the Prince of This World has usurped are really his own as Son of God.

Satan now affects a casual dismissal of these kingdoms and directs his astonishing ingenuity to the construction of a new and even more remarkable pageant, just when the reader is sure that he has exhausted all his skill in displaying Roman grandeur. He offers Athens in all of its fourth- and fifth-century glory as the compendium of classical learning, equating this with 'wisdom' and presenting it as precisely the non-material good needed for Christ's accomplishment of all the lofty ideals and functions he himself has just defined. Satan proposes that Christ learn eloquence from the classical orators, moral prudence from the tragedians, and wisdom from Socrates who turned philosophy away from idle speculation and toward ethics and who was himself the source of the ethical teachings of the various schools (IV, 272–4). But Christ, in what appears to be an exaltation of narrow Biblicism and a bitter derogation of humanistic learning, repudiates the offer and asserts the sufficiency and superiority of Scripture in all these areas and for all these purposes. The divinely inspired prophets and the Law educate a king better than the orators do; the classical poets are inferior to biblical poets as moral teachers and even as artists because they write about 'The vices of thir Deities, and thir own'; and Greek philosophy is 'false, or little else but dreams' since the philosophers are 'Ignorant of themselves, of God much more' (IV, 291–310).

To understand the denunciation it is necessary to examine very closely the terms of the offer. Satan directs it in part to Christ's kingly office of 'ruling by persuasion' and to his prophetic (teaching) office, both of which continue in some sense in his kingdom, the Church:

> with the Gentiles much must thou converse,
> Ruling them by persuasion as thou means't
> Without thir learning how wilt thou with them,
> Or they with thee hold conversation meet?
> How wilt thou reason with them, how refute
> Thir Idolisms, Traditions, Paradoxes?   (IV, 229–34)

Relevant to this aspect of the offer is an argument, central to reformed Protestantism and elaborated at length by Milton in his contribution to the so-called 'learned-ministry' controversy,[16] to the effect that human learning is wholly irrelevant to both the minister and his auditory in pursuing or conveying spiritual truth, which derives only from above and ought not to be commingled with the doctrines of human learning. Christ in the poem takes just such a position:

> Think not but that I know these things; or think
> I know them not; not therefore am I short
> Of knowing what I ought: he who receives
> Light from above, from the fountain of light,
> No other doctrine needs.   (IV, 286–90)

Satan also offers classical learning for other purposes: to achieve the wisdom appropriate to the life of contemplation for which Christ showed an early propensity, and to complete the kingdom within the self:

>   Be famous then
> By wisdom; as thy Empire must extend,
> So let extend thy mind o'er all the world,
> In knowledge, see things in it comprehend . . .
> These rules will render thee a King complete
> Within thyself.   (IV, 221–4, 283–4)

It has not been generally noted that these statements make of wisdom a wholly mundane thing, and that Athens, despite the exaltation and refinement of its lures, is like Rome a compendium of the earlier worldly enticements. Instead of political rule over a kingdom, Christ is urged to desire dominion of the mind 'O'er all the world' (IV, 223); instead of military glory, the opportunity is offered to 'Be famous . . ./By wisdom' (IV, 221–2); instead of the voluptuous banquet, the Olive Grove of Academe has sensory delights attractive to a much more refined sensibility. The Satanic conception of wisdom as knowledge of all things 'in the world' and as knowledge relating to moral virtue (ethics) is much too limited even for the Stoics and Plato, but it is quite foreign to medieval or Renaissance Christians in the Augustinian tradition, such as Filelfo, Nicolas of Lyra, John Colet, Ficino, and many others.[17] Following Augustine, these men labelled the first sort of knowledge *scientia* rather than *sapientia*, called the second sort *prudentia* or else an aspect of *scientia*, and held that true wisdom, *sapientia*, comes only from above. The distinction was often developed through commentary upon Job xxviii, 12, 13, 18: 'But where shall wisedome be found? and where is the place of understanding? / Man knoweth not the price thereof; neither is it found in the land of the living. . . ./ Behold, the feare of the Lord, that is wisedome: and to depart from evill, is understanding.' Augustine's seminal exegesis of these verses defines wisdom as discourse of divine things, and knowledge as human ethical teaching, on the basis of the Septuagint rendering of Job xxviii:

> Having examined a great number of passages from Holy Scriptures, I find it written in the Book of Job, that holy man being the speaker, 'Behold, piety, that is wisdom; but to depart from evil is knowledge'. . . . In this place he meant by piety the worship of God. . . . And what is the worship of Him except the love of Him, by which we now desire to see Him, and we believe and hope that we shall see Him. . . . Discourse about these and the like subjects seems to me to be the discourse itself of wisdom. But to depart from evil, which Job says is knowledge, is without doubt of temporal things. . . . And therefore, whatsoever we do prudently, boldly, temperately, and justly, belongs to that knowledge or discipline wherewith our action is conversant in avoiding evil and desiring good. . . . When a discourse then relates to these things, I hold it to be a discourse belonging to knowledge.[18]

Augustinian Christians who wrote from this perspective, and especially commentators upon Job, often enumerated the errors of the classical schools and contrasted Greek ethical knowledge with Job's wisdom in terms very closely resembling Christ's language in *Paradise Regained*.[19]

We can now perceive more clearly the function of this episode. At the conclusion of the banquet-wealth-glory sequence, Christ appealed both to Socrates and Job as teachers and exemplars of the highest moral and ethical knowledge, affirming Job as the more perfect. Satan, using his accustomed strategy, at this point invites Christ to identify himself with the lesser type, Socrates, and changes the terms of discourse so as to equate the moral knowledge (*scientia*) for which Christ had earlier honoured Socrates, with wisdom (*sapientia*). Christ, offered knowledge in place of true wisdom from above, and offered it as a means of attaining goods which only true wisdom can gain – the life of contemplation, the perfection of the kingdom within, and the accomplishment of his kingly and prophetic offices – disparages as lacking in wisdom the same classical philosophers whose ethical knowledge he had before praised, and vehemently denying that wisdom can be of mundane origin, identifies himself with the more adequate conception of wisdom associated with Job in the Augustinian tradition. Moreover his reference to himself as one receiving 'Light from above, from the fountain of light' (IV, 289) may allude to a status of which he himself is not yet fully aware and one which surpasses and supersedes Job's wisdom – Christ's own unique role as Image of the Father's wisdom, whereby he may manifest such of the Father's wisdom as God devolves upon him, just as he expressed the Father's power by special delegation at the Creation of the world (*Paradise Lost*, VII, 163–96).

In the storm-tower sequence many earlier motifs are subsumed. Christ endures here, with a patience surpassing that of Job, the ultimate test of the kingdom within, violence and the threat of death. Satan challenges the prophetic role anew by his efforts to induce Christ to believe in portents and the Satanic interpretation of them (IV, 382–8, 451–66), and he casts doubts upon Christ's kingdom as merely 'Allegoric . . . as without end, / Without beginning' (IV, 390–92). But chiefly, building upon precedents in some biblical exegesis of the tower temptation, Milton contrives his storm-tower sequence to foreshadow and epitomize Christ's passion and death, the sacrificial priesthood which is the essence of the third function of his office.

Milton prepares the reader for such an interpretation by indicating that after the learning temptation Satan's 'darts' and 'devices' were all spent and he returned to Christ only to 'vent his rage'; Thomas Aquinas and many others had already explained that after the temptation episode the devil left Christ 'for a season' (Luke iv, 12) but returned at the Passion 'not to tempt Him but to assail Him openly'.[20] Satan predicts the events of Christ's passion before sending the storm which, he says, confirms that prediction: 'Sorrows, and labors, opposition, hate, / Attends thee, scorns, reproaches, injuries, / Violence and stripes, and lastly cruel death' (IV, 386–8). The circumstances of the storm – the darkness, 'louring Night', violent upheavals of nature – suggest those of the Crucifixion: the three hours' darkness over the earth, the splitting of rocks, the opening of graves (Matthew xxvii, 51–2). The reference to Christ as 'ill . . . shrouded' looks forward to his death and burial, while the description of him as sustaining the attack of 'Hellish Furies' suggests the descent to Hell. In this context the marvellous beauty, holiness, and peace of all nature after the nocturnal storm provides an image of the first Easter.[21]

Following the storm Satan returns in his 'wonted shape' to Christ – which evidently means in his own demonic shape, appropriate to him now that he has no more guiles and gifts to offer but can only display the violence and brutality which comprise his essential self. The tower episode actualizes the violence threatened and portended in the storm: Satan here attempts murder, for he places Christ on the very pinnacle of the temple where, he makes clear, by human strength alone Christ cannot stand. The incident is thereby made to suggest the Crucifixion, in which Christ submitted himself wholly to satanic violence and paradoxically overthrew it by that very submission, as his escape from death suggests the Resurrection, and his decisive defeat 'in air' of Satan Prince of the Air foreshadows the Ascension.[22] Moreover, in the extended typological perspective of the poem which sees the history of the Church reflected in the actions of her founder, the storm scene is suggestive of the Church subject to persecution by Satan and the world, the glorious dawn after the storm foreshadows the millennial reign of Christ with his saints, the tower episode images the final battle of Christ and Antichrist, and the angelic

banquet is at once a figure of the Church's communion commemorating Christ's priestly sacrifice, and also of the great
'marriage supper of the Lamb'.

Besides all this, the tower temptation serves also as an identity
test, as Satan's ultimate challenge to Christ's divine sonship
whose true meaning he has not yet fathomed. In his scornful
challenge to Christ –

> There stand, if thou wilt stand; to stand upright
> Will ask thee skill; . . .
> Now show thy progeny; if not to stand,
> Cast thyself down, safely if Son of God (IV, 551–5)

– Satan supposes that he has allowed for all the possibilities. If
Christ is a mere man he must fall from the spire upon which he
has been placed; if he is divine he will save himself by miracle;
and if he is uncertain he may cast himself down to test himself
and God. But what happens is quite beyond the limited
Satanic imagination. Christ shows his divinity not by miraculous
escape on Satan's terms, but by calmly maintaining the impossible position into which Satan has thrust him. Christ's response
to the tower challenge – 'Tempt not the Lord thy God; he
said and stood' (IV, 561) – suggests I believe by its confident
and commanding tone that Christ here completes his journey to
self-understanding through the teaching of the Father, and that
as he here images forth the passive endurance he will display at
the Crucifixion he is permitted to turn this very passion into a
dramatic act of conquest over Satan. He is permitted to exercise
the power of his Almighty Father in standing, as he exercised it
before in the victory over Satan in heaven, and will do so again
at the end of time. Satan's fall, 'smitten with amazement',
indicates that at last in total defeat he knows his victor, and the
angelic hymn celebrates Christ unequivocally as the 'True
Image of the Father' no less in the wilderness than in the bosom
of bliss (IV, 596–7).

The fact that the temptation episode has epitomized Christ's
entire role, and thus has been given the large significance and

scope appropriate to a brief epic, is emphasized again by the ambiguities of time and conflations of tense in the angelic hymn. Christ has '*now* . . . aveng'd / Supplanted Adam' and has '*regain'd* lost Paradise', but has yet '*to* reinstall' Adam's sons in that paradise where they '*shall* dwell secure'. He is already 'heir of both worlds' and 'Queller of Satan', but he has yet to '*begin* to save mankind'. Eden is already restored but Christ has yet to restore it; he has saved mankind but has yet to do so. The angelic hymn suggests that since all that is to be has been epitomized in this episode, Christ has indeed already gained the victory and has now merely to work out the history here foreshadowed. The poem makes further claim to large epic significance by its ambitious and for the most part successful attempt to incorporate, evaluate and order the whole complex of Classical-Judeo-Christian values which constitute the intellectual heritage of Western man. The particular ordering vision, like all human things, is partial. But the action of the poem – Christ's search in the wilderness to comprehend his nature and discover his mission, his subsumption of the past but rejection of its dead literalisms, his abjuration of the many evil or ignoble or imperfect or less perfect modes of action that would preclude attainment of the highest concept of personal excellence and mission – presents a myth of human process, of human striving toward ideals of comprehension and order, of wisdom and noble action, which must remain relevant and powerful as long as such ideals hold any meaning for us.

NOTES

1. See Milton's *De doctrina christiana*, in *Works*, ed. F. A. Patterson *et al.* (New York, 1931–8), especially XIV, 187, 189, 193, 219, 311–21, 337–43; XV, 275–7. I have argued this point at length in ch. VI of my *Milton's Brief Epic: The Genre, Meaning, and Art of 'Paradise Regained'* (Providence, R.I., and London, 1966).

2. I, 100–105, 111–15, 154–5; II, 131–5, 140–43, 348–9, 369–71; IV, 57, 613–15.

3. See Elizabeth M. Pope, *'Paradise Regained': The Tradition and the Poem* (Baltimore, 1947).

4. See for example, Gregory the Great, *Moralia in Job* (Library of the Fathers, vol. xviii (Oxford, 1844)), Preface.

5. I, 364–70, 407–26; III, 60–68, 88–95.

6. Chs. VIII–XII of *Milton's Brief Epic*.

7. *Works*, XV, 287–9, 291, 297, 299–301.

8. See for example, John Calvin, *A Harmonie upon the Three Evangelistes*, trans. E. P. (London, 1610), p. 125; Lancelot Andrewes. *The Wonderfull Combate . . . betweene Christ and Satan* (London, 1592), pp. 14–15; William Perkins, *Combate betweene Christ and the Devill*, in *Workes* (Cambridge, 1616–18), III, 372.

9. Milton defends gathered churches of the regenerate against the parochial church principle in his tracts *Of Civil Power* and *The Likeliest Means*.

10. See Michael Fixler, 'The Unclean Meats of the Mosaic Law and the Banquet Scene in *Paradise Regained*', *Modern Language Notes*, LXX (1955), 573–7.

11. 'And in this mountaine shall the LORD of hostes make unto all people a feast of fat things, a feast of wines on the lees well refined.' See Luther, *The Prefaces to . . . Luther's Bible*, ed. T. A. Readwin (London, 1863), p. 6.

12. Xenophon, *Memorabilia*, II, i, 21–6. See also Erwin Panofsky, *Hercules am Scheidewege* (Berlin, 1930), pl. xxv, fig. 46; pl. xl, fig. 61; pl. xxxix, fig. 60.

13. Epictetus, *Discourses*, III, xxvi, 30–32; Dio Chrysostom, 'The First Discourse on Kingship' (London, 1932), I, 31–47.

14. A. R. Anderson, 'Heracles and His Successors', *Harvard Studies in Classical Philology*, XXXIX (1928), 7–58.

15. Plato, *Republic*, IX, 580c.

16. See Howard Schultz, *Milton and Forbidden Knowledge* (New York, 1955); Lewalski, 'Milton on Learning and the Learned-Ministry Controversy', *Huntington Library Quarterly*, XXIV (1961), 267–81.

17. See Eugene F. Rice, *The Renaissance Idea of Wisdom* (Cambridge, Mass., 1958).

18. Augustine, *De Trinitate*, XII, xiv, 22–3, trans. A. W. Hadden, *Works*, ed. M. Dods (Edinburgh, 1877), VII, 302–3.

19. See Theodore Beza, *Job Expounded*, trans. anon. (1599?), sigs. B6–B6ᵛ, C7; sig. B (Preface).

20. *Summa Theologica*, pt III, Q. 41, art. 4.

21. The dawn passage has close verbal resemblances to the description of Easter Morn in Giles Fletcher's poem, *Christs Victorie and Triumph* (Cambridge, 1610), bk IV, stanzas 1–3.
22. See *Paradise Lost*, X, 187–9: 'and with ascension bright / Captivity led captive through the Air, / The Realm itself of Satan long usurpt.'

Louis L. Martz

PARADISE REGAINED:
THE INTERIOR TEACHER*

> When we have to do with things which we behold with
> the mind, that is, with the intelligence and with reason, we
> speak of things which we look upon directly in the inner
> light of truth which illumines the inner man and is inwardly
> enjoyed.   Augustine, *De Magistro*

MILTON's nephew, Edward Phillips, tells us that even in the
seventeenth century *Paradise Regained* was 'generally censur'd
to be much inferiour to' *Paradise Lost*, though he notes that the
poet 'could not hear with patience any such thing when related
to him'. 'Possibly', the nephew adds, 'the Subject may not
afford such variety of Invention, but it is thought by the most
judicious to be little or nothing inferiour to the other for stile
and decorum.'[1] But it is exactly the style and decorum that have
troubled Milton's readers. For Milton was given to writing in
clearly defined genres: the pastoral elegy, the classical epic, the
Greek drama; and for all these kinds of poetry he well knew the
appropriate style and decorum. But what kind of poem is
Paradise Regained? Usually, after the hint given by Milton thirty
years before the poem appeared, it has been called a 'brief epic'
modelled on the book of Job.[2] But Tillyard has argued that it
has a closer affinity with the old Morality plays; and, more
recently, Arnold Stein, in a persuasive book, has made an
extended effort to show that the poem is truly a drama, though
the stage is set in the hero's mind: a true drama in the usual
terms of character, motivation, incident, and dramatic surprise.[3]
Now all these epic and dramatic aspects are truly there in the

* From *The Paradise Within: Studies in Vaughan, Traherne and Milton*
(1964), ch. IV; revised from the *Journal of English Literary History*, XXVII
(1960), 223–47. Some slight changes have been made with the author's
permission.

poem; the trouble is that in the actual reading they seem to be only the vestiges, the echoes, the attenuated sketches of what might have made a true epic or drama; the possibilities of the action are strangely muted, deliberately underplayed, as though the centre of the action lay elsewhere.

Yet another suggestion, advanced by Tillyard thirty years ago, has not thus far received the attention it deserves. Tillyard noted (*Milton*, p. 322) that *Paradise Regained* and Vergil's *Georgics* were poems of almost exactly the same length, a little more than two thousand lines, and that both poems were divided into four books; moreover, some kind of Vergilian analogy, he thought, must reside in the fact that Milton's opening line, 'I who e're while the happy Garden sung', clearly echoes the lines that used to open the *Aeneid* in Renaissance editions:

> Ille ego, qui quondam gracili modulatus avena
> carmen, et egressus silvis vicina coegi
> ut quamvis avido parerent arva colono,
> gratum opus agricolis, at nunc horrentia Martis . . .

– lines, now widely regarded as authentic, which allude to Vergil's earlier works in the pastoral and georgic kinds. It is indeed a happy thought that Milton may thus have concluded his poetical career by publishing three poems in what his age regarded as the three great classical modes: the epic, the georgic and the drama in the manner of the Greeks.

The more we brood over the possibility, the more fruitful it seems. For *Paradise Regained*, as everyone has noticed, is not written in the grand style of *Paradise Lost*; it has its flashes of grandeur, but on the whole its writing is simpler, more subdued, more direct. This is just what the man of the Renaissance was trained to feel in comparing the *Aeneid* to the *Georgics*; in the classic definition of 'the three styles' handed down from late Roman critics, Vergil's *Aeneid* was the model of the grand style, his *Georgics*, the model of the middle style, and his *Eclogues*, the model of the low style. As Servius said:

tres enim sunt characteres, humilis, medius, grandiloquus: quos omnus in hoc invenimus poeta: nam in Aeneide grandiloquum habet, in georgicis medium, in bucolis humilem pro qualitate negotiorum et personarum.[4]

Thus at the outset of *Paradise Lost* Milton asks the Heavenly Muse to aid his 'adventrous Song, / That with no middle flight intends to soar / Above th' *Aonian* Mount'; but now, it seems, in *Paradise Regained*, he chooses to make a middle flight in the georgic style, which Vergil himself may be said to define at the outset of his Second Book:

> non ego cuncta meis amplecti versibus opto,
> non, mihi si linguae centum sint oraque centum,
> ferrea vox. (42-4)[5]

Furthermore, the two works share a common ethical theme: the praise of the temperate, disciplined, frugal life, as opposed to the grandeur, luxury, and vice of empires. Thus, as Milton's Tempter offers Jesus the power and the glory of the Roman Empire, Milton's hero answers by scorning

> That people victor once, now vile and base,
> Deservedly made vassal, who once just,
> Frugal, and mild, and temperate, conquer'd well,
> But govern ill the Nations under yoke,
> Peeling thir Provinces, exhausted all
> By lust and rapine; first ambitious grown
> Of triumph that insulting vanity;
> Then cruel, by thir sports to blood enur'd
> Of fighting beasts, and men to beasts, expos'd,
> Luxurious by thir wealth, and greedier still,
> And from the daily Scene effeminate. (IV, 132-42)

It is very close to the warning that Vergil implies throughout the *Georgics*, and indeed makes openly at the end of his second book, along with an allusion to the degrading effects of the theatre, Milton's 'daily Scene':

                              But happy
Too is he who knows the gods of nature,
Old man Silvanus, Pan, the sister nymphs.
Not for him 'the mandate of the people,'
The royal cloak of kings, not dissonance
Creating civil wars, the swift onslaught
From Balkan coalitions; not for him
The Roman State or Empires doomed to die . . .
Others lash the unknown seas with oars,
Rush at the sword, pay court in royal halls.
One destroys a city and its homes
To drink from jeweled cups and sleep on scarlet;
One hoards his wealth and lies on buried gold.
One gapes dumbfounded at the speaker's stand;
At the theatre, still another, open-mouthed,
Reels before crescendos of applause
From the tiers where mob and dignitaries sit . . .
    The farmer drives his curved plough through the earth:
His year's work lies in this; thus he sustains
His homeland . . .
Such a life the Sabines once embraced,
And Romulus and Remus; in this way
Etruria grew strong; thus Rome was formed . . . [6].

A georgic form, a georgic style, a georgic theme: everything combines to suggest that Milton, in *Paradise Regained*, is following out the same design that he set for himself in *Paradise Lost* and *Samson Agonistes*: to convert the modes of classic poetry into the service of Christianity. In *Paradise Regained* he has done this, I believe, by converting Vergil's georgic mode into a channel for religious meditation, with the result that the poem belongs, simultaneously, to the classical mode of didactic, instructive poetry,[7] and to the Christian genre of formal meditations on the Gospel.

From this standpoint we can understand the meaning of the basic style in which the poem is written: a ground-style that Milton carefully announces in his opening lines and maintains with strong consistency throughout the First Book:

> I who e're while the happy Garden sung,
> By one mans disobedience lost, now sing
> Recover'd Paradise to all mankind,
> By one mans firm obedience fully tri'd
> Through all temptation, and the Tempter foil'd
> In all his wiles, defeated the repuls't,
> And *Eden* rais'd in the wast Wilderness.

The allusion to *Paradise Lost* here asks us to recall that poem, and to note how different this new poem will be in its theme and hence in its style. We need only recall the latinate suspension and compression of that first enormous sentence of *Paradise Lost* to feel the contrast with the normal movement and scope of educated English speech in *Paradise Regained*. This new poem, then, as Tillyard says, 'is not an epic, it does not try to be an epic, and it must not be judged by any kind of epic standard' (*Milton*, p. 316). It is a simple 'I' who sings this new poem: a plain man without those bardic 'robes' that C. S. Lewis sees as characteristic of the high style of *Paradise Lost*. The voice of the narrator now speaks in the middle style appropriate to a personal meditation prompted not at all by emulation of the epic Muse, but purely by the 'Spirit who ledst this glorious Eremite / Into the Desert'. Reversing the order of Vergil's two great poems, the Christian poet will now 'tell of deeds / Above Heroic, though in secret done'.

Hence the trappings of *Paradise Lost* recede from view in Book I of *Paradise Regained*: as the opening lines prophesy, the syntax will tend to display the normal, supple, easy movement of an educated mind. Furthermore, when we recall the vast range of elaborate epic similes in the opening book of *Paradise Lost*, it is significant to notice that the opening book of *Paradise Regained* contains not a single simile of this kind; indeed it contains no classical allusions whatsoever, except near the close of the book, where the pagan oracles are mentioned only in order to announce their demise, as Jesus says to Satan:

> No more shalt thou by oracling abuse
> The Gentiles; henceforth Oracles are ceast,
> And thou no more with Pomp and Sacrifice
> Shalt be enquir'd at *Delphos* or elsewhere,
> At least in vain, for they shall find thee mute.
> God hath now sent his living Oracle
> Into the World, to teach his final will,
> And sends his Spirit of Truth henceforth to dwell
> In pious Hearts, an inward Oracle
> To all truth requisite for men to know.   (I, 455–64)

The firm and quiet manner of these lines, dignified, yet modest, is representative of the ground-style laid down in Book I of *Paradise Regained* as a central principle of the whole poem's action. To be sure, the difference from *Paradise Lost* is not complete. The language is less obviously latinate, though there is still plenty of latinity, since this is part of the Renaissance heritage and is also appropriate, in moderation, to a poem with a georgic model. And there are still a good many of those peculiar Miltonic compressions, transcending and defying grammar. The style, in short, reminds us, at a distance, of the manner of *Paradise Lost*: but it is all deliberately muted, thoroughly absorbed into another texture of writing:

> So spake our Morning Star then in his rise,
> And looking round on every side beheld
> A pathless Desert, dusk with horrid shades;
> The way he came not having mark'd, return
> Was difficult, by humane steps untrod;
> And he still on was led, but with such thoughts
> Accompanied of things past and to come
> Lodg'd in his brest, as well might recommend
> Such Solitude before choicest Society.
> Full forty days he pass'd, whether on hill
> Sometimes, anon in shady vale, each night
> Under the covert of some ancient Oak,
> Or Cedar, to defend him from the dew,
> Or harbour'd in one Cave, is not reveal'd . . . .
>   (I, 294–307)

We can recognize the voice and the manner as Miltonic: but the language is essentially that of any educated man. This effect, both common and peculiar, is characteristic of Vergil's georgic style, and is also essential to the meditative genre. This meditative kind of poetry consists of 'current language heightened' (Hopkins's phrase) – heightened by a voice that is at once that of a unique individual and yet still the voice of a man searching inwardly in common ways for the common bond of mankind. The muted, chastened style thus announced in the First Book of *Paradise Regained* seems appropriately developed out of Vergil's middle style, in order to pursue a work that is essentially a meditation on the Gospel.

From beginning to end of this poem the meditative mind of the narrator roams freely over the past, present, and future life of its hero. We begin, after the brief prologue, with a memory of the scene at Jordan during the baptism of Jesus by John: a scene that Satan recapitulates only forty lines later when he addresses his Council and warns them that he has heard 'the Sov'raign voice' at Jordan pronounce this man 'my Son'. And only forty lines after this (130 ff.) we hear the 'Sov'raign voice' itself, addressing Gabriel in Heaven, and summing up the whole life of the Son, from the mission of Gabriel at the Annunciation, through the coming temptation in the Wilderness, where the hero will 'lay down the rudiments / Of his great warfare', in which he will destroy the power of Sin and Death 'By Humiliation and strong Sufferance'. Thus prepared by the Father's own summation of the Son's career, we now come to 'the Son of God' himself:

> Mean while the Son of God, who yet some days
> Lodg'd in *Bethabara* where *John* baptiz'd,
> Musing and much revolving in his brest,
> How best the mighty work he might begin
> Of Saviour to mankind, and which way first
> Publish his God-like office now mature,
> One day forth walk'd alone, the Spirit leading;
> And his deep thoughts, the better to converse

> With solitude, till far from track of men,
> Thought following thought, and step by step led on,
> He entred now the bordering Desert wild,
> And with dark shades and rocks environ'd round,
> His holy Meditations thus persu'd.   (I, 183–95)

The period of temptation, we see, is primarily a mental retirement – 'thought following thought' – and what follows
now (196 ff.) is a meditation on the entire life of Jesus, given in
the person of the hero himself, as he meditates on the meaning
of his existence:

> O what a multitude of thoughts at once
> Awakn'd in me swarm, while I consider
> What from within I feel my self, and hear
> What from without comes often to my ears,
> Ill sorting with my present state compar'd.

He recalls his childhood, his visit to the Temple, his early aspirations when 'victorious deeds / Flam'd in my heart, heroic acts';

> Yet held it more humane, more heavenly first
> By winning words to conquer willing hearts,
> And make perswasion do the work of fear;
> At least to try . . . .

Then he recalls how his mother had 'inly rejoyc'd' at his youthful thoughts, how she had informed him that he was the son of
Heaven's Eternal King, how she had told him of the Annunciation and the Nativity: when

> a glorious Quire
> Of Angels in the fields of *Bethlehem* sung
> To Shepherds watching at their folds by night,
> And told them the Messiah was now born,
> Where they might see him, and to thee they came;
> Directed to the Manger where thou lais't,
> For in the Inn was left no better room . . . .

A biblical simplicity is thus interwoven with the subdued Miltonic and latinate idiom of this poem. And we learn of the Wise

Men, of Simeon and Anna, and how Jesus, pondering these things, along with the Scriptures, came to realize he was the promised Messiah:

> this chiefly, that my way must lie
> Through many a hard assay even to the death,
> E're I the promis'd Kingdom can attain,
> Or work Redemption for mankind, whose sins
> Full weight must be transferr'd upon my head.

Then finally, after this glimpse of the Passion, he remembers the central scene at Jordan:

> But as I rose out of the laving stream,
> Heaven open'd her eternal doors, from whence
> The Spirit descended on me like a Dove,
> And last the sum of all, my Father's voice,
> Audibly heard from Heav'n, pronounc'd me his,
> Me his beloved Son, in whom alone
> He was well pleas'd; by which I knew the time
> Now full, that I no more should live obscure,
> But openly begin, as best becomes
> The Authority which I deriv'd from Heaven.
> And now by some strong motion I am led
> Into this wilderness, to what intent
> I learn not yet, perhaps I need not know;
> For what concerns my knowledge God reveals.

This meditative poem, we see, first of all, concerns the self-discovery of the hero: what it means to be pronounced the Son of God. And indeed, as we read and re-read this poem, we are struck by the way in which that phrase 'Son of God' resounds throughout the poem as the chief title by which Milton alludes to the hero. The phrase 'Son of God' occurs no less than 39 times; 10 times in Book I and 21 times in the concluding book. A few statistics may be in order here to make an important point. Milton calls his hero Jesus only 6 times; he calls him Saviour 21 times, Messiah 7 times – but he never once calls his hero by the name of Christ. This is not simply because he prefers to use the Hebrew equivalent, Messiah, for as I have said, this term is not used often, nor does he use the translated title 'Anointed' more than once.

Why not use the term 'Christ'? I think Milton avoids the term here because he is not writing only about the life of Christ, that unique being, Prophet, Priest, and King; he is writing about a composite generalized being whom he calls the Son of God in such an insistent way as to recall the opening of John's Gospel: 'But as many as received him, to them gave he power to become the sons of God' (i, 12); or the promise of Paul in Romans viii, 14: 'For as many as are led by the Spirit of God, they are the sons of God.' Or, best of all, the words of John's first Epistle (iii, 1–3): 'Behold, what manner of love the Father hath bestowed upon us, that we should be called the sons of God: therefore the world knoweth us not, because it knew him not. Beloved, now are we the sons of God, and it doth not yet appear what we shall be: but we know that, when he shall appear, we shall be like him; for we shall see him as he is. And every man that hath this hope in him purifieth himself, even as he is pure.'

After tantalizing us with the phrase throughout the poem, Milton finally clarifies the issues for us at the very close, as Satan is about to make his last desperate effort: the temptation of the pinnacle. Here, with a wonderful irony, Milton matches the opening meditation of the hero by giving now Satan's own sardonic commentary on the Gospel story, Satan's version of what it means to be the Son of God:

> To whom the Fiend now swoln with rage reply'd:
> Then hear, O Son of *David*, Virgin-born;
> For Son of God to me is yet in doubt,
> Of the Messiah I have heard foretold
> By all the Prophets; of thy birth at length
> Announc't by *Gabriel* with the first I knew,
> And of the Angelic Song in *Bethlehem* field,
> On thy birth-night, that sung thee Saviour born.
> From that time seldom have I ceas'd to eye

Thy infancy, thy childhood, and thy youth,
Thy manhood last, though yet in private bred;
Till at the Ford of *Jordan* whither all
Flock'd to the Baptist, I among the rest,
Though not to be Baptiz'd, by voice from Heav'n
Heard thee pronounc'd the Son of God belov'd.
Thenceforth I thought thee worth my nearer view
And narrower Scrutiny, that I might learn
In what degree or meaning thou art call'd
The Son of God, which bears no single sence;
The Son of God I also am, or was,
And if I was, I am; relation stands;
All men are Sons of God; yet thee I thought
In some respect far higher so declar'd.   (IV, 499–521)

He has not long to wait: placed on the pinnacle and faced with
the final temptation, the hero answers in the words of the Bible:
'Tempt not the Lord thy God, he said and stood. / But Satan
smitten with amazement fell.' Into those brief words, 'Tempt
not the Lord thy God,' Milton has packed a trinity of meanings:
they bear no single sense.[8] First of all, in the traditional interpretation, the words give the answer that any man might give:
that is, one must not ask God for unreasonable help, one must
not ask for unnecessary evidence of divine favour. But secondly,
in Milton's strategic placing of the words, they show why Satan
fell, stupefied, 'strook with dread and anguish', filled with
'Ruin, and desperation, and dismay'. Satan is confounded by
the revelation that he has been tempting divinity incarnate.
And thirdly, we may take the words to indicate the full self-
realization of the hero: he understands now what he has not
known earlier, or has known by glimpses only: that he is himself divine.

Certainly the critics are right who have said that this invulnerable hero makes it very difficult to produce a dramatic
development in the poem. As D. C. Allen has pointed out,[9]
Satan is 'aghast' from the opening and feels his forces shattered
from the outset; his 'motivation' for the temptations seems to

be the curiosity of desperation rather than any real hope of victory. How, then, can the poem sustain our interest?

I believe the answer lies in watching the movements of the meditative mind as it defines the nature of the Son of God. The whole poem presents a mind that uses the 'characters' to explore the problems and besetting sins of any potential Son of God among men: a mind that conveys the process of temptation by creating what might be called a contest of styles. The ground of this great warfare is laid down, stylistically, in Book I; what we feel here, I think, is the presence of a mind engaged in an immense effort at self-control, a mind held in leash, poised, tense, alert, watching any tendency toward elaboration, luxury, self-indulgence: alert to control any temptation that might lead the meditator far away from the ground that he strikes, ethically, theologically, and stylistically, at the end of Book I, in answer to Satan's opening manoeuvres:

> To whom our Saviour with unalter'd brow.
> Thy coming hither, though I know thy scope,
> I bid not or forbid; do as thou find'st
> Permission from above; thou canst not more.

Book I is a prelude: it draws the scene; it establishes the middle style: it sets the problems to be explored, and foresees their conclusion. The action proper begins with Book II, where the life of Jesus is considered from many different perspectives. First, from the viewpoint of the new-born Christians who had been baptized at Jordan – Andrew, Simon Peter, and others, whom we meet in a properly georgic setting:

> Then on the bank of *Jordan*, by a Creek:
> Where winds with Reeds, and Osiers whisp'ring play
> Plain Fishermen, no greater men them call,
> Close in a Cottage low together got
> Thir unexpected loss and plaints out breath'd.   (II, 25–9)

They speak appropriately on the lower edge of the middle style, in language that moves gracefully out of the biblical toward the latinate:

>   our eyes beheld
> Messiah certainly now come, so long
> Expected of our Fathers; we have heard
> His words, his wisdom full of grace and truth,
> Now, now, for sure, deliverance is at hand,
> The Kingdom shall to *Israel* be restor'd:
> Thus we rejoyc'd, but soon our joy is turn'd
> Into perplexity and new amaze .... (II, 31–8)

But they end with simple faith: 'Soon we shall see our hope, our joy return.'

From these we turn to 'Mother *Mary*' (II, 60 ff.), whom we find pondering in her heart all the major events in her son's life to this point: the Annunciation, the Nativity –

> In such a season born when scarce a Shed
> Could be obtain'd to shelter him or me
> From the bleak air; a Stable was our warmth,
> A Manger his . . .

the flight into Egypt, his acknowledgement as Son at Jordan, the prophecy of Simeon, and that time when Jesus visited the Temple:

> when twelve years he scarce had seen,
> I lost him, but so found, as well I saw
> He could not lose himself; but went about
> His Father's business . . . .

And now as Mary 'with thoughts / Meekly compos'd awaited the fulfilling', we have a glimpse of her son, at the centre of the poem's inward action, as he,

>   tracing the Desert wild,
> Sole but with holiest Meditations fed,
> Into himself descended .... (II, 109–11)

After all these humble, inward scenes, so frequently marked by a biblical simplicity of phrasing, the process of temptation now bursts upon us in the high oratorical style of *Paradise Lost*, as we hear Satan addressing his host of devils and consulting with them over how to proceed in the face of such dangerous self-mastery:

> Princes, Heavens antient Sons, Aethereal Thrones,
> Demonian Spirits now, from the Element
> Each of his reign allotted, rightlier call'd,
> Powers of Fire, Air, Water, and Earth beneath . . . .
>
> (II, 121–4)

That touch of the old fallen oratory leads us quickly down to the lowest level of sensuality, as Belial moves to suggest that the Son of God be tempted by sexual appetite. Thus Milton skilfully manages to include in his poem an aspect of human weakness that could not be associated with Jesus. Milton has Satan reject Belial's suggestion in such a way as to remind us of lust's long history, bringing in the first strong colouring from classical mythology that has been allowed thus far in the poem:

> Before the Flood thou with thy lusty Crew,
> False titl'd Sons of God –

note how Milton keeps the problem ever before us: what it means to be a Son of God –

> roaming the Earth
> Cast wanton eyes on the daughters of men,
> And coupl'd with them, and begot a race.
> Have we not seen, or by relation heard,
> In Courts and Regal Chambers how thou lurk'st,
> In Wood or Grove by mossie Fountain side,
> In Valley or Green Meadow to way-lay
> Some beauty rare, *Calisto, Clymene,*
> *Daphne,* or *Semele, Antiopa,*
> Or *Amymone, Syrinx,* many more
> Too long, then lay'st thy scapes on names ador'd,
> *Apollo, Neptune, Jupiter,* or *Pan,*
> Satyr, or Fawn, or Silvan?   (II, 178–91)

That brilliant cluster of old Ovidian myths, rejected here even by Satan, prepares us for the meditative combat that will now develop in a long contest of styles, as the rich, sensuous colouring and the high rhetoric of the world rises up against the 'frugal' ground-style set in Book I: that middle, georgic style which represents the way of temperance struggling against the self-indulgence of an elaborate style.

Thus the vision of the Banquet now arises (II, 337 ff.) in an effort to obliterate the hero's self-control. It is a step upward from Belial's sensuality, but it includes a touch of Belial's suggestion in the vision of

> Nymphs of *Diana's* train, and *Naiades*
> With fruits and flowers from *Amalthea's* horn,
> And Ladies of th' *Hesperides* . . . .

Its appeal to hunger of course relates back to the preliminary temptation of Book I, while the whole scene looks forward to the following temptations of wealth and regal power; for it is 'A Table richly spred, in regal mode'. Milton is offering a Roman banquet to all the quickened senses:

> And at a stately side-board by the wine
> That fragrant smell diffus'd, in order stood
> Tall stripling youths rich clad, of fairer hew
> Then *Ganymed* or *Hylas* . . . .

The worlds of classic myth and medieval romance are ransacked for physical allurement and brought to a climax in those superbly over-wrought lines of Spenserian motif and alliteration, carrying the appeal of sound to its furthest poetical extreme:

> And Ladies of th' *Hesperides,* that seem'd
> Fairer then feign'd of old, or fabl'd since
> Of Fairy Damsels met in Forest wide
> By Knights of *Logres,* or of *Lyones,*
> *Lancelot* or *Pelleas,* or *Pellenore* . . . .

We return with a shock to the frugal ground-style, as Jesus rejects the offer, renouncing imagery in favour of irony – except for a brief suggestion of the communion table:

> To whom thus Jesus temperately reply'd:
> Said'st thou not that to all things I had right?
> And who withholds my pow'r that right to use?
> Shall I receive by gift what of my own,
> When and where likes me best, I can command?
> I can at will, doubt not, as soon as thou,
> Command a Table in this Wilderness,
> And call swift flights of Angels ministrant
> Array'd in Glory on my cup to attend . . . .

So the central contest, the full excitement, of the poem lies in the movements, the fluctuations, of the meditative mind itself. It is an inward combat created by Milton's brilliant manipulation of styles, a contest in which the flights of poetic splendour are consistently drawn back by the prevailing net of a frugal, georgic style to the ground of renunciation and temperance.[10] The way in which this ground-style represents the controlling ideal of the poem is clearly shown now in the speech of Jesus that closes Book II, in answer to the temptation of wealth. Here Milton gives, exactly in the centre of the poem, a definition of true Kingship, true Sonship. Jesus first alludes to Gideon, Jephthah, and David, and then places them beside certain men 'Among the Heathen' who are also 'Worthy of Memorial': *'Quintius, Fabricius, Curius, Regulus'*. This collocation of Roman and biblical heroes of the simple life points the way toward the association of Job with Socrates that is soon to follow in Book III, as Jesus rejects the temptation of glory by praising higher conquests won

> By deeds of peace, by wisdom eminent,
> By patience, temperance; I mention still
> Him whom thy wrongs with Saintly patience born,
> Made famous in a Land and times obscure;
> Who names not now with honour patient *Job*?
> Poor *Socrates* (who next more memorable?) . . . .

> (III, 91–6)

Anticipating this open praise of Socrates, the great ethical speech of the Son ending Book II proceeds to show how the

Socratic reliance on the inner man (Socrates' 'discovery of the soul', as Cornford has called it)[11] leads onward into the Christian concept of highest kingship: we note the quiet implication of the 'wreath of thorns' and the 'burden' of Second Isaiah:

> What if with like aversion I reject
> Riches and Realms; yet not for that a Crown,
> Golden in shew, is but a wreath of thorns,
> Brings dangers, troubles, cares, and sleepless nights
> To him who wears the Regal Diadem,
> When on his shoulders each mans burden lies;
> For therein stands the office of a King,
> His Honour, Vertue, Merit and chief Praise,
> That for the Publick all this weight he bears.
> Yet he who reigns within himself, and rules
> Passions, Desires, and Fears, is more a King;
> Which every wise and vertuous man attains:
> And who attains not, ill aspires to rule
> Cities of men, or head-strong Multitudes,
> Subject himself to Anarchy within,
> Or lawless passions in him which he serves.
> But to guide Nations in the way of truth
> By saving Doctrine, and from errour lead
> To know, and knowing worship God aright,
> Is yet more Kingly, this attracts the Soul,
> Governs the inner man, the nobler part,
> That other o're the body only reigns,
> And oft by force, which to a generous mind
> So reigning can be no sincere delight.
> Besides to give a Kingdom hath been thought
> Greater and nobler done, and to lay down
> Far more magnanimous, then to assume.   (II, 457–83)

' – to lay down' – with his careful placing of those words at the end of a line, Milton forces us to pause and complete the phrase in the familiar words of John. And thus the Greek virtue of magnanimity is redefined in terms of Christian sacrifice. It is important that thus, in the middle of the poem, Milton should pay tribute to classic virtue and classic thought, for the tribute helps to qualify the renunciation of Greek culture that follows in Book IV.

From this steadfast centre of the poem, a centre defined both by concept and by style, Satan now attempts to move the hero by rhetorical and imagistic elaborations that gradually rise toward the height of Milton's grand style. The temptation of glory begins on a higher pitch of rhetorical insinuation than anything we have seen earlier, especially in contrast with the long, straightforward, temperate speech we have just heard:

> I see thou know'st what is of use to know,
> What best to say canst say, to do canst do;
> Thy actions to thy words accord, thy words
> To thy large heart give utterance due, thy heart
> Conteins of good, wise, just, the perfect shape.
>   . . . wherefore deprive
> All Earth her wonder at thy acts, thy self
> The fame and glory, glory the reward
> That sole excites to high attempts the flame
> Of most erected Spirits, most temper'd pure
> Aetherial, who all pleasures else despise,
> All treasures and all gain esteem as dross,
> And dignities and powers all but the highest?
>
>   (III, 7–30)

In line with such artifice and convolution the first half of the Third Book is devoted to abstract argument at a very high level of rhetorical elaboration and oratorical prowess.

Jesus answers this challenge with a burst of blunt oratory that has puzzled many readers, since the harshness here seems out of line with the charity of a Saviour, seems rather to voice the bitter disillusionment of John Milton himself, who had once tried to win a victory of the Just with the help of the many, and had seen the whole effort fail:

> For what is glory but the blaze of fame,
> The peoples praise, if always praise unmixt?
> And what the people but a herd confus'd,
> A miscellaneous rabble, who extol

Things vulgar, & well weigh'd, scarce worth the praise,
They praise and they admire they know not what;
And know not whom, but as one leads the other;
And what delight to be by such extoll'd,
To live upon thir tongues and be thir talk,
Of whom to be disprais'd were no small praise?
His lot who dares be singularly good.
Th' intelligent among them and the wise
Are few, and glory scarce of few is rais'd.
This is true glory and renown, when God
Looking on the Earth, with approbation marks
The just man, and divulges him through Heaven
To all his Angels, who with true applause
Recount his praises . . . .   (III, 47–64)

We are right, I think, if we hear in these words the voice of the
fierce old Cromwellian, elected even in defeat. But is it a flaw in
the fabric of the poem? Is it a flaw like that which Arnold Stein
has seen in Milton's later description of the Parthian power,
where he feels that 'Milton has tampered with the perspective',
so that a 'narrative voice seems to have intruded without
warrant'?[12] But that narrative voice, or that meditative voice,
has been in control of the action from the poem's outset, where
we met at the first word the meditative 'I' whose inward
thoughts enact the poem. In such a poem we are bound to hear
throughout a personal voice. In a pure drama, properly so
called, it would indeed be a flaw if one felt another voice
coming through instead of the voice appropriate to a given
character in that drama. But in this inward speaking of the
meditative mind, all 'characters', all speeches, are enveloped
within, and suffused with, the controlling voice of the meditator
himself. That mind is exploring its own problems, as well as
those of mankind, through the speeches of the 'characters',
who have indeed no separate existence, whose very function is
to take upon themselves the meditative voice of the narrator.

That is why the poem never shows any extended effort to
present a drama of characters in the usual sense. Satan and the

Son of God in this poem speak within the mind of one who hopes to be himself a Son of God; both these actors use the human voice that this particular possible Son of God, John Milton, possesses; for the meditative voice must speak as a particular meditative man himself would speak. So I think it is hardly valid to object that this poem does not present the Christ of the Gospels. For this is not a rehearsal of the Gospels; it is rather (as Hopkins would say) a rehearsal of the self, where the voice of the inner man discovers what a true Son of God ought to reply to such temptations.

Thus earlier we have heard Satan speak, as it might seem, 'out of character', when he rebukes Belial for suggesting a temptation through female beauty:

> or should she confident,
> As sitting Queen ador'd on Beauties Throne,
> Descend with all her winning charms begirt
> To enamour, as the Zone of *Venus* once
> Wrought that effect on *Jove*, so Fables tell;
> How would one look from his Majestick brow
> Seated as on the top of Vertues hill,
> Discount'nance her despis'd, and put to rout
> All her array; her female pride deject,
> Or turn to reverent awe? For Beauty stands
> In the admiration only of weak minds
> Led captive; cease to admire, and all her Plumes
> Fall flat and shrink into a trivial toy .... (II, 211–23)

If this strikes us as more Miltonic than Satanic, it need not worry us: the 'characters' of this poem exist, not for their own points of view, but as occasions, as channels, by which the personal meditation can make its way.

Now, after this brilliant battle of rhetoric has ended with the defeat of worldly glory, so, in another mode of temptation, Milton moves onward, in the second half of Book III, to show a richer, higher style arising out of the temperate ground. It is a significant touch that Milton should have the grand tableau of

Parthian power, with its echoes of the grand style of *Paradise Lost*, literally rise up from a georgic plain:

> With that (such power was giv'n him then) he took
> The Son of God up to a Mountain high.
> It was a Mountain at whose verdant feet
> A spatious plain out strech't in circuit wide
> Lay pleasant; from his side two rivers flow'd,
> Th' one winding, the other strait and left between
> Fair Champain with less rivers interveind,
> Then meeting joyn'd thir tribute to the Sea:
> Fertil of corn the glebe, of oyl and wine,
> With herds the pastures throng'd, with flocks the hills,
> Huge Cities and high towr'd, that well might seem
> The seats of mightiest Monarchs . . . .   (III, 251–62)

And so we come to those grandly over-wrought displays of proper names that sum up worldly power and empire:

> *Ecbatana* her structure vast there shews,
> And *Hecatompylos* her hunderd gates,
> There *Susa* by *Choaspes*, amber stream,
> The drink of none but Kings; of later fame
> Built by *Emathian*, or by *Parthian* hands,
> The great *Seleucia, Nisibis,* and there
> *Artaxata, Teredon, Tesiphon* . . . .   (III, 286–92)

> From *Arachosia,* from *Candaor* East,
> And *Margiana* to the *Hyrcanian* cliffs
> Of *Caucasus,* and dark *Iberian* dales,
> From *Atropatia* and the neighbouring plains
> Of *Adiabene, Media,* and the South
> Of *Susiana* to *Balsara's* hav'n.   (III, 316–21)

It is appropriate, I think, that near the close of all this splendid panoply, Milton should bring in (at line 329) the poem's outstanding example of a pompous and affected latinism: 'Chariots or Elephants *endorst* with Towers'. And it is even more appropriate that at the very end of the vision we should meet the poem's first example of an epic comparison, one that clearly

reminds us of the allusions to chivalric romance in the opening
book of *Paradise Lost* (582–7, 763–6):

> Such forces met not, nor so wide a camp,
> When *Agrican* with all his Northern powers
> Besieg'd *Albracca*, as Romances tell;
> The City of *Gallaphrone*, from thence to win
> The fairest of her Sex *Angelica*
> His daughter, sought by many Prowest Knights,
> Both *Paynim*, and the Peers of *Charlemane*.
> Such and so numerous was thir Chivalrie . . . .

(III, 337–44)

This great passage on the Parthians demonstrates, as the
banquet scene has earlier shown, that this writer is still at the
peak of his powers. All the strength of *Paradise Lost* is still
there; he can use it when he chooses; but here the Son of God
condemns the grand vision as 'argument / Of human weakness
rather then of strength'.

As the Fourth Book opens, Milton announces the imminent
climax of the grand style by introducing a cluster of similes.
They are not quite heroic similes; they are rather subdued echoes
of the heroic mode; but they serve to prepare for the epic
manner of the following tableau of Rome, where Milton bends
his heroic bow still further, carrying the compressed richness of
his high style to its absolute and appropriate limit:

> Thence to the gates cast round thine eye, and see
> What conflux issuing forth, or entring in,
> Pretors, Proconsuls to thir Provinces
> Hasting or on return, in robes of State;
> Lictors and rods the ensigns of thir power,
> Legions and Cohorts, turmes of horse and wings:
> Or Embassies from Regions far remote
> In various habits on the *Appian* road,
> Or on the *Aemilian,* some from farthest South,
> *Syene,* and where the shadow both way falls,
> *Meroe Nilotic* Isle, and more to West,
> The Realm of *Bocchus* to the Black-moor Sea;

> From the *Asian* Kings and *Parthian* among these,
> From *India* and the golden *Chersoness,*
> And utmost *Indian* Isle *Taprobane,*
> Dusk faces with white silken Turbants wreath'd:
> From *Gallia, Gades,* and the *Brittish* West,
> *Germans* and *Scythians,* and *Sarmatians* North
> Beyond *Danubius* to the *Tauric* Pool.   (IV, 61–79)

This vision of Rome is more than the climax of the high style:
it is a culmination of all the many threads of temptation that
have been weaving their way toward this highest 'grandeur and
majestic show / Of luxury', of 'wealth and power, / Civility of
Manners, Arts, and Arms'. For the Son's answer recalls the
Banquet scene of Book II:

> though thou should'st add to tell
> Thir sumptuous gluttonies, and gorgeous feasts
> On *Cittron* tables or *Atlantic* stone;
> (For I have also heard, perhaps have read)
> Their wines of *Setia, Cales,* and *Falerne,*
> *Chios* and *Creet,* and how they quaff in Gold,
> Crystal and Myrrhine cups imboss'd with Gems
> And studs of Pearl, to me should'st tell who thirst
> And hunger still . . . .   (IV, 113–21)

It has all been one sustained temptation, from the point where
Belial first spoke of sexual appetite, up through the more refined
appetites of the banquet, and onward to this moment of final
rejection for these kingdoms of the flesh, the world, and the
devil.

For this, we must note, is the end of Satan's kingdoms,[13] as
Satan himself three times says: first, in concluding his vision of
Rome:

> These having shewn thee, I have shewn thee all
> The Kingdoms of the world, and all thir glory.
>
>   (IV, 88–9)

Next, in his answer to the Son's rejection, where Milton concludes the whole sequence by bringing in the ending of the

second temptation in Luke's account: 'The Kingdoms of the world to thee I give . . . if thou wilt fall down, / And worship me'; with the answer: 'Get thee behind me . . .' (IV, 163–7, 193–4). And thirdly, by way of prologue to the next vision:

> Therefore let pass, as they are transitory,
> The Kingdoms of this world; I shall no more
> Advise thee, gain them as thou canst, or not.
>
> (IV, 209–11)

But just as he had offered to the meditative mind the sexual suggestion of Belial, before the temptation of the Kingdoms, properly so called, here Milton adds another temptation. What implications lie in this placing of the final tableau of Greek culture outside of the Kingdoms of the World? First of all, we should note, with some relief, perhaps, that these realms of Greek culture do not lie within Satan's gift: he does not control them, he does not offer to give them. Satan can only urge the Son of God to use Greek culture on the wrong terms, that is, to value Greek learning and art beyond the bounds proper to a Son of God. Thus: shall the Son of God concede that Athens is truly 'Mother of Arts / And Eloquence', that her Tragedians are 'teachers best / Of moral prudence', 'High actions, and high passions best describing'? Shall the Son of God concede that Socrates was really 'Wisest of men' and that Greek thought is all in all because 'These rules will render thee a King compleat / Within thy self'?

The Son has already anticipated his answer in the long speech at the end of Book II. The Son of God can never rest within the ideal of being 'compleat / Within thy self'. This, he has implied, is a right beginning, but the Son of God must look beyond himself to the thorns, the burden, the weight of mankind's incompleteness.

The Son's answer at first should cause us no discomfort: he does not at first deny the value of Greek culture: he says only that it is not necessary to the good life:

> To whom our Saviour sagely thus repli'd.

371

> Think not but that I know these things, or think
> I know them not; not therefore am I short
> Of knowing what I aught: he who receives
> Light from above, from the fountain of light,
> No other doctrine needs, though granted true . . . .
>
> (IV, 285–90)

Milton could have avoided all our modern worries over this scene if he had only had the consideration to stop here; but, as in Satan's scorn of sexual weakness, or in Jesus' denunciation of glory, so here the personal involvement of the meditator runs beyond the bounds of an easy propriety. For the Christian Humanist and Platonist this is the greatest challenge: can he be brought to say that truth resides in Greek achievements, in and by themselves? The Son of God is thus driven to make, at this point, a judgement more drastic and more violent than that made by the rest of the poem. For the whole poem qualifies and moderates this fierce renunciation, while at the same time this particular episode shows the speaker's readiness to make the ultimate sacrifice, if it should be demanded. The tone is tense, vehement, almost savage in places:

> But these are false, or little else but dreams,
> Conjectures, fancies, built on nothing firm.
> The first and wisest of them all profess'd
> To know this only, that he nothing knew;
> The next to fabling fell and smooth conceits . . .
> Alas what can they teach, and not mislead;
> Ignorant of themselves, of God much more,
> And how the world began, and how man fell
> Degraded by himself, on grace depending?
> Much of the Soul they talk, but all awrie,
> And in themselves seek vertue, and to themselves
> All glory arrogate, to God give none . . . .
>
> (IV, 291–315)

And as for learning the 'secret power / Of harmony' and 'moral prudence' from Greek poetry:

> All our Law and Story strew'd
> With Hymns, our Psalms with artful terms inscrib'd,
> Our Hebrew Songs and Harps in *Babylon,*
> That pleas'd so well our Victors ear, declare
> That rather *Greece* from us these Arts deriv'd;
> Ill imitated, while they loudest sing
> The vices of thir Deities, and thir own
> In Fable, Hymn, or Song, so personating
> Thir Gods ridiculous, and themselves past shame.
> Remove their swelling Epithetes thick laid
> As varnish on a Harlots cheek, the rest,
> Thin sown with aught of profit or delight,
> Will far be found unworthy to compare
> With *Sion's* songs, to all true tasts excelling,
> Where God is prais'd aright, and Godlike men,
> The Holiest of Holies, and his Saints;
> Such are from God inspir'd, not such from thee;
> Unless where moral vertue is express't
> By light of Nature not in all quite lost.   (IV, 334–52)

The violence of the charge, followed by the curt qualification, suggests that here is the hardest renunciation of all; but if necessary, the Son of God is prepared to lay down all. It is the same action that Milton's older contemporary, Nicholas Ferrar, performed on his deathbed, where, as the scene has come down to us, he said at last to his brother:

When you have measured out the place for my grave, then goe and take out of my Study, those three great Hampers full of Bookes that have stood there locked up these many yeares: They were not many scores but many Hundreths in all kind of Languages, which he had in all places gotten with great search, and some cost. They were Comedies, Tragedies, Love-Hymns, Heroicall Poems, and such like. Carry (sayd he) those Hampers to the place of my grave, and upon it, see you burn them all: and this he spake with some vehemency and passion of Indignation. Goe, Let it be done, Let it be done . . . .

And after the books had been burned, John Ferrar returned to his brother's bedside and 'told him, all was done, as he had required'. 'Then he suddenly lifting up himself, sat up in his Bed, gave God hearty thanks, and called for Pen, Inke, and Paper,' and wrote out the following document:

November 28th 1637. I.H.S. In the name of God, Amen.

In as much as all the Comedyes, Tragedyes, Pastoralls etc: and all those they call Heroicall Poems, none excepted; and like wise all the Bookes of Tales, which they call Novells, and all feigned Historyes written in Prose, all Love Hymns, and all the like Bookes are full of Idolatry, and especially tend to the Overthrow of Christian Religion, undermining the very Foundations thereof, and corrupt and pollute the minds of the Readers, with filthy lusts, as, woe is me, I have proved in my self. In this regard therefore, to shew my detestation of them to the World, and that all others may take warning, I have burned all of them, and most humbly have, and doe beseech God, to forgive me all my mispent time in them, and all the sinns that they have caused in me, which surely, but for his infinite Grace, had carried my soule down into Hell long ere this. . . . I beseech all that truly feare God, that love Jesus Christ, to consider these things well. Amen, Amen, Amen.[14]

So Milton's Son of God must also enact this final renunciation: a stern demand, but just, in terms of the whole poem; for what has the poem been saying if it has not said that the elaborations of classical literature are unnecessary dangerous, and unreliable? Milton has constantly affirmed this in the ground-style of his poem, where 'swelling Epithetes' are removed, and a basic idiom is achieved approaching the 'majestic unaffected stile' that Milton here praises in the Hebrew prophets. 'So spake the Son of God' and Satan finds himself now 'Quite at a loss, for all his darts were spent'.

With those words (IV, 366) Milton marks the close of his long meditative analysis of human temptation. What remains is prophecy, epiphany, and praise, which Milton gives in three symbolic scenes. First Satan arouses a tremendous storm which shadows forth the Passion and the Resurrection, as Milton makes clear by having Satan allude to the future sufferings of Jesus immediately before and after the storm (IV, 386–8, 477–

83). Next comes the full revelation of divine power, suggesting the Day of Judgement, as the Son of God stands on the pinnacle, and Satan falls, accompanied to his doom by a pair of true epic similes which drive home the absolute finality of the defeat. And lastly, the 'Angelic Quires' sing their concluding hymn of praise, which Milton phrases in a way that allows the Son of God in this poem to suggest the restored Image of God in man, the Paradise within.

> True Image of the Father whether thron'd
> In the bosom of bliss, and light of light
> Conceiving, or remote from Heaven, enshrin'd
> In fleshly Tabernacle, and human form,
> Wandring the Wilderness, whatever place,
> Habit, or state, or motion, still expressing
> The Son of God, with Godlike force indu'd
> Against th' Attempter of thy Fathers Throne,
> And Thief of Paradise; him long of old
> Thou didst debel, and down from Heav'n cast
> With all his Army, now thou hast aveng'd
> Supplanted *Adam*, and by vanquishing
> Temptation, hast regain'd lost Paradise . . .
> For though that seat of earthly bliss be fail'd,
> A fairer Paradise is founded now
> For *Adam* and his chosen Sons, whom thou
> A Saviour art come down to re-install.
> Where they shall dwell secure, when time shall be
> Of Tempter and Temptation without fear.

(IV, 596–617)

NOTES

1. See *The Early Lives of Milton*, ed. Helen Darbishire (London, 1932), pp. 75–6.
2. See the famous prologue to the second book of *The Reason of Church Government* (1642).
3. E. M. W. Tillyard, *Milton* (London, 1930), pp. 317–18; Arnold Stein,

Heroic Knowledge (Minneapolis, 1957). See also the presentation of an adverse view of the poem by W. W. Robson, 'The Better Fortitude', in *The Living Milton*, ed. Kermode; and the study of the poem from the standpoint of Christ's mediatorial role by Barbara Kiefer Lewalski, 'Theme and Structure in *Paradise Regained*', *Studies in Philology*, LVII (1960), 186–220 [reprinted above, pp. 322 ff.].

4. *Servis Grammatici Qui Feruntur in Vergilii Carmina Commentarii*, ed. G. Thilo and H. Hagen (4 vols., Leipzig, 1881–1902), vol. 3, fasc. 1, pp. 1–2.

5.   'I choose not to enfold
        All things within my verse, not though I had
        A hundred tongues and mouths, a voice of iron.'
From the translation of the *Georgics* by Smith Palmer Bovie (Chicago, 1956).

6. *Georgics*, II, 493–534, in the translation by Bovie. See the whole famous passage beginning '*O fortunatos nimium, sua si bona norint, | agricolas!*' (II, 458 f.).

7. See Addison's essay on the *Georgics*, first published in Dryden's translation of Vergil (1697): 'No rules therefore that relate to *Pastoral*, can any way affect the *Georgics*, since they fall under that class of Poetry, which consists in giving plain and direct instructions to the reader; whether they be Moral duties, as those of *Theognis* and *Pythagoras*: or Philosophical speculations, as those of *Aratus* and *Lucretius*: or Rules of practice, as those of *Hesiod* and *Virgil*.' Addison, *Miscellaneous Works*, ed. A. C. Guthkelch (2 vols., London, 1914), II, 4.

8. For the wide range of interpretations possible here see the study of the third temptation given by Elizabeth Marie Pope in her valuable book, '*Paradise Regained': The Tradition and the Poem* (Baltimore, 1947), ch. 7. Also the admirable article by A. S. P. Woodhouse, 'Theme and Pattern in *Paradise Regained*', *University of Toronto Quarterly*, XXV (1955–6), 167–82; esp. p. 181.

9. Don Cameron Allen, *The Harmonious Vision* (Baltimore, 1954), pp. 110–15.

10. I believe that this functional view of the basic style of *Paradise Regained* was suggested to me by certain remarks of W. Menzies in his essay, 'Milton: the Last Poems', *Essays and Studies*, XXIV (1938), 80–113; see esp. pp. 109–11. A similar view is developed by Jacques Blondel in the introduction (really a sizeable monograph) prefaced to his bilingual edition of *Paradise Regained* (Paris, 1955); see esp. pp. 92–110 *passim*.

11. F. M. Cornford, *Before and after Socrates* (Cambridge, 1950), ch. 2, esp. pp. 50–51.

12. Stein, *Heroic Knowledge*, p. 89. For a discussion of the ways in which

Milton 'intrudes' throughout the poem, see the adverse criticism by W. B. C. Watkins, *Anatomy of Milton's Verse*, pp. 113–25.

13. See Allan H. Gilbert, 'The Temptation in *Paradise Regained,*' *Journal of English and Germanic Philology,* XV (1916), 599–611, esp. pp. 606–7. Also Miss Pope's book (above, note 8), p. 67.

14. *The Ferrar Papers,* ed. B. Blackstone (Cambridge, 1938), pp. 60–63; I have expanded abbreviations and altered the punctuation slightly.

An Annotated
Reading List

CONTENTS

ABBREVIATIONS

Abbreviations used for Milton's works are: *DDC = De doctrina christiana; PL = Paradise Lost; PR = Paradise Regained;* and *SA = Samson Agonistes.* Other abbreviations:

CE	*College English*	*MLQ*	*Modern Language Quarterly*
CJ	*Cambridge Journal*	*MLR*	*Modern Language Review*
DR	*Dalhousie Review*	*MP*	*Modern Philology*
EC	*Essays in Criticism*	*NQ*	*Notes and Queries*
ELH	*Journal of English Literary History*	P	Paperback edition
ES	*English Studies*	*PBA*	*Proceedings of the British Academy*
E&S	*Essays and Studies* by members of the English Association	*PM-LA*	*Publications of the Modern Language Association of America*
HLQ	*Huntington Library Quarterly*	*PQ*	*Philological Quarterly*
HTR	*Harvard Theological Review*	*RES*	*Review of English Studies*
JEGP	*Journal of English and Germanic Philology*	*SAQ*	*South Atlantic Quarterly*
JHI	*Journal of the History of Ideas*	*SEL*	*Studies in English Literature*
		SN	*Studia Neophilologica*
		SP	*Studies in Philology*
JWCI	*Journal of the Warburg and Courtauld Institutes*	*SQ*	*Shakespeare Quarterly*
		SR	*Sewanee Review*
KR	*Kenyon Review*	*S Ren*	*Studies in the Renaissance*
MA	*Papers of the Michigan Academy of Science, Arts, and Letters*	*TSLL*	*Texas Studies in Literature and Language*
		UTQ	*University of Toronto Quarterly*
MLN	*Modern Language Notes*		

I

GENERAL AND BACKGROUND STUDIES, WITH SOME ANTHOLOGIES

THERE are detailed bibliographies in C. S. Lewis, *English Literature in the Sixteenth Century excluding Drama* (1954), and Douglas Bush (below, *23*). More modest bibliographies will be found in the various Folger Booklets on Tudor and Stuart Civilization, and in *A Guide to English Literature*, ed. Boris Ford, II: *The Age of Shakespeare*, and III: *From Donne to Marvell* (P: Penguin Books, 1955–6; rev. ed., 1961–2). Cf. J. H. Summers, 'Notes on Recent Studies in English Literature of the Earlier Seventeenth Century', *MLQ*, XXVI (1965), 135–49, and Ernest Sirluck, 'Recent Studies in the English Renaissance', *SEL*, VI (1966), 159–92.

Annual bibliographies include: The English Association's *The Year's Work in English Studies* (1919 ff.); the Modern Humanities Research Association's *Annual Bibliography of English Language and Literature* (1920 ff.); *PMLA* (1922 ff.); and especially *SP* (1922 ff.).

1. Adams, R. P.: *More, Erasmus, Colet, and Vives, on Humanism, War, and Peace, 1496–1535* (1962). Brilliantly comprehensive. Cf. *9, 27, 123*.

2. Allen, D. C.: *Doubt's Boundless Seas: Skepticism and Faith in the Renaissance* (1964). On the 'atheists' of the period: Pomponazzi, Montaigne, Bodin, *et al*. See also the author's *The Legend of Noah: Renaissance Rationalism in Art, Science and Letters* (P: 1949; repr. 1963).

3. Allen, D. C.: *The Star-Crossed Renaissance: The Quarrel about Astrology and its Influence in England* (1941). An excellent introduction.

4. Anderson, R. L.: *Elizabethan Psychology and Shakespeare's Plays* (P: 1927; repr. 1964). Cf. *12, 30*.

5. Ashley, Maurice: *England in the Seventeenth Century*, being vol. VI of *The Pelican History of England* (P: Penguin Books, 1952; 2nd ed., 1954). A useful survey. Cf. *7, 50, 181, 188, 198*.

6. Atkins, J. W. H.: *English Literary Criticism: The Renascence* (1947; 2nd ed., 1951). A survey, concluding with a few pages on Milton. Cf. *71, 175, 199*.

7. Aylmer, G. E.: *The Struggle for the Constitution: England in the Seventeenth Century* (1963; American ed.: *A Short History of Seventeenth-Century England*, P: 1963). The best recent general history of the period. Cf. *5, 50, 181, 188, 198*.

8. Babb, Laurence: *The Elizabethan Malady: A Study of Melancholia in*

English Literature from 1580 to 1642 (1951). See also the same author's essay, *309*.

9. Baker, Herschel: *The Dignity of Man* (1947; repr. as *The Image of Man*, P: 1961), and *The Wars of Truth* (1952). Companion volumes on the climax and decay of Renaissance Christian humanism. Cf. *1, 27, 109, 123, 127*.

10. Baldwin, T. W.: *William Shakespere's Small Latine and Lesse Greeke* (1944; repr. 1956), 2 vols. The most comprehensive study of Renaissance grammar school education. Cf. *37, 224; 38, 44, 93; 248*.

11. Baldwin, C. S.: *Renaissance Literary Theory and Practice: Classicism in the Rhetoric and Poetic of Italy, France, and England, 1400–1600* (1939; repr. 1959). Cf. *38, 44, 93*.

12. Bamborough, J. B.: *The Little World of Man* (1952). On Renaissance psychological theory. Cf. *4, 30*.

13. Baroway, Israel: 'The Bible as Poetry in the English Renaissance: An Introduction', *JEGP*, XXXII (1933), 447–80; and three related studies in *ELH*, II (1935), 66–91; VIII (1941), 119–42; and XVII (1950), 115–35. Standard essays.

14. Bennett, H. S.: *English Books & Readers 1475 to 1557* (1952), and *English Books & Readers 1558 to 1603* (1965). Companion volumes on the history of the book trade from Caxton to the end of the Elizabethan era.

15. Blau, J. L.: 'The Diffusion of the Christian Interpretation of the Cabala in English Literature', *Review of Religion*, VI (1942), 146–68, and especially *The Christian Interpretation of the Cabala in the Renaissance* (1944). The only introductions to the subject available in English; it is to be hoped someone will translate the brilliant survey by F. Secret, *Les Kabbalistes chrétiens de la Renaissance* (1964). Cf. *169*.

16. Blench, J. W.: *Preaching in England in the late Fifteenth and Sixteenth Centuries: A Study of English Sermons 1450–c.1600* (1964). A thorough survey, with full bibliography. Cf. *120, 133*.

17. Boyd, M. C.: *Elizabethan Music and Musical Criticism* (1940). The standard work on English theory and practice 1558–1625. Cf. *157, 161, 170*.

18. Bredvold, L. I.: *The Intellectual Milieu of John Dryden* (1934; P: 1956). Useful on seventeenth-century 'philosophical scepticism', i.e., anti-rationalism. Cf. *153, 209*.

19. Briggs, K. M.: *The Anatomy of Puck: An Examination of Fairy Beliefs among Shakespeare's Contemporaries and Successors* (1959).

20. Brinkley, R. F.: *Arthurian Legend in the Seventeenth Century* (1932). With an important account of Milton's gradual revision of his plans for an epic (pp. 126–41). Cf. *102*.

21. Buckley, G. T.: *Atheism in the English Renaissance* (1932; repr. 1965). Introductory. Cf. *107*.

22. Burtt, E. A.: *The Metaphysical Foundations of Modern Physical Science*

(1924; rev. ed., 1932; P: 1954). A seminal study of the rise of the 'new science'. Cf. *140*.

23. Bush, Douglas: *English Literature in the Earlier Seventeenth Century* (1945; 2nd rev. ed., 1962). The best single survey of Milton's age, with indispensable bibliographies.

24. Bush, Douglas: *Mythology and the Renaissance Tradition in English Poetry* (1932; rev. ed., P: 1963). A standard work; with a chapter on Milton.

25. Bush, Douglas: *Prefaces to Renaissance Literature* (P: 1965). Five essays: two on classical influences on Renaissance literature, the others on 'God and Nature', 'Time and Man', and 'The Isolation of the Renaissance Hero'.

26. Bush, Douglas: *Science and English Poetry: A Historical Sketch, 1590–1950* (1950). A survey; with two chapters on the Renaissance.

27. Bush, Douglas: *The Renaissance and English Humanism* (1939; P: 1962). Four lectures on Renaissance humanism, the last on Milton. Cf. *9, 96, 108, 109, 122, 123, 127*.

28. Camden, Carroll (ed.): *Literary Views: Critical and Historical Essays* (1964), pp. 1–43. Includes the essays by Harry Levin, 'The Golden Age and the Renaissance', and A. E. Barker, 'An Apology for the Study of Renaissance Poetry'.

29. Campbell, L. B.: *Divine Poetry and Drama in Sixteenth Century England* (1959). On Renaissance attempts to make the Bible part of English literature. Cf. *111*.

30. Campbell, L. B.: *Shakespeare's Tragic Heroes: Slaves of Passion* (1930; P: 1962). An outline of Elizabethan psychology. Cf. *4, 12*.

31. Campbell, L. B.: 'The Christian Muse', *Huntington Library Bulletin*, VIII (1935), 29–70. The history of Urania's christianization.

32. Carré, M. H.: 'The New Philosophy', in *Phases of Thought in England* (1949), ch. VII. A survey of seventeenth-century philosophy.

33. Cassirer, Ernst: *The Individual and the Cosmos in Renaissance Philosophy*, trans. Mario Domandi (1963; P: 1964). An influential study of early Renaissance philosophy as a systematic unity.

34. Cassirer, Ernst: *The Platonic Renaissance in England*, trans. J. P. Pettegrove (1953). The best study of the Cambridge Platonists who exerted a decisive influence on Milton. Cf. *190, 210, 274*.

35. Cassirer, Ernst, with P. O. Kristeller and J. H. Randall (eds.): *The Renaissance Philosophy of Man* (P: 1948). An anthology of important treatises by Petrarch, Valla, Ficino, Pico, Pomponazzi and Vives; with a useful bibliography. Cf. *69, 200*.

36. Cawley, R. R.: *Unpathed Waters: Studies in the Influence of the Voyages on Elizabethan Literature* (1940). For its sequel, see *236*.

37. Charlton, Kenneth: *Education in Renaissance England* (1965). A comprehensive survey. Cf. *11, 37*.

38. Clark, D. L.: *John Milton at St. Paul's School: A Study of Ancient Rhetoric in English Renaissance Education* (1948; repr. 1964). Cf. *11, 44, 93, 248.*

39. Clark, Sir George: *The Seventeenth Century* (1929; 2nd ed., 1947: P: 1960). An excellent survey. Cf. *60, 124, 145.*

40. Coffin, C. M.: *John Donne and the New Philosophy* (1937; repr. 1958). On Donne's response to the emerging world of science. Cf. *97; 140.*

41. Colie, R. L.: *Paradoxia Epidemica: The Renaissance Tradition of Paradox* (1966). The most important study of the subject. Cf. *415.*

42. Cowie, L. W.: *Seventeenth-Century Europe* (1960). An introductory survey. Cf. *39, 124, 145.*

43. Craig, Hardin: *The Enchanted Glass: The Renaissance Mind in English Literature* (1936), and its sequel, *New Lamps for Old* (1960). Difficult but rewarding surveys of the cross-currents of ideas.

44. Crane, W. G.: *Wit and Rhetoric in the Renaissance: The Formal Basis of Elizabethan Prose Style* (1937). Cf. *11, 38, 93.*

45. Croll, M. W.: *Style, Rhetoric, and Rhythm*, ed. J. M. Patrick *et al.* (1966). Important essays on Renaissance prose and rhetoric. Cf. *99, 133, 216.*

46. Crombie, A. C.: *Augustine to Galileo: The History of Science A.D. 400–1650* (1952; 2nd ed., 1961; P: 1961). A standard work. Cf. *97, 110, 208.*

47. Cross, F. L., and P. E. More (eds.): *Anglicanism: The Thought and Practice of the Church of England, illustrated from the religious literature of the Seventeenth Century* (1954). An indispensable anthology.

48. Cruttwell, Patrick: *The Shakespearean Moment and its Place in the Poetry of the Seventeenth Century* (1954; P: 1960). A comprehensive study demonstrating the unity of seventeenth-century poetry.

49. Curry, W. C.: *Shakespeare's Philosophical Patterns* (1937; 2nd ed., 1959). A useful survey of some themes in Shakespearean drama and Renaissance literature generally. Cf. *420.*

50. Davies, Godfrey: *The Early Stuarts 1603–1660*, being vol. IX of *The Oxford History of England* (1937; 2nd ed., 1959). The standard work. Cf. *181, 198.*

51. Dickens, A. G.: *The English Reformation* (1964). The standard work. Cf. *94, 114.*

52. Ellis-Fermor, Una: *The Jacobean Drama: An Interpretation* (1936; 4th ed., 1958; P: 1964). A comprehensive survey. Cf. *146.*

53. Farmer, D. L.: *Britain and the Stuarts* (1965). A survey. Cf. *50, 181, 198.*

54. Farnham, W. E.: *The Medieval Heritage of Elizabethan Tragedy* (1936; repr. 1956). Also useful on Renaissance literature generally, this work studies a variety of widely-accepted assumptions.

55. Ferguson, W. K.: *The Renaissance* (P: 1940). An introductory survey.

56. Ferguson, W. K.: *The Renaissance in Historical Thought* (1948). An excellent survey of Renaissance historiography. Cf. *62, 150.*

57. Ferguson, W. K., *et al.*: *The Renaissance* (1953; P: 1962). Six essays on various aspects of the period by Ferguson, R. S. Lopez, George Sarton, R. H. Bainton, Leicester Bradner, and Erwin Panofsky. Cf. *202*.

58. Finney, G. L: *Musical Backgrounds for English Literature, 1580–1650* (1962). Seven comprehensive chapters on the period generally, and four important chapters on Milton. Cf. *128, 178*.

59. Fisch, Harold: *Jerusalem and Albion: The Hebraic Factor in Seventeenth-Century Literature* (1964). A comprehensive subject single-mindedly pursued; with three chapters on Milton.

60. Friedrich, C. J.: *The Age of the Baroque 1610–1660* (1952; P: 1962). An excellent survey. Cf. *39, 124, 145*.

61. Frye, R. M.: 'The Teachings of Classical Puritanism on Conjugal Love', *SRen*, II (1955), 148–59. A basic study. Cf. *74*.

62. Fussner, F. S.: *The Historical Revolution: English Historical Writing and Thought 1580–1640* (1962). An excellent survey. Cf. *56, 150*.

63. George, C. H. and K.: *The Protestant Mind of the English Reformation 1570–1640* (1961). One of the best studies of the period's 'fascinating world of religious ideas'. Cf. *73*.

64. Gilmore, M. P.: *The World of Humanism 1453–1517* (1952; P: 1962). An excellent survey of the background to the Renaissance in England. Cf. *39, 60*.

65. Gilson, Etienne: *History of Christian Philosophy in the Middle Ages* (1955). The best survey of the medieval background to the Renaissance. Cf. *162*.

66. Gooch, G. P.: *English Democratic Ideas in the Seventeenth Century* (1898; 2nd ed., 1927; P: 1959). A survey.

67. Greene, T. M.: *The Descent from Heaven: A Study in Epic Continuity* (1963). An attractive study of the convention of divine and angelic epiphanies; with a chapter on Milton.

68. Grierson, Sir Herbert: *Cross-Currents in English Literature of the XVIIth Century* (1929; P: Penguin Books, 1966). The best work of a great humanist; with a chapter on Milton.

69. Gundersheimer, W. L. (ed.): *The Italian Renaissance* (P: 1965). An anthology of extracts from Salutati, Valla, Pico, Bembo, Castiglione, *et al.* Cf. *35, 200*.

70. Hägin, Peter: *The Epic Hero and the Decline of Heroic Poetry: A Study of the Neoclassical English Epic with special reference to Milton's 'PL' (1964)*.

71. Hall, Vernon, jr.: *Renaissance Literary Criticism: A Study of its Social Context* (1945). Cf. *6, 175, 199*.

72. Haller, William: *Foxe's Book of Martyrs and the Elect Nation* (1963). An excellent study expanding far beyond Foxe. Cf. *62, 150*.

73. Haller, William: *The Rise of Puritanism* (1938; P: 1957), and *Liberty and Reformation in the Puritan Revolution* (1955; P: 1963). Indispensable volumes; with chapters on Milton. Cf. *63, 87, 104, 143, 223, 234, 302*.

74. Haller, William and Malleville: 'The Puritan Art of Love', *HLQ*, V (1941–2), 235–72. Cf. *61, 449.*

75. Hamilton, G. K.: *The Two Harmonies: Poetry and Prose in the Seventeenth Century* (1963). A study of the period's views on the nature and function of poetry.

76. Harbison, E. H.: *The Christian Scholar in the Age of the Reformation* (P: 1956). Studies of Erasmus, Luther, Calvin, *et al.* Cf. *9, 109, 123.*

77. Harris, Victor: *All Coherence Gone* (1949; repr. 1966). The most thorough study of the controversy over nature's decay. Cf. *82, 98.*

78. Hay, Denys (ed.): *The Renaissance Debate* (P: 1965). Statements and discussions of the notion of 'Renaissance'. Cf. *80, 202.*

79. Haydn, Hiram: *The Counter-Renaissance* (1950). A study of 'a radical anti-intellectual revolution' that set in during the Renaissance.

80. Helton, Tinsley (ed.): *The Renaissance: A Reconsideration of the Theories and Interpretations of the Age* (1961; P: 1964). Six useful surveys by Garrett Mattingly, P. O. Kristeller, Earl Rosenthal, Edward Rosen, Bernard Weinberg, and Harry Levin. Cf. *78, 202.*

81. Heninger, S. K.: *A Handbook of Renaissance Meteorology, with particular reference to Elizabethan and Jacobean literature* (1960). The standard work.

82. Hepburn, R. W.: 'Godfrey Goodman: Nature Vilified', *CJ,* VII (1954), 424–34, and 'George Hakewill: The Virility of Nature', *JHI,* XVI (1955), 135–50. On the two protagonists of the controversy over nature's decay. Cf. *77.*

83. Heppe, Heinrich (ed.): *Reformed Dogmatics, set out and illustrated from the sources,* ed. Ernst Bizer, trans. G. T. Thomson (1950). Difficult but indispensable for anyone aspiring to master the intricacies of seventeenth-century theology. Cf. *182.*

84. Herrick, M. T.: *Italian Tragedy in the Renaissance* (1965). Useful as a background study to *S A.*

85. Herrick, M. T.: *The Poetics of Aristotle in England* (P: 1930). A survey, with a chapter on seventeenth-century interpretations.

86. Highet, Gilbert: *The Classical Tradition: Greek and Roman Influences on Western Literature* (1949; P: 1957). The standard survey; with some pages on Milton. Cf. *25, 109.*

87. Hill, Christopher: *Puritanism and Revolution* (1958; P: 1962); *Society and Puritanism in Pre-Revolutionary England* (1964; P: 1966); and *Intellectual Origins of the English Revolution* (1965). Three of the author's most important contributions to the subject. Cf. *73, 234, 302.*

88. Hill, Christopher, and Edmund Dell (eds.): *The Good Old Cause – The English Revolution of 1640–60: Its Causes, Course and Consequences* (1949). Wide-ranging extracts from contemporary sources.

89. Hirst, Désirée: *Hidden Riches: Traditional Symbolism from the Renaissance to Blake* (1964). One of the best studies of Renaissance thought; especially relevant are chs. I–V.

90. Hollander, John: *The Untuning of the Sky: Ideas of Music in English Poetry 1500–1700* (1961). The standard work; with a discussion of Milton's views, pp. 315–31 (partially repr. in *228*). Cf. *177.*

91. Hoopes, Robert: *Right Reason in the English Renaissance* (1962). The history of an idea from its classical origins to Milton.

92. Howarth, W. D.: *The Seventeenth Century* (1965), being vol. I of the series *Life and Letters in France*, gen. ed. Austin Gill. A comprehensive survey based on twenty-one extracts with commentary.

93. Howell, W. S.: *Logic and Rhetoric in England, 1500–1700* (1956). An authoritative survey, with some pages (211–19) on Milton ('the last of England's Ramist scholars'). Cf. *11, 38, 44.*

94. Hughes, Philip: *The Reformation in England* (1950–54), 3 vols. A massive and brilliant study from the Catholic point of view. Cf. *51.*

95. Hurstfield, Joel (ed.): *The Reformation Crisis* (P: 1965). Surveys of various aspects of the Reformation by Denys Hay, Gordon Rupp, G. R. Potter, A. G. Dickens, *et al.* Cf. *51, 114.*

96. Hyma, Albert: 'The Continental Origins of English Humanism', *HLQ,* I (1940), 1–25. Largely a bibliographical study. See also *1, 9, 27, 76, 108, 109, 123, 127, 160.*

97. Johnson, F. R.: *Astronomical Thought in Renaissance England* (1937). The standard work. Cf. *46, 208.*

98. Jones, R. F.: *Ancients and Moderns: A Study of the Rise of the Scientific Movement in Seventeenth-Century England* (1936; 2nd ed., 1961; P: 1965). An influential study, including an account of the controversy over nature's decay. Cf. *77, 82.*

99. Jones, R. F.: *The Seventeenth-Century: Studies in the History of English Thought and Literature from Bacon to Pope* (1951), pp. 75–160. Three basic studies of the period's prose styles. See also the author's 'The Rhetoric of Science in England of the Mid-Seventeenth Century', in *Restoration and Eighteenth-Century Literature*, ed. Carroll Camden (1963), pp. 5–24. Cf. *45, 133, 216.*

100. Jones, R. M.: *Spiritual Reformers in the 16th and 17th Centuries* (1914; P: 1959). On Sebastian Franck, Castellio, Weigel, Boehme, the Cambridge Platonists, Traherne, *et al.*

101. Jordan, W. K.: *The Development of Religious Toleration in England* (1932–40), esp. vols. II–IV. The standard work.

102. Kendrick, Sir Thomas: *British Antiquity* (1950). Fundamental for the understanding of the background to the Renaissance attitude toward Brut and King Arthur. Cf. *20.*

103. Kernan, Alvin: *The Cankered Muse: Satire of the English Renaissance* (1959). A survey.

104. Knappen, M. M: *Tudor Puritanism: A Chapter in the History of Idealism* (1939; P: 1965). The best account. Cf. *73, 87.*

105. Knights, L. C.: *Drama and Society in the Age of Jonson* (1937; P: Penguin Books, 1962). Select dramatists studied in relation to their times.

106. Knights, L. C.: *Explorations: Essays in Criticism mainly on the literature of the seventeenth century* (1946; P: Penguin Books, 1964). Noteworthy is the essay on 'Bacon and the Seventeenth-Century Dissociations of Sensibility'.

107. Kocher, P. H.: *Science and Religion in Elizabethan England* (1953). The standard work. Cf. *204.*

108. Kristeller, P. O.: *Studies in Renaissance Thought and Letters* (P: 1956). A collection of important essays, among them 'The Philosophy of Man in the Italian Renaissance'; 'Ficino and Pomponazzi on the Place of Man in the Universe'; 'Music and Learning in the Early Italian Renaissance'; etc. (The last two essays are reprinted with others in *Renaissance Thought II: Papers on Humanism and the Arts* (P: 1965)). Cf. *27, 35, 160.*

109. Kristeller, P. O.: *The Classics and Renaissance Thought* (1955); rev. ed. as *Renaissance Thought: The Classic, Scholastic, and Humanistic Strains* (P: 1961). Highly recommended as an introductory study. Cf. *9, 25, 123.*

110. Kuhn, T. S.: *The Copernican Revolution: Planetary Astronomy in the Development of Western Thought* (1957; P: 1959). The best general account. Cf. *46, 97, 208.*

111. Kurth, B. O.: *Milton and Christian Heroism: Biblical Epic Themes and Forms in Seventeenth-Century England* (P: 1959). Cf. *29.*

112. Lamprecht, S. P.: 'The Role of Descartes in Seventeenth-Century England', in *Studies in the History of Ideas* (1935), III, 181–240. A survey of the influence of, and reactions to, Cartesianism.

113. Lee, Sir Philip (ed.): *Shakespeare's England: An Account of the Life & Manners of his Age* (1916), 2 vols. Still the best single survey of every aspect of life in Renaissance England. Cf. *138, 219, 221.*

114. Léonard, É. G.: *A History of Protestantism*, ed. H. H. Rowley, trans. J. M. H. Reid. (1965–6), 2 vols. A magisterial survey of developments to the end of the seventeenth century; with bibliographies. Cf. *51.*

115. Levi, Anthony: *French Moralists: The Theory of the Passions 1585 to 1649* (1964). Much more comprehensive than the subtitle indicates.

116. Lewis, C. S.: *The Discarded Image: An Introduction to Medieval and Renaissance Literature* (1964). An excellent survey.

117. Lovejoy, A. O.: *The Great Chain of Being: A Study in the History of an Idea* (1936; P: 1960). A classic of modern scholarship, on one of the most persistent ideas in Western thought.

118. McAdoo, H. R.: *The Spirit of Anglicanism: A Survey of Anglican Theological Method in the Seventeenth Century* (1965).

119. McAdoo, H. R.: *The Structure of Caroline Moral Theology* (1949). The best study of seventeenth-century Anglican moral theology.

120. MacLure, Millar: *The Paul's Cross Sermons 1534–1642* (1958). A useful survey, with a register of the relevant sermons. Cf. *16, 133.*

121. Maddison, Carol: *Apollo and the Nine: A History of the Ode* (1960). Useful as a background study to Milton's *Nativity Ode* (discussed here, pp. 320 ff.).

122. Mahood, M. M.: *Poetry and Humanism* (1950). Thoughtful chapters on Marlowe, Donne, Vaughan, Milton ('The Baroque Artist' and 'Milton's Heroes'), *et al.* Cf. *136, 180, 324.*

123. Major, J. M.: *Sir Thomas Elyot and Renaissance Humanism* (1964). Most useful on the nature of Renaissance humanism. Cf. *1, 9, 27, 96, 109, 127.*

124. Maland, David: *Europe in the Seventeenth Century* (1966). A general survey. Cf. *39, 42, 60, 145.*

125. Martz, L. L.: *The Paradise Within: Studies in Vaughan, Traherne, and Milton* (1964; P: 1966). Includes a chapter on *PL* ('The Journey of the Mind') and another on *PR* (reprinted above, pp. 348 ff.).

126. Martz, L. L.: *The Poetry of Meditation: A Study in English Religious Literature of the Seventeenth Century* (1954; P: 1962). Concerned in the main with 'metaphysical' poetry, but relevant to the discussion of *PR* (above, pp. 348 ff.).

127. Mason, H. A.: *Humanism and Poetry in the Early Tudor Period* (1959). A good account of the prelude to the high Renaissance in England. Cf. *27, 96.*

128. Mellers, Wilfrid: *Harmonious Meeting: A Study of the Relationship between English Music, Poetry and Theatre, c. 1600–1900* (1965). With a consideration of *Comus* (pt II, ch. II: 'The Genesis of Masque'). Cf. *58, 178.*

129. Mercer, Eric: *English Art 1553–1625*, being vol. VII of *The Oxford History of English Art* (1962). An authoritative survey, with bibliography. Cf. *206.*

130. Miles, Josephine: *The Primary Language of Poetry in the 1640s* (P: 1948), being pt I of *The Continuity of Poetic Language* (P: 1951). With some observations on Milton's minor poems (pp. 86–90). Cf. the author's essay on *Lycidas*, in *361.*

131. Miller, Perry: *The New England Mind: The Seventeenth Century* (1939; repr. 1954). The best study of various leading ideas in colonial New England, but also useful for students of the Age of Milton. Cf. *135.*

132. Mintz, S. I.: *The Hunting of Leviathan: Seventeenth-Century Reactions to the Materialism and Moral Philosophy of Thomas Hobbes* (1962). The standard account.

133. Mitchell, W. F.: *English Pulpit Oratory from Andrewes to Tillotson: A Study of its Literary Aspects* (1932). The standard work. Cf. *45, 99, 216; 16, 120.*

134. Morris, Christopher: *Political Thought in England: Tyndale to Hooker* (1953). A substantial introduction, with a bibliography.

135. Murdock, K. B.: *Literature & Theology in Colonial New England* (1949; P: 1954). The best account of the relationship between theological ideas and literary practice in New England, but also useful for students of the Age of Milton. Cf. *131.*

136. Nelson, Lowry, jr.: *Baroque Lyric Poetry* (1961). An excellent study, focusing on the poetic practice of Donne, Milton (in the *Nativity Ode* and *Lycidas*), and select Continental poets. Cf. *122, 180, 324.*

137. New, J. F. H.: *Anglican and Puritan: The Basis of their Opposition, 1558–1640* (1964). Introductory.

138. Nicoll, Allardyce: *The Elizabethans* (1957). An introductory survey, with the Elizabethans giving 'an image of their times in their own words'. Cf. *113, 219, 221.*

139. Nicolson, M. H.: *Mountain Gloom and Mountain Glory: The Development of the Aesthetics of the Infinite* (1959; P: 1963). An absorbing study of the changing attitudes toward mountains from the Renaissance to the nineteenth century.

140. Nicolson, M. H.: *The Breaking of the Circle: Studies in the Effect of the 'New Science' upon Seventeenth-Century Poetry* (1950; rev. ed., 1960; P: 1962). A comprehensive study concerned with the 'basic Renaissance preconceptions about man, the world, and the universe'. Cf. *495.*

141. Notestein, Wallace: *A History of Witchcraft in England from 1558 to 1718* (1911). Still one of the best surveys. See also G. L. Kittredge, *Witchcraft in Old and New England* (1929). Cf. *185.*

142. Notestein, Wallace: *The English People on the Eve of Colonization 1603–1630* (1954). A survey of life in early seventeenth-century England.

143. Nuttall, G. F.: *The Holy Spirit in Puritan Faith and Experience* (1946). An excellent study that expands to a survey of the Puritan movement. Cf. *73.*

144. Nuttall, G. F.: *Visible Saints: The Congregational Way, 1640–1660* (1957). The definitive study. (The New England Congregationalists are discussed in a book with a similar title, E. S. Morgan's *Visible Saints: The History of a Puritan Idea* (1963; P: 1965).)

145. Ogg, David: *Europe in the Seventeenth Century* (1925; 8th ed., 1960; P: 1962). A general survey. Cf. *39, 42, 60, 124.*

146. Ornstein, Robert: *The Moral Vision of Jacobean Tragedy* (1960; P: 1965). A comprehensive survey. Cf. *52.*

147. Panofsky, Erwin: *Studies in Iconology: Humanistic Themes in the Art of the Renaissance* (1939; P: 1962). Extremely important and influential. Cf.

172, 220. See also the author's *Renaissance and Renascences in Western Art* (P: 1960), 2 vols.

148. Parry, Sir Charles: *The Music of the Seventeenth Century*, being vol. III of *The Oxford History of Music* (1902; 2nd ed., rev. by E. J. Dent, 1938)· A survey. Cf. *157, 158, 161*.

149. Patrides, C. A.: 'Renaissance Thought on the Celestial Hierarchy: The Decline of a Tradition', *JHI*, XX (1959), 155–66; XXIII (1962), 265–7. Cf. *203*.

150. Patrides, C. A.: *The Phoenix and the Ladder: The Rise and Decline of the Christian View of History* (P: 1964). The development of a fundamental idea from ancient Israel to Renaissance England. Cf. *62, 72*.

151. Pinto, V. de S.: *The English Renaissance 1510–1688* (1938; 2nd rev. ed., 1951). Four chapters, being introductory surveys and detailed bibliographies arranged by author (superseded by the bibliographies cited in the headnote on p. 383, above).

152. Plumb, J. H., *et al.* (eds.): *The Horizon Book of the Renaissance* (1961). A sumptuously illustrated survey of the Renaissance in Italy. The text is reprinted, with drastically reduced illustrations, in *The Penguin Book of the Renaissance* (P: 1964).

153. Popkin, R. H.: *The History of Scepticism from Erasmus to Descartes* (1960). A competent survey. Cf. *18, 209*.

154. Powell, C. L.: 'Contemporary Attitudes Towards Woman', in *English Domestic Relations 1487–1653* (1917), pp. 147–78. A survey; see also the relevant chapters in *63, 225*. Cf. *289*.

155. Praz, Mario: '"The Politic Brain": Machiavelli and the Elizabethans', in *The Flaming Heart* (P: 1958), pp. 90–145. One of the best surveys of Machiavelli's impact on Renaissance England; with numerous further references. Cf. *156*.

156. Raab, Felix: *The English Face of Machiavelli: A Changing Interpretation 1500–1700* (1964). The most thorough survey to date. Cf. *155*.

157. Reese, Gustave: *Music in the Renaissance* (1954). The standard survey of European developments, with two chapters devoted to England. Cf. *17, 108, 148, 158, 161*.

158. Rhys, H. H. (ed.): *Seventeenth Century Science and the Arts* (1961). Four essays relating science and literature (by D. Bush), music (C. V. Palisca), visual art (J. S. Ackerman), and the arts generally (S. Toulmin).

159. Rice, E. F.: *The Renaissance Idea of Wisdom* (1958). The history of the idea from Petrarch's *De sapientia* through Charron's *De la Sagesse* (1601).

160. Robb, Nesca: *Neoplatonism of the Italian Renaissance* (1935). Possibly the best introduction available in English to a subject of fundamental importance. Cf. *35, 108, 202*.

161. Robertson, Alec, and Denis Stevens (eds.): *Renaissance and Baroque*, being vol. II of *The Pelican History of Music* (P: 1963). An excellent introduction: 'an account of music seen against its various backgrounds'. Cf. *17, 108, 148, 157, 158*.

162. Robertson, D. W., jr.: *A Preface to Chaucer: Studies in Medieval Perspective* (1963). A magisterial work, extremely useful for the understanding of the medieval background to the Renaissance. Cf. *65*.

163. Røstvig, M.-S.: *The Happy Man: Studies in the Metamorphoses of a Classical Ideal* (1954; rev. ed., 1962), vol. I: *1600–1700*. A survey of the *beatus ille* tradition, with a section on *L'Allegro* and *Il Penseroso* (pp. 100 ff.).

164. Ross, M. M.: *Poetry and Dogma: The Transfiguration of Eucharistic Symbols in Seventeenth Century English Poetry* (1954). The effect of revisions in theology on 'the analogical mode of the poetic symbol'.

165. Roth, Cecil: *The Jews in the Renaissance* (1959; P: 1965). The standard work. Cf. *300*.

166. Sarton, George: *Appreciation of Ancient and Medieval Science during the Renaissance, 1450–1600* (1955; P: 1961). An indispensable survey.

167. Sarton, George: *Six Wings: Men of Science in the Renaissance* (1957). A survey of the work of the greatest scientists.

168. Saunders, J. L.: *Justus Lipsius* (1955). A substantial introduction to Renaissance stoicism.

169. Scholem, Gershom: *Major Trends in Jewish Mysticism* (1941; P: 1961). An outstanding study of the background to Renaissance cabbalistic thought. See also the same author's *On the Kabbalah and its Symbolism*, trans. Ralph Manheim (1965). Cf. *15*.

170. Scholes, P. A.: *Music and Puritanism* (1934). Explodes the legend of the Puritan opposition to music. Cf. *17*.

171. Sells, A. L.: *The Paradise of Travellers: The Italian Influence on Englishmen in the Seventeenth Century* (1964).

172. Seznec, Jean: *The Survival of the Pagan Gods: The Mythological Tradition and its Place in Renaissance Humanism and Art*, trans. B. F. Sessions (1953; P: 1961). Cf. *147, 220*.

173. Smith, Hallett: *Elizabethan Poetry: A Study in Convention, Meaning, and Expression* (1952). An authoritative exposition of the nature of the creative process in Elizabethan England.

174. Spencer, Theodore: *Shakespeare and the Nature of Man* (1942; 2nd ed., 1949; P: 1961). On 'the framework that gave Shakespeare his terms and his values', but also useful for Renaissance literature generally. Cf. *49*.

175. Spingarn, J. E.: *A History of Literary Criticism in the Renaissance* (1899; 2nd ed., 1908; P: 1963). An excellent introductory survey. Cf. *6, 71, 199*.

176. Spingarn, J. E. (ed.): *Critical Essays of the Seventeenth Century* (1908–9; repr. 1957), 3 vols. The standard collection. For a more modest anthology, see *English Literary Criticism: The Renaissance*, ed. O. B. Hardison (P: 1963).

177. Spitzer, Leo: *Classical and Christian Ideas of World Harmony,* ed. A. G. Hatcher (1963). The standard account. Cf. *90.*

178. Stevens, John: *Music and Poetry in the Early Tudor Court* (1961). A thorough study of the relationship between words and music. (No similar work exists on the later Renaissance.) Cf. *58, 128.*

179. Summerson, Sir John: *Architecture in Britain 1530 to 1830,* being vol. III of the *Pelican History of Art* (1954; 4th rev. ed., 1963). An authoritative survey; pts I–II cover the period 1530–1660.

180. Sypher, Wylie: *Four Stages of Renaissance Style: Transformations in Art and Literature 1400–1700* (P: 1955). The four 'styles' – renaissance, mannerism, baroque, and late-baroque – analysed in their relation to literature; with some comments on *PL* ('baroque'). Cf. *122, 136, 324.*

181. Tanner, J. R.: *English Constitutional Conflicts of the Seventeenth Century 1603–1689* (1928; P: 1962). See also his edition of *Constitutional Documents of the Reign of James I, with an historical commentary* (1930; P: 1961). Cf. *5, 7, 50, 188, 198.*

182. Tappert, T. G. (ed.): *The Book of Concord: The Confessions of the Evangelical Lutheran Church* (1959). An indispensable collection. Cf. *83.*

183. Tawney, R. H.: *Religion and the Rise of Capitalism* (1926; P: Penguin Books, 1938; repr. 1964). A classic study of the relationship between religious ideas and social ethics, fifteenth to seventeenth centuries.

184. Thompson, E. N. S.: 'Mysticism in Seventeenth-Century English Literature', *SP*, XVIII (1921), 170–231. A useful survey.

185. Thorndike, Lynn: *A History of Magic and Experimental Science* (1941, 1958). A magisterial survey; the sixteenth and seventeenth centuries are considered in vols. V–VIII. Cf. *141.*

186. Tillyard, E. M. W.: *The Elizabethan World Picture* (1943; P: Penguin Books, 1963). A 'popular' but over-simplified account of the 'great chain of being' (see *117*). Cf. *138, 221.*

187. Tillyard, E. M. W.: *The English Epic and its Background* (1954; P 1967). A useful survey, from Homeric Greece to Augustan England; with a brief chapter on Milton.

188. Trevelyan, G. M.: *England under the Stuarts* (1904; 19th rev. ed., 1947; P: 1966). A useful survey. Cf. *5, 7, 50, 181, 198.*

189. Trevor-Roper, H. R.: *Archbishop Laud 1573–1645* (1940; 2nd ed., 1962; P: 1965). A comprehensive biography.

190. Tulloch, John: *Rational Theology and Christian Philosophy in England in the Seventeenth Century* (1872; rev. ed., 1874; repr. 1965–6), 2 vols. Still useful introductory chapters on Hales, Chillingworth, the Cambridge Platonists, *et al.* Cf. *34.*

191. Tuve, Rosemond: *Elizabethan and Metaphysical Imagery: Renaissance Poetic and Twentieth-Century Critics* (1947; P: 1961). One of the finest products of modern critical scholarship, on the Renaissance theories and practice of figurative language.

192. Tuveson, E. L.: *Millennium and Utopia: A Study in the Background of the Idea of Progress* (1949; P: 1964). A pioneer study, calling attention to the importance of apocalyptic ideas in Renaissance literature.

193. Walker, D. P.: *The Decline of Hell: Seventeenth-Century Discussions of Eternal Torment* (1964). One of the most important contributions to our understanding of Renaissance eschatology.

194. Wallerstein, Ruth: 'The Laureate Hearse: The Funeral Elegy and Seventeenth-Century Aesthetic', in *Studies in Seventeenth-Century Poetic* (1950; P: 1965), pt I. On the theory and practice of a frequently misunderstood form; with a study of *Lycidas*.

195. Waterhouse, E. K.: *Painting in Britain 1530–1790*, being vol. I of the *Pelican History of Art* (1953). An authoritative survey; pts I–II cover the period to 1688.

196. Wedgwood, C. V.: *Poetry and Politics under the Stuarts* (1960; P: 1964). A survey of seventeenth-century political verse.

197. Wedgwood, C. V.: *Seventeenth-Century English Literature* (1950). An introductory survey.

198. Wedgwood, C. V.: *The Great Rebellion*, vol. I: *The King's Peace* (1955); vol. II: *The King's War* (1958; P: 1966). The best history of the turbulent decade 1637–47.

199. Weinberg, Bernard: *A History of Literary Criticism in the Italian Renaissance* (1961), 2 vols. The most thorough survey of a complex subject. Cf. *6, 71, 175.*

200. Weinstein, Donald (ed.): *The Renaissance and the Reformation 1300–1600* (P: 1965). An anthology of extracts representing the period's significant points of view and developments. Cf. *35, 69.*

201. Welsford, Enid: *The Court Masque: A Study in the Relationship between Poetry and the Revels* (1927). Useful as a background study to *Comus*.

202. Werkmeister, W. H. (ed.): *Facets of the Renaissance* (1959; P: 1963). Five lectures: by W. K. Ferguson on the reinterpretation of the Renaissance, M. P. Gilmore on conceptions of the lessons of history, Garrett Mattingly on changing attitudes toward the State, E. H. Harbison on Machiavelli and More, and P. O. Kristeller on Renaissance Platonism. Cf. *57, 78, 80.*

203. West, R. H.: *The Invisible World: A Study of Pneumatology in Elizabethan Drama* (1939). The standard work. Cf. *297.*

204. Westfall, R. S.: *Science and Religion in Seventeenth-Century England* (1958). Cf. *107.*

205. Whinney, Margaret: *Sculpture in Britain 1530 to 1830*, being vol. XXIII of the *Pelican History of Art* (1964). An authoritative survey; pts I–II cover the sixteenth and early seventeenth centuries.

206. Whinney, Margaret, and Oliver Millar: *English Art 1625–1714*, being vol. VIII of *The Oxford History of English Art* (1957). An authoritative survey, with bibliography. Cf. *129*.

207. White, H. C.: *The Tudor Books of Private Devotion* (1951), and *English Devotional Literature, Prose, 1600–1640* (1931; repr. 1966). Excellent surveys.

208. Whitehead, A. N.: 'The Century of Genius', in *Science and the Modern World* (1925; P: 1948), ch. III. A survey of seventeenth-century advances in science. Cf. *46*.

209. Wiley, M. L.: *The Subtle Knot: Creative Scepticism in Seventeenth-Century England* (1952). On writers – Donne, Browne, Baxter, *et al.* – who shared 'a belief in the wholesome effect of doubt'. Cf. *18, 153*.

210. Willey, Basil: *The English Moralists* (1964; P: 1965). With five chapters on Hooker, Bacon, Hobbes, Browne, and the Cambridge Platonists.

211. Willey, Basil: *The Seventeenth Century Background: Studies in the Thought of the Age in Relation to Poetry and Religion* (1934; P: Penguin Books, 1962). With a section on Milton ('The Heroic Poem in a Scientific Age').

212. Williams, Arnold: *The Common Expositor: An Account of the Commentaries on Genesis; 1527–1633* (1948). The standard work on hexameral literature. Cf. *418, 479*.

213. Williamson, George: *Milton and Others* (1965). A collection of essays, among them 'Milton the Anti-romantic', 'The Context of *Comus*', 'The Education of Adam' (repr. in *228*), 'Plot in *PR*', 'Tension in *SA*'. The 'others' are Donne, Vaughan, Marvell, *et al.*

214. Williamson, George: *Seventeenth Century Contexts* (1960). A collection of important essays, among them 'Mutability, Decay and Jacobean Melancholy', 'Milton and the Mortalist Heresy', etc.

215. Williamson, George: *The Donne Tradition: A Study in English Poetry from Donne to the Death of Cowley* (1930; P: 1958). A comprehensive survey.

216. Williamson, George: *The Senecan Amble: A Study in Prose Form from Bacon to Collier* (1951; P: 1966). One of the basic studies of the period's prose styles. Cf. *45, 99, 133*.

217. Wilson, F. P.: *Elizabethan and Jacobean* (1946). A survey of the period of transition: an excellent introduction.

218. Wilson, F. P.: *Seventeenth Century Prose: Five Lectures* (1960). The best survey, with individual chapters on Burton, Browne, biography, and the sermon.

219. Wilson, J. D. (ed.): *Life in Shakespeare's England* (1911; P: Penguin Books, 1944). Extracts from Elizabethan prose on various aspects of the high Renaissance. Cf. *113, 138, 221*.

220. Wind, Edgar: *Pagan Mysteries in the Renaissance* (1958). A study of

Renaissance works of art, including 'philosophical arguments in their own terms'. Cf. *147, 172*.

221. Winny, James (ed.): *The Frame of Order: An Outline of Elizabethan Belief taken from treatises of the late sixteenth century* (1957). The texts relate to ideas discussed in *12, 117, 138, 186,* etc.

222. Woodhouse, A. S. P.: *The Poet and his Faith: Religion and Poetry in England from Spenser to Eliot and Auden* (1965). With a chapter on Milton.

223. Woodhouse, A. S. P. (ed.): *Puritanism and Liberty* (1938). An important collection of extracts on the political thought of the Puritan revolution. Cf. *73, 87*.

224. Woodward, W. H.: *Studies in Education during the Age of the Renaissance 1400–1600* (1906; repr. 1924 and 1965). An excellent survey of humanist education and educators. Cf. *11, 37*.

225. Wright, L. B.: *Middle-Class Culture in Elizabethan England* (1935; repr. 1958). A magisterial survey of popular literature.

226. Yates, F. A.: *Giordano Bruno and the Hermetic Tradition* (1964). The best introduction to Renaissance hermetic thought.

227. Yates, F. A.: *The French Academies of the Sixteenth Century* (1947). An excellent study of their thought and influence.

II

EDITIONS OF MILTON

THE standard edition is *The Works of John Milton*, gen. ed. F. A. Patterson (1931–40), 20 vols.; in part being superseded by the fully annotated *Complete Prose Works of John Milton*, gen. ed. D. M. Wolfe (1953 ff.), 7 vols. An indispensable work for the scholar is *John Milton's Complete Poetical Works reproduced in photographic facsimile*, ed. H. F. Fletcher (1943). Adequate editions of Milton's poetry include those by H. F. Fletcher (1941), J. H. Hanford (2nd ed., 1953), Douglas Bush (1949), Northrop Frye (1951), E. S. Le Comte (P: 1961), M. H. Nicolson (P: 1962), and J. M. Shawcross (P: 1963). The fully annotated edition by M. Y. Hughes (1957) is widely used in the United States; in Britain something less formidable is likely to establish itself in time, such as the edition by Douglas Bush in the 'Oxford Standard Authors' (1966) or perhaps the forthcoming edition by John Carey and A. D. S. Fowler in the new series 'Longman's Annotated English Poets'. Helen Darbishire's edition (1952–5), 2 vols., is a controversial but important contribution to textual criticism. J. S. Smart's edition of Milton's sonnets (1921; P: 1966) has been replaced by E. A. J. Honigmann's (1966). On the changing patterns of editorial work on Milton, see Ants Oras, *Milton's Editors and Commentators from Patrick Hume to Henry John Todd: 1695–1801* (1931; repr. 1964). J. Blondel's *Le 'Comus' de John Milton, masque neptunien* (Paris, 1964) provides a translation, a comprehensive essay and full annotation.

A Variorum edition of Milton's poetry is in preparation, ed. M. Y. Hughes *et al.* (1967 ff.). Two editions for schools are also being prepared; the respective general editors: J. B. Broadbent (for Cambridge University Press) and C. A. Patrides (for Macmillan). Among the available collections of essays are the following:

228. Barker, A. E. (ed.): *Milton: Modern Essays in Criticism* (P: 1965).
229. Martz, L. L. (ed.): *Milton, 'PL': A Collection of Critical Essays* (P: 1966).
230. Thorpe, James (ed.): *Milton Criticism: Selections from Four Centuries* (1950; P: 1965).
Other collections are cited below (*329, 343, 361, 378, 579*).

III

STUDIES OF MILTON

THE principal bibliographical works include: D. H. Stevens, *Reference Guide to Milton: 1800–1930* (1930); H. F. Fletcher, *Contributions to a Milton Bibliography: 1800–1930* (1931); and Calvin Huckabay, *John Milton: A Bibliographical Supplement, 1929–1957* (1960). The works listed above (headnote, p. 383) include sections on Milton. See also J. H. Hanford, *Milton* (Goldentree Bibliographies, P: 1966), and the annotated survey by David Daiches, *Humanistic Scholarship in America: English Literature* (The Princeton Studies, 1964), ch. II.

The Life Records of John Milton have been edited by J. M. French (1949–58), 5 vols. The first biographies of the poet are in *The Early Lives of Milton*, ed. Helen Darbishire (1932; repr. 1965); seventeenth-century comments are in W. R. Parker, *Milton's Contemporary Reputation* (1940). Modern critical biographies range from Hilaire Belloc's absurd performance (1935) and Rex Warner's superficial one (1949), through Kenneth Muir's much better estimate (1955; 2nd ed., 1961), to the excellent studies by E. M. W. Tillyard (1930), J. H. Hanford (1949; P: 1961), David Daiches (1957; rev. repr. 1959; P: 1963), Emile Saillens (1959; trans. 1964), and Douglas Bush (1964, 1965). W. R. Parker's *Milton: A Biography* (1966), 2 vols., is the only work comparable to Masson's monumental labours.

R. D. Havens has written a survey of *The Influence of Milton on English Poetry* (1922; repr. 1961), but a more thorough study is very much needed.

(a) On Milton's prose works, with general studies of his thought

231. Adamson, J. H.: 'Milton's Arianism', *HTR*, LIII (1960), 269–76. Supports, and qualifies, Hunter's thesis (*261*).

232. Adamson, J. H.: 'Milton and the Creation', *JEGP*, LXI (1962), 756–78. On the tradition underlying Milton's views.

233. Barker, A. E.: 'Christian Liberty in Milton's Divorce Pamphlets', *MLR*, XXXV (1940), 153–61.

234. Barker, A. E.: *Milton and the Puritan Dilemma 1641–1660* (1942; repr. 1955). A study of the development of Milton's views 'in the light of the changing climate of opinion among his Puritan contemporaries'. Cf. *73, 87, 302.*

235. Bryant, J. A.: 'Milton and the Art of History: A Study of two Influences on *A Brief History of Moscovia*', *PQ*, XXIX (1950), 15–30.

Cf. G. B. Parks, 'Milton's *Muscovia* not History', *PQ*, XXXI (1952), 218–21, and Bryant's rejoinder, ibid., pp. 221–3. Cf. *251*.

236. Cawley, R. R.: *Milton and the Literature of Travel* (1951). Cf. *36*.

237. Clair, J. A.: 'A Note on Milton's "Arianism"', in *Essays and Studies in Language and Literature*, ed. H. H. Petit (Duquesne Studies: Philological Series, V: 1964), pp. 44–8. Cf. *261, 266*.

238. Conklin, G. N.: *Biblical Criticism and Heresy in Milton* (1949). On philological aspects of Milton's exegesis in *DDC*.

239. Duhamel, P. A.: 'Milton's Alleged Ramism', *PMLA*, LXVII (1952), 1035–53. Cf. *93, 245*.

240. Eisenring, A. J. T.: *Milton's 'DDC': An Historical Introduction and Critical Analysis* (1946). Elementary and misleading. Cf. *265, 288*.

241. Ekfelt, F. E.: 'Latinate Diction in Milton's English Prose', *PQ*, XXVIII (1949), 53–71.

242. Fink, Z. S.: *The Classical Republicans: An Essay in the Recovery of a Pattern of Thought in Seventeenth Century England* (1945; 2nd ed., 1962). Reprints, in ch. IV, part of 'The Theory of the Mixed State and the Development of Milton's Political Thought', *PMLA*, LVII (1942), 705–36.

243. Fiore, A. P.: 'The Problem of Seventeenth-Century Soteriology in Reference to Milton', *Franciscan Studies*, XV (1955), 48–59, 257–82. Not reliable on Protestant theology.

244. Firth, Sir Charles: 'Milton as an Historian', in *Essays Historical & Literary* (1938), pp. 61–102. The best evaluation of Milton's *History of Britain* (publ. 1670, but written in 1632–8 – at least according to L. S. Berry, *RES*, n.s., XI (1960), 150–56).

245. Fisher, P. F.: 'Milton's Logic', *JHI*, XXIII (1962), 37–60. On Milton's Ramist affiliations in his *Artis logicae* (publ. 1672). Cf. *239; 287*.

246. Fisher, P. F.: 'Milton's Theodicy', *JHI*, XVII (1956), 28–53.

247. Fletcher, H. F.: *Milton's Semitic Studies* (1926), and *Milton's Rabbinical Readings* (1930). Good surveys.

248. Fletcher, H. F.: *The Intellectual Development of John Milton* (1956 ff.), 2 vols.; in progress. The second volume of this massive work carries us only to Milton's twenty-fourth year (1632). Cf. *38*.

249. Frank, Joseph: 'John Milton's Movement toward Deism', *Journal of British Studies*, I (1961), 38–51.

250. French, J. M.: 'Milton as a Historian', *PMLA*, L (1935), 469–79. Cf. *244*.

251. Gleason, J. B.: 'The Nature of Milton's *Moscovia*', *SP*, LXI (1964), 640–49. On the possibility that the work was 'a preparatory stage' in an abandoned project. Cf. *235*.

252. Grace, W. J.: 'Milton, Salmasius, and the Natural Law', *JHI*,

XXIV (1963), 323–36. On the central thesis of Milton's *Defensio pro populo anglicano* (1651).

253. Graves, Robert: 'The Ghost of Milton', in *The Common Asphodel* (1949), pp. 315–25. The author of the wildly unhistorical biography of Mary Powell (*Wife to Mr. Milton*, 1943; P: 1962) here expresses his 'dismay at the recent revival of Milton-worship' and states his own view of the poet (' a monster anda renegade').

254. Greaves, Margaret: 'Magnanimous to Correspond with Heaven', in *The Blazon of Gentry* (1964), ch. VI. On Milton's view of 'magnanimity'; superficial.

255. Hanford, J. H.: *A Milton Handbook* (1926; 4th ed., 1946; repr. 1961). This sometime useful survey is now in need of drastic revision.

256. Hanford, J. H.: 'The Date of Milton's *DDC*', *SP*, XVII (1920), 309–19. Argues for 1655–60. Cf. *265, 288.*

257. Harding, D. P.: *Milton and the Renaissance Ovid* (1946). Milton's debt to the christianized Ovid.

258. Henry, N. H.: 'Milton and Hobbes: Mortalism and the Intermediate State', *SP*, XLVIII (1951), 234–49. Cf. *214.*

259. Henry, N. H.: 'Milton's Last Pamphlet: Theocracy and Intolerance', in *A Tribute to G. C. Taylor*, ed. Arnold Williams (1952), pp. 197–210, On the pamphlet *Of True Religion, Heresy, and Schism* (1673).

260. Hughes, M. Y.: *Ten Perspectives on Milton* (1965). A very important collection of essays, among them 'Lydian Airs', 'Milton and the Sense of Glory', 'Milton and the Symbol of Light', 'The Filiations of Milton's Celestial Dialogue', and 'Milton's Treatment of Reformation History in *The Tenure of Kings and Magistrates*'. Cf. *580.*

261. Hunter, W. B.: 'Milton's Arianism Reconsidered', *HTR*, LII (1959), 9–35. Milton in *DDC* is indebted to the 'subordinationism' current throughout the pre-Nicene period and revived in modified form by the rationalists of the later Renaissance. Cf. *277.*

262. Hunter, W. B.: 'Some Problems in John Milton's Theological Vocabulary', *HTR*, LVII (1964), 353–65. On the complex terminology of *DDC*.

263. Huntley, J. F.: '*Proairesis, Synteresis,* and the Ethical Orientation of Milton's *Of Education*', *PQ*, XLIV (1965), 40–46.

264. Jones, C. W.: 'Milton's "Brief Epic"', *SP*, XLIV (1947), 209–27. On Milton's allusion to the Book of Job in *The Reason of Church Government*.

265. Kelley, Maurice: *This Great Argument: A Study of Milton's 'DDC' as a Gloss upon 'PL'* (1941). The 'gloss' rests on the assumption that Milton's treatise (here dated *c.* 1658–60) contains 'a less ambiguous statement of the dogma, aims, and argument of his epic'. Cf. *288.*

266. Kelley, Maurice: 'Milton's Arianism Again Reconsidered', *HTR*, LIV (1961), 195–205. An angry reply to Hunter (*261*).

267. Kranidas, Thomas: '"Decorum" and the Style of Milton's Antiprelatical Tracts', *SP*, LXII (1965), 176–87. See also the author's 'Milton and the Rhetoric of Zeal', *TSLL*. VI (1965), 423–32.

268. Lewalski, B. K.: 'Milton: Political Beliefs and Polemical Methods, 1659–60', *PMLA*, LXXIV (1959), 191–202.

269. Liljegren, S. B.: *Studies in Milton* (1918). Asserts that Milton (1) falsely claimed to have visited Galileo, and (2) forged a prayer in the *Eikon Basilike*. On (1), see the replies by B. A. Wright, *MLR*, XXVIII (1933), 308–14, and M. H. Nicolson, *ELH*, II (1935), 8–10; and on (2): J. S. Smart, *RES*, I (1925), 385–91, and M. Y. Hughes, *RES*, III (1927), 130–40.

270. MacCallum, H. R.: 'Milton and Figurative Interpretation of the Bible', *UTQ*, XXXI (1962), 397–415. On the exegetical principles of *DDC*.

271. Mutschmann, Heinrich: *The Secret of John Milton* (1925). The author's notorious claim that Milton was an albino has rightly been described as 'German scholarship run mad' (A. Pompen, *Neophilologus*, VII, 276).

272. Neumann, J. H.: 'Milton's Prose Vocabulary', *PMLA*, LX (1945), 102–20. Its chief features.

273. Nicolson, M. H.: 'Milton and Hobbes', *SP*, XXIII (1926), 405–33. Cf. *301; 132*.

274. Nicolson, M. H.: 'The Spirit World of Milton and More', *SP*, XXII (1925), 433–52; 'Milton and the *Conjectura Cabbalistica*', *SP*, VI (1927), 1–18. The first – and in many ways still the best – studies of Milton's relationship with the Cambridge Platonists. Cf. *34*.

275. Parker, W. R.: 'Education: Milton's Ideas and Ours', *CE*, XXIV (1962), 1–14.

276. Patrick, J. M. (ed.): *SAMLA Studies in Milton* (P: 1953). Includes J. A. Bryant's 'Milton's Views on Universal and Civil Decay'; A. H. Gilbert's 'Milton's Defense of Bawdry'; Alwin Thaler's 'Milton and Shakespeare Once More'; Ants Oras's 'Milton's Blank Verse and the Chronology of his Major Poems'; etc.

277. Patrides, C. A.: 'Milton and Arianism', *JHI*, XXV (1964), 423–9. *DDC* is said to diverge significantly from all the major Arian tenets. Cf. *261*.

278. Patrides, C. A.: *Milton and the Christian Tradition* (1966). Chapters on 'Milton's conception and presentation of the principal themes of the Christian faith'.

279. Praz, Mario: 'Milton and Poussin', in *Seventeenth Century Studies presented to Sir Herbert Grierson* (1938), pp. 192–210. On their 'neo-classicism'.

280. Price, A. F.: 'Incidental Imagery in *Areopagitica*', *MP*, XLIX (1952), 217–22.

281. Reesing, John: 'The Materiality of God in Milton's *DDC*', *HTR*, L (1957), 159–73. Milton's position is 'not exactly heretical'.

282. Røstvig, M.-S.: 'The Hidden Sense: Milton and the Neoplatonic Method of Numerical Composition', in *The Hidden Sense and Other Essays* (1963), pp. 1–112. An attempt to enlist Milton among Renaissance numerologists. (All other relevant studies are mentioned by the same author in 'Renaissance Numerology: Acrostics or Criticism?' *EC*, XVI (1966), 6–21.

283. Rusk, R. R.: 'Milton', in *The Doctrines of the Great Educators* (1918; 3rd ed., 1965), ch. VI. Introductory.

284. Sasek, L. A.: 'Milton's Patriotic Epic', *HLQ*, XX (1959), 1–14. 'Milton's prose works represent a definite fulfilment of his patriotic aims'.

285. Saurat, Denis: *Milton: Man and Thinker* (1925; rev. ed., 1944; repr. 1964). Often far-fetched on Milton's 'sources', but important as a pioneer study. (A chapter is repr. in *230*.)

286. Schultz, Howard: *Milton and Forbidden Knowledge* (1955). On the influence of various 'formulas of piety' on Milton and his contemporaries.

287. Scott-Craig, T. S. K.: 'The Craftsmanship and Theological Significance of Milton's *Art of Logic*', *HLQ*, XVII (1953), 1–16. Cf. *245*.

288. Sewell, Arthur: *A Study in Milton's Christian Doctrine* (1939). Not yet entirely superseded as the most reasonable study of *DDC*, which is here dated in three stages (1640 ff., 1658–60, and after 1660). See also the author's essay in *E&S*, XIX (1934), 40–65. Cf. *256, 265*.

289. Siegel, P. N.: 'Milton and the Humanistic Attitude toward Women', *JHI*, XI (1950), 42–53. The best study of a frequently misunderstood subject. Cf. *154*.

290. Sims, J. H.: *The Bible in Milton's Epics* (1962). Introductory.

291. Sirluck, Ernest: 'Milton Revises the *Faerie Queene*', *MP*, XLVIII (1950), 90–96. The implications of Milton's misquotation of Spenser in *Areopagitica*.

292. Sirluck, Ernest: 'Milton's Political Thought: The First Cycle', *MP*, LXI (1964), 209–24. On Milton's changing attitude toward natural law.

293. Spaeth, S. G.: *Milton's Knowledge of Music* (1913; P: 1963). Cf. *90*.

294. Stapleton, Laurence: 'Milton's Conception of Time in *The Christian Doctrine*', *HTR*, LVII (1964), 9–21.

295. Svendsen, Kester: *Milton and Science* (1956). One of the finest studies of the background to Milton's thought.

296. Taylor, Dick: 'Grace as a Means of Poetry: Milton's Pattern for Salvation', *Tennessee Studies in English*, IV (1954), 57–90. Superficial.

297. West, R. H.: *Milton and the Angels* (1955). The best study of the subject. Cf. *149, 203*.

298. Whiting, G. W.: *Milton's Literary Milieu* (1939; repr. 1964). On some aspects of 'the contemporary setting of Milton's work'. A sequel, *Milton and this Pendant World* (1958), is marred by excessive sermonizing.

299. Williams, Arnold: '*Areopagitica* Revisited', *UTQ*, XIV (1944), 67–74. One of the better tributes on the tercentenary of the oration's publication in 1644. See also William Haller, 'For the Liberty of Unlicens'd Printing', *American Scholar*, XIV (1945), 326–33.

300. Wolfe, D. M.: 'Limits of Miltonic Toleration', *JEGP*, LX (1961), 834–46. The limits: 'undeviating hostility toward freedom of Catholic conscience, and failure to speak for the Jews'. Cf. *165*.

301. Wolfe, D. M.: 'Milton and Hobbes: A Contrast in Social Temper', *SP*, XLI (1944), 410–26. Cf. *273*.

302. Wolfe, D. M.: *Milton in the Puritan Revolution* (1941; repr. 1963). An excellent study of Milton's political beliefs in the light of 'both the historical events and the social ideas of his influential contemporaries'. Cf. *73, 87, 234*.

303. Woodhouse, A. S. P.: 'Milton, Puritanism, and Liberty', *UTQ*, IV (1935), 483–513. On 'the reasons for Milton's position and its limitations'.

304. Woodhouse, A. S. P.: 'Notes on Milton's View of the Creation: The Initial Phases', *PQ*, XXVIII (1949), 211–36. Cf. *232*.

See further *59, 62, 73, 102, 150, 214, 418, 420, 424, 457, 479, 510, 570, 591, 603, 609,* etc.

(b) On Milton's 'minor' poems, with general studies of his poetry

305a. Abrams, M. H.: *The Mirror and the Lamp: Romantic Theory and the Critical Tradition* (1953; repr. P: 1960), pp. 250–56. On the romantic critics' view of Milton.

305b. Adams, R. M.: 'Reading *Comus*', in *Ikon: John Milton and the Modern Critics* (1955; P: 1966), ch. I. A caveat against the frequent 'overreading' of the masque.

306. Allen, D. C.: *The Harmonious Vision: Studies in Milton's Poetry* (1954), chs. I–II. Uneven essays on the most important 'minor' poems.

307. Arthos, John: *On a Mask presented at Ludlow-Castle* (P: 1954). On the imaginative forming of the masque together with a consideration of its sources and of the adaptation of certain literary conventions to its primary ideas.

308. Arthos, John: 'The Realms of Being in the Epilogue of *Comus*', *MLN*, LXXVI (1961), 321–4. On the epilogue's Platonic burden.

309. Babb, Laurence: 'The Background of *Il Penseroso*', *SP*, XXXVII (1940), 257–73. See also *8*.

310. Barker, A. E.: 'The Pattern of Milton's *Nativity Ode*', *UTQ*, X (1941), 167–81. A basic study.

311. Beer, John: 'Milton, Lost and Regained', *PBA*, L (1964), 143–68. A survey.

312. Bridges, Robert: *Milton's Prosody, with a Chapter on Accentual Verse,* rev. ed. (1921; repr. 1965). Still the best introduction. Cf. *374, 460.*

313a. Broadbent, J. B.: *Milton: 'Comus' and 'S A'* (P: 1961). Introductory.

313b. Brockbank, Philip: '*Comus* and the Trials of Our Youth', in *Eng. Lit. and English Literature,* Bulletin of the National Association for the Teaching of English, vol. III, no. 2 (Summer 1966), pp. 42–54.

314. Brooks, Cleanth: 'Milton and the New Criticism', *SR*, LIX (1951), 1–22, and 'Milton and Critical Re-estimates', *PMLA*, LXVI (1951), 1045–54. Appraisals of the changing critical attitudes. Cf. *392.*

315. Brooks, Cleanth, and J. E. Hardy: 'Essays in Analysis', in *Poems of Mr. John Milton* (1951), pt II. Studies of all the 'minor' poems; particularly noteworthy is the essay on *Comus.* (The essay on *L'Allegro* and *Il Penseroso* is taken from Brooks's *The Well Wrought Urn: Studies in the Structure of Poetry* (1947; P: 1956), ch. III; the essay on *Lycidas* is reprinted in Hardy's *The Curious Frame* (1962), pp. 22–44).

316. Bruser, Fredelle: 'Comus and the Rose Song', *SP*, XLIV (1947), 625–44. On the *carpe diem* tradition voiced by Comus (ll. 743–4).

317. Carpenter, N. C.: 'The Place of Music in *L'Allegro* and *Il Penseroso*', *UTQ*, XXII (1953), 354–67. Music clarifies the form, content and meaning of the twin lyrics.

318. Carrithers, G. H.: 'Milton's Ludlow *Mask*: From Chaos to Community', *ELH*, XXXIII (1966), 23–42. The poem's movement is primarily from 'threatened isolation' to 'charitable commitment'.

319. Chambers, R. W.: 'Poets and their Critics: Langland and Milton', *PBA*, XXVII (1941), 109–54. A modest defence.

320. Clark, E. M.: 'Milton's English Poetical Vocabulary', *SP*, LIII (1956), 220–38. An enlightening statistical survey. Cf. *349, 407.*

321. Condee, R. W.: 'The Structure of Milton's *Epitaphium Damonis*', *SP*, LXII (1965), 577–94.

322. Cope, J. I.: 'Fortunate Falls as Form in Milton's *Fair Infant*', *JEGP*, LXIII (1964), 660–74. The best study of a neglected poem. Cf. *351.*

323. Cormican, L. A.: 'Milton's Religious Verse', in *A Guide to English Literature,* ed. B. Ford, III: *From Donne to Marvell* (P: Penguin Books, 1956; rev. ed., 1962), pp. 165–84. Introductory.

324. Daniells, Roy: *Milton, Mannerism and Baroque* (1963). A comprehensive survey of an important subject. Cf. *122, 136, 180.*

325. Darbishire, Helen: 'Milton's Poetic Language', *E&S*, n.s., X (1957), 31–52. An attractive lecture on the *Nativity Ode, Lycidas,* and *PL.*

326. Diekhoff, J. S.: 'Critical Activity of the Poetic Mind: John Milton', *PMLA*, *LV* (1940), 748–72. The Trinity MS. of Milton's minor poems reveals the poet's concern 'to find the right word'.

327. Dyson, A. E.: 'The Interpretation of *Comus*', *E&S*, VIII (1955), 89–114. An important essay, its emphasis on the 'dramatic and poetic context'.

328. Emma, R. D.: *Milton's Grammar* (1964). On the 'characteristic grammatical practice' of Milton's works.

329. Emma, R. D., and J. T. Shawcross (eds.): *Language and Style in Milton: A Symposium in Honor of the Tercentenary of 'PL'* (1967). Essays by Robert Beum, Christine Brooke-Rose, M. A. DiCesare, E. J. Dobson, Harold Fisch, K. G. Hamilton, H. M. Hume, C. A. Patrides, J. M. Steadman, and the two editors.

330. Garrod, H. W.: 'Milton's Lines on Shakespeare', *E&S*, XII (1926), 1–23.

331. Gordon, George: 'The Youth of Milton', in *The Lives of Authors* (1950), pp. 44–86. Three graceful lectures on Milton's early development.

332. Groom, Bernard: 'Milton', in *The Diction of Poetry from Spenser to Bridges* (1955), ch. IV. On aspects of Milton's various styles.

333. Hanford, J. H.: 'The Youth of Milton: An Interpretation of his Early Literary Development', *Studies in Shakespeare, Milton, and Donne*, University of Michigan Publications: Language and Literature, I (1925; repr. 1964), pp. 87–163. Still one of the most useful studies. (This and other essays by Hanford have been reprinted in his *John Milton: Poet and Humanist* (1966).)

334. Hardison, O. B.: 'Milton's *On Time* and its Scholastic Background', *TSLL*, III (1961), 107–22.

335. Haun, Eugene: 'An Inquiry into the Genre of *Comus*', in *Essays in Honor of W. C. Curry* (1954), pp. 221–39. Concludes that *Comus* is one of many 'musical dramatic pieces . . . thoroughly familiar to the sophisticated theatre-going audience of the time'.

336. Holmes, Elizabeth: 'Some Notes on Milton's Use of Words', *E&S*, X (1924), 97–121. On 'the interplay of distinct but related shades of meaning in some of Milton's characteristic words'.

337. Hunter, W. B.: 'Milton translates the Psalms', *PQ*, XL (1961), 485–94. Cf. *377*.

338. Hunter, W. B.: 'New Words in Milton's English Poems', in *Essays in Honor of W. C. Curry* (1954), pp. 241–59. A useful roll-call.

339. Hyman, L. W.: 'Milton's *On the Late Massacre in Piedmont*', *English Language Notes*, III (1965), 26–9. The poem manifests 'Milton's faith in the ultimate triumph of the saints'. Cf. *379*.

340. Jarrett-Kerr, Martin: 'Milton, Poet and Paraphrast', *EC*, X (1960),

373–89. Some comments on the ways Milton 'injured himself' in *PL* and other poems.

341. Jayne, Sears: 'The Subject of Milton's Ludlow *Mask*', *PMLA*, LXXIV (1959), 533–43 (repr. in *228*). Considers *Comus* as 'a Platonic Masque of Chastity'.

342. Jones, W. M.: 'Immortality in Two of Milton's Elegies', in *Myth and Symbol: Critical Approaches and Applications*, ed. Bernice Slote (P: 1963), pp. 133–40. On the 'thought progression' of *On the Death of a Fair Infant* and *Epitaphium Damonis*.

343. Kermode, Frank (ed.): *The Living Milton* (1960; P: 1963), chs. I–III, IX–X. Essays by John Wain, 'Strength and Isolation: Pessimistic Notes of a Miltonolater'; J. B. Broadbent, '*The Nativity Ode*'; G. S. Fraser, 'Approaches to *Lycidas*'; Michael Hamburger, 'The Sublime Art: Notes on Milton and Hölderlin'; and Bernard Bergonzi, 'Criticism and the Milton Controversy'. See further *465, 584*.

344. Klein, J. L.: 'Some Spenserian Influences on Milton's *Comus*', *Annuale Mediaevale*, V (1964), 27–47.

345. Kranidas, Thomas: *The Fierce Equation: A Study of Milton's Decorum* (1965). The best work on the subject to date.

346. Langdon, Ida: *Milton's Theory of Poetry and Fine Art: An Essay with a collection of illustrative passages from his works* (1924; repr. 1965). A useful compendium.

347. Leishman, J. B.: '*L'Allegro* and *Il Penseroso* in their Relation to Seventeenth-Century Poetry', *E&S*, n.s., IV (1951), 1–36.

348. Lewis, C. S.: 'A Note on *Comus*', *RES*, VIII (1932), 170–76; repr. in his *Studies in Medieval and Renaissance Literature,* ed. Walter Hooper (1966), ch. XIV. Implications of the changes introduced by Milton after 1634.

349. Lumiansky, R. M.: 'Milton's English Again', *MLN*, LV (1940), 591–4. A study of *L'Allegro* 'to refute the prevailing notion of the alien quality of Milton's words'. Cf. *320*.

350. Mabley, A. H.: 'Milton's Latin Poems', *Western Reserve University Bulletin*, II, 49–72. On the poems' biographical significance and 'considerable poetical merit'. Cf. *365, 369*.

351. Maclean, H. N.: 'Milton's *Fair Infant*', *ELH*, XXIV (1957), 296–305 (repr. in *228*). On the poem's structure and imagery. Cf. *322*.

352. Major, J. M.: '*Comus* and *The Tempest*', *SQ*, X (1959), 177–83. Cf. *368*.

353. Maxwell, J. C.: 'The Pseudo-Problem of *Comus*', *CJ*, I (1948), 376–80. Protests against some excessive readings of the masque, and argues that its main theme is Virtue.

354. Murry, J. M.: 'Milton', in *Heaven – and Earth* (1938; American ed.: *Heroes of Thought*), chs. XI–XIII. Three essays, largely on Milton's 'curious version of Christian morality'.

355. Nelson, Lowry, jr.: 'Góngora and Milton: Toward a Definition of the Baroque', *CL*, VI (1954), 53–63. A consideration of the *Nativity Ode* and Góngora's *Polifemo*. Cf. *136*.

356. Nicolson, M. H.: *A Reader's Guide to John Milton* (1964). A good introduction.

357. Ogden, H. V. S.: 'The Principles of Variety and Contrast in Seventeenth Century Aesthetics, and Milton's Poetry', *JHI*, X (1949), 159–82.

358. Osgood, C. G.: *The Classical Mythology of Milton's English Poems* (1900; repr. 1964). Still the best work of reference.

359. Parker, W. R.: 'Milton's Last Sonnet', *RES*, XXI (1945), 235–8. Claims that the 'late espoused Saint' in Sonnet XXIII is not Mary Powell, Milton's first wife, but Katherine Woodcock, his second. On the ensuing controversy, see the references in Thomas Wheeler, 'Milton's Twenty-Third Sonnet', *SP*, LVII (1961), 510–15. Cf. *373*.

360. Patrides, C. A.: 'The Cessation of the Oracles: The History of a Legend', *MLR*, LX (1965), 500–507. On the background to the *Nativity Ode*, ll. 173–228 (cf. *PL*, I, 455–64).

361. Patrides, C. A. (ed.): *Milton's 'Lycidas': The Tradition and the Poem* (P: 1961). Includes fourteen essays (by Dr Johnson, J. H. Hanford, E. M. W. Tillyard, P. E. More, J. Miles, D. Daiches, R. P. Adams, W. Shumaker, C. Brooks and J. E. Hardy, F. T. Prince, R. Tuve, N. Frye, and M. H. Abrams); with full annotated bibliography.

362. Prince, F. T.: *The Italian Element in Milton's Verse* (1954). Chs. VII–VIII deal with Milton's blank verse (ch. VII is repr. in *229*); the rest deal with the minor poems and *SA*. The standard work.

363. Pyle, Fitzroy: 'Milton's First Sonnet on his Blindness', *RES*, n.s., IX (1958), 376–87. On Sonnet XIX ('When I consider'), here linked with Sonnet XXII ('Cyriack, this three years' day').

364. Rajan, B.: '"Simple, Sensuous and Passionate"', *RES*, XXI (1945), 289–301 (repr. in *228*). A sensitive study of Milton's unified views – in theory and practice – of 'the nature and limits of his profession'.

365. Rand, E. K.: 'Milton in Rustication', *SP*, XIX (1922), 109-35. Still the best study of Milton's Latin poems. Cf. *350*, *369*.

366. Read, Sir Herbert: 'Milton', in *A Coat of Many Colours* (1945), pp. 132–3. A note on Milton's 'artificiality'.

367. Saunders, J. W.: 'Milton, Diomede and Amaryllis', *ELH*, XXII (1955), 254–86. An interesting survey of Milton's development in terms of the worlds symbolized by jocund Amaryllis, and wise, courageous Diomede.

368. Seaton, Ethel: '*Comus* and Shakespeare', *E&S*, XXXI (1945), 68–80. Argues the influence of *Romeo and Juliet*. Cf. *352*.

369. Semple, W. H.: 'The Latin Poems of John Milton', *Bulletin of the John*

Rylands Library, XLVI (1963), 217–35. A lecture on 'the natural vigorous output of a young but powerful mind'. Cf. *350, 365*.

370. Sensabaugh, G. F.: 'The "Milieu" of *Comus*', *SP*, XLI (1944), 238–49. Sees the masque as 'an answer to the court in the current debate on matters of marriage and love'.

371. Shawcross, J. T.: 'What we can learn from Milton's Spelling', *HLQ*, XXVI (1963), 351–61. One of the more interesting of the author's series of studies on Milton's texts.

372. Sherburn, George: 'The Early Popularity of Milton's Minor Poems', *MP*, XVII (1919–20), 259–78, 515–40. On the critical views ventured to 1740.

373. Spitzer, Leo: 'Understanding Milton', in *Essays on English and American Literature*, ed. Anna Hatcher (1962), ch. VII. Argues that Sonnet XXIII ('Methought I saw') is 'perfectly understandable without the hypothesis of [Milton's] blindness'. Cf. *359*.

374. Sprott, S. E.: *Milton's Art of Prosody* (1953). Complements *312*.

375. Stapleton, Laurence: 'Milton and the New Music', *UTQ*, XXIII (1954), 217–26 (repr. in *228*). On Milton's adaptation of traditional themes in the *Nativity Ode*.

376. Stoehr, Taylor: 'Syntax and Poetic Form in Milton's Sonnets', *ES*, XLV (1964), 289–301. The 'particularly moving quality' of the sonnets resides in Milton's ability to match sound and sense.

377. Studley, M. H.: 'Milton and his Paraphrases of the Psalms', *PQ*, IV (1925), 364–72. Cf. *337*.

378. Summers, J. H. (ed.): *The Lyric and Dramatic Milton* (1965), pt I. Three essays: by L. L. Martz, 'The Rising Poet, 1645'; C. L. Barber, '*A Mask presented at Ludlow Castle*: The Masque as Masque'; and I. G. MacCaffrey, '*Lycidas*: The Poet in a Landscape'. See further *620*.

379. Svendsen, Kester: 'Milton's Sonnet on the Massacre in Piedmont', *Shakespeare Association Bulletin*, XX (1945), 147–55. Cf. *339*.

380. Tate, Eleanor: 'Milton's *L'Allegro* and *Il Penseroso* – Balance, Progression, or Dichotomy?' *MLN*, LXXVI (1961), 585–90. Supports, and qualifies, Allen's study (*306*).

381. Tillyard, E. M. W.: 'Milton: *L'Allegro* and *Il Penseroso*', *English Association Pamphlet*, LXXXII (1932). Links the two poems with Milton's first academic exercise (prolusion). (Repr. in *The Miltonic Setting* (1938), ch. I, where other aspects of Milton's poetry are also discussed. Cf. *537*.)

382. Tillyard, E. M. W.: *The Metaphysicals and Milton* (1956). An introductory exploration. Cf. *529*.

383. Tuve, Rosemond: *Images and Themes in Five Poems by Milton* (1957). Very important essays on *L'Allegro* and *Il Penseroso* (repr. in *228*), *Lycidas* (repr. in *361*), *Nativity Ode*, and *Comus*.

384. Wallace, J. M.: 'Milton's *Arcades*', *JEGP*, LVIII (1959), 627–36 (repr. in *228*). Sees the poem as 'a pilgrimage from the profane to the religious'.

385. Watkins, W. B. C.: *An Anatomy of Milton's Verse* (1955). A good introduction. (A chapter on *PL* ('Creation') is repr. in *229*).

386. Whiteley, M.: 'Verse and its Feet', *RES*, n.s., IX (1958), 268–79. On Milton's prosody; with a note by F. T. Prince. Cf. *312, 362*.

387. Wilkinson, David: 'The Escape from Pollution: A Comment on *Comus*', *EC*, X (1960), 32–43. On 'the ritual effect' in *Comus*, seen here as less than successful because of Milton's 'half-dramatic, half-allegorical presentation'. Cf. W. Leahy's rejoinder in *EC*, XI (1961), 111.

388. Williams, Charles: 'Introduction' to *The English Poems of John Milton* (1940), pp. vii–xx (repr. in *230*). An influential essay, one of the landmarks in twentieth-century Milton criticism.

389. Williams, Charles: 'Milton', in *The English Poetic Mind* (1932; repr. 1963), ch. IV (repr. in his *Selected Writings*, ed. Anne Ridler (P: 1961), pp. 23–55). A sympathetic review of Milton's poetic performance.

390. Woodhouse, A. S. P.: 'Notes on Milton's Early Development', *UTQ*, XIII (1943), 66–101. A suggestive survey.

391. Woodhouse, A. S. P.: 'The Argument of Milton's *Comus*', *UTQ*, XI (1941), 46–71. An influential though overstated study of the orders of nature and grace.

392. Woodhouse, A. S. P.: 'The Historical Criticism of Milton', *PMLA*, LXVI (1951), 1033–44. Cf. *314*.

393. Wrenn, C. L.: 'The Language of Milton', in *Studies in English Language and Literature presented to Professor Dr. Karl Brunner*, ed. Siegfried Korninger (1957), pp. 252–67. On Milton's 'use and exploitation of the utmost powers of his native English'.

On *Comus* see further: *19, 58, 128, 201, 213, 577*: on *Lycidas*: *58, 130, 136, 194*: on the *Nativity Ode*: *121, 136*: and on the 'minor' poems generally: *90, 130, 163, 164, 228, 230, 260, 282, 293*, etc.

(c) On 'Paradise Lost'

394. Adams, R. M.: 'Milton's Verse: Efforts at a Judgement', in *Ikon* (1955), ch. VI. A lively account of shortcomings in Milton criticism. Cf. *305*.

395. Allen, D. C.: 'Description as Cosmos: The Visual Image in *PL*', in *The Harmonious Vision* (1954), ch. V. On Milton's 'visual imagery' *pace* T. S. Eliot (*429*) *et al.*

396. Allen, D. C.: 'Milton and the Descent to Light', *JEGP*, LX (1961), 614–30 (repr. in *228*). On Milton's 'poetic realization of the themes of descent and ascent'.

Milton's Epic Poetry

397. Arthos, John: *Dante, Michelangelo and Milton* (1963), pp. 90–120. On the nature of the 'sublime' in *PL*.

398. Banks, T. H.: *Milton's Imagery* (1950). A catalogue.

399. Barker, A. E.: 'Structural Pattern in *PL*', *PQ*, XXIII (1949), 17–30 (repr. in *228*). On the regrouping of the ten books of *PL* (1667) into twelve (1674). See also the author's essay in *481*.

400. Bell, Millicent, and Wayne Shumaker: 'The Fallacy of the Fall in *PL*', *PMLA*, LXVIII (1953), 863–83, and LXX (1955), 1185–1203. An exchange of views on whether Adam and Eve had 'fallen' before the Fall.

401. Benham, A. R.: '"Things Unattempted Yet in Prose or Rime"', *MLQ*, XIV (1953), 341–7. An 'extended note' on *PL*, I, 16, in relation to the poem's structure.

402. Bodkin, Maud: *Archetypal Patterns in Poetry: Psychological Studies of Imagination* (1934; P: 1963), *passim*. A rewarding study relating psychology and literature.

403. Bowra, Sir Maurice: 'Milton and the Destiny of Man', in *From Virgil to Milton* (1948; P: 1963), ch. V. One of the most solid essays on *PL*, here studied within context of the changing epic tradition.

404. Broadbent, J. B.: 'Milton's Rhetoric', *MP*, LVI (1959), 224–42. Aspects of the 'formal rhetoric' of *PL*.

405. Broadbent, J. B.: *Some Graver Subject: An Essay on 'PL'* (1960). Part of a chapter is reprinted above, pp. 132 ff.

406. Brooks, Cleanth: 'Eve's Awakening', in *Essays in Honor of W. C. Curry* (1954), pp. 281–98. A reading of *PL*, IV, 449 ff.

407. Brown, J. R.: 'Some Notes on the Native Elements in the Diction of *PL*', *NQ*, CXCVI (1951), 424–8. Cf. *320*.

408. Bryan, R. A.: 'Adam's Tragic Vision in *PL*', *SP*, LXII (1965), 197–214. A reading of *PL*, XI, 385–411.

409. Bush, Douglas: *'PL' in our Time: Some Comments* (1945; repr. 1948). One chapter is reprinted above, pp. 33 ff.; another ('Religious and Ethical Principles') in *228*; a third ('Characters and Drama') in *229*.

410. Bush, Douglas: 'Ironic and Ambiguous Allusion in *PL*', *JEGP*, LX (1961), 631–40.

411. Butler, A. Z.: 'The Pathetic Fallacy in *PL*', in *Essays in Honor of W. C. Curry* (1954), pp. 269–79. A roll-call of some 'striking instances'.

412. Chambers, A. B.: 'Chaos in *PL*', *JHI*, XXIV (1963), 55–84. On Milton's adaptation of the traditional views.

413. Champion, L. S.: 'The Conclusion of *PL* – A Reconsideration', *CE*, XXVII (1966), 384–94. A summary of various interpretations.

414. Coffin, C. M.: 'Creation and the Self in *PL*', ed. C. A. Patrides, *ELH*, XXIX (1962), 1–18 (repr. with a Prefatory Note by John Crowe Ransom in the *Kenyon Alumni Bulletin*, XX, *4* (1962), 11–17). On the implications of the exchanges between God and Adam in *PL*, VIII, 204 ff.

415. Colie, R. L.: 'Time and Eternity: Paradox and Structure in *PL*', *JWCI*, XXIII (1960), 127–38 (repr. in *41*). The 'inexplicable theological paradoxes' of *PL* are transcended through 'the poem itself', 'the experience of reading it'. Cf. *41*.

416. Cook, Albert: 'Milton's Abstract Music', *UTQ*, XXIX (1960), 370–85 (repr. in *228*). On the rhythm of *PL* and *SA*.

417. Cope, J. I.: *The Metaphoric Structure of 'PL'* (1962). On *PL* as the 'richest expression' of metaphoric vision.

418. Corcoran, Sister M. I.: *Milton's Paradise with Reference to the Hexameral Background* (P: 1945; repr. 1966). Detailed and comprehensive. Cf. *212*, *479*.

419. Corcoran, Sister M. I.: 'Milton: *PL*', in *The Great Books: A Christian Appraisal*, ed. H. C. Gardiner (1951), III, 89–96. For the Catholic student of Milton. Cf. *492*.

420. Curry, W. C.: *Milton's Ontology, Cosmogony and Physics* (1957; P: 1966). Among these essays on the intellectual background of *PL* are 'Milton's Chaos and Old Night', 'The Lordship of Milton's Sun', 'Milton's Scale of Nature', etc.

421. Daniells, Roy: 'Humour in *PL*', *DR*, XXXIII (1953), 159–66. Cf E. M. W. Tillyard, *Studies in Milton* (1951), pp. 71–81.

422. Darbishire, Helen: *Milton's 'PL'* (P: 1951). A lively lecture, focusing on the characterization of Adam and Eve.

423. Day, Douglas: 'Adam and Eve in *PL*, IV', *TSLL*, III (1961), 369–81. 'To look just beneath the lyrical surface of the passage [IV, 411 ff.. is to see the Fall of Man in its embryonic stages'.

424. Diekhoff, J. S.: 'Eve, the Devil, and *Areopagitica*', *MLQ*, V (1944), 429–34. On the echoes of the treatise in *PL*, esp. IX, 322 ff.

425. Diekhoff, J. S.: *Milton's 'PL': A Commentary on the Argument* (1945; repr. 1958). A reliable introduction.

426. Douglas, J. W.: 'Milton's Dance of Life', *Downside Review*, LXXX (1962), 243–9. On freedom and obedience in *PL*.

427. Duncan, E. H.: 'The Natural History of Metals and Minerals in the Universe of Milton's *PL*', *Osiris*, XI (1954), 386–421.

428. Eisenstein, Sergei: *The Film Sense*, trans. Jay Leyda (1943), pp. 52–7 (also in *Film Form and The Film Sense*, P: 1957). The celebrated film-director's view of *PL* as 'a first-rate school in which to study montage and audio-visual relationships'.

429. Eliot, T. S.: 'A Note on the Verse of John Milton', *E&S*, XXI (1935), 32–40, and 'Milton', *PBA*, XXXIII (1947), 61–79. Both of these influential essays are readily available in *T. S. Eliot: Selected Prose*, ed. John Hayward (P: Penguin Books, 1953), pp. 116–41. The first is also reprinted in *229*; and the second in both *230*, and *SR*, LVI (1948), 185–209.

430. Empson, William: 'All in *PL*', in *The Structure of Complex Words* (1951), ch. IV. Observes the frequency of 'all' in III, 318–43, X, 817–50, etc.

431. Empson, William: 'Milton and Bentley: The Pastoral of the Innocence of Man and Nature', in *Some Versions of Pastoral* (1935; P: Penguin Books, 1966), ch. V (repr. in *229*). Detailed examination of Milton's language in relation to the celebrated observations ventured by Richard Bentley in 1732.

432. Empson, William: *Milton's God* (1961; rev. ed., 1965). Part of a chapter is reprinted above, pp. 157 ff.

433. Ferry, A. D.: *Milton's Epic Voice: The Narrator in 'PL'* (1963).

434. Fish, Stanley: 'The Harassed Reader of *PL*', and 'Further Thoughts on Milton's Christian Reader', *Critical Quarterly*, VII (1965), 162–82, 279–84. 'The main action of the poem is the discovery by the reader of his limitations'.

435. Fox, R. C.: 'Satan's Triad of Vices', *TSLL*, II (1960), 261–80. On the traditional 'triad' of pride, envy, wrath.

436. Fox, R. C.: 'The Allegory of Sin and Death in *PL*,' *MLQ*, XXIV (1963), 354–64. 'Sin and Death represent the respective sins of lust and gluttony in addition to their nominal concepts'.

437. Fox, R. C.: 'The Character of Mammon in *PL*', *RES*, n.s., XIII (1962), 30–39, and 'The Character of Moloc in *PL*', *Die neueren Sprachen*, IX (1962), 389–95.

438. Fraser, John: '*PL*, Book IX: A Minority Opinion', *Melbourne Critical Review*, No. 7 (1964), pp. 22–32. On Milton's frequent 'failures of mind'.

439. Frye, Northrop: *Five Essays on Milton's Epics* (1965; in U.K., 1966). Four lectures on *PL* – not merely for 'relatively inexperienced readers' – with an essay on *PR* revised from *MP*, LIII (1956), 227–38 (reprinted above, pp. 301 ff.).

440. Frye, R. M.: *God, Man, and Satan* (1960), pt I. A stimulating study of *PL* as a 'great work of Christian imagination'.

441. Gardner, Helen: *A Reading of 'PL'* (1965). The Alexander Lectures in the University of Toronto (1962), on the 'permanent greatness' of *PL*.

442. Gardner, Helen: 'Milton's First Illustrator', *E&S*, n.s., IX (1956), 27–38 (repr. in *441*). The first study of an important subject. Cf. Kester Svendsen, 'John Martin and the Expulsion Scene in *PL*', *SEL*, I (1961), 63–74, and M. Y. Hughes, 'Some Illustrators of Milton: The Expulsion from Paradise', *JEGP*, LX (1961), 670–79 (repr. in *228*).

443. Gardner, Helen: 'Milton's "Satan" and the Theme of Damnation in Elizabethan Tragedy', *E&S*, n.s., I (1948), 46–66 (repr. in *228, 441*).

Milton created in Satan 'the last great tragic figure in our literature' and destroyed 'the unity of the poem in doing so'.

444. Gilbert, A. H.: 'Critics of Mr C. S. Lewis on Milton's Satan', *SAQ*, XLVII (1948), 216–25. A convenient summary of the 'Satanist controversy' of the 1930s and early 1940s; with references to the relevant essays.

445. Gilbert, A. H.: *On the Composition of 'PL': A Study of the Ordering and Insertion of Material* (1947). Interesting speculations on the poem's 'inconsistencies'.

446. Gilbert, A. H.: 'The Theological Basis of Satan's Rebellion and the Function of Abdiel in *PL*', *MP*, XL (1942), 19–42. Milton's use of traditional ideas.

447. Greenlaw, Edwin: 'A Better Teacher than Aquinas', *SP*, XIV (1917), 196–217, and 'Spenser's Influence on *PL*', *SP*, XVII (1920), 320–59. An over-stated thesis but still useful.

448. Grierson, Sir Herbert: *Milton and Wordsworth: Poets and Prophets – A Study of their Reaction to Political Events* (1937).

449. Haller, William: '"Hail Wedded Love"', *ELH*, XIII (1946), 79–97. On Milton's idealistic view of marriage in *PL*. Cf. *74*.

450. Hanford, J. H.: 'Milton and the Return to Humanism', *SP*, XVI (1919), 126–47 (repr. in *230* and in *333*: *John Milton: Poet and Humanist*, ch. IV). One of the finest statements of the enduring qualities of Milton's thought.

451. Hanford, J. H.: '"That Shepherd, who First Taught the Chosen Seed": A Note on Milton's Mosaic Inspiration', *UTQ*, VIII (1939), 403–19. On Milton's conception of his function as poet-prophet.

452. Harding, D. P.: *The Club of Hercules: Studies in the Classical Background of 'PL'* (P: 1962).

453. Hart, Jeffrey: '*PL* and Order', *CE*, XXV (1964), 576–82. *PL* 'contains an elegiac representation of the old order and the old worldview'.

454. Hartmann, Geoffrey: 'Milton's Counterplot', *ELH*, XXV (1958), 1–12 (repr. in *228, 229*). On Milton's indirect manner of expressing the 'divine imperturbability'.

455. Hobsbaum, Philip: 'The Criticism of Milton's Epic Similes', *SN*, XXXVI (1964), 220–31. Cf. *472, 545*.

456. Horrell, Joseph: 'Milton, Limbo, and Suicide', *RES*, XVIII (1942), 413–27. On the implications of the 'Paradise of Fools' (*PL*, III, 416 ff.). Cf. *461, 487*.

457. Howard, Leon: '"The Invention" of Milton's "Great Argument": A Study of the Logic of "God's Ways to Men"', *HLQ*, IX (1946), 149–73. On the claims of Milton in *PL*, in relation to his arguments in *Artis logicae*. Cf. *93*.

458. Hunter, W. B.: 'Eve's Demonic Dream', *ELH*, XIII (1946), 255–65, and 'Prophetic Dreams and Visions in *PL*', *MLQ*, IX (1949), 277–85. On the influence of contemporary dream and demon lore on *PL*. Cf. J. M. Steadman, 'Eve's Dream and Witchcraft Conventions', *JHI*, XXVI (1965), 567–74.

459. Hunter, W. B.: 'The Meaning of "Holy Light" in *PL* III', *MLN*, LXXIV (1959), 589–92, and 'Milton's Urania', *SEL*, IV (1964), 35–42. Suggests that Milton addresses the Son of God at the outset of Books I, III, VII, IX.

460. Hunter, W. B.: 'The Sources of Milton's Prosody', *PQ*, XXVIII (1949), 125–44. The principal sources are Joshua Sylvester and the metrical psalters. Cf. *312.*

461. Huntley, F. L.: 'A Justification of Milton's "Paradise of Fools"', *ELH*, XXI (1954), 107–13. Cf. *456, 487.*

462. Huntley, J. F.: 'The Ecology and Anatomy of Criticism: Milton's Sonnet XIX and the Bee Simile in *PL*, I, 768–76', *Journal of Aesthetics and Art Criticism*, XXIV (1966), 383–91.

463. Kelley, Maurice: 'Milton's Use of "Begot" in *PL*, V, 603', *SP*, XXXVIII (1941), 252–65. The word is used metaphorically.

464. Maurice, Kelley: 'The Theological Dogma of *PL*, III, 173–202', *PMLA*, LII (1937), 75–9 (repr. in *228*). Cf. *265.*

465. Kermode, Frank (ed.): *The Living Milton* (1960; P: 1963), chs. IV–VI. Essays by David Daiches, 'The Opening of *PL*'; Donald Davie, 'Syntax and Music in *PL*'; and Frank Kermode, 'Adam Unparadised'. See also *343, 584.*

466. Kirkconnell, Watson (ed.): *The Celestial Cycle: The Theme of 'PL' in World Literature, with translations of the major analogues* (1952).

467. Knight, Douglas: 'The Dramatic Center of *PL*', *SAQ*, LXIII (1964), 44–59. On the nature of the reader's 'involvement' in *PL*.

468. Knight, G. W.: 'The Frozen Labyrinth: An Essay on Milton', in *The Burning Oracle: Studies in the Poetry of Action* (1939), ch. III. *PL* is seen as 'artistically fallacious', displaying 'a rejection of the specifically vital'.

469. Koehler, G. S.: 'Milton on "Numbers", "Quantity", and Rime', *SP*, LV (1958), 201–17. On the terminology of the prefatory note to *PL*.

470. Kranidas, Thomas: 'Adam and Eve in the Garden: A Study of *PL*, Book V', *SEL*, IV (1964), 71–83 (repr. in *345*). Argues the presence in the poem of 'the magnificent and tragic and the modest and comic'.

471. Leavis, F. R.: 'Mr Eliot and Milton', and 'In Defence of Milton', in *The Common Pursuit* (1952; P: Penguin Books, 1962), pp. 4–43. Observations on Milton's poetry *pace* T. S. Eliot (*429*), Tillyard (*537*), Grierson (*448*), *et al.*

472. Learner, L. D.: 'The Miltonic Simile', *EC*, IV (1954), 297–308. The similes of *PL* 'provide a sense of context'. Cf. *455, 545.*

473. Lewalski, B. K.: 'Structure and the Symbolism of Vision in Michael's Prophecy, *PL*, Books XI–XII', *PQ*, XLII (1963), 25–35. Cf. *481, 519,* and F. T. Prince (above, pp. 233 ff.).

474. Lewis, C. S.: *A Preface to 'PL'* (1942; P: 1960). An influential defence of Milton's tradition-bound thought and style. Chs. VII–VIII ('The Style of Secondary Epic'; 'Defence of this Style') are reprinted in *229* and *230*, and ch. XIII ('Satan') in *228.*

475. Lovejoy, A. O.: 'Milton's Dialogue on Astronomy', in *Reason and the Imagination*, ed. J. A. Mazzeo (1962), pp. 129–42. On the 'extreme expression' of Milton's 'pragmatism' in *PL*, VIII, 5 ff.

476. Lumpkin, B. G.: 'Fate in *PL*', *SP*, XLIV (1947), 56–68. A superficial look at the 'two opposed senses' in which the word is used in *PL*.

477. MacCaffrey, I. G.: *'PL' as 'Myth'* (1959). A detailed and stimulating 'descriptive analysis' of *PL* whose 'myth' is treated as 'history' and 'in a spiritual sense'.

478. McColley, Grant: 'Milton's Dialogue on Astronomy: The Principal Immediate Sources', *PMLA*, LII (1937), 728–62. On the background of *PL*, VIII, 5 ff.

479. McColley, Grant: *'PL'*, *HTR*, XXXII (1939), 181–235. On the epic's traditional themes, with a wealth of references. See also the author's *'PL': An Account of its Growth and Major Origins* (1940; repr. 1963). Cf. *212, 418.*

480. MacKenzie, Phyllis: 'Milton's Visual Imagination: An Answer to T. S. Eliot', *UTQ*, XVI (1947), 17–29. Cf. *429.*

481. MacLure, Millar, and F. W. Watt (eds.): *Essays in English Literature ... presented to A. S. P. Woodhouse* (1964), pp. 125–94. Three important essays, by M. Y. Hughes, 'Satan and the "Myth" of the Tyrant'; H. R. MacCallum, 'Milton and Sacred History: Books XI and XII of *PL*'; and A. E. Barker, 'Structural and Doctrinal Pattern in Milton's Later Poems'.

482. McNamee, M. B.: 'Magnanimity in Milton', in *Honor and the Epic Hero* (1960), ch. IX. A survey.

483. Madsen, W. G.: 'Earth the Shadow of Heaven: Typological Symbolism in *PL*', *PMLA*, LXXV (1960), 519–27 (repr. in *228*). Cf. *620.*

484. Madsen, W. G.: 'The Fortunate Fall in *PL*', *MLN*, LXXIV (1959), 103–5. On the implications of *PL*, XII, 473–8. Cf. *488.*

485. Madsen, W. G.: 'The Idea of Nature in Milton's Poetry', in *Three Studies in the Renaissance* (1958), pp. 181–283.

486. Marilla, E. L.: 'Milton's Pandemonium', *Die neueren Sprachen*, IV (1960), 167–74. Books I–II are said to anticipate 'the calamitous situation that confronts fallen Adam'. See also the author's 'The

Central Problem in *PL*: The Fall of Man', *Essays and Studies on English Language and Literature*, XV (Upsala, 1953).

487. Marilla, E. L.: 'Milton's "Paradise of Fools"', *ES*, XLII (1961), 1–6. Cf. *456, 461.*

488. Marshall, W. H.: '*PL*: *Felix Culpa* and the Problem of Structure', *MLN*, LXXVI (1961), 15–20 (repr. in *228*). Cf. *484*, and A. O. Lovejoy (above, pp. 55 ff.).

489. Miller, D. D.: 'Eve', *JEGP*, LXI (1962), 542–7. Milton's attitude toward his heroine is far more favourable than it is often thought to be. Cf. *289.*

490. Miller, Milton: 'Milton's Imagination and the Idyllic Solution', *Western Review*, XIII (1948), 35–43. Some implications of 'the strength and certainty of [Milton's] faith'.

491. Miller, Milton: '*PL*: The Double Standard', *UTQ*, XX (1951), 183–99. On the 'heroic' and the 'super-heroic' by which 'action is judged in *PL*'.

492. Miriam Joseph, Sister: 'Orthodoxy in *PL*', *Laval théologique et philosophique*, VIII (1952), 243–84. For the Catholic student. Cf. *419.*

493. Mohl, Ruth: 'The Theme of *PL*', and 'Milton and the Idea of Perfection', in *Studies in Spenser, Milton and the Theory of Monarchy* (1949), pp. 66–132.

494. Morris, J. M.: '*PL* Now', *American Scholar*, XXXIII (1963–4), 65–83. 'Milton's moral notions, viewed in all their complication, have in them something interesting and immediately valuable to us'.

495. Nicolson, M. H.: 'Milton and the Telescope', in *Science and Imagination* (P: 1956), ch. IV. The effect of telescopic astronomy on Milton's conception of space. Cf. *140.*

496. Nott, Kathleen: *The Emperor's Clothes* (1953; P: 1958), ch. VI *passim.* Among her most typical comments on *PL* ('not essentially Christian') as well as on Milton's responsibility for 'the devastation of poetic language'.

497. Ogden, H. V. S.: 'The Crisis of *PL* Reconsidered', *PQ*, XXXVI (1957), 1–19 (repr. in *228*). The Fall is 'the climax of the narrative' after all. Cf. *536; 400.*

498. Oras, Ants: 'Spenser and Milton: Some Parallels and Contrasts in the Handling of Sound', in *Sound and Poetry: English Institute Essays 1956* (1957), pp. 109–33.

499. Paolucci, Anne: 'Dante's Satan and Milton's "Byronic Hero"', *Italica*, XLI (1964), 139–49. Dante's poetic representation is 'intensified' in *PL*.

500. Parish, J. E.: 'Pre-Miltonic Representations of Adam as a Christian', *Rice Institute Pamphlet*, XL (1953), No. 3, pp. 1–24. On the theme of the 'Christian Adam' – further discussed by the same author in 'Milton and

God's Curse on the Serpent', *JEGP*, LVIII (1959), 241–7; by J. M. Steadman, 'Adam and the Prophesied Redeemer', *SP*, LVI (1959), 214–25; and by C. A. Patrides, 'The "Protevangelium" in Renaissance Theology and *PL*', *SEL*, III (1963), 19–30.

501. Patrides, C. A.: 'Renaissance and Modern Thought on the Last Things', *HTR*, LI (1958), 169–85, and 'Renaissance and Modern Views on Hell', *HTR*, LVII (1964), 217–36. Surveys of the background to Milton's conceptions. See further *278*.

502a. Patrides, C. A.: 'The Godhead in *PL*: Dogma or Drama?' *JEGP*, LXIV (1965), 29–34. Milton is said to have satisfied the demands of 'drama' even while preserving the unity of the Godhead. Cf. *517*.

502b. Patrides, C. A. (ed.): *Approaches to 'PL': The York Tercentenary Lectures* (1968). Thirteen lectures delivered at the University of York in 1967 by John Arthos, J. B. Broadbent, J. P. Brockbank, Bernard Harris, M. Y. Hughes, F. L. Huntley, Brian Morris F. T. Prince, M. A. Radzinowicz, Irene Samuel, T. J. B. Spencer, J. H. Summers, and J. B. Trapp.

503. Pearce, D. R.: 'The Style of Milton's Epic', *Yale Review*, LII (1963), 427–44 (repr. in *228*). Wide-ranging, from the 'prose element' in *PL* to Milton's handling of classical allusions.

504. Pecheux, Mother M. C.: 'Abraham, Adam, and the Theme of Exile in *PL*', *PMLA*, LXXX (1965), 365–71. On the significance of the Abraham-Adam parallel in Books XI–XII.

505. Pecheux, Mother M. C.: '"O Foul Descent!": Satan and the Serpent Form', *SP*, LXII (1965), 188–96. On the contrast between Satan's 'incarnation' in the serpent and the Son of God's in man (cf. *PL*, IX, 163 ff.).

506. Pecheux, Mother M. C.: 'The Concept of the Second Eve in *PL*', *PMLA*, LXXV (1960), 359–66. Cf. *602*.

507. Pecheux, Mother M. C.: 'The Conclusion of Book VI of *PL*', *SEL*, III (1963), 109–17. On the importance of Satan's defeat at the epic's half-way mark.

508. Peter, John: *A Critique of 'PL'* (1960). An uneven work: at times most perceptive but just as often merely destructive.

509. Pound, Ezra: *Literary Essays*, ed. T. S. Eliot (1954; P: 1960), pp. 201, 216 f., 237 f., etc. Among his most typical comments on 'the abominable dogbiscuit of Milton's rhetoric'.

510. Rajan, B.: *'PL' and the Seventeenth Century Reader* (1947; repr. 1962). A noteworthy attempt to see *PL* 'through the eyes of Milton's contemporaries'.

511. Raleigh, Sir Walter A.: *Milton* (1900). Representative of past dismissals of Milton's thought ('a monument to dead ideas') but still useful on the style of *PL*. (Parts of chs. V–VI are repr. in *230*.)

512. Ransom, John Crowe: 'The Idea of a Literary Anthropologist and what he might say of the *PL* of Milton', *KR*, XXI (1959), 121–40. A wide-ranging, urbane and witty lecture. See also the author's neglected observations on *PL* and *PR* in *God without Thunder: An Unorthodox Defence of Orthodoxy* (1931), pp. 130–49.

513. Ricks, Christopher: *Milton's Grand Style* (1963). Part of a chapter is reprinted above, pp. 249 ff.

514. Rudrum, Alan: *Milton: 'PL'* (P: 1966). A 'point-by-point critical exposition' for sixth-formers.

515. Samuel, Irene: *Dante and Milton: The 'Commedia' and 'PL'* (1966). The most systematic comparison of the two poems to date.

516. Samuel, Irene: *Plato and Milton* (1947; P: 1965). On the poetic and ethical theories of *PL* and *PR*, investigated in the light of Milton's 'avowed study of Plato'.

517. Samuel, Irene: 'The Dialogue in Heaven: A Reconsideration of *PL*, III, 1–417', *PMLA*, LXXII (1957), 601–11 (repr. in *228*). On the 'drama' of the Council in Heaven. Cf. *502a*.

518. Samuels, C. T.: 'Tragic Vision in *PL*', *University of Kansas City Review*, XXVII (1960), 65–78. On 'the limits of assertion possible for tragedy'.

519. Sasek, L. A.: 'The Drama of *PL*, Books XI and XII', in *Studies in English Renaissance Literature*, ed. W. F. McNeir (Baton Rouge, 1962), pp. 181–96 (repr. in *228*). The last books 'present a drama in which the character of Adam is moulded into an example of Christian fortitude'. Cf. *473, 481*, and F. T. Prince (above, pp. 233 ff.).

520. Shawcross, J. T.: 'The Balanced Structure of *PL*', *SP*, LXII (1965), 696–718.

521. Shumaker, Wayne: '*PL*: The Mythological Dimension', *Bucknell Review*, X (1961), 75–86. Argues the necessity of granting *PL* 'suspended disbelief as a record of divine events which have determined the nature of the world'. (Forthcoming from the same author: a major study tentatively entitled *Unpremeditated Verse: Feeling and perception in Milton's 'PL'*.)

522. Smith, Hallett: 'No Middle Flight', *HLQ*, XV (1962), 159–72. A lecture, on the elements that constitute the enduring greatness of *PL*.

523. Smith, L. P.: *Milton and his Modern Critics* (1940). A modest defence.

524. Steadman, J. M.: 'Heroic Virtue and the Divine Image in *PL*', *JWCI*, XXII (1959), 88–105. Milton's fusion of the two concepts, studied in the light of traditional theology and Renaissance critical theory.

525. Steadman, J. M.: 'Image and Idol: Satan and the Element of Illusion in *PL*', *JEGP*, LIX (1960), 640–54. Milton uses the 'image' – the Son – to discredit the 'idol' – Satan

526. Steadman, J. M.: '"Man's First Disobedience": The Causal Structure of the Fall', *JHI*, XXI (1960), 180–97. Reconsiders Howard's thesis (*457*), directing attention to Renaissance conceptions of the causes of man's first disobedience.

527. Steadman, J. M.: 'The "Suffering Servant" and Milton's Heroic Norm', *HTR*, LIV (1961), 29–43. 'In the Messiah's ministry of redemption Milton found the norm of Christian heroism for both his epics'.

528. Stein, Arnold: *Answerable Style: Essays on 'PL'* (1953). One chapter is reprinted above, pp. 92 ff.; another ('Milton's War in Heaven') in *228* and *229*.

529. Stein, Arnold: 'Milton and Metaphysical Art: An Exploration', *ELH*, XVI (1949), 120–34.

530. Stein, Arnold: 'Structures of Sound in Milton's Verse', *KR*, XV (1953), 266–77. An excerpt from *528*.

531. Stoll, E. E.: *Poets and Playwrights* (1930), chs. VII, IX, and *From Shakespeare to Joyce* (1944), chs. II, XIX–XXI. The first work contains the essays 'Was Paradise Well Lost?' and 'Milton, Puritan of the Seventeenth Century'; the second: 'Belial as an Example', 'Milton as a Romantic', 'Time and Space in Milton', and – the best of all – 'From the Superhuman to the Human in *PL*' (repr. in *230*).

532. Summers, J. H.: *The Muse's Method: An Introduction to 'PL'* (1962). A chapter is reprinted above, pp. 179 ff.; another ('The Final Vision') in *229*. Highly recommended.

533. Svendsen, Kester: 'Adam's Soliloquy in Book X of *PL*', *CE*, X (1949), 366–70 (repr. in *228*). Considers the soliloquy (X, 720–844) as a dramatic monologue and in relation to the entire poem.

534. Svendsen, Kester: 'Epic Address and Reference and the Principle of Decorum in *PL*', *PQ*, XXVIII (1949), 185–206.

535. Taylor, G. C.: *Milton's Use of Du Bartas* (1934). Overstates the influence of Du Bartas's 'epic' (translated by Joshua Sylvester in the 1590s), but is still useful. Cf. H. Ashton, *Du Bartas en Angleterre* (1908), pt III, ch. I, 'L'Influence sur Milton'.

536. Tillyard, E. M. W.: 'The Crisis of *PL*', in *Studies in Milton* (1951), pp. 8–52 (repr. in *229*). The reported 'crisis' occurs in *PL*, X, 937–65. Cf. *497*.

537. Tillyard, E. M. W.: *The Miltonic Setting* (1938), ch. VI. On Milton's 'visual imagination', *pace* T. S. Eliot (*429*). Cf. *480*.

538. Toliver, H. E.: 'Complicity of Voice in *PL*', *MLQ*, XXV (1964), 153–70. On the linguistic elements that contribute to the poem's 'human style'.

539. Tung, Mason: 'The Abdiel Episode: A Contextual Reading', *SP*, LXII (1965), 595–609. Cf. *446*.

540. Van Doren, Mark: '*PL*', in *The Noble Voice* (1946; repr. as *Ten Great Poems*, P: 1962), ch. IV. Argues that Milton's style ('more successful than his story') suffers from 'a sense of strain'.

541. Waddington, R. B.: 'Appearance and Reality in Satan's Disguises', *TSLL*, IV (1962), 390–98.

542. Waldock, A. J. A.: '*PL* and its Critics* (1947; P: 1961). Part of a chapter is reprinted above, pp. 74 ff.; another chapter ('Satan and the Technique of Degradation') is in *229*.

543. Watson, J. R.: 'Divine Providence and the Structure of *PL*', *EC*, XIV (1964), 148–55. Argues Milton's 'unfailing grasp of the various interconnecting elements' of *PL*.

544. Werblowsky, R. J. Z.: 'Milton and the *Conjectura Cabbalistica*', *JWCI*, XVIII (1955), 90–113. Denies the influence of the Zohar on *PL*, VII, 168 ff., *pace* Saurat (*285*).

545. Whaler, James: 'Compounding and Distribution of Similes in *PL*', *MP*, XXVIII (1931), 313–27; 'Grammatical *Nexus* of the Miltonic Simile', *JEGP*, XXX (1931), 327–34; 'The Miltonic Simile', *PMLA*, XLVI (1931), 1034–74; and 'Animal Simile in *PL*', *PMLA*, XLVII (1932), 534–53. The most thorough studies of the subject. Cf. *455, 472*.

546. Whaler, James: *Counterpoint and Symbol: An Inquiry into the Rhythm of Milton's Epic Style* ('Anglistica', VI) (P: 1956).

547. Whiting, G. W., and Ann Gossman: 'Siloa's Brook, the Pool of Siloam, and Milton's Muse', *SP*, LVIII (1961), 193–205. The 'real source of Milton's poetic inspiration' is his 'intimate spiritual communion with the Divine'.

548. Wilkes, G. A.: *The Thesis of 'PL'* (P: 1961). Indicates how the weight of Milton's conception is supported by the poem's twelve books equally.

549. Williams, Arnold: 'The Motivation of Satan's Rebellion in *PL*', *SP*, XLII (1945), 253–68. On traditional aspects of Milton's conception.

550. Williams, Charles: 'The Deification of Reason', in *Reason and Beauty in the Poetic Mind* (1933), ch. VIII. See also *388, 389*.

551. Winters, Yvor: *The Function of Criticism* (1957), pp. 42–3. Among his most typical comments on *PL* ('It requires more than a willing suspension of disbelief to read most of Milton; it requires a willing suspension of intelligence').

552. Woodhouse, A. S. P.: *Milton the Poet* (P: 1955). A lecture, being an authoritative survey of Milton's performance. Cf. *222*.

553. Woodhouse, A. S. P.: 'Pattern in *PL*', *UTQ*, XXII (1953), 109–27. On Milton's adaptation of traditional epic patterns to his general theme.

554. Worden, W. S.: 'Milton's Approach to the Story of the Fall', *ELH*,

XV (1948), 295–305. The approach was historical, psychological and allegorical.

555. Wright, B. A.: *Milton's 'PL'* (1962). An introduction.

On *PL* see further Sections I and III (a), (b), (d), *passim*.

(d) On 'Paradise Regained' & 'Samson Agonistes'

556. Allen, D. C.: *The Harmonious Vision* (1954), chs. IV, VI. Two essays: 'Realization as Climax: *PR*', and 'The Idea as Pattern: Despair and *SA*'.

557. Baumgartner, P. R.: 'Milton and Patience', *SP*, LX (1963), 203–13. Considers Milton's Adam, Christ and Samson as exemplars of patience.

558. Beum, Robert: 'The Rhyme in *SA*', *TSLL*, IV (1962), 177–82. Argues a 'distinct pattern' in the distribution of the rhyming passages in *SA*.

559. Boughner, D. C.: 'Milton's Harapha and Renaissance Comedy', *ELH*, XI (1944), 297–306. On similarities between the giant in *SA* and the braggarts of Continental comic literature.

560. Bowra, Sir Maurice: '*SA*', in *Inspiration and Poetry* (1955), ch. VI. *SA* 'displays much of a Greek spirit' but is not 'truly tragic'.

561. Bywater, Ingram: 'Milton and the Aristotelian Definition of Tragedy', *Journal of Philology*, XXVII (1901), 267–75. On possible precedents for Milton's interpretation in *SA*. Cf. *84, 614.*

562. Chambers, A. B.: 'Wisdom and Fortitude in *SA*', *PMLA*, LXXVIII (1963), 315–20. Milton's use of the tradition of *sapientia et fortitudo*.

563. Clare, Sister Miriam: '*SA*': *A Study in Contrast* (1964). On Milton's use of antithesis. Dull.

564. Cleveland, Edward: 'On the Identity Motive in *PR*', *MLQ*, XVI (1955), 232–6. On Satan's attempt to discover the identity of Jesus.

565. Cox, L. S.: 'Food-Word Imagery in *PR*', *ELH*, XXVIII (1961), 225–43. Such imagery reveals Milton's 'primary concern', namely, 'the nature and office of the Word Incarnate and of the Word'.

566. Daube, David: 'Three Notes on *PR*', *RES*, XIX (1943), 205–13. The first two notes concern Milton's agreement with the conclusions of many modern theologians; the last is on *PR* and Schiller's *Fiesco*.

567. Dyson, A. E.: 'The Meaning of *PR*', *TSLL*, III (1961), 197–211. 'In Christ . . . Milton dramatizes his sense that one man can hold a world's destiny in his hands, if he is big enough'.

568. Ellis-Fermor, Una: '*SA* and Religious Drama', in *The Frontiers of Drama* (1945; 2nd ed., 1964; P), ch. II (repr. in *579*). The best evaluation of *SA* as a major work of a 'distinctive kind' of religious drama.

569. Fell, Kenneth: 'From Myth to Martyrdom: Towards a View of

Milton's *S A*', *ES*, XXXIV (1953), 145–55. Sees *S A* as a step 'in the long ascent towards man's interpretation of the related puzzles of the divine mission and the need for a forgiving spirit'.

570. Fixler, Michael: *Milton and the Kingdoms of God* (1964). On Milton's apocalyptic expectations, with the resolution he finally achieved in *P R*.

571. Gilbert, A. H.: 'Is *S A* Unfinished?' *PQ*, XXVIII (1949), 98–106. Claims that *S A* is an unrevised early work.

572. Gohn, E. S.: 'The Christian Ethic of *PL* and *S A*', *SN*, XXXIV (1962), 243–68. Discusses 'the doctrinal ends of Milton's poems . . . viewed against a background of Renaissance ethical theory'.

573. Gossman, Ann: 'Milton's Samson as the Tragic Hero Purified by Trial', *JEGP*, LXI (1962), 528–41.

574. Gossman, Ann: 'Samson, Job, and "the Exercise of Saints"', *ES*, XLV (1964), 212–24.

575. Grenander, M. E.: '*Samson*'s Middle: Aristotle and Dr Johnson', *UTQ*, XXIV (1955), 377–89. *S A* has a 'middle' after all.

576. Hanford, J. H.: '*S A* and Milton in Old Age', *Studies in Shakespeare, Milton, and Donne*, University of Michigan Publications: Language and Literature, I (1925; repr. 1964), pp. 165–89 (repr. in *579* and in *333: John Milton: Poet and Humanist*, ch. VIII).

577. Hanford, J. H.: 'The Temptation Motive in Milton', *SP*, XV (1918), 176–94. (repr. in *333: John Milton: Poet and Humanist*, ch. VII.) A survey, culminating in a discussion of *P R* and *S A*.

578. Harris, W. O.: 'Despair and "Patience as the Truest Fortitude" in *S A*', *ELH*, XXX (1963), 107–20. On the importance of fortitude, the virtue opposed to the sin of despair (cf. *556*).

579. Hone, R. E. (ed.): *John Milton's 'S A': The Poem and Materials for Analysis* (P: 1966). Includes some antecedents (from the Bible, Josephus, Lydgate, etc.) and essays on various aspects of the poem (by Dr Johnson, R. C. Jebb, J. H. Hanford, Una Ellis-Fermor, *et al.*).

580. Hughes, M. Y.: 'The Christ of *P R* and the Renaissance Heroic Tradition', in *Ten Perspectives on Milton* (1965), ch. III. Cf. *622*.

581. Jebb, Sir Richard: '*S A* and the Hellenic Drama', *PBA*, 1907–8, pp. 341–8 (repr. in *579*). On the Hebraic nature of *S A* ('neither as poem nor as drama is it Hellenic'). Cf. *601*.

582. Kermode, Frank: 'Milton's Hero', *RES*, n.s., IV (1953), 317–30. *P R* is concerned to establish 'the character of Christian heroic virtue as distinct from pagan, and . . . the heavenly nature of the rewards which supersede the earthly recompense of the old heroes'.

583. Kermode, Frank: '*S A* and Hebrew Prosody', *Durham University Journal*, n.s., XIV (1953), 59–63. When Milton deviates from blank verse in *S A* he is imitating 'Hebrew lyric measures and rhymes as he understood them'.

584. Kermode, Frank (ed.): *The Living Milton* (1960; P: 1963), chs. VII–VIII. Essays on *PR* by W. W. Robson, 'The Better Fortitude', and F. W. Bateson, '*PR*: A Dissentient Appendix'. See also *343, 465*.

585. Kirkconnell, Watson (ed.): *That Invincible Samson: The Theme of 'SA' in World Literature with translations of the major analogues* (1964).

586. Kliger, Samuel: 'The "Urbs Aeterna" in *PR*', *PMLA*, LXI (1946), 474–91. Milton's interpretation of a persistent classical and early Christian theme.

587. Kranidas, Thomas: 'Dalila's Role in *SA*', *SEL*, VI (1966), 125–37.

588. Krouse, F. M.: *Milton's Samson and the Christian Tradition* (1949; repr. 1963). Mainly on the traditional view of Samson as a type of Christ.

589. Landy, Marcia: 'Character Portrayal in *SA*', *TSLL*, VII (1965), 239–53.

590. Leavis, F. R.: 'The Verse of *SA*', in *Revaluation* (1936; P: Penguin Books, 1964), pp. 64–7. The second of the appendices to the essay reprinted above (pp. 15 ff.), claiming that the rhythm of *SA* is 'stiff and mechanical'.

591. Lewalski, B. K.: *Milton's Brief Epic: The Genre, Meaning, and Art of 'PR'* (1966). The most thorough study of the poem to date. Cf. *603*.

592. Marilla, E. L.: '*SA*: An Interpretation', *SN*, XXIX (1957), 67–76. On *SA* as 'a corollary to *PR* and an extension of *PL*'.

593. Martz, L. L.: '*PR*: The Meditative Combat', *ELH*, XXVII (1960), 223–47. The original version of the essay reprinted above, pp. 348 ff. (from *125*).

594. Menzies, W.: 'Milton: The Last Poems', *E&S*, XXIV (1938), 80–113. Introductory.

595. Moss, Leonard: 'The Rhetorical Style of *SA*', *MP*, LXII (1965), 296–301. Lists some rhetorical techniques.

596. Mueller, M. E.: '"Pathos" and "Katharsis" in *SA*', *ELH*, XXXI (1964), 156–74. On the play's 'crucial problem' – 'its *pathos*, the deed of violence which constitutes the catastrophe'.

597. Mueller, M. E.: 'Sixteenth-Century Italian Criticism and Milton's Theory of Catharsis', *SEL*, VI (1966), 139–50. Denies Sellin's thesis (*614*).

598. Orange, L. E.: 'The Role of the Deadly Sins in *PR*', *Southern Quarterly*, II (1964), 190–201. On the possibility that the seven sins appear in *PR*.

599. Parker, W. R.: '"Misogyny" in Milton's *SA*', *PQ*, XVI (1937), 139–44. Denies the charge.

600. Parker, W. R.: 'The Date of *SA*', *PQ*, XXVIII (1949), 145–66 (repr. in *579*). Claims that *SA* was composed in 1646–8 and 1652–3. Cf. *629*.

601. Parker, W. R.: 'The Greek Spirit in Milton's *SA*', *E&S*, XX (1935), 21–44, and especially *Milton's Debt to Greek Tragedy in 'SA'* (1937; repr.

1963). The most thorough study of the subject; incidentally demolishes Jebb's theory (*581*).

602. Petit, H. H.: 'The Second Eve in *PR*', *MA*, XLIV (1959), 365-9. Cf. *506*.

603. Pope, E. M.: '*PR*: *The Tradition and the Poem* (1947; repr. 1962). Indispensable for the understanding of the poem's background. Cf. *591*.

604. Radzinowicz, Mary Ann: 'Eve and Dalila: Renovation and the Hardening of the Heart', in *Reason and the Imagination*, ed. J. A. Mazzeo (1962), pp. 155-81. On the 'realistic psychological complexity' of Milton's heroines.

605. Radzinowicz, Mary Ann: '*SA* and Milton the Politician in Defeat', *PQ*, XLIV (1965), 454-71. *SA* is 'an epic of defeat' with a 'moral addressed to the politically responsible'.

606. Raphael, D. D.: *The Paradox of Tragedy* (P: 1960), pp. 57 ff. Discusses *SA* and Corneille's 'tragédie chrétienne' *Polyeucte*, summarizing the doubts often expressed concerning the possibility of Christian tragedy. But cf. A. F. Glencross, 'Christian Tragedy', *Downside Review*, LXXIV (1956), 228-33. Cf. *568*.

607. Rice, W. G.: '*PR*', *MA*, XXII (1936), 493-503 (repr. in *229*). General observations.

608. Sackton, A. H.: 'Architectonic Structure in *PR*', *University of Texas Studies in English*, XXXIII (1954), 33-45. On the poem's series of 'parallels and contrasts'.

609. Samuel, Irene: 'Milton on Learning and Wisdom', *PMLA*, LXIV (1949), 708-23. Three passages seemingly repudiating learning (*PL*, VIII, 66 ff.; XII, 575 ff.; *PR*, IV, 286 ff.) are studied within context of Milton's theories concerning learning in relation to wisdom and the good life.

610. Samuels, C. T.: 'Milton's *SA* and Rational Christianity', *DR*, XLIII (1963), 495-506. The 'last and most telling stage in Milton's thought' is also 'his most unlovely and irrational'.

611. Schultz, Howard: 'Christ and Antichrist in *PR*', *PMLA*, LXVII (1952), 790-808. On 'the progressively more deadly manifestations of Antichrist', here seen as part of the poem's 'churchly theme'. See also the author's 'A Fairer Paradise? Some Recent Studies of *PR*', *ELH*, XXXII (1965), 275-302.

612. Scott-Craig, T. S. K.: 'Concerning Milton's *Samson*', *Renaissance News*, V (1952), 45-53. Sees in *SA* 'the major themes of Calvinistic scholasticism'.

613. Sellin, P. R.: 'Milton's Epithet *Agonistes*', *SEL*, IV (1964), 137-62. Implications of the epithet's traditional meanings.

614. Sellin, P. R.: 'Sources of Milton's Catharsis: A Reconsideration', *JEGP*, LX (1961), 712-30. Daniel Heinsius's treatise (1611) is said to be 'one of the likely sources of Milton's ideas on drama'. Cf. *561, 597*.

615. Sensabaugh, G. F.: 'Milton on Learning', *SP*, XLIII (1946), 258–72. A survey. Cf. *609*.

616. Steadman, J. M.: '"Faithful Champion": The Theological Basis of Milton's Hero of Faith', *Anglia*, LXXVII (1959), 12–28 (repr. in *228*). Samson's trials constitute a 'test of faith'.

617. Steadman, J. M.: 'Milton's Harapha and Goliath', *JEGP*, LX (1961), 786–95. Argues Milton's 'primary source'.

618. Steadman, J. M.: '*PR*: Moral Dialectic and the Pattern of Rejection', *UTQ*, XXXI (1962), 416–30. On the poem as 'a crisis of judgement' in relation to the pattern of systematic rejection ('a standard method of Western ethical tradition').

619. Stein, Arnold: *Heroic Knowledge: An Interpretation of 'PR' and 'SA'* (1957; repr. 1965). Extremely stimulating essays.

620. Summers, J. H. (ed.): *The Lyric and Dramatic Milton* (1965), pt II. Three essays on *SA*: by W. G. Madsen, 'From Shadowy Types to Truth'; Edward Weismiller, 'The "Dry" and "Rugged" Verse' (the best single essay on the verse of *SA*); and J. H. Summers, 'The Movements of the Drama'. Cf. *378*.

621. Taylor, Dick, jr.: 'The Storm Scene in *PR*: A Reinterpretation', *UTQ*, XXIV (1955), 359–76.

622. Tillyard, E. M. W.: 'The Christ of *PR* and the Renaissance Heroic Tradition', in *Studies in Milton* (1951), pp. 100–106. Cf. *580*.

623. Tinker, C. B.: '*SA*,' in *Tragic Themes in Western Literature*, ed. Cleanth Brooks (1955; P: 1960), pp. 59–76. Notes the transformation of the 'repulsive' Hebrew legend into 'the best of the Greek tragedies in English'.

624. Tupper, J. W.: 'The Dramatic Structure of *SA*', *PMLA*, XXXV (1920), 375–89. 'The power of *SA* lies . . . in the poetic content of certain speeches'.

625. Whiting, G. W.: 'Christ's Miraculous Fast', *MLN*, LXVI (1951), 12–16. Observes that Milton's Jesus is 'divine' as well as human.

626. Wilkenfeld, R. B.: 'Act and Emblem: The Conclusion of *SA*', *ELH*, XXXII (1965), 160–68. On the significance of the phoenix emblem (ll. 1687–1707).

627. Wilkes, G. A.: 'The Interpretation of *SA*', *HLQ*, XXVI (1963), 363–79. Invites us to see the action in a perspective larger than Samson's regeneration.

628. Wolfe, D. M.: 'The Role of Milton's Christ', *SR*, LI (1943), 467–75. On 'temperance and self-mastery as the supreme virtues' of the hero of *PR*.

629. Woodhouse, A. S. P.: '*SA* and Milton's Experience', *Transactions of the Royal Society of Canada*, 3rd s., XLIII (1949), sect. II, pp. 157–75.

Dates *SA* in 1660–61 (cf. *600*), and endeavours to describe the inter-relation between aesthetic and religious experience.

630. Woodhouse, A. S. P.: 'Theme and Pattern in *PR*', *UTQ*, XXV (1956), 167–82. One of the better readings of *PR*.

631. Woodhouse, A. S. P.: 'Tragic Effect in *SA*', *UTQ*, XXVIII (1959), 205–22 (repr. in *228*). On viewing *SA* as 'a classical tragedy with a Christian theme and outlook'.

632. Zwicky, Laurie: 'Kairos in *PR*', *ELH*, XXXI (1964), 271–7. On the theme of 'time'.

On *PR* see further *13, 122, 126, 213, 228, 230, 264, 286, 360, 388*, etc.

On *SA* see further *84, 213, 228, 230, 313, 362*, etc.

MORE ABOUT PENGUINS
AND PEREGRINES

If you have enjoyed reading this book you may wish to know that *Penguin Book News* appears every month. It is an attractively illustrated magazine containing a complete list of books published by Penguins and still in print, together with details of the month's new books. A specimen copy will be sent free on request.

Penguin Book News is obtainable from most bookshops; but you may prefer to become a regular subscriber at 3s. for twelve issues. Just write to Dept EP, Penguin Books Ltd, Harmondsworth, Middlesex, enclosing a cheque or postal order, and you will be put on the mailing list.

Some other books published by Penguins are described on the following pages.

Note: *Penguin Book News* is not available in the U.S.A., Canada or Australia

The Pelican Guide to English Literature

EDITED BY BORIS FORD

What this work sets out to offer is a guide to the history and traditions of English Literature, a contour-map of the literary scene. It attempts, that is, to draw up an ordered account of literature that is concerned, first and foremost, with value for the present, and this as a direct encouragement to people to read for themselves.

Each volume sets out to present the reader with four kinds of related material:

   (i) An account of the social context of literature in each period.
  (ii) A literary survey of the period.
 (iii) Detailed studies of some of the chief writers and works in the period.
 (iv) An appendix of essential facts for reference purposes.

The *Guide* consists of seven volumes, as follows:

a Peregrine Book

Cross Currents in English Literature
of the Seventeenth Century

HERBERT GRIERSON

This century, in which (if ever) 'new philosophy calls all in doubt', has found itself in inescapable sympathy with the seventeenth century. The English literature of that period was the special province of Sir Herbert Grierson, as evidenced by his editions of Donne and Milton, and by his well-known collection, *The Metaphysical Poets*.

Grierson's deep scholarship and peculiar powers of sympathy and exposition enable him, in *Cross Currents*, to trace the interaction of three main elements – the world, the flesh, and the spirit – in the century's literature. Among the major poets and dramatists he discusses in detail are Spenser, Shakespeare, Donne, Milton, and Dryden, but he also devotes space to Vaughan, Herbert, Marvell, Bunyan, Crashaw, Wither, and the Anglican preachers.